I0889360

Mimetic Lives

SRLT

NORTHWESTERN UNIVERSITY PRESS

Studies in Russian Literature and Theory

SERIES EDITORS

Caryl Emerson

Gary Saul Morson

William Mills Todd III

Andrew Wachtel

Justin Weir

Mimetic Lives

Tolstoy, Dostoevsky, and Character in the Novel

Chloë Kitzinger

Northwestern University Press / Evanston, Illinois

Northwestern University Press
www.nupress.northwestern.edu

This publication was made possible with a generous subvention from the Rutgers Research Council.

Copyright © 2021 by Northwestern University Press. Published 2021. All rights reserved.

Printed in the United States of America

10 9 8 7 6 5 4 3 2 1

Library of Congress Cataloging-in-Publication Data
Names: Kitzinger, Chloë, author.
Title: Mimetic lives : Tolstoy, Dostoevsky, and character in the novel / Chloë Kitzinger.
Other titles: Studies in Russian literature and theory.
Description: Evanston, Illinois : Northwestern University Press, 2021. | Series: Northwestern University Press studies in Russian literature and theory | Includes bibliographical references and index
Identifiers: LCCN 2021018397 | ISBN 9780810143968 (paperback) | ISBN 9780810143975 (cloth) | ISBN 9780810143982 (ebook)
Subjects: LCSH: Tolstoy, Leo, graf, 1828–1910—Criticism and interpretation. | Tolstoy, Leo, graf, 1828–1910—Characters. | Dostoyevsky, Fyodor, 1821–1881—Criticism and interpretation. | Dostoyevsky, Fyodor, 1821–1881—Characters. | Characters and characteristics in literature.
Classification: LCC PG3412 .K58 2021 | DDC 891.73/30927—dc23
LC record available at https://lccn.loc.gov/2021018397

Except where otherwise noted, this book is licensed under a Creative Commons Attribution-NonCommercial-NoDerivatives 4.0 International License. To view a copy of this license, visit http://creativecommons.org/licenses/by-nc-nd/4.0/.

In all cases attribution should include the following information:
Kitzinger, Chloë. *Mimetic Lives: Tolstoy, Dostoevsky, and Character in the Novel.* Evanston, IL: Northwestern University Press, 2021.

The following material is excluded from the license:
Cover art and previously published material described in the acknowledgments

For permissions beyond the scope of this license, visit http://www.nupress.northwestern.edu/

Knowledge Unlatched
An electronic version of this book is freely available, thanks to the support of libraries working with Knowledge Unlatched. KU is a collaborative initiative designed to make high-quality books open access for the public good. More information about the initiative and links to the open-access version can be found at www.knowledgeunlatched.org.

For my parents, with gratitude and love

Contents

Acknowledgments

I HAD THE rare good fortune to begin work on this book as a doctoral student at the University of California, Berkeley. My greatest thanks to Irina Paperno, for her extraordinary scholarship and intellectual generosity; to Eric Naiman, for sharing the delight of literary discovery; and to Dorothy Hale, for asking me so many questions that I am still trying to answer. I'm grateful for their advice, conversation, and friendship, as well as that of other teachers and mentors at Berkeley: Ronelle Alexander, Ian Duncan, Catherine Gallagher, Luba Golburt, Joachim Klein, Lisa Little, Olga Matich, Anna Muza, Anne Nesbet, Johanna Nichols, Harsha Ram, and the late Viktor Zhivov. Discussions at Slavic Kruzhok and Townsend Center for the Humanities Fellows meetings shaped the project and provided invaluable feedback on parts of the argument.

I was equally fortunate to pursue this project as a postdoctoral fellow in the Princeton Society of Fellows, and then to find an exciting and collegial professional home in the Department of German, Russian, and East European Languages and Literatures at Rutgers University. At Princeton, I would like to thank Susan Stewart and Mary Harper for the transformative scholarly community they created and all the postdoctoral and faculty fellows for making it a space of lively exploration. My particular thanks to the Slavic Department (especially Caryl Emerson, Ilya Vinitsky, and Michael Wachtel); to Deborah Nord and Esther Schor; and to Nijah Cunningham, Stefan Eich, Grace Helton, and Monica Huerta. At Rutgers, I am grateful for the conversation, friendship, and advice of colleagues in and beyond my department, especially Emily Van Buskirk, Martha Helfer, Pavel Khazanov, Cori Anderson, Nicola Behrmann, Daniel Brooks, Tom Dyne, Lauren Goodlad, Regina Karl, Michael Levine, Fatima Naqvi, Andy Parker, Alexander Pichugin, Nicholas Rennie, and Janet Walker. I also thank the students whose ideas and questions have enriched and challenged my thinking about the writers in this book.

I gratefully acknowledge the financial and practical support the project has received: at Berkeley, a Dean's Normative Time fellowship and a dissertation completion fellowship from the Mabelle McLeod Lewis Memorial Fund; at Princeton, a Perkins-Cotsen Postdoctoral Fellowship; at LMU Munich, a short-term fellowship with the International Doctoral Program Mimesis; and at Rutgers, a semester's leave from teaching through the Faculty Sabbatical Leave Program and a subvention from the Rutgers University Research Council.

Sections of every chapter have benefitted from presentation at AATSEEL, ASEEES, ACLA, and MLA conferences and at the Slavic Alumni Conference at UC Berkeley; special thanks to all the participants in the "Mimesis" stream at AATSEEL. I am grateful to the following colleagues for other opportunities to present the project: Galina Alekseeva (Iasnaia Poliana); Riccardo Nicolosi, Tobias Döring, and Christopher Balme (LMU Munich); Nancy Ruttenberg (Stanford University); Robin Feuer Miller (Brandeis University); and Ilya Kliger and Anne Lounsbery (NYU).

I would like to thank Trevor Perri, Gary Saul Morson, and everyone at Northwestern University Press who expertly shepherded this book into print (and Jessica Hinds-Bond for the splendid index). Warmest thanks to the press's readers, Yuri Corrigan and Alex Woloch, for their attentive and illuminating responses to the manuscript and sound advice on revising it. An earlier version of chapter 1 appeared in the *Slavic and East European Journal* as "Dinner at the English Club: Character on the Margins in *War and Peace*" (vol. 61, no. 2 [2017]: 311–30). Thanks to the editor for permission to reprint and to Irene Masing-Delic and the anonymous reviewers for their thought-provoking questions.

Finally, I want to thank the many other colleagues who have responded to portions of this book or who guided work that later became relevant to it. They include Carol Apollonio, Anna Berman, Katia Bowers, Peter Brooks, Lindsay Ceballos, Mikhail Dolbilov, Karsten Harries, Kate Holland, Zach Johnson, Ilya Kliger, Michael Kunichika, David Kurnick, Emma Lieber, Deborah Martinsen, Susan McReynolds, Robin Feuer Miller, Riccardo Nicolosi, Donna Orwin, Vadim Shneyder, Sasha Spektor, Amir Tevel, and Ilya Vinitsky. I'm enduringly grateful to Chiara Ricciardone, Tatyana Gershkovich, Greta Matzner-Gore, and Jillian Porter for writing exchanges that have sustained both progress and excitement. Thanks to librarians at UC Berkeley, Northwestern, Princeton, and Rutgers for their invaluable assistance—and heartfelt thanks to Jeffrey Brooks, who generously furnished a copy of the cover image during a summer when libraries worldwide were closed.

Writing this book would have been dreary work without friends in Berkeley and New Jersey, especially Katy Sosnak and Kostas Goulas, Irina Kogel, Lily Scott, and Tom Dyne. It would have been impossible without my family—especially my sister Beatrice Kitzinger (who long ago gave me a copy of Auerbach's *Mimesis* with a prophetic inscription) and brother-in-law

Charlie Barber; my mother-in-law Mel Shedlock; and my parents Elizabeth and Adrian Kitzinger, who inspired and encouraged my earliest adventures with nineteenth-century novels and to whom this book is gratefully dedicated. There are no words to thank my husband Jordan Shedlock, whose love has carried me through its writing; or our daughters Nadezhda and Talia, who are just beginning to discover both characters and language, and whose exuberance makes them new again.

Mimetic Lives

Mimetic Life as Narrative Illusion

> [Tolstoy] notices the blue or red of a child's frock; the way a horse shifts its tail; the sound of a cough; the action of a man trying to put his hands into pockets that have been sewn up. And what his infallible eye reports of a cough or a trick of the hands his infallible brain refers to something hidden in the character so that we know his people, not only by the way they love and their views on politics and the immortality of the soul, but also by the way they sneeze and choke. Even in a translation we feel that we have been set on a mountain-top and had a telescope put into our hands. Everything is astonishingly clear and absolutely sharp. Then, suddenly, just as we are exulting, breathing deep, feeling at once braced and purified, some detail—perhaps the head of a man—comes at us out of the picture in an alarming way, as if extruded by the very intensity of its life.
> —Virginia Woolf

WHAT MAKES SOME characters seem to be so real?

In the *Poetics*, Aristotle conceived of narrative poetry as a fiction: the plot structure created by the representation of an action, with the power to intellectually and emotionally engage an audience regardless of its fidelity to factual truth.[1] With this idea, the mimetic narrative gains two opposing faces; it becomes both "world reflecting" (depicting a world knowable outside itself) and "world creating" (forming a world of its own that temporarily removes its audience from everyday life).[2] Thus understood, the term *mimesis* (representation) brings together a set of foundational questions—originating with Plato and continuing through Derrida, Ricoeur, and beyond—about verisimilitude, form, and aesthetic response. A mimetic work of art draws us in partly thanks to its own formal properties, but it engages interpretive categories and strategies grounded in daily life and so also makes extra-aesthetic claims on the person experiencing it. How does one kind of engagement intensify or interfere with the other? What does an audience bring *to* the experience of a fiction, what can they carry *away* from it, and what belongs to the moments of captivation *inside* particular fictional worlds?

The realist novel was a dominant mimetic art form of nineteenth-century Europe, and of all its devices, it is character that most sharply awakens the tension between the inward and outward faces of mimesis.[3]

Paradoxically blending "utter embeddedness and radical detachability," realist characters claim both a reality within and a reality outside the act of reading.[4] They belong to the fictional world that the captivated reader creates, according to the instructions and within the frame of the narrative. But they also offer images of human existence that stand out from this frame, available to be related to what the reader knows, believes, or does in the course of her everyday life.

In this book, I trace the technical sources and practical limits of the mimetic illusion of character in the novel, through readings of major works by Fyodor Dostoevsky and Leo Tolstoy. Although many novels invite similar theoretical questions, late Russian realism offers unparalleled ground for their investigation. Tolstoy's and Dostoevsky's novels are poised at the height of the Russian realist tradition, at a time when both institutional and political circumstances gave fiction a central role in public discourse. Arbiters and innovators within this tradition, Tolstoy and Dostoevsky each—in opposite ways—mastered the illusion of the lifelike character while pushing it toward the novel's generic bounds: philosophy, history, journalism, theology, myth. Their works lead into the underexplored territory where literary character meets the essential problems of mimesis itself. Where does the mimetic illusion of character begin? What sustains it, and what makes it falter? And what can this illusion do in the world outside the novel? Can a reader's experience of mimetic novelistic characters be used to transform her, beyond the actual moment of her reading?

These questions have bearing on the problem of why novels are written and read today. Twentieth-century philosophers and critics from Mikhail Bakhtin to Martha Nussbaum (and beyond) have argued that the social and ethical potential of the novel form lies in its power to give us portable, vivid models for the perspectives of autonomous Others, creating richer and more empathetic moral vision.[5] This idea has taken on the status of a cultural trope, repeated by no less a reader than then-president Barack Obama in conversation with the novelist Marilynne Robinson.[6] Tracing Tolstoy's and Dostoevsky's experimental techniques of characterization, I propose an account of *how* realist novels foster and sustain the impression of characters who live with their own individual, autonomous "lives." But I argue that contrary to our intuition as readers, this life effect begins and ends with our absorption in novelistic narrative. Dostoevsky and Tolstoy themselves were acutely aware of how unreliably mimetic character bridges the act of reading to a lasting transformation of the reader. Seen close, the realist novel's power to create a world of sensuously solid and autonomous fictional persons underscores its resources as a form for thought, and its limits as a direct source of spiritual, social, or political change.

"MIMETIC LIFE" AND REALIST CHARACTER-SYSTEMS

Theories of character and characterization have long been hampered by two linked extremes—a naïvely humanizing approach that exaggerates the likeness between characters and people, and a formalizing approach that exaggerates the difference.[7] Although most novel readers remain convinced of the primacy of character, influential structuralist and narratological critics have often subordinated the character to the event; symptomatically, Gérard Genette organizes his comprehensive theory of narrative around "categories borrowed from the grammar of verbs."[8] Meanwhile, deconstructionist essays published throughout the 1960s and 1970s posed penetrating challenges to the ideas of both "character" and "mimesis," with roots in the earliest statements of Russian formalism.[9] As Roland Barthes writes in *S/Z* (1970), the realist novel's seductive game is to fill the "impersonal network of symbols combined under the proper name" with an illusory plenitude.[10] For Barthes, Genette, Derrida, and others, character became a focus of the tenet that the "real" invoked in realist prose is a construct that supports a shared contract or code, reinforcing the ideologies that make novels legible.[11]

In the wake of such challenges, contemporary scholars remain wary of how shifting conventions, dynamics of political power, and the instabilities of language itself puncture the aura of correspondence between reality and representation that is key to mimetic character. Nevertheless, interest in character has reawakened over the past thirty years, as theorists pursue a balance between naïve and skeptical approaches. Rather than debating the truth or falsity and virtue or vice of reading for character, there has been a productive shift toward asking what makes a given reader prone to receive a given character as personlike and exploring the historical consequences of this mode of reading.[12]

However, as widely as the contemporary renewal of critical interest in mimetic character ranges—with studies rooted in new historicism, narratology, moral philosophy, rhetoric, cognitive science, and more—it has been dominated by a concern with the outward, "world-reflecting" face of mimesis.[13] Scholars emphasize the question of what mimetic characters tell us about the worlds in which they are written and read—from Chaucer's England on to Manley's, Fielding's, and Austen's. This line of approach was recently extended in John Frow's transcultural, transtemporal study *Character and Person* (2014), whose title gets to the heart of an investment in mimetic character as world reflection: how do changing ways of conceptualizing and experiencing character expose changing concepts of what it is to be human? Seen in this light, the study of character across genres, languages, and eras becomes a key to the study of authors and readers, and what is most telling about character, as a model of human existence, is also what is most "detachable" from narrative and text.

The *inward* face of mimetic character—the aspect of illusion that depends on the character's "embeddedness" in narrative and text—has less often occupied the center of scholars' attention. But it too affects the experience of character, and especially of characters in realist novels. How can we designate the specific sense of a character's "reality" that is lost when the character is described at second hand, and regained when he is encountered within the complex web of words that makes up a realist narrative?

As a first step toward foregrounding this inward aspect of the illusion of character, I propose summarizing it under the term *mimetic life*. By "mimetic life," I mean the reader's sense of a character's autonomous, embodied existence in and for himself, not only free from authorial control, but even independent of the words of narrative.

The effect of the character's physical solidity and moral autonomy has been discussed, although never conclusively named. Some theorists attribute it to the descriptive set of "distinctive, mostly human characteristics" assigned to many characters, which prompt readers to think of them as autonomous persons.[14] Others appeal to characters' conformity with a widely shared rhetoric of literary being and behavior, which then seems to control them independently of their authors' intentions.[15]

I want to suggest that these narratological and rhetorical perspectives downplay a key aspect of the "life" of novelistic characters: its status, above all, as an aesthetic construct—woven, sustained, and controlled by running narrative interrelationships that are perceived most fully in the act and moment of reading.[16] On the face of it, our sense of the autonomous existence and "rights" of characters seems to conflict with the strictures of aesthetic form.[17] Nevertheless, the very illusion of autonomy harks back to what M. H. Abrams calls the "organic metaphor" in aesthetics: the enduring habit of describing beauty by analogy with a living and self-sufficient body. Rooted in some of Plato's dialogues and (especially) in Aristotle's *Poetics*, and continuing via Kant into German romantic aesthetics, the "organic metaphor" underlies the definition of beauty as the synthesis of parts into a working whole, where each part seems to have been necessarily chosen and none of what is necessary has been left out.[18] By analogy, for some readers of realist novels, the seemingly autonomous life of characters offers a sign of the novel's own organic self-determination and coherence. The success with which this illusion is maintained sets a standard for the novel's worth as a work of art.

Like the organic metaphor in its post-Kantian guise, and also like realist novels themselves, the perception of mimetic life is shot through with what Terry Eagleton calls the "ideology of the aesthetic."[19] Not all kinds of narrative work as tirelessly as does the quintessentially bourgeois form of the realist novel to foster readers' impressions of the characters' autonomous life.[20] But within the conventions of novel reading, the idea of the character's life has undeniable intuitive force. We can list everything there is to know about Anna Karenina or Tertius Lydgate, as kinds of characters or as implied persons, without actually reading from *Anna Karenina* or *Middlemarch*. But to reference the specific sense that many readers share of Anna or Tertius as vivid, solid, and individual presences, I suggest, we have to be consciously or unconsciously recalling the experience of aesthetic absorption that the novel genre invites. The effect of lifelikeness emerges from and within our willing submission to what Tolstoy—with both admiration and dislike for the Western European narrative form that he had mastered—dubbed the realist novel's "labyrinth of linkages."[21]

If we are willing to consider the character's autonomous, embodied life as an effect to which readers are predisposed by the conventional aesthetic practices of novel reading, we can turn to a less mystical question: how do texts *regulate* and *distribute* the powerful, amorphous illusion of life over the course of a multicharacter narrative? A robust set of theoretical tools already exists for exploring such labyrinthine narrative interrelationships among characters, or as they have generally been called, character-systems.

The idea of the character-system has a predecessor in Georg Lukács's writings on the novel, particularly his mid-twentieth-century Marxist essays on European realism:

> In the works of a great realist everything is linked up with everything else. Each phenomenon shows a polyphony [*Vielstimmigkeit*] of determinations, a polyphony in the intertwinement of the individual and social, of the physical and the psychical, of private and public, and so on. And because the polyphony of their composition goes beyond immediacy, the number of their *dramatis personae* is always more numerous than any playbill could show. The great realists always regard society from the viewpoint of a grasped living and mobile centre. And this centre is present, visibly or invisibly, in every phenomenon. Think of Balzac. He shows how capital . . . takes over power in France. From Gobseck to Nucingen, Balzac creates a long procession of the immediate representatives of this demoniacal force. . . . But does this exhaust

> the power of financial capital in Balzac's world? Does Gobseck cease to rule when he leaves the stage? No, Balzac's world is permanently saturated with Gobseck and his like. . . . Tolstoy is the poet of the peasant revolt that lasted in Russia from 1861 to 1905. In his life-work the exploited peasant is this visible-invisible ever-present protagonist [*Gestalt*].[22]

Alongside the overt political claims of this passage, Lukács uses "polyphony" as a flexible metaphor—not incidentally, itself strongly associated with romantic aesthetics—to tie the representation of a realist novel's characters to the organization of its themes.[23] Within a large and complex cast, realist novels hide a "living and mobile center" that may coincide with the actual protagonist, but that also works as a life force animating the entire "polyphonic" composition. In order to discern this center, the figure or force that defines the novel's picture of history and the world, Lukács implies that readers must read in wholes. Conversely, behind the image of the "living center" stands the Aristotelian promise that the realist novel will *be* a whole: the "visible-invisible protagonist" is a principle drawing the novel's diverse cast of characters together, propelling their intersecting movements through the plot.

In the 1970s, describing similar formal relationships among characters in the language of structuralist criticism, Philippe Hamon and Fredric Jameson each independently coined the term "character system" to talk about how narrative configurations of characters convey thematic, ideological, and political meaning. For Hamon, the systematic arrangement of characters (like that of morphemes in a word and words in a sentence) ensures the legibility of narrative; narratives are read in characters, just as sentences are read in words.[24] For Jameson, characters' patterned interactions point to the historical, social, and political dynamics that underlie a novel's plot (dynamics that the biographical author in person might deny).[25] Looking through the "personalities" of characters to the social conditions and forces they evoke, we can see their systematic configuration as an index of the historical moment that a novel represents.

Most recently, the term "character-system" has been revived by Alex Woloch in his pathbreaking study *The One vs. the Many: Minor Characters and the Space of the Protagonist in the Novel* (2003). Deallegorizing the concept of the character-system, Woloch reinterprets it as the narrative and thematic field in which mimetic characterizations themselves unfold. Characters closest to the center of the narrative's (and so the reader's) attention emerge more completely than those at the periphery. Accordingly, no panoramic realist novel has enough "space" for all the people it sets out to represent. The pragmatic suppression or fragmentation of minor characters allows the novel's protagonists to emerge more completely as fictional persons, by a perspectival contrast that is at once social, thematic, and narrative. The ideological parameters of the character-systems that Jameson and Hamon describe thus make themselves felt, according to Woloch, as degrees of protagonicity. Realist novels map particular worlds by placing some figures closer to the vivifying center, and consigning others to the formulaic margins.

Spanning more than seventy years of literary theory, these approaches to the systematic or "polyphonic" aspect of realist characterization can hardly be arranged into teleological progression.[26] But taken together, Hamon's, Jameson's, and Woloch's theories develop and draw out the aspects of Lukács's hypercondensed image, the "visible-invisible ever-present protagonist" at the living heart of a realist narrative. Their differing explications of the character-system are united by a commitment to reading mimetic novelistic characters through bounded novelistic wholes. As the distance from Hamon to Jameson makes clear, radical disagreement is possible about how such literary wholes mirror, remake, and comment on reality. But that disagreement arises on the back of a common insight: novelistic characters owe much of their significance to the textual bounds that set them in relation to one another—defining an enclosed field, as in Saussurean linguistics, where differences among characters can be made to count toward the creation of a vividly populated fictional world.

It is a small step beyond this theoretical foundation to argue that the effect I call "mimetic life"—the concentrated impression of any one character's vivid and autonomous existence—is fostered and controlled by bounded narrative systems. Like Woloch (and Wolfgang Iser before him), I assume the aesthetic model of an absorbed reader, who follows the text's instructions about what to imagine and where to direct her attention—and so, even if unconsciously, picks up on a building set of cues and reads with reference to the boundaries in which those cues operate.[27] One of the effects that they direct is the illusion of a character's autonomous "life."

However, while Hamon and Jameson tend to abstract away this life effect and Woloch treats it as an absolute quality proper to every character, I suggest that individual realist narratives set up their *own* rules for creating and distributing it. In many cases, a strong narrative focus on the protagonist indeed suppresses or distorts the "lives" of minor characters. In others, it may leave them unaffected, or even enhanced.

As Barthes long ago averred, the mimetic life of characters—the magic trick by which characters become "Proper Names"—thus lies at the heart of a "readerly" approach to the realist novel. It is the product of a mode of reading governed by near-devotional faith in the novelist's creative powers, and so also by the desire not to "omit a connection" or miss a single instruction.[28] If we want to explore the much-critiqued but persistent illusion of mimetic life, we should understand it as a powerful resource, which nineteenth-century realist novelists virtuosically modulated and used.

We have only begun to explain how novelistic character-systems enact the complex work of representation. How do novels construct the networks—of names, repeated descriptions, thematic associations—that shape, color, or warp the distribution of narrative "space," and let it correspond to a particular mimetic effect? What makes a character (in Woolf's evocative phrase) "come at us out of the picture in an alarming way, as if extruded by the very intensity of its life"? And how does dependence *on* a bounded system condition this effect of life—the character propelled outward by the composition of the very picture that fails to contain it?

MIMETIC LIFE AND RUSSIAN REALISM (I)

Recent studies of character, characterization, and character-systems have focused chiefly on the Western European and Anglophone canons. But Tolstoy's and Dostoevsky's novels offer an unmatched lens for theorizing mimetic life more fully. The roots of this assertion lie in early novel theory: in the East European branch, Mikhail Bakhtin's account of Dostoevsky's preternaturally autonomous characters; in the Anglo-American, the work of pioneering theorizers of the novel like Woolf, Henry James, and Percy Lubbock, who held Tolstoy up—sometimes disapprovingly—as a paradigm of unbounded novelistic vitality.[29]

It bears remembering that these and other twentieth-century critical statements were tied to the specific historical, literary, philosophical, and political circumstances of Tolstoy's and Dostoevsky's early reception in Russia and the West. Bakhtin's argument about the "freedom" and indeterminacy of Dostoevsky's characters grows in part from turn-of-the-century Russian Symbolist criticism, in which Dostoevsky appears as a prophet of the divine symbiosis between art and life.[30] Meanwhile, Woolf's, James's, and Lubbock's responses to Tolstoy say as much about Woolf and James, and Anglo-American modernism, as they do about Tolstoy himself.[31]

However, these early accounts hardly exhaust Tolstoy's and Dostoevsky's unique place in transnational imaginations of the nineteenth-century realist tradition—summed up in a breathless blurb (attributed to Isaac Babel) on the back of the Oxford's World Classics paperback edition of *War and Peace*: "If life could write, it would write like Tolstoy."[32] My argument takes seriously this overwhelming impression of represented life, and the course it has set for scholarly and popular approaches to both Dostoevsky's and Tolstoy's novels. I believe that it springs from their experimental methods of representing people and human worlds, which *appear* in different ways to open the aesthetic frame of novelistic narrative and to do away with the inherent boundedness of character-systems, while also relying on this boundedness for the very illusions that they create. A brief survey of how the tension between mimetic experimentation and aesthetic limits took shape in nineteenth-century Russian literature, particularly during Tolstoy's and Dostoevsky's careers, will clarify the basis for my argument.

The strong extra-aesthetic orientation of the nineteenth-century Russian novel, its claim to authority about reality and the inner truth of things, can be traced to specific historical circumstances.[33] Although subject to government oversight and censorship, literature and literary criticism offered singularly open forums for the discussion of social, cultural, and philosophical questions. Moreover, throughout the second half of the nineteenth century, most fiction was published in "thick journals," monthly magazines available by subscription, where installments of novels were printed side by side with memoirs, scientific articles, works of history and theology, and more.[34] The novel's intersection with nonfictional genres, which reduced the distance between literature and other kinds of writing, was a feature of serial publication throughout Europe from the 1830s on (Balzac's and Sue's *romans-feuilletons* in *La presse* and *Journal des débats*, Dickens's weekly periodical *Household Worlds*, and so on). However, scholars agree that it took on particular weight in Russia in the absence of other avenues for expression, where thick journals became a crucial gathering place for their readers.

The idiosyncratic development of the novel—and of secular literature itself—in eighteenth- to nineteenth-century Russia is also part of this landscape. Before and in the immediate wake of Peter I's westernizing reforms (1682–1725), writing and publication lay primarily under the aegis of the tsarist government and the Russian Orthodox Church. Secular folk literature was oral, and the vast majority of serfs (themselves a majority of the population) were illiterate.[35] When the novel came to Russia, it was as an import from France and England, where the genre had developed under stronger traditions of secular literature and popular literacy—and where it became the dominant literary form for a middle class that Russia never fully acquired.[36] Beginning with early forays such as M. D. Chulkov's *The Comely Cook* (*Prigozhaia povarikha*, 1770), which is often likened to Defoe's *Moll Flanders* (1722), "the novel" remains a self-conscious problem for Russian writers well into the 1850s. One might be wary of Tolstoy's self-serving pronouncement that "the history of Russian literature since the time of Pushkin not merely affords many examples of . . . deviation from European forms, but does not offer a single example of the contrary . . . rising at all above mediocrity" (16:7; "A Few Words about the Book *War and Peace*" ["Neskol'ko slov po povodu knigi *Voina i mir*"], 1868). Nevertheless, from Pushkin's "novel in verse" *Eugene Onegin* (1833) to Lermontov's story cycle

A Hero of Our Time (*Geroi nashego vremeni*, 1840) and Gogol's unfinished "*poema*" *Dead Souls* (*Mertvye dushi*, part 1, 1842), the novel emerged in Russia as contentious ground—assertions of Russian difference coexisting with assertions of European belonging, and novelistic narrative conventions ostentatiously juxtaposed with the forms and ingredients of other genres.[37]

Shaped as much by influential literary critics as by authors themselves, Russia's approach toward the novel remained fitful and strange throughout the 1840s–60s.[38] Ivan Goncharov published the fragment "Oblomov's Dream" in 1849, and the novel built around it, *Oblomov*, a full ten years later. Turgenev began with the sketches in *A Hunter's Notebook* (*Zapiski okhotnika*, 1847–51; 1852), continued on to novellas like *Rudin* (1856), and published the full-length novel *Fathers and Children* (*Otsy i deti*) only in 1862. Meanwhile, the dominant critic Vissarion Belinsky and his successors lamented the absence in Russia of a more robust novel tradition. Throughout this period, the problem of "the Russian novel" was intertwined with the problem of its hero(es). Like Pushkin, Lermontov, and Gogol before them, Turgenev and Goncharov explored this question self-consciously: if no meaningful action is possible for Russia's "superfluous men," what kind of biographical plots can be built around them? In the case of *A Hunter's Notebook* and *Oblomov*, striking narrative idiosyncrasies result from these questions about what protagonicity in nineteenth-century Russia could mean: the series of rural sketches held together by the perspective of a wandering narrator; the novel whose hero—for an astonishing number of pages—fails to take the fundamental action of getting out of bed.

By the late 1850s, the interchange between realist novelists and the critics and readers of Russian thick journals had cohered around the discussion of realist protagonists in their guise as literary "types."[39] In European realist aesthetics, "type" combined the Hegelian sense of the ideal—a concretely embodied idea or principle—with the newer sense of the representative of a sociological class; the type was a fictional figure in whom an entire group and way of being were thought to be represented and crystallized.[40] In Russia, critics thus treated "typical" heroes as occasions to expand on social developments, most famously in Nikolai Dobroliubov's review of Goncharov's *Oblomov* ("What Is Oblomovitis?" ["Chto takoe Oblomovshchina?"], 1859) and Dmitrii Pisarev's review of Turgenev's *Fathers and Children* ("Bazarov," 1862). Taking up the critics' invitation, some readers indeed began modeling their behavior and apprehensions of contemporary life on Turgenev's nihilist Bazarov, or Nikolai Chernyshevsky's variations on the nihilist type in his unabashedly clumsy, enormously influential novel *What Is to Be Done?* (*Chto delat'?*, 1863). The trajectories of protagonists like Turgenev's Bazarov, or Chernyshevsky's visionary seamstress Vera Pavlovna, trace a literal conversion of character into person, demonstrating how fictional figures might come to designate people who actually exist.

Tolstoy and Dostoevsky were near the beginning of their mature careers as novelists at the height of these debates around Goncharov's, Turgenev's, and Chernyshevsky's protagonists.[41] Only Dostoevsky entered directly and publically into the fray. But both authors objected on principle to the topical cooption of literature and fictional characters, while continuing to probe the question of literature's place in spiritual, social, and political life. In the chapters that follow, I trace Tolstoy's and Dostoevsky's mimetic techniques and ambitions primarily through the novels they wrote. However, a digression here into the authors' own comments on mimetic character and the work of art will provide a helpful preliminary context.

The tangle of continuities and ruptures in Tolstoy's aesthetic thought, from early, private writings in diaries and letters to the scandalous public statement of *What Is Art*? (1898), has been richly documented.[42] One central continuous thread is the idea that the author's task is to communicate his vision and experience of reality. In an early diary entry, Tolstoy doubts the possibility of fulfilling this ideal, because of the inadequacies of written language:

> I thought: I'll go and describe what I see. But how to write this. One has to go and sit at an ink-stained table, take up a gray sheet of paper, ink; stain one's fingers and mark letters on the paper. The letters make words; the words—sentences; but is it really possible to convey a feeling [*peredat' chuvstvo*]. Isn't there any way to pour one's own gaze onto nature into someone else? Description is not enough. (46:65; July 3, 1851)[43]

When Tolstoy published *What Is Art?*, almost fifty years and two major novels later, he still praised works that he felt could directly "infect" the reader with the feeling that inspired the artist's creation—pointedly excluding most of his own fiction.

However, despite Tolstoy's emphasis on the communication between author and reader, he was anything but sympathetic to the utilitarian approach to writing, reading, and criticism that centered in the 1860s around Nikolai Nekrasov's thick journal the *Contemporary*, and its short-lived but explosive competitor the *Russian Word*.[44] As Tolstoy wrote in an unsent letter to the literary editor and novelist P. D. Boborykin, topical political questions "waver in a small puddle of dirty water, which looks like the ocean only to those whom fate put down in the middle of this puddle. . . . The aim of the artist is not to definitively solve a question, but to move [the reader] to love life in all its innumerable, inexhaustible manifestations" (July–August 1865; 61:100).[45] This dedication to the ideal of the "artistic" as it overlaps with the mimetic coexisted, throughout Tolstoy's life, with his doubts about the social and moral value of his own aesthetic activity.

Far from presenting his fictional characters as authorial mouthpieces or instruments for working through contemporary problems, Tolstoy often referred to them as invented "people"—sometimes by explicit analogy (or in competition) with his biological children.[46] The author controls his people's fictional lives, but any narrative choice has its own unpredictable ramifications. In one letter, Tolstoy compared this kind of reckoning to a mathematical puzzle, a matter of "sorting through a million combinations . . . to choose the 1/1,000,000" right one.[47] Glimpsing a fictional world that lies adjacent to his own, the author strains toward his characters like someone "trying to hear the sounds of whispering and trying to see rays of light in the gloom."[48] The fictional world and characters thus demand the author's attention as an *index* of reality—to be reclaimed from the falsity of literary convention and subjected to the author's judgment, but on their own and the work's autonomous terms.

Tolstoy clearly laid out this vision of his characters' "self"-determination relative to the observing and judging author in a draft preface to the first part of *War and Peace*:

> The work at hand comes closest to a novel or story, but it is not a novel, because I cannot in any way and do not know how to place certain limits on the characters [*litsam*] I have invented—like marriage or death, after which the interest of the narrative would be spent. It ineluctably appeared to me that the death of one character only awakened interest in the others, and marriage appeared more as the opening than the resolution of an interest. I cannot call my composition a short story, because I do not know how to and cannot make my characters act only with the aim of proving or clarifying some thought or succession of thoughts. (13:55; tentatively dated late 1863)

Here the character's autonomy works as a guarantee against both artificial literary convention and the arbitrariness of the author's own "thoughts." Tolstoy's understanding of the autonomy of fictional characters figures still more clearly in a famous letter to another close correspondent, the critic and philosopher Nikolai Strakhov, in which he describes the aesthetic structure of *Anna Karenina* (April 23 and 26, 1876). There Tolstoy recalls the suicide of his character Vronsky, which he says entered spontaneously into the proofs of the final chapters of part 5: "I went about correcting [the chapter] and completely unexpectedly for me, but unmistakably, Vronsky proceeded to shoot himself." As Tolstoy tells it, the character's unexpected suicide serves as a proof of the work's "organic" form, which he evocatively describes as a "labyrinth of linkages": "Now it turns out that [Vronsky's suicide] was organically necessary for what followed" (62:269).[49] This statement has been quoted in testaments to the irreducible intricacy of literary structure and what it communicates.[50] But as a recent scholar has pointed out, in the context of

Strakhov and Tolstoy's religious and philosophical correspondence, the letter can also be taken to express Tolstoy's frustration with the unpredictability of artistic form.[51] The problem with conveying ideas through characters is that their "self"-directed aesthetic activity muddies the clarity of the very message it enlivens. Seen in this light, Tolstoy's genius for creating "living" characters—rather than characters that, like Chernyshevsky's Vera Pavlovna, can be made to speak directly for the writer's views—is one explanation for his ever more resolute turns away from fiction.[52]

Dostoevsky shared Tolstoy's keen interest in using his novels, as well as the public stature they gave him, to communicate with readers. In the wake of his early idol Friedrich Schiller, Dostoevsky cherished the hope that art and beauty would shape and educate the viewer. However, this ambition was not a matter of formal Schillerian aesthetic education only; as Dostoevsky's letters and journalistic writings make clear, he also sometimes assigned himself and his contemporaries the task of conveying specific content. (Consider his avowed goal in *The Idiot* of creating a "positively beautiful man," as well as his pride in later "positive types" such as Father Zosima; consider too his scathing criticism of Tolstoy's "insufficiently Russian" hero Levin.[53]) In canonical Soviet and Western twentieth-century criticism, the open-ended discord of Dostoevsky's novels takes precedence over their bombastic authorial messages.[54] But as early as 1861, Dostoevsky himself articulated an aesthetic standard close to what Tolstoy would later call "infection": "artistry, at least for example in a novelist, is the ability to express his thought so clearly in the characters and images of a novel that the reader, reading the novel, understands the writer's thought exactly as the writer himself understood it while creating the work" (18:80; Dostoevsky, "Mr. —bov and the Question of Art"). Later, in the 1877 *Diary of a Writer* essay in which Dostoevsky mythologized his own debut, he highlighted Vissarion Belinsky's praise for his novella *Poor Folk* in still more suggestive terms. As Belinsky supposedly told him, "You have penetrated to the very heart of the matter, you have at once pointed out the most important thing. We publicists and critics only pontificate . . . but you, an artist, present the essence in a single stroke, all at once in an image, so that one could feel it with one's hand, so that even to the least penetrating reader, everything suddenly at once becomes clear!" (25:30). Ventriloquizing Belinsky, Dostoevsky shows that his urge to replicate the ideological chaos of postreform Russia was rivaled by his sense of the novel genre's potential as a space of mimetic image making, and so also of intellectual and spiritual conversion.

However, like Tolstoy, Dostoevsky roundly condemned the utilitarian cooption of art, and for him too, the index of "organic," untrammeled aesthetic form in the novel was often mimetic characters themselves. This association is clearest in the important 1861 credo cited above, "Mr. —bov and the Question of Art." Discussing the tendentious stories of Marko Vovchok, whom the radical critical Dobroliubov praised, Dostoevsky objects to the stiffness, generality, and artifice of Vovchok's peasant characters:

> Tell me: have you ever read anything more unrealistic, more monstrous, more incoherent than this story? What kind of people are these? *Are* they people, in the end? . . . Imagine that instead of this farcical clown, instead of this line of text [*stroki*] Masha, there had emerged for the story's author a vivid, faithful character [*iarkoe, vernoe litso*], so that you would immediately in waking reality see that which you're so hotly arguing about,—would you reject such a story just because it was artistic? Indeed, such a story would be a thousand times more useful. (18:90, 93)

If the pinnacle of Dostoevsky's moral-aesthetic scale is the compelling beauty of the embodied Christ, further down lies the "vivid, faithful" fictional character or type, who compels readers toward the author's vision of reality precisely *because* she emerges within a self-determining work of art.[55]

As we have already seen, the common conceptual vocabulary of organic aesthetics is a thread connecting Tolstoy's and Dostoevsky's conceptions of mimetic character to that of later novelists like Woolf and theorists like Lukács, and also to the assumptions of present-day novel readers. The organic metaphor was widely spread in nineteenth-century Russian criticism by Belinsky, and also in the air more generally, in a critical period shaped by Kant, Hegel, and German Romanticism. It is prominent, for example, in Schiller's *Letters on the Aesthetic Education of Man* (1794–1801)—a text especially close to Dostoevsky's heart, but key for his entire generation—where beauty is defined as "living form" (*lebende Gestalt*).[56]

In mid-nineteenth-century Russia, when writers and critics sought to apply a version of this standard to realist novels, the slide between the aesthetic and the mimetic—between the "organic" integrity of the entire work and the mimetic life of individual characters—was extraordinarily common. When the radical critic Dobroliubov writes that he values Turgenev's novella *On the Eve* (*Nakanune*, 1860) as art "in which life has spoken of its own accord, and not according to an author's preconceived program," he is using an aesthetic standard similar to the one Dostoevsky invokes in his screed about Marko Vovchok's characters, which was aimed to rebuke Dobroliubov himself. A similar logic permeates Tolstoy's unpublished preface to *War and Peace* and his later comments on Vronsky's suicide in *Anna Karenina*.[57] For Tolstoy, Dostoevsky, and Dobroliubov alike, an aesthetically successful work is one in which "life has spoken of its own accord," and there is a tendency to see autonomous life and the aesthetic worth it signals as embodied, in turn, in the *characters'* seeming autonomy.

In the Russian realist tradition, then, the long-standing philosophical problem of how aesthetic experience can be understood in relation to extra-aesthetic experience becomes refreshingly trivial in some senses, unusually acute in others. For the radical critics, the "autonomous" world and characters of artistic fiction served as a viable if paler proxy for actual life. In a subtler position closer to the one that Dostoevsky worked out in his criticism, readers might understand real and fictional worlds on distinct but equal (and equally urgent) terms. In his first published essay (1919), Dostoevsky's seminal interpreter Bakhtin extended this logic: "Art and life are not one, but they must become united in myself—in the unity of my answerability."[58]

Nevertheless, it is striking that Bakhtin's aphorism takes the form of an exhortation. In actuality, the realist novel's passage between art and life may be just as uncertain as it is desired. This is particularly true if the novel's most compelling rhetorical strength does indeed lie in the creation of vivid mimetic characters—rather than (say) retellable plots or, as in the case of Chernyshevsky's *What Is to Be Done?*, characters intended to offer didactic social and political models. If a condition of creating "living" characters is the novel's coherence and autonomy from overt and purposeful polemics, and if the "living" character also functions as a *marker* of aesthetic coherence and autonomy, then there is no guarantee that well-made novels will serve any extra-aesthetic purposes at all. It is worth lingering with so stark a paradox. For Tolstoy and Dostoevsky—as still for some theorists and many readers of realist novels today—the strongest force urging us to take the novel as *more* than a novel depends on figures who live most fully in the act and moment of reading. The novel's surest and most direct power over its readers is bounded by the aesthetic limitations of character-systems themselves.

More visibly than any of their great contemporaries, Tolstoy and Dostoevsky explored this paradox through the medium of novelistic narrative. They realized new and exhilarating potentials of realist technique in an effort to disguise the complex narrative systems on which mimetic characterization in the novel depends. For example, they employed narrative "side shadowing"—having a narrator tell not just what did happen to a character, but also what could have happened, and what might or might not have happened, in ways that emphasize the fundamental contingency of being and behavior.[59] Like other Russian realist authors, they gave some works projected but unwritten sequels, and so also protagonists who seem to live beyond the text, whose undetermined futures make a claim on readers' imaginations.[60] Still more fundamentally, they experimented with expanding the kinds of human figures that realist novels can represent and the ground that mimetic illusion can cover—from Natasha Rostova, to Napoleon, to the crowds of *War and Peace*; from the Christlike Prince Myshkin to Ivan Karamazov's devil.

Each of these experiments in mimesis requires its own generic and technical innovations. In particular, as I will argue, both authors found a range of strategies for loosening the linear correspondence between the intensity of the effect of a character's life and the size of the narrative space allotted to him. Their novels thus asymptotically approach the goal of making readers forget the bounded narrative systems in which the illusion of mimetic life itself takes shape. The resulting characterizations move the critical and readerly dramas of the early 1860s—the blurring between life and fiction, reader and type, manual and novel—back between the covers of individual works.

At the same time, by so virtuosically staging the extension of realist characterization to the outer boundaries of the novel genre, Dostoevsky and Tolstoy marked the *project* of extension as problematic. Written near the end of the period of the realist novel's ascension in Russia, by authors drawn throughout their lives to more direct ways of shaping their readers, these experiments with characterization spring from a shared anxiety. What if the very success of mimetic characterizations within a novel signals that novel's self-containment, its supreme capacity to involve the reader in a world created by and sealed within text?

Closer attention to what creates the exceptional vividness of Tolstoy's and Dostoevsky's characters, surprisingly, reveals the *challenge* that character posed to the exceptional spiritual and conceptual ambition of their novels. It has long been accepted that these novels' claim to truth about and penetration into the reader's world rests on the capacity to evoke unplotted, indeterminate life, yielding unprecedented insights into physical and psychological experience. One reason why Tolstoy's and Dostoevsky's novels add to what we know about mimetic character-systems, is that they often test just how far from the center of individual written narratives this illusion of life can be realized. Conversely, however, the very idea of the character-system sounds a note of caution about the scope of such fictional experiments. Tolstoy's and Dostoevsky's novels subvert the protagonist-centered European realist character-system from within, but they also demonstrate how life effects depend on economies of attention that *only* a character-system, set into the bounds of a fictional world, can support. And they sharply manifest the tension between these two conditions. As much as they show realist characters "jostl[ing] for, and within" the narrative's attention,[61] these novels stage their authors' vexed struggles to move beyond the limits of realist character-systems themselves.

MIMETIC LIFE AND RUSSIAN REALISM (II)

In the chapters that follow, I explore a variety of ways in which Tolstoy and Dostoevsky destabilized the protagonist-centered character-systems that anchor Western European realist novels. This idea of destabilization requires another word of introduction.

As Alex Woloch has argued, the Western European realist tradition, as built around British and French nineteenth-century novels, uneasily balances an impulse toward "social expansiveness" with an impulse toward "individual interiority and depth." This tension results from a core feature of narrative: in any single narrative of a particular *agon* there will be fewer protagonists than actors (and in the strictest definition, only one). Authors from Homer to Joyce have constructed their narratives so as to register this asymmetry and often, to unsettle it—by weaving together multiple plots, by imagining a single narrative world from multiple perspectives, by calling the reader's attention to the fact of minorness or (conversely) to the potential "flatness" of protagonicity.[62] Woloch frames the realist tradition's particular discomfort with narrative asymmetry as sociological, political, and moral, reflecting anxieties that grew over the course of the nineteenth century. What does it mean that realist novels place so many implied persons outside the center of narrative attention? Conversely, how socially encyclopedic can the realist narrative tradition become before it collapses under the weight of all the minor characters pressing in upon its chosen individual protagonist(s)?

A key assumption underlying Woloch's approach—and also, it seems fair to agree, underlying the basic project of European realist narrative—is that more narrative means more mimesis. Longer narratives embrace greater swaths of "world and time"; characters toward the perspectival center of the narrative are more fully drawn than those toward the margins. These assumptions are of a piece, as Woloch argues, with the historical and political conditions in which realist novels arose:

> The realist novel is infused with the sense that any character is a potential hero, but simultaneously enchanted with the freestanding individual, defined through his or her interior consciousness. . . . On the one hand, the asymmetric structure of realist characterization . . . reflects actual structures of inequitable distribution. On the other hand, the claims of minor characters on the reader's attention—and the resultant tension between characters and their functions—are generated by the democratic impulse that forms a horizon of nineteenth-century politics.[63]

In realist novels written from a political tradition whose "democratic impulses" are (to say the least) uncertain, the dialectic between major and minor might well look different.[64] Consider the realist novel as a genre imported into Russia from the European West—the cultural sphere in relation to which many post-Petrine Russian intellectuals consciously defined themselves—and difference begins to seem inevitable. I do not mean a difference within the logic of how characters are created and conceived in the realist novel, but rather a difference in Russian novelists' estimation of what realist novels are and do. George Eliot, writing *Middlemarch* soon after the Second Reform Bill, was ready to question what Woloch calls the "asymmetric norm . . . of nineteenth-century omniscient narrative"; but Tolstoy, writing during and after the Crimean War, was ready to question the underlying terms of "asymmetry" as such.[65] In different ways but for some of the same reasons, both Tolstoy and Dostoevsky came to idealize the *mir* (community) of Russian peasants ("the many") while struggling against the alienated condition of Europeanized nobles ("the ones"). If it is better to be "many" than "one"—if *less* individualized narrative is better than *more*—then the very terms of realist characterization ought to be reversed. However, there is no guarantee that this reversal can be accomplished from within the European novel form.[66] Any approach toward realizing it then becomes a titanic work of illusion—illusion that operates at once with and against the mimetic resources of realism and the novel themselves.

From the beginnings of their careers, Dostoevsky (*Poor Folk* [*Bednye liudi*], 1846) and Tolstoy (*Childhood* [*Detstvo*], 1852) approached this work of illusion in diametrically opposing ways. *Poor Folk*, narrated in letters sent between the destitute titular councilor Makar Devushkin and his beloved neighbor Varvara, endows a conventional Gogolian type with a plausible self-consciousness. To an unprecedented extent, the character seems to be aware of, and to attempt to control, his own literary image. *Childhood*, by contrast, is narrated in the first person of "pseudo-autobiography."[67] Fictional characters so clearly serve the author's account of his own lived experience that when the novella was published in the *Contemporary*, the editor Nekrasov (to Tolstoy's disgust) retitled it "The History of My Childhood ("Istoriia moego detstva").[68]

In later novels too, Tolstoy set his characterizations into the frame of stably and often obtrusively omniscient narrative; Dostoevsky, into a frame that challenges the reader's assumption of omniscience and works to disguise the implied author's hand.[69] Tolstoy favored "direct" characterization, through the overt and repeated naming of qualities by an authoritative narrator, in conjunction with representations of the characters' inner lives. Dostoevsky more often relied on "indirect" techniques—indicating characters through the "evidence" of a speech, emotion, action, or thought, rather than through extensive authoritative description.[70] As Bakhtin in particular emphasizes, Tolstoy and Dostoevsky thus represent the character's autonomous "subjective perception" of his or her world differently.[71] In Tolstoy, it is a mimetic effect like any other, produced "monologically" by the omniscient narrator's activity.[72] In Dostoevsky, characters appear in the guise of speaking subjects, as the "dialogic" narrative creates the impression that the character's "own word about himself" stands on a par with the words of the narrator and other characters. However, through these opposed techniques, both Tolstoy and Dostoevsky intensified the illusion of extratextual presence and autonomous self-consciousness that I call "mimetic life." It is precisely because they used such different strategies to render and regulate mimetic life, while nurturing such far-reaching ambitions for it, that I place their paired example at the center of this study.

Tolstoy's direct and Dostoevsky's indirect techniques of characterization offer equally powerful ways of destabilizing the assumption that more narrative means more mimesis. Tolstoy tugged readers' attention from the center toward the margins of his novels' narratives—reflecting his lifelong conviction, and suspicion, that the relationship between truth and narrative is not linear. Dostoevsky's dialogic novels challenge the conventional vision of implied personhood as a limited resource, distributed by a single central authority. A formidable group of literary theorists (among them Bakhtin, Viktor Shklovsky, Lydia Ginzburg, and Gary Saul Morson) have analyzed and named the innovative techniques that Tolstoy and Dostoevsky used to create their vivid characters.[73] My attention to the authors' manipulations of realist character-systems allows me to add to this gallery of mimetic techniques. Because I argue that these techniques are essentially relational, working within and throughout the course of the narrative, I concentrate my analysis not on individual passages but on entire texts.

However, in the case of each novel I analyze, I am equally concerned with the inherent incompleteness of Tolstoy's and Dostoevsky's destabilizing projects. If it were ever to take place, a total rupture in the linear proportion between narrative attention and mimesis would also mean a divorce between illusion and text: an exit from the enchanted circle of what Lukács called the "totality" between the novel's beginning and its end, which raises the individual protagonist "to the infinite heights of one who must create an entire world through his experience."[74] In other words (and here I imagine a different end point than Lukács), novelistic characters would become independent of text-based systems, taking equally vivid, equally compelling, and equally controlled shape as a lens for the reader's experience whether she is reading or not. In the most extreme case of this translation of authority, the novel's world would wholly merge with the reader's: a vision of divine creation mediated by the modern metaphor of authorship.[75] I argue that some version of this dream propels both Tolstoy and Dostoevsky into new realms of experimentation with mimetic character, and newly bewitching versions of the illusion of solid and autonomous "life." But these illusions are the by-product of an ultimately impossible ambition: that bounded character-systems might be so fully transformed as to lead the novel reader entirely beyond the genre's aesthetic bounds.

The constellations of characters that result from this ambition are unconventional, often unsustainable, and certainly unrepeatable. The figures I will highlight—the marginal character who seems to live precisely because he is so little narrated, the narrator who obscures characters rather than portraying them, the protagonist who must be untangled from plot and narrative description in order to fulfill his most pivotal role in the novel—are not the building blocks of a continuing realist tradition. On the contrary, they help explain what Boris Eikhenbaum calls the "crisis of narrative prose" that Dostoevsky and Tolstoy brought about in Russia toward the end of the nineteenth century, which serves as a capstone to the story of European realism itself.[76] Specific forms of this crisis are the subjects of the chapters that follow.

THE LIVES OF CHARACTERS IN DOSTOEVSKY AND TOLSTOY

Chapter 1 gives an account of mimetic characterization in Tolstoy's great historical novel *War and Peace* (1865–69). A crystalline structure of repeated contrasts between central and minor characters, organized by family name, generation, and theme, helps create and sustain the relational illusion of mimetic life throughout the novel's fictional world. But Tolstoy is increasingly drawn to a problem that taxes this conventional character-system past its limits: how to represent the life of historical people in a crowd, army, or nation—the *marginal* figures that take shape only at the periphery of the named characters' experience? In the notorious theoretical digressions that gradually overwhelm the novel's plot, Tolstoy attempts to work out a new logic, from the perspective of a different genre and discipline, for the vivid representation of marginal characters. Tolstoy's preoccupation with this challenge creates a productive but unsupportable tension. The richly narrated mimetic life of the protagonists at the narrative's center strains toward the barely sketched mimetic life of the crowds at its margins, but the fulfillment of this desire could only mean an escape from the novel genre and a rejection of the compelling vividness that text-bound novelistic representation makes possible. Because Tolstoy explicitly draws attention to this paradox, *War and Peace* clarifies the pattern that I trace through all the chapters of the study: mobilization of the character-system's capacity to create, sustain, and regulate mimetic illusion, followed by frustration with the limits of characterization and the novel themselves.

Chapter 2 traces Dostoevsky's representations of a set of characters cut off from the twin anchors of conventional realist narrative: the social order of "landowner literature" (29.I:216) and the literary order of narrative omniscience. To capture protagonists that defied existing literary form, Dostoevsky created the techniques that Bakhtin describes as dialogic, projecting his characters backward from their "own" utterances about "themselves" in an illusion of totally unsystematic flexibility. However, despite their apparent repudiation of stable character-systems, his novels reveal a longing for the seductive mimetic solidity that character-systems support. I argue that Dostoevsky saw severance from the image-making authority of omniscient narrative—which mirrors postreform Russia's divorce from its traditional religious, moral, and social foundations—as a condition not of freedom, but of *narrative illegitimacy*: the state of estrangement from one's rightful origins and name. First posed in *Notes from Underground* (1864), the problem of narrative illegitimacy comes to a head in *The Adolescent* (1875), which recounts the moral decay of an impoverished landowner as narrated by his illegitimate son. *The Adolescent* exaggerates the Dostoevskian protagonist's detachment from narrative design, but in doing so, it reveals the contrasting utopian fantasy of a novel that would arrest modern spiritual and social dissolution simply by transforming it into a mimetic work of art—an extra-aesthetic creative power that Dostoevsky knew neither his own novels nor anyone else's could reliably wield.

Chapters 3 and 4 turn to each author's furthest-reaching attempt, in the face of such representational challenges, to push vivid characterization past the limits of the novel genre: Tolstoy's *Anna Karenina* (1875–77), and Dostoevsky's *The Brothers Karamazov* (1879–80).

In chapter 3, I show how Tolstoy manipulates the double narrative of *Anna Karenina* as he works to sever the aesthetic experience of imagining a character from the practical model for living life that a character can embody. In Anna's half of the novel, Tolstoy highlights what he sees as the seductive but false terms of conventional realist characterization. He intensifies the illusion of Anna's living body, while painting minor characters (in her lover Vronsky's telling phrase) as "parasites" upon this body, vainly competing for the reader's limited attention. In the narrative centered on the novel's other protagonist, Konstantin Levin, Tolstoy stages a reversal of convention. He asks whether a protagonist could become a new kind of parasite on the main body of the novel—nurtured by one host, the novel *Anna Karenina*, and then delivered to another, the novel reader. Tolstoy thus attempts to make Levin, a character central to the novel's action, into a lure that compels us beyond the bounds of fiction itself: a model for seeing and thinking about the world that becomes ineluctably compelling because the character is so vivid. But at its most ambitious, Tolstoy's attempt to remake the terms of realist characterization fails. Anna's and Levin's intertwined narrative lines depend on one another for their vividness, and the protagonist who "lives" beyond the text thus turns out to be an irresistible but unrealizable dream. It was recognition of this failure, in part, that drove Tolstoy in the second half of his career away from writing novels, toward polemical and philosophical tracts, religious parables, and other more reliable modes of communication with his readers.

Chapter 4 shows how in *The Brothers Karamazov*, his final novel, Dostoevsky uses indirect techniques of characterization to draw the reader into a universal story of spiritual transcendence. Each Karamazov, left to negotiate his "own" fluid position in relation to a family identity, opens a site for a redemptive narrative of religious conversion—a narrative for which the secular forms of nineteenth-century European realism must be reworked. With the Karamazovs, Dostoevsky hoped to give his readers a set of portable types that could guide them toward a new vision of human nature as perfectible and divine. But this sweeping ambition is threatened by the textbound character-system that structures the Karamazovs' plot. *The Brothers Karamazov* broke ground for later theorists who would embrace Dostoevsky the journalist and thinker's vision of the novel's potential to transform readers. However, it also cements the distrust of the limitations of form and character that Dostoevsky the *novelist* shared with Tolstoy. This distrust is balanced only precariously with narrative techniques that further Dostoevsky's ideal of turning the realist novel into the matrix for a new Russian myth.

The outcome of the struggle against the limits of character and the novel is thus uncertain. Bounded networks of characters organized around a vivid protagonist or small group of protagonists structure Tolstoy's and Dostoevsky's novels, just as they do Austen's, Dickens's, or Balzac's. But in Tolstoy's and Dostoevsky's novels, the mimetic ideal embodied by a protagonist at the center of an absorbing fictional heterocosm competes with the ideal of characters that continue, in predictable ways, to capture the attention of a reader *un*bound from the novel's text. The trick these novels continually attempt—which necessarily remains incomplete—is to extend the power of vividness beyond the aesthetic act of novel reading.

Because some of Tolstoy's and Dostoevsky's most influential readers have argued for the conclusive success of this project (with implications not just for Russian realism, but for the theory of the novel itself), I must embrace a degree of reinterpretive hubris. The thrust of my analysis will be, pace Lukács, that Dostoevsky did write novels; and pace Bakhtin, that realist novels do (like other kinds of art) work within the bounds of aesthetic experience. Tolstoy's and Dostoevsky's novels do not count on a Bakhtinian reader who would "make art and life one" by force of conviction. On the contrary, they chart new territory in the attempt to *create* such a reader, extending the power of vivid novelistic characterization to the borders of nonfictional genres. In the process, they reveal an insuperable tension between the constructed illusion of a character's independent life, and the dream of turning that illusion into a path leading outward from the fictional text.

In a brief afterword, I reflect on this argument's implications for contemporary readers of realist novels. It is often said that encounters with novelistic characters should make readers more empathetic, but the real moral consequences of novel reading remain elusive.[77] The systematic, self-contained nature of mimetic life helps account for this disjunction. Novels offer compelling models of "possible people" with particular perspectives, but these model people belong to the moment of reading: they are shaped by the authored systems in which they become so vivid. We should thus question the contemporary tenet that novels like Tolstoy's and Dostoevsky's endow readers with visions of Others that carry directly into ethical encounters in day-to-day life. Instead, we should value realist novels for what they do offer: an invitation into the inexhaustible work of reading.

By focusing on techniques of mimetic characterization, this book aims to retell the story of Tolstoy's and Dostoevsky's place in the history of representing reality in European literature. There is no better point of departure for this project than the gap that Erich Auerbach left for a chapter on Russian realism in his canonical history *Mimesis* (1947).

Auerbach begins his history of mimetic representation from two opposing origins, Homer's epics and the Hebrew Bible. In Homer, narrative events are "foregrounded," each circumstance and cause fully illuminated for the audience in turn. The sensory vividness of Homer's reality, his "delight in physical existence," has no claim to lasting persuasion; it "ensnares us, weaving its web around us, and that suffices him." Biblical narrative, by contrast, leaves many of its events and its characters' motivations opaque. It thus demands interpretation, and still more, assent: "Far from seeking, like Homer, merely to make us forget our own reality for a few hours, [the Bible] seeks to overcome our reality: we are to fit our lives into its world, feel ourselves to be elements in its structure of universal history."[78] Auerbach finds the climactic crossroads of these world-creating and world-reflecting mimetic impulses in Dante's *Divine Comedy*, where human characters and biographies are set into the cosmic order of Christian judgment and salvation, but narrated with sensory detail so vivid as to eclipse it.[79] By the time of Balzacian realism, he suggests, the framework of salvation and the afterlife is no longer present to lend overwhelming and communal ("tragic") weight to everyday detail; weight comes, rather, from the potential in individual characters and narratives to reveal the essential dynamics of human history. And by the time of Woolf's or Proust's modernism, not even so large a frame as history is offered: instead, the sheer sensory richness of "each moment to which we surrender ourselves without prejudice" lends significance to the narration of an individual life.[80]

As Auerbach tells it, Russia is absent from his study only because he could not read Russian works in the original. But in a suggestive digression, he likens the high spiritual stakes attached to the everyday in Russian realist literature, and the widely oscillating "pendulum of [the characters'] vitality, of their actions, thoughts, and emotions," to pre-Dantean "Christian realism": the Bible, Augustine, and medieval mystery plays.[81] He places this claim into the context of a specific Western European reaction: "When the great Russians, especially Dostoevski, became known in Central and Western Europe, the immense spiritual potential and the directness of expression which their amazed readers encountered in their works seemed like a revelation of how the mixture of realism and tragedy might at last attain its true fulfillment."[82]

The "amazement" that Auerbach describes is worth dwelling on. If *Mimesis* had had a chapter on the Russian novel, midway between Flaubert and Woolf, it might have developed the idea of characters so intensely vivid that they recall the spiritual and epistemological force of "Christian realism." But midway between Flaubert and Woolf, within the secular genre of the European novel, this narrative mode looks like a paradox—a fictional world real enough to its readers to demand not just absorbed reflection but transformative belief. By marking in their novels the problem of expanding character beyond the bounds of system, Tolstoy and Dostoevsky themselves drew attention to the complex lines of connection among character, novel, and reader. Retracing these lines, we see not just the conditions that create the effect of lifelike persons, but also the conditions that contain it: a collision between the plenitude and the discontents of mimesis that few novelists have made so compellingly clear.

Chapter One

Dinner at the English Club: Character on the Margins in *War and Peace*

TOLSTOY'S EARLY SHORT story "Sevastopol in May" ("Sevastopol' v mae," 1855)—among the dispatches from the Crimean War that cemented his reputation as a leading realist writer—ends with a famous provocation:

> Where in this story is the evil that should be avoided, and where the good that should be imitated? Who is the villain and who the hero? All are good and all are bad. Not Kalugin . . . nor Praskukhin . . . not Mikhaylov . . . nor Pest . . . can be either the villain or the hero of the story. The hero of my story—whom I love with all the power of my soul, whom I have tried to portray in all his beauty, who has been, is, and will be beautiful—is truth.[1]

Like the narrative as a whole, this passage plays on the slip between virtue and centrality inherent in the imported word "hero" (*geroi*). The contemporaneous four-volume *Dictionary of the Church Slavonic and Russian Language* (*Slovar' tserkovno-slavianskago i russkago iazyka*, 1847) gives three meanings: a valiant warrior; a person who has distinguished himself with great feats or selflessness; and "in poems, novels, or stories, the main person about whom the story is told."[2] Tolstoy's story undermines both the concept and the narrative position of the hero. It is divided among five named officer protagonists, whose reported thoughts contradict their most cherished and romanticized self-conceptions. Its rhetorical climax is not the dramatic death of one of these protagonists, Praskukhin, but rather the foray of an unnamed peasant child to gather blue flowers on the battlefield. The coda thus spells out the story's premise: military and narrative "heroism" are two sides of the same deceit. But it blurs a crucial equivocation: in order to evoke the lived experience of a battle, Tolstoy has no choice but to draw our attention to a set of individual, internally focalized main characters—

the very kinds of protagonists that realist narrative is so well designed to construct. If narrative centrality itself courts falsehood, then how could the hero of such a story be truth?

Characterization is not the only dimension of this Tolstoyan paradox. The inescapable limits of embodied, individual selfhood were Tolstoy's preoccupation from the beginning to the end of his life as a writer.[3] But fictional "heroism" concentrates these anxieties in peculiar ways. As early as "Sevastopol in May," Tolstoy challenged the principle that the *center* of a narrative is the site of its fullest and most privileged acts of representation. However, he drew on the resources of realist characterization and realist protagonicity even as he revised their conventions. He attempted both to use and to transcend the bounds of fiction.

Although all its elements are already present by the time of "Sevastopol in May," the history of the novel holds no more thrilling example of this balancing act than Tolstoy's *War and Peace* (*Voina i mir*, 1865–69).

That *War and Peace* is a novel (and not, as Tolstoy maintained, an unclassifiable "book") is one of the arguments of this chapter. It is a novel in the sense that, like *Madame Bovary* (1856) or *Don Quixote* (1615), it confronts us with the problematic romance of mimetic illusion itself. This confrontation takes shape not through the image of a reading hero or heroine, but over the course of our own reading. Tolstoy creates the illusion of a vast and vividly populated fictional world using systematic contrasts between major and minor characters, which make his major characters seem to live. As the novel continues, his attention is increasingly drawn toward the equally "living" historical scene, with all its unnamed actors, unfolding in the margins of his own characters' stories—and from there, to theoretical digressions on historiography and the problem of free will that become longer and longer as the novel continues. Tolstoy's provocative hybrid text suspends us between a fictional world and its ever more urgently omniscient narrator. He imagines a fiction that would encapsulate reality, and so no longer need to be fiction. But as I will show, Tolstoy's absorbing act of mimesis depends on the unequal distribution of *limited* narrative space and attention—that is, on the very fictional bounds that his novel also attempts to escape. *War and Peace* thus exposes the triumphant early credo, "The hero of my story is truth," as an enduring problem. It models the clash between mimetic life and transformational reading—the compelling illusion of living characters, and the uncertain practical, epistemological, or rhetorical uses of this illusion—that all the chapters of this book set out to address.

DINNER AT THE ENGLISH CLUB: APPROACHING THE CHARACTER-SYSTEM OF *WAR AND PEACE*

Soon after Alexander I's army has lost the Battle of Austerlitz in *War and Peace*, Tolstoy's character Count Ilya Rostov organizes a banquet at the English Club in Moscow in honor of Prince Bagration. Collecting together fictional and historical players, the novel's most central protagonists and evanescent incidental figures, the scene of this banquet extends an invitation into *War and Peace*'s vast web of characters. A brief reading will establish some basic terms for describing how this web is constructed.

Bagration's dinner is narrated three times, in three successive chapters. The first narrative is just one sentence long: "Next day, the 3rd of March, soon after one o'clock, two hundred and fifty members of the English Club and fifty guests were awaiting the guest of honor and hero of the Austrian campaign, Prince Bagration, to dinner."[4] With this sentence, almost three hundred new characters enter *War and Peace*. The guests and members then receive a collective biography. We see them placed on the second highest tier of a social hierarchy that follows the lead of Count Rastopchin, Prince Dolgorukov, and other historical figures. The fictional characters we already know illuminate this group within the novel's own self-contained terms: some pass on stories about the heroics of the minor character Berg, Count Rostov's officious future son-in-law; only a few lament the major character Andrei Bolkonsky, whom the narrative has left wounded on the field at Austerlitz.

The second narrative brings the guests and members of the English Club more concretely into the novel:

> On the third of March all the rooms in the English Club were filled with a hum of conversation, like the hum of bees swarming in spring-time. The members and guests of the club wandered hither and thither, sat, stood, met, and separated, some in uniform and some in evening dress. . . . Most of those present were elderly respected men with broad self-confident faces, fat fingers, and resolute gestures and voices. (329)[5]

Having first encountered these figures from a distance, we are now close enough to hear the drone of their voices and see their fat fingers. All three hundred guests and members now emerge as fully embodied, although extremely minor, characters—as do the "powdered footmen in livery with buckled shoes and smart stockings . . . anxiously noting visitors' every movement in order to offer their services" (329; 10:16). The narrative descriptions of these crowds intersperse the collective with the individual and the alien with the known. The scattered guests assemble to watch Bagration's entrance "like rye shaken together in a shovel" (330; 10:17), but when the company toasts the emperor, the "ecstatic voice" of another major fictional character, Count Rostov's son Nikolai, can "be heard above all the three hundred others." Such moments group the guests around Nikolai Rostov in the discourse as surely as, in the story, they take their places around Bagration, "the more important nearer to the honored guest, as naturally as water flows deepest where the land lies lowest" (332; 10:19).

The third and final narrative starts again from the beginning of Bagration's banquet, this time moving the scene from the public sphere of ceremonious toasts at the head of the table to the private level of the guests sitting at its middle: Pierre Bezukhov, Nikolai Rostov, and Fyodor Dolokhov. Focalized mainly through Pierre, this rendition barely touches on Bagration; the banquet becomes a backdrop to Pierre's realization that Dolokhov is cuckolding him, and to Dolokhov's insult and the challenge Pierre issues him at the end of the night. We learn not only that Pierre looks preoccupied, but also what thoughts are preoccupying him and how these thoughts sound: "He seemed to see and hear nothing of what was going on around him and to be absorbed by some depressing and unsolved problem. The unsolved problem that tormented him was caused by hints given by the princess, his cousin, at Moscow, concerning Dolokhov's intimacy with his wife" (334; 10:21). The second narrative used named fictional characters to construct an idiosyncratic perspective on a historical scene; the third makes one of these same characters the center of its attention, allowing his subjective experience to dictate our view.

Dolokhov's voice, by contrast, never enters the narrator's discourse. We read him only as Pierre does, from the outside: "Dolokhov looked at Pierre with clear mirthful cruel eyes, and that smile of his which seemed to say, 'Ah! This is what I like!'" (335; 10:23). This external focalization limits Dolokhov's presence in the narrative of the scene. In one respect, however, his role is more important to that narrative than either Pierre's or Nikolai's: it is Dolokhov who initiates the scene's main plot development by snatching away Pierre's copy of Kutuzov's cantata, the final insult that precipitates Pierre's challenge and (the next morning) their duel.

The contrast between the representation of Pierre and the representation of Dolokhov, against the background of the footmen, guests, and members of the English Club, throws into relief the lines that separate three basic categories of character in *War and Peace*. I will call them *major*, *minor*, and *marginal*.

The concept of a novelistic "character-system," as defined in Alex Woloch's *The One vs. the Many*, makes it possible to formalize these categories.[6] Woloch focuses on the distortion of minor characters relative to the fuller rendering of central protagonists: on the fact that no realist novel has enough narrative "space" for all the people it purports to represent. His study develops two linked concepts. The "character-space" is the "charged encounter" between the designation of an "individual human personality," and the space and position into which the representation of this personality must fit within the narrative. The "character-system" is the "arrangement of multiple and differentiated character-spaces . . . into a unified narrative structure."[7] As Woloch stresses, the difference between major and minor characters in any narrative is, fundamentally, a difference of character-spaces: a novel's main protagonist(s) lie(s) closest to the center of its narrative attention, and its most minor characters, furthest toward the periphery.

In *War and Peace*, Tolstoy both exploits and experiments with the conventional shape of a realist character-system. The terms of the exploitation and the experiment emerge in the triple narration of Bagration's banquet at the English Club. Of the eight pages it occupies in the Jubilee edition, about three attend mainly to Pierre and his perception of Dolokhov, while the other three hundred guests and members are squeezed into forty scattered lines of collective description. Moreover, they comprise a group continually in need of differentiation, arrangement around a vivid point like Nikolai Rostov's cheer. In each narration of the banquet, we are aware of the fictional characters' organizing centrality. Yet the moments when Pierre and Nikolai are central to the scene combine with others when they sink into the crowd of guests and members, all pressed alike into the service of making Bagration's banquet part of Tolstoy's novel. While reinforcing a configuration of characters centered on Pierre and the Rostovs, these scenes also reveal a parallel configuration, centered on a particular presentation of Bagration.

The center of narrative attention in *War and Peace* is thus divided—not only among its protagonists (Pierre Bezukhov, Marya and Andrei Bolkonsky, and Natasha and Nikolai Rostov), but *between* these protagonists and the other material that the novel brings to life.[8] With sweeping ambition, Tolstoy distributes the space of *War and Peace* among five major characters, dozens of named minor characters, and thousands of soldiers, officers, serfs, tradesmen, workers, doctors, provincial officials, lunatics, children, horses, dogs—even (as we will see) stars.[9] He relies on named protagonists to organize a narrative that stretches out to encompass the myriad around them; while the protagonists' centrality helps construct this world, its very dimensions work to dismantle their centrality. As a contemporary reviewer of *War and Peace* remarked, "To his heroes and their private lives [Tolstoy] gives as much space, light and air as is necessary for the bare support of their existence."[10]

Because of this peculiarity, which springs from (but also heightens) the demands of historical fiction, *War and Peace* calls for a third interpretive category that could bypass Woloch's opposition between major characters, and characters that are minor in comparison with them. These are the characters that I will call *marginal*, by which I mean "located at the fringes," both of the narrative and of the reader's consciousness. Most (if not all) realist novels have incidental or marginal characters, but Tolstoy, unusually, is drawn to marginality for its mimetic potential: a form of vividness and authenticity that depends upon *exclusion* from the fictional plot and its organizing terms.[11] Seen in this light, Tolstoy's protagonists function not just to occupy their own proper space, but also to create a crucially peripheral space for the representation of others.[12] In the first half of *War and Peace*, its marginal characters remain (like the guests, members, and footmen of the English Club) largely dormant. But throughout the novel's second half, they evoke an ever more enticing representational ideal: the mimetic horizon that Tolstoy refers to as the "history of *all*" (1278; 12:305).

To Tolstoy scholars, the proposal that his protagonists are not the sole defining center of his texts will come as no surprise. As Viktor Shklovsky wrote in his 1928 study of *War and Peace*, "The employment of 'heroes' in Tolstoy generally is to draw in and transform material, and not to display themselves. . . . In [Tolstoy] the hero's role is secondary: he is summoned by the action, rather than determining it."[13] Lydia Ginzburg later argued that "the Tolstoian hero is not indivisibly attached to his particular personality nor is the novel itself indivisibly attached to its hero. . . . Tolstoi was a great master of individual personality, but he went beyond that personality in order to see and reveal the nature of 'life in general' [*obshchaia zhizn'*] . . . the very processes of life itself."[14] Still later, Gary Saul Morson showed how *War and Peace* (like "Sevastopol in May") exposes the folly of heroism in all its guises, training the reader to redirect her attention from the agents who seem to be controlling the narrative, to the truer vision of limited human agency that Tolstoy "hides in plain view."[15]

My reading of *War and Peace* aims both to extend and to redirect this seminal line of argument. I suggest that the distinctions *among* major, minor, and marginal characters are more important to Tolstoy's mimetic project than has yet been acknowledged, in a novel long praised for its miraculously complete fictional world. Using both fictional narrative and an explicit theory of historical narration, Tolstoy assembles a system of relations and contrasts among his characters that supports the illusion of his protagonists' lives and offers a crucial—although crucially limited—glimpse of the life beyond them. We can begin to understand the power and the limitations of this experiment by turning to the question of how *War and Peace*'s narrative "space" is divided among its major, minor, and marginal characters.

MAJOR VERSUS MINOR CHARACTERS: THE FICTIONAL FAMILIES OF *WAR AND PEACE*

Early readers found it hard to identify the major characters in the first serial installments of *War and Peace*.[16] Their confusion points to the success of an important aspect of the mimetic project Tolstoy undertakes: his move to exchange the conventional trappings of form for an appearance of the disorder and indeterminacy of extraliterary life.[17]

The hindsight that comes with multiple readings of the published novel yields a different kind of perspective into the techniques Tolstoy uses to build his illusions.[18] The most basic of these techniques is Tolstoy's division of the novel's fictional characters into eight named families: the scaffolding of the character-system that, in turn, supports the novel's represented world. By the end of the novel's first part, these major and minor families, and the techniques that signal their persistent narrative positions and tasks, are already in place. Tolstoy begins to establish this narrative division in the very first scene of *War and Peace*, set in Anna Pavlovna Scherer's Saint Petersburg salon.

The novel opens like a play, with urbane political dialogue (in French) between Mlle. Scherer, a maid of honor attached to Tsar Alexander I's mother, and Prince Vasili Kuragin, a high-ranking nobleman and courtier.[19] From the first, Tolstoy discourages us from delving beneath this polished dramatic surface. Not only are the characters described in external focalization; they are also continually related to the categories to which they belong. Thus, Vasili Kuragin "spoke in that refined French in which our grandfathers not only spoke but thought, and with the gentle, patronizing intonation natural [*svoistvennyi*] to a man of importance who had grown old in society and at court" (3–4; 9:4); "to be an enthusiast had become [Anna Pavlovna's] social vocation" (4; 9:5); "Anna Pavlovna, with the womanly and courtier-like quickness and tact habitual [*svoistvennoiu*] to her" (6; 9:7); "Prince Vasili did not reply though, with the quickness of memory and perception befitting [*svoistvennoiu*] a man of the world, he indicated" (7; 9:8). The adjective *svoistvennyi* (characteristic, typical of) tolls through these passages like a bell. Vasili Kuragin and Anna Pavlovna Scherer lend themselves to easy characterization because they are types of all the sets they belong to, types (in a sense) of their very selves.[20]

Indeed, as the guests pass through Anna Pavlovna's salon—compared to a "workshop" whose "conversational machine" Anna Pavlovna keeps smoothly running (11; 9:12)—the salon itself is revealed as a machine for the mass production of characters, created in transit between instance and type. *Each* guest is led up to greet Anna Pavlovna's maiden aunt, and *all* escape with a feeling of relief; *all* are cheered to see Andrei Bolkonsky's lively, pregnant wife Lise, and her smile encourages *each* to think he is being "especially amiable" (9; 9:10).

It is this machine, both social and narrative, whose works Pierre Bezukhov threatens to gum as soon as he enters the novel:

> One of the next arrivals was a stout, heavily built young man with close-cropped hair, spectacles, the light-colored breeches fashionable at that time, a very high ruffle and a brown dress-coat. . . . Anna Pavlovna greeted him with the nod she accorded to the lowest hierarchy in her drawing-room. But in spite of this lowest grade greeting, a look of anxiety and fear, as at the sight of something too large and uncharacteristic of the place, came over her face when she saw Pierre enter. Though he was certainly rather bigger than the other men in the room, her anxiety could only have reference to the clever though shy, observant and natural expression which distinguished him from everyone else in that drawing-room. (10)[21]

The early clue to Pierre's exceptionality in the discourse is not in the initial description of him; it is in Anna Pavlovna's immediate inkling of something "uncharacteristic" (*nesvoistvennogo*) of the space of her salon. Pierre's observant, unstudied gaze sets him off socially from all the other guests, and just as importantly, it sets him off technically from all the other characters. There is a visible gap between Pierre "himself" and the public figure that the salon allows him to present. The impression this strategy produces is not so much that Pierre *is* not narrated purely from the outside, as that—alone among all the well-defined social players around him—he *cannot* be.

If a flat character (in E. M. Forster's tenacious formulation) is one who "never surprises," then Tolstoy introduces his first protagonist into a room full of flat minor characters who imply willfully flat people, invested in performing their own conformity to a stable, preestablished type.[22] In this sense, the opening in Anna Pavlovna Scherer's salon makes an exceptionally strong mimetic claim: it primes us to believe that the aspects of *War and Peace*'s represented world that appear artificial are artificial of their own accord, not of the narrative's. Conversely and comparatively, through Pierre, we see the standard that this narrative sets for what is substantial, natural, and alive. Given this opposition, Andrei Bolkonsky's later characterization of Pierre approaches the level of the metafictional: "You are dear to me, especially since you are the one living person [*zhivoi chelovek*] among our whole circle" (31; 9:36). The imbalance that shapes these opening chapters is less an unequal distribution of narrative attention than an unequal distribution of the capacity to resemble a living person.[23]

These relational techniques for establishing the illusion of the living person are not confined to the space of the salon. Natasha Rostova first appears in a different setting, but under strikingly similar conditions. She interrupts the empty formalities of her parents' conversation with the Karagins to run, apparently by accident, into the pages of Tolstoy's novel:

> A silence ensued. . . . The visitor's daughter was already smoothing down her dress with an inquiring look at her mother, when suddenly from the next room were heard male and female feet running to the door and the crash of a chair falling over, and a girl of thirteen, hiding something in the folds of her short muslin skirt, darted in and stopped short in the middle of the room. It was evident that she had not intended her flight to bring her so far. Behind her in the doorway appeared a student with a crimson coat-collar, an officer of the Guards, a girl of fifteen, and a plump rosy-faced boy in a short jacket. (41)[24]

It is as much the background of silence and formality as the figure of Natasha that creates such a strong impression of animated motion. She stands out in relief against not only the Rostovs and Karagins sitting in the salon but also the figures framed behind her in the doorway, and even the doll hidden under her skirt. More than any other named protagonist, Natasha appears to *stumble* into form, both social and narrative—as she is first described, "not pretty, but full of life" (*nekrasivaia, no zhivaia*; 41; 9:47).

Of the novel's eventual protagonists, Andrei's sister Princess Marya Bolkonskaya is the only one who does not enter in the middle of a large gathering. She appears instead out of the long opening portrait of Prince Bolkonsky, her father:

> With those about him, from his daughter to his serfs, the prince was sharp and invariably exacting . . . every high official appointed to the province in which the prince's estate lay considered it his duty to visit him, and waited in the lofty antechamber just as the architect, gardener, or Princess Marya did . . . Everyone sitting in this antechamber experienced the same feeling of respect and even fear . . . On the morning of the day that [Andrei and Lise] were to arrive, Princess Marya entered the antechamber as usual at the time appointed for the morning meeting, crossing herself with trepidation and repeating a silent prayer. Every morning she came in like that, and every morning she prayed that the daily interview might pass off well. (93–94)[25]

The stroke that at once distinguishes Marya from her father and the uniform group around him, and integrates her perspective into the narrative, is the inner prayer she says daily before knocking on her father's door. The quality of spiritual activity enlivens Marya just as the quality of physical motion enlivens Natasha: just as we are prompted to imagine Natasha's body, we are prompted to imagine Marya's soul.

Most strongly developed in protagonists like Pierre, Natasha, and Marya, although not exclusive to them, is the illusion that I summarize under the term "mimetic life." A character's mimetic life is the reader's sense of his autonomous, embodied existence in and for himself, not only free from authorial control, but even independent of the words of narrative.[26] Natasha's mimetic life rests in the degree to which we feel that she runs into the salon (and the novel) by accident, from some other place where she could have existed just as well. Marya's rests in the voice in which her inner prayer can be imagined, before we have even heard her speak aloud in the novel. Pierre's rests in in his "shy, observant, natural" gaze. Heightened by contrast with the dead or uniform social world around them, these appeals to the protagonists' minds and bodies explicitly affirm that they "themselves" transcend the language that narrates them.

I will return in more detail to the two sides of this novel-wide contrast: Tolstoy's techniques for amplifying the signals of mental and physical "mimetic life" in the major characters of *War and Peace*, and of formulaic, mechanistic, ghostlike, or fragmentary existence in the minor ones. It is helpful, however, to begin by laying out the same organizing framework for this discussion that Tolstoy himself uses—the character-system's division into families.

Of the four figures who appear behind Natasha in the doorway when she enters, two are Rostovs, one is a Drubetskoy, and one (Sonya, Count Rostov's orphaned niece) never explicitly gets a surname. These facts have consequences in the character-system of *War and Peace*, a novel where more than one family is described as a "breed" (*poroda*).[27] Descriptions of the characters fall into narrative soil that may or may not sustain the illusion of mimetic life and the possibility of narrative centrality.

There are only about a dozen fictional families in *War and Peace*, if a family is defined as two or more characters represented in the discourse of the novel and sharing the same known family name. Eight come readily (enough) to mind: the Rostovs, the Bolkonskys, the Bezukhovs, the Bergs, the Drubetskoys, the Kuragins, the Karagins, and the Dolokhovs.[28] There are also several story orphans, like Sonya and old Prince Bolkonsky's companion Mlle. Bourienne; and a number of discourse orphans, whose families never appear in person. The scarcity of such characters who play significant roles, however, underscores the extent to which *War and Peace* thinks in families. The thematic functions associated with each family name, which in turn tend to dictate conditions of representation, are contained enough to be given here as a list.[29]

The Rostovs are associated with a conscious and unbounded, sometimes excessive, instinct for living life. The traits of life in excess are passed down in generations: the count's lavish but ruinous hospitality and gambling;

the countess's weariness from bearing twelve children and her jealous affection for the living ones; Nikolai's innate skill as a soldier, hunter, and manager of his estates, and also his gambling; the untaught beauty of Natasha's singing and dancing, and her susceptibility to male admiration, sexuality, and love; Petya's love of the hunt, the emperor, and the army, and his extravagant impulse to share all his raisins and flints. The Rostovs' thematic association with excessive vitality also defines the sphere that the novel leaves open for unplotted *narrative* excess: Count Rostov dancing the Daniel Cooper, Nikolai and then Petya falling asleep on the eve of battle, the wolf hunt, the Christmas masquerade, the notorious yellow diaper that Natasha shows off to Pierre in part 1 of the epilogue. The odd Rostov out is Vera, whose primness sets her apart from her family and so throws their identity into relief. Appropriately, midway through the novel, she changes from a Rostov to a Berg.

The Bolkonskys are thematically associated with intellect and the life of the spirit, life as lived in proximity to birth and death. Old Prince Nikolai Bolkonsky pursues "activity and intelligence" to the exclusion of all else, especially of open affection toward his family; this dryness endures through his capricious senility and weakens only on his deathbed. His son Andrei inherits the problem of reconciling intellect and ambition with human ties, played out through the disappointment of his first marriage and his broken engagement to Natasha; he too finds regeneration only when he is near death, on the field of Austerlitz and after Borodino. Marya, intensely religious, shelters pilgrims but never manages to become one herself: she arrives instead at a marriage made possible by the deaths of her father and brother. In all, the Bolkonskys bring one birth, three deaths, and three near deaths into the novel. Throughout this family trajectory, we become aware of a door between life and death swinging open and closed—represented explicitly in Andrei's famous dream (1059; 12:63–64).[30] Just as the Rostovs define a sphere for the representation of excessive life, the Bolkonskys create space for representing this mysterious passageway. Andrei's wife Lise, who dies in childbirth, is drawn into the family function (and name) by marriage, although she presents problems worthy of a separate discussion.

The Bezukhovs are less readily described. Count Bezukhov appears in the novel only on his deathbed, in a scene of singular ambiguity.[31] He is rumored to have lost count of his illegitimate children, among whom only Pierre has taken his name. Thus, although Pierre inherits his father's tendency to violent rages and governing "passion" for women, his central inheritance may be the very fact of his illegitimacy, the ambiguous possession of an indefinite family line. Pierre enters the novel with the potential for a fixed position in its social (and thematic) system, but he is characterized by the search for this position—for the meaning of the name "Bezukhov." He finds it partly by testing his own character against those of the Bolkonskys and Rostovs. If the Rostovs and the Bolkonskys divide between them experiences tied to the basic binaries of the novel's represented world—earthly life and the life of the spirit—then Pierre Bezukhov is a needle swinging over and around the areas they define. His narrative function as a *Bildungshero* is to be changed by what he sees and undergoes, and this instability and capacity for change most nearly define his family name as he embodies it.[32]

I have sketched the Rostovs, the Bolkonskys, and Pierre Bezukhov as a kind of thematic compass; this metaphor suggests itself, even if only temporarily, because of the elegance at the heart of the sprawling representational system of *War and Peace*. Two Rostovs and two Bolkonskys begin the novel at the right age to carry out its main action between 1805 and 1812, and each is associated with a complementary aspect of the family's thematic function, determined partly by gender.[33] These four characters, with Pierre, are the novel's main points of contact with historical events, with the natural world, and with fundamental aspects of conscious experience: thinking, praying, singing, falling in love, falling asleep, dreaming, dying. Reductive as this schema becomes, the novel's structure lends itself to such abstractions.

What helps to shade and solidify these abstractions is the mimetic system of the named families themselves, ranged behind the protagonists to create the sense that centrality is hereditary, its particulars determined only by the demands of historical material. The Rostovs demonstrate this continuity most clearly: by books 3 and 4 of the novel, set in 1812, Petya Rostov is old enough to retrace some of Nikolai Rostov's steps in books 1 and 2. For the other families, it works in glimpses. If the novel had been about Suvorov's campaigns, one of its protagonists would have been old Prince Bolkonsky; we catch sight of this novel in his memories of Potemkin, shortly before his death (742; 11:110–11). If the novel had been (as Tolstoy originally planned) about the Decembrists, one of its protagonists would have been Nikolenka Bolkonsky; we see this novel in Nikolenka's dream at the end of the first epilogue. When the Rostovs and the Bolkonskys cross into one another's thematic territory within this stable generational structure (Andrei's vision of the oak tree that leads to his courtship of Natasha, Natasha's suicide attempt and prayers after her break with Andrei, Petya's death in a partisan raid), these events gain additional emotional power by departing from the expectations the novel has set—gradually moving the major families toward the tightly knotted combined family group with which the narrative ends.

Nevertheless, the categories "instinct" and "spirit," "life" and "death" are so elemental as to risk becoming meaningless. They establish the foundation of the world the narrative represents, but they cannot account for the architecture of the novel's plot and strong thematic oppositions. Four other fictional families provide this additional structure.

The Bergs, a family formed midway through book 2, mark a transitional point between the organic foundations of the novel and what stands for artificiality within it. Separately, Vera and Berg are each associated primarily with their own pointlessness. As Vera's mother asks her, "Don't you see that you are superfluous here [chto ty zdes' lishniaia]?" (48; 9:55). (Chapters later, Nikolai says much the same thing to Berg [255; 9:293].) As a pair, they encapsulate what the novel itself codes as superfluous; they give a family name, it might be said, to the typicality of Anna Pavlovna Scherer's salon. At their housewarming party, "Berg and Vera could not repress their smiles of satisfaction. . . . Everything was just as everybody always has it. . . . The old people sat with the old, the young with the young. . . . Everything was just as it was everywhere else" (502–3; 10:215–16). Essential neither to the story nor to the discourse, Vera and Berg embody the principle on which the novel's character-system is divided. They are a passageway from the inner core to the outer surface of Tolstoy's representation of human life.[34]

The Karagins (Marya L'vovna and her daughter Julie) play a similar role, but in particular relation to the artifice of style. They are associated with false sentiment, coded through the stylized sentimental novels of the eighteenth century. Initiated in their first visit to the Rostovs' name day party, the theme is developed fully through Julie Karagina's later appearances—from her long, rapturous epistle to Marya Bolkonskaya, to her affected religious melancholy at the time of Boris's courtship, to her heavy-handed comparison of Pierre to a "knight" from a novel by Mme. de Souza (803; 11:178).[35] By cordoning such patterned feeling off in one family's sphere—and linking it with the prosaic image of Julie's round red face and powdered chin—Tolstoy is able to attack it, even as *War and Peace* itself spins plotlines that would not be out of place in a sentimental novella.[36]

The Drubetskoys (Anna Mikhailovna and her son Boris) play a more dynamic role in building the novel's artifice, related to the mechanics of its discourse—to the necessity of moving from one place to another and reaching the right place at the right narrative time. Thematically, they are associated with grasping ambition—less for "glory" (*slava*) than for the social and political connections that Andrei and Pierre have no need to pursue.[37] This thematic function also lets the Drubetskoys introduce the narrative itself into new circles. In book 1, as she builds the foundations of her son's career, Anna Mikhailovna leads us from Anna Pavlovna Scherer's Petersburg salon to the Rostovs' name day party in Moscow, and from the Rostov house to the deathbed of Pierre's father, Count Bezukhov. In book 2, Boris manages to be among the few present when Alexander and Napoleon meet at the Niemen River; in book 3, he is one of the first to learn that Napoleon has crossed the Niemen into Russia. The Drubetskoys' instinct to expand their given sphere simultaneously extends the novel's own flexibility and grasp.

Finally, the Kuragins (Prince Vasili, his wife Aline, and their children Hippolyte, Anatole, and Hélène) pull many of the strings behind the novel's fictional plot; in this way, their function parallels the Karagins', whose name differs from theirs by only one letter. They are associated with a cunning animal sensuality that expresses itself in a range of qualities, from Vasili's skill at social manipulation, to Hippolyte's ingratiating stupidity, to Anatole's licentiousness. (Hélène—manipulative, stupid, and sensuously beautiful—combines these family traits.) They orchestrate two central seductions, Hélène's of Pierre and Anatole's of Natasha—the episode that Tolstoy, in an often-cited letter to his editor P. I. Bartenev (November 26, 1867) called the novel's "hub" or "knot" (*uzel*; 61:184). Their seductions of Pierre and Natasha might, indeed, be characterized as a seduction *into* plot: in Vladimir Propp's terms, their "villainy" creates "the actual movement of the tale."[38] While Hélène and Anatole occasionally become complex enough to surpass this fairy-tale villainy, the vicious characterization of the family as a whole—accomplished, for example, by the otherwise gratuitous inclusion of the strikingly ugly Hippolyte (13; 9:15)—helps condense them into the functional terms of Propp's schema.

The Bergs, Karagins, Drubetskoys, and Kuragins carry out thematic functions that both complement and parody those of the families at the novel's center. The Drubetskoys' striving and the Karagins' false sentiment distort the ambition and spiritual depth of the Bolkonskys; the Bergs' superfluity and the Kuragins' sensuality distort the Rostovs' structurally excessive, instinctive physical life.[39] (Similarly, Dolokhov can be read as Pierre Bezukhov's minor double, an unrealized and unrealizable protagonist, as I discuss further below.) The behavior associated with these families' thematic functions shifts them from the core of the novel's represented life—from births and deaths, sleeping and dreaming—out toward the marked artifices of discourse and plot; although they provide a context and impetus for the unplotted inner experiences of the Rostovs, the Bolkonskys, and Pierre, such experiences never enter their fictional lives. They form, in this sense, the "proletariat" of Tolstoy's novel—a doubling, functional outer compass in the system of families that structures *War and Peace*.[40]

What this broad framework cannot yet encompass is how Tolstoy deals with the literary facts of majorness and minorness themselves. To understand the expansion and reversal of conventional realist character-systems that Tolstoy attempts in *War and Peace*, we need first to look more closely at how he uses the contrast between major and minor characters as a tool of mimetic representation.

MAJOR AND "POTENTIALLY" MAJOR CHARACTERS: SUSTAINING THE ILLUSION OF MIMETIC LIFE

Mimetic life arises in the context of an absorbed, attentive encounter with a work of fiction. In the introduction, I have proposed that the illusion of the character's life draws on an age-old aesthetic metaphor: the instinct to envision an artwork's coherence by analogy with the coherence of a living body. While this readerly instinct itself is rather mystical, we can clearly define the narrative techniques that authors use to modulate and control it. Tolstoy invokes and manipulates these techniques unusually directly. The character's entrance is only the beginning of a narrative process by which the effect of her life can be saturated, renewed, and used.

At the heart of any life effect is a tautology: the assertion of a fictional person equal precisely and only to herself. Like real persons, "living" characters seem to resist total characterization, or reduction to a particular set of words (whether the narrator's or their own). The creation of such a character both depends upon and bolsters the narrative's capacity to weave an imaginary fictional world. The living character thus seems to be a fantasy on the same order, and of the same kind, as the omniscient narrator, and in fact these two fantasies work together: there is a mutually reinforcing similarity between the image-making authority of the narrator's word and the imaged authority of the character's being.[41] In *War and Peace*, Natasha Rostova's characterization shows this collusion at its height.

In one remarkable passage, Natasha has just gone to bed after talking with her mother about her flirtation with Boris Drubetskoy:

> It was a long time before she could sleep. She kept thinking that no one could understand all that she understood and all there was in her. "Sonya?" she thought, glancing at the curled-up, sleeping little kitten with her enormous plait of hair. "No, how could she? She's virtuous. She fell in love with Nikolenka and does not wish to know anything more. Even Mama does not understand. It is wonderful how clever I am and how . . . charming she is," she went on, speaking of herself in the third person, and imagining it was some very wise man—the wisest and best of men—who was saying it of her. "There is everything, everything in her,' continued this man. 'She is unusually intelligent, charming . . . and then she is pretty, uncommonly pretty, and agile—she swims and rides splendidly . . . and her voice! One can really say it's a wonderful voice!" She hummed a scrap from her favorite opera by Cherubini, threw herself on her bed, laughed at the pleasant thought that she would immediately fall asleep, called Dunyasha, the maid, to put out the candle, and before Dunyasha had left the room had already passed into another yet hap-

> pier world of dreams, where everything was as light and beautiful as in reality, only better, because it was different. (483–84; ellipses in original)[42]

Placed on the eve of the ball where Andrei Bolkonsky's courtship of Natasha begins, this passage represents the height of her romance with the narrative itself. The "no one" who *does* understand "all that [Natasha] understood and all there was in her"—if it is anyone—is the novel's omniscient narrator. He presents what there is to understand by relaying Natasha's game of self-characterization, mediated by a second, mock`omniscient voice of her own creation. The thinking character Natasha exceeds the list of qualities she attributes to herself just as clearly as the novel's actual omniscient narrator exceeds her imaginary one. And the beginning and the end of the passage establish a conspiracy between the "reality" of Natasha and this "real" omniscient voice. It is the narrator who habitually describes Sonya as a kitten with a long tail, but it is Natasha looking at her. It is the narrator who continues the narration after Natasha falls asleep, but Natasha's reported dream is enigmatic in her own capricious vein: "everything was as light and beautiful as in reality, only better, because it was different."

The passage thus plays on the ellipsis hidden within the novelistic convention of interior representation. "All there was in" Natasha, it seems, cannot be listed. This device reasserts the fiction behind Natasha's entrance, where she seemed to be waiting to run into the narrative from somewhere else. Describing Natasha, the novel's verbal narrative can only gesture at what it claims is there—and by gesturing seem to demonstrate that there, indeed, it is. Natasha's life, irreducible to language, is one of the terms in which this fictional world unfolds.

Even Natasha knows that she points only to herself. The enigmatic circularity behind her interior monologue is echoed in the self-exultation that she sees when she looks into a mirror: "'There, that's me!' ['Vot ona ia!'] the expression of her face seemed to say as she caught sight of herself" (510; 10:224; see also 367; 10:59). This infinite loop again sums up the tautology—the "self-enclosed circularity without escape of the experience of character"—that both constitutes and reinforces the illusion of mimetic life.[43]

Such scenes provide the foundation for understanding and assenting to other characters' responses to Natasha—Nikolai's rapturous "but this is real" ("a vot ono nastoaiashchee") (367; 10:60), when Natasha's singing breaks in on his despair over his gambling loss to Dolokhov; or Andrei's pleasure when he dances with Natasha at having met something in society "that did not have the general social stamp upon it" ("vstrechat' v svete to, chto ne imelo na sebe obshchego svetskogo otpechatka") (493; 10:205). Andrei's image of Natasha as unstamped material reaches back to the etymology of "character" and *kharakter*, both from the Greek χαρακτήρ, "an instrument for marking or engraving."[44] With Andrei's remark, we arrive back at the difference Tolstoy's novel makes between the flattened "type" already primed for signifying abstraction, and the figure that signifies the individual, raw, or real. To imply that Natasha is yet to be stamped is also to imply that she is made of some substance that *could* be stamped; standing behind the novel's strict thematic division between the natural and the artificial is the realist pretense that fiction can include what has not already been made by language.

The construction and reinforcement of Natasha's mimetic life throughout the first half of the novel stands out, because it is so explicitly physical as well as mental. More insistently than with any other character, Tolstoy repeats assertions that Natasha is self-sufficient and "alive" alongside evocations of her sensations and thoughts. However, the novel also employs other strategies for creating the impression of an uncharacterizable or living character and for using the collusion between living characters and omniscient narrative to weave a fictional world.

The most common of these strategies, which Tolstoy shares with many other realist novelists, is a particular way of signifying consciousness through narrative: a loose internal focalization created through a mixture of quoted monologue, psychonarration, and narrated monologue (free indirect discourse).[45] Thus, waiting in the post station at Torzhok after his duel with Dolokhov, Pierre gazes at the post master and a woman trying to sell her embroidery,

> unable to understand what they wanted or how they could go on living without solving the problems that so absorbed him. . . . It was as if the thread of the chief screw which held his life together were *stripped*. The screw could not get in or out, but went on twirling, without catching on anything, in the same groove, and it was impossible to stop twirling it. The post-master came in and began obsequiously to beg his Excellency to wait only two little hours. . . . It was plain that he was lying and only wanted to get more money from the traveler. "Is this good or bad?" Pierre asked himself. ". . . What is bad? What is good? What should we love and what hate? What do we live for? And what am I? What is life, and what is death? What power governs it all?" he asked himself. (371–72)[46]

Unlike the post master, whose speech in free indirect discourse is clearly marked off from the surrounding narrative, Pierre's thoughts mingle indistinguishably with the narrator's analysis of them. Who envisions the stripped "chief screw" of Pierre's life twirling endlessly in his head—Pierre, or the narrator? The italics suggest that it is Pierre, but what Pierre says about himself closely approaches what the narrator might say about him; the questions that preoccupy him here are the same ones which will soon drive the narrator's own philosophical digressions. The illusion of Pierre's life thus cannot be primarily based on identification of his particular voice or language. It stems, rather, from a narrative fiat, which conjures up the activity of Pierre's mind as a part of the same speech act that conjures up the fictional world as a whole.[47]

A similar technical continuity between the inner life of characters and the represented physical world of *War and Peace* emerges in two famous landscapes—one glimpsed by Nikolai Rostov during his first skirmish at Enns, the other by Andrei Bolkonsky at Austerlitz:

> Nikolai Rostov turned away and, as if searching for something, gazed into the distance, at the waters of the Danube, at the sky, and at the sun. How beautiful the sky looked; how blue, calm, and deep! How bright and solemn the setting sun! . . . And fairer still were the far away blue mountains beyond the river, the nunnery, the mysterious gorges, and the pine forests veiled in mist to their summits . . . "I would wish for nothing else, nothing, if only I were there," thought Rostov. "In myself alone and in that sunshine there is so much happiness." (158; second ellipsis in original)[48]

> It seemed to [Andrei] as though one of the soldiers near him hit him on the head with the full swing of a bludgeon. . . . Above him there was now nothing but the sky—the lofty sky, not clear yet still immeasurably lofty, with grey clouds gliding slowly across it. "How quiet, peaceful, and solemn, not at all as I ran," thought Prince Andrei—"not as we ran, shouting and fighting, not at all as the gunner and the Frenchman with frightened and angry faces struggled for the mop: how differently do those clouds glide across that lofty infinite sky!" (299)[49]

The language in which each character thinks is consistent with that character's familiar voice: the careful ascending, rhetorical logic of Andrei's reflections differs from Nikolai's impassioned outburst. However, the difference between Andrei and Nikolai as characters is also reflected in the fact that Andrei's revelation comes from the moving clouds, and Nikolai's, from the brightly setting sun.[50] Their thoughts take shape in a natural world that, like Andrei and Nikolai, can only be imaginatively present in language—but in their engagement with this natural world, Andrei and Nikolai too seem to transcend the words that evoke them.

These passages narrating Natasha, Pierre, Andrei, and Nikolai thus set an absolute limit of mimetic characterization in the novel: the naming of a fictional being whose individuality and coherence are marked primarily *by* a proper name and the sensations and thoughts that are organized under it. Such characterization is the opposite of caricature—in particular, of the kind of speech tic that cordons a character's "own" word off from the omniscient narrative, what Gérard Genette calls a "too-perfect mimesis of language."[51] Where Tolstoy's contemporary Dostoevsky habitually links verbal tics to markers of ideological worldview, implying that the character is characterizing "himself," Tolstoy relies on narrative fiat to produce his protagonists' mimetic lives. It is their very compatibility with the omniscient narrative producing the novel's fictional world that links them to the "real" as the novel defines it.

The result is a set of techniques for marking life that thrive on abundant narrative space and attention, but do not require it on the scale of the novel as a whole. For example, Captain Tushin, whom Andrei overhears talking with his fellow officers about the possibility of life after death on the eve of the Battle of Schön Grabern, later becomes the focalizing center of one of the most vivid scenes describing the experience of this battle:

> Amid the smoke, deafened by the incessant reports which always made him jump, Tushin, not taking his pipe from his mouth, ran from gun to gun. . . . Owing to the terrible uproar and the necessity for concentration and activity, Tushin did not experience the slightest unpleasant sense of fear. . . . It seemed to him that it was a very long time ago, almost a day, since he had first seen the enemy and fired the first shot. . . . The enemy's guns were in his imagination not guns but pipes from which occasional puffs were blown by an invisible smoker. . . . "Come along, our Matveevna!" he said to himself. (204–5)[52]

By narrating Tushin in the same kind of loose internal focalization as Natasha or Nikolai, Tolstoy temporarily magnifies his figure to let him function as the scene's protagonist. Conversely, a character who might as well have been a protagonist (for example, Natasha's mother Countess Rostova) can be shrunk through techniques that cordon her perspective off from that of the omniscient narrative, even in free indirect discourse: "How strange, how extraordinary, how joyful it seemed, that her son, the scarcely perceptible motion of whose tiny limbs she had felt twenty years ago within her . . . that this son should now be away in a foreign land amid strange surroundings, a virile warrior doing some kind of man's work of his own without help or guidance" (251; 9:289).

From only these two examples, it becomes clear that the narrative evocation of solid and autonomous life does not always correspond to a character's position within the surrounding system. Tolstoy reinforces this illusion for Natasha as for no other character in *War and Peace*, but he uses similar techniques of representation whenever he needs a character to occupy the relatively unmarked watching or experiencing position of "protagonist" within a particular scene—and withdraws these techniques whenever he needs a character *not* to.

War and Peace is constructed from this remarkably flexible network of gazes, which encompasses an ever-widening field of figures, places, and events. We follow Andrei Bolkonsky to Kutuzov's council of war on the eve of the Battle of Austerlitz and the opening of the battle on the left flank; when Andrei falls, we follow Nikolai Rostov, stationed on the right flank with Bagration. We follow Natasha Rostova from the Otradnoe wolf hunt to the opera boxes of Moscow, and old Prince Bolkonsky's overseer Alpatych to Smolensk, under attack by Napoleon. Tolstoy thus rests his novel's illusion of limitless scope on the trajectories of familiar characters, who invite us into much larger scenes or whom we tend to find there once we have arrived. Wherever there is any named character capable of assuming the attributes and function of a protagonist, Tolstoy uses her perspective to construct the scene of which she is a part.

However, the flexibility of this network is far from limitless. Named characters as fleeting as Captain Tushin—or as vilified as Napoleon—are sometimes narrated like living narrative protagonists, but some characters, such as Dolokhov, never are. As the novel's opening scene at Anna Pavlovna Scherer's salon suggests, consistent and system-wide differences in how different figures are represented have a perspectival function: Tolstoy underscores and intensifies the inevitable flattening of minor characters. Repeated contrasts with what is artificial, ghostlike, fragmentary, or dead help create and sustain the technical illusion of life. My discussion of the novel's character-system as divided into families lays out the most general logic by which characters become major or minor. I want now to look in more detail at the techniques Tolstoy uses to reinforce "minorness" itself as a narrative condition in *War and Peace*.

MINOR AND DIMINISHING CHARACTERS: THE PRODUCTIVE CONTRAST TO MIMETIC LIFE

Tolstoy implies that Drubetskoys are represented differently from Bolkonskys because the quality of their experience is different; this difference makes them suitable for functions that have to do with the evident constructedness of the novel, rather than with its declared reality. However, at moments throughout *War and Peace*, this mimetic justification for the asymmetrical representation of minor characters is disrupted. Two characters who are less clearly tied to particular functions, and thus less limited within the novel's system of named fictional identities, lie at the crux of this problem: the Rostovs' ward Sonya and her suitor Fyodor Dolokhov.

In his first appearance, Dolokhov stands out from a crowd of eight men at Anatole Kuragin's party: "Another voice, from a man of medium height with clear blue eyes, particularly striking among all these drunken voices by its sober ring, cried from the window . . . This was Dolokhov, an officer of the Semyonov regiment, a notorious gambler and duelist" (33; 9:38). The "two distinct smiles" at the corners of Dolokhov's mouth "produced an effect which made it impossible not to notice this face" (34; 9:39). And yet, when the whole room turns to Dolokhov as he drinks a bottle of rum on a high windowsill, the narrator pointedly looks elsewhere: "One of the footmen who had stooped to pick up some broken glass, remained in that position without taking his eyes from the window. . . . The Englishman looked on sideways pursing up his lips. . . . Pierre hid his face, and a faint smile, forgotten, stayed on his face, although it now expressed horror and fear" (36; 9:41). This episode sets a lasting pattern. Each time Dolokhov resurfaces in book 1, he is at the center of someone's attention, but each reappearance is framed as a surprise to the narrator himself. The range of Dolokhov's character and experience appears only obliquely, in contrast with the fixed trademark of his duplicitous smile.[53] When he loses his duel with Pierre, we learn that he "lived in Moscow with an old mother and a hunchback sister, and was the most affectionate of sons and brothers" (339; 10:27). When he appears at the opera, we learn that he has been in Persia, "acting as minister to some ruling prince" (600; 10:323).

Dolokhov's mother, Marya Ivanovna, enters the novel in person so briefly that she has time only to point out this asymmetry, the fictional world's unfairness to her son:

> "Yes, Count," she would say, "he is too noble and pure-souled for our present, depraved world. No one nowadays loves virtue, it seems like a reproach to everyone. Now tell me, Count, was it right, was it honorable, of Bezukhov? . . . Those pranks in Petersburg when they played some tricks on a policeman, didn't they do it together? And there! Bezukhov got off scot free, while Fedya had to bear the whole burden on his shoulders. . . . And now—this duel! Have these people no feeling, or honor? Knowing him to be an only son, to challenge him and to shoot so straight!" (352)[54]

Her sole act in *War and Peace* is to sketch the outlines of a different novel, of which Dolokhov could be the hero. The comic irony around Marya Ivanovna's account discourages us from taking this possibility seriously, but what would happen if we tried?

Thematically, Dolokhov can be associated with an "appetite for personal power"—a desire that alienates him, like the Drubetskoys and Kuragins, from Tolstoy's conception of a moral life.[55] But treated as a family, the Dolokhovs also bring the fact of narrative asymmetry itself to our attention. In the course of marking the kind of story the novel does not tell, they expand its fictional universe, pointing into recesses of the story world that the discourse leaves hidden. However, their minorness also points to the limitations of that universe—to the sense in which telling Pierre's story *has* to exclude telling Dolokhov's.

The figure of Dolokhov catches the novel in a crisis between the thematic rigidity that sets the terms of its represented world, and the mirage of unlimited representational possibility that makes this world so convincing. As Morson points out, Dolokhov helps demonstrate that in *War and Peace*, as in real life, "characters, like incidents, do not have significance, only potential significance. For some, that potential is great; for others, small."[56] However, Morson avoids saying that such a character is also a sign of the *in*flexibility of Tolstoy's character-system: "potential significance" tends in turn to be distributed by proximity (familial or thematic) to the novel's actual protagonists. Petya Rostov and even Captain Tushin could have been protagonists of a novel recognizable as *War and Peace*, but Dolokhov could not, and this is exactly Tolstoy's point. His potential for centrality, and for the kind of representation associated with it, is embedded in a system where it cannot possibly be fulfilled.

The power of this system to anchor so comprehensive a represented world thus comes, again, from its stability. The centrality of *War and Peace*'s protagonists is so closely woven into the novel's fabric that it becomes invisible: the narrative condition of "potential protagonicity" merges with the condition of living life as the novel defines it. Dolokhov demonstrates this stability by his exile from that vision; Sonya, by her crucially incomplete integration.

Many readers have tried to account for Sonya's suppression in *War and Peace*.[57] But more striking than any particular explanation is the sheer clarity with which Sonya is placed off-center in the novel's character-system. Her minorness begins with the lack of a family name, a semiotic poverty more essential than her dependent state in the story world.[58] It continues with the image, at once memorable and distracting, of Sonya as "a pretty, half-grown kitten which promises to become a beautiful little cat" (43; 9:49). This recurring metaphor displaces the accompanying description of her body and forestalls lengthy forays into her mind. Its self-containment captures Sonya's defining stasis, which takes the form of her desire to become a Rostov by marriage: as she tells Natasha, "I am in love with your brother once for all, and whatever may happen to him or to me I shall never cease to love him as long as I live" (250; 9:287). When she refuses Dolokhov's marriage proposal, the flattening force of this self-definition shows through the eyes of Nikolai, who thinks, "My Sonya could not have done otherwise" (356; 10:47); and of Natasha, who (as we have already seen) dismisses Sonya: "She fell in love with Nikolenka and does not wish to know anything more" (483; 10:194).

However, the innate difference between Sonya and the Rostovs, which makes her inclusion in the family impossible, is explicit: "Sonya, as always, did not keep pace with [the Rostovs], though they shared the same reminiscences. Much that they remembered had slipped from her mind, and what she recalled did not arouse the same poetic feeling as they experienced. She simply enjoyed their pleasure and tried to fit in with it" (558; 10:278). At Natasha's first ball, "the two girls in their white dresses, each with a rose in her black hair, both curtsied in the same way, but the hostess's eye involuntarily rested longer on the slim Natasha" (488; 10:199). Indeed, Nikolai only seriously entertains the possibility of making Sonya a Rostov in the context of the temporary "magical kingdom" of the Christmas (*sviatki*) masquerade, where the world is turned literally on its head: Sonya cross-dresses as a Circassian soldier, and "the snow sparkled with so many stars, that one did not wish to look up at the sky and the real stars were unnoticed. The sky was black and dreary, while the earth was gay. 'I am a fool, a fool! what have I been waiting for?' thought Nikolai" (567; 10:287). There could be no clearer inversion of *War and Peace*'s fictional order.[59]

In the epilogue, Sonya's unrealizable desire to become a Rostov is fossilized as she fulfills the promised turn from kitten to cat: "She seemed to be fond not so much of individuals as of the family as a whole. Like a cat, she had attached herself not to the people but to the home" (1235–36; 12:260). In this sense, she is Dolokhov's inverse: because her key defining quality is her sense of the Rostovs' centrality, her character could *only* have been realized in this novel of which they are indeed the center.

The representation of major protagonists brings us to the foundation of *War and Peace*'s mimetic power—the point where the author must simply assert the names of his central characters and the vitality of their figures. Dolokhov and Sonya, in turn, define two outer ends of its range. These characters mark the text as a text, by pointing to the absolute and arbitrary lines along which it distributes the illusion of mimetic life. Such figures show minorness to be a problem that *War and Peace*, no less than any other novel, must negotiate. If the sheer authorial assertion of a reality beyond text and convention is necessary to make a character like Natasha, a character like Sonya results from dampening this impression of reality, the potentially distracting vividness that must be contained within characterizing language.

It is worth dwelling on this point, because Tolstoy's novel has so often been described as a simulacrum of life in which everyone, and even everything, lives.[60] A closer look shows that the novel depends for its formal coherence on a set of characters whose function is *not* to mimetically live—even though Tolstoy also motivates this sterility by making it part of their (or their families') self-determining "natures."[61] The suppression of mimetic life is absolute in the cases of Sonya and Dolokhov, written into their characters from the beginning. I turn now to a few key minor characters for whom it is less firm, fluctuating throughout their interactions with the novel's protagonists. These figures demonstrate the dynamic negotiation of illusion as *War and Peace*'s character-system unfolds throughout the first half of the narrative.

When Hélène Kuragina first appears at Anna Pavlovna Scherer's salon, she is constantly attended by the epithet *krasavitsa* ("the beauty"). The Homeric overtones of *La belle Hélène* (217; 9:249) are, of course, ironic—intimating that Hélène's "antique" beauty has been imported from another narrative where it would have mattered more.[62] But early in the novel, the passage in which she seduces Pierre by leaning her shoulders forward enacts her conversion from classical statue into flesh:

> Her bust, which had always seemed like marble to Pierre, was so close to him that his shortsighted eyes could not but perceive the living charm of her neck and shoulders, so near to his lips that he need only have bent his head a little to have touched them. He was conscious of the warmth of her body, the scent of perfume, and the creaking of her corset as she moved. He did not see her marble beauty forming a complete whole with her dress, but all the charm of her body only covered by her garments. And having once seen this he could not help being aware of it, just as we cannot renew an illusion we have once seen through. "So you never before noticed how beautiful I am?" Hélène seemed to say. "You had not noticed that I am a woman?" (219)[63]

Pierre's multisensory recognition of the live woman beneath Hélène's clothes also embodies her, startlingly vividly, within Tolstoy's narrative. The shining white shoulders that have acted as her metonymic identifying trait take on a "living charm," coupled with her warmth and the smell of her perfume. For us, both Hélène's symbolic abstraction and her embodiment are illusory, but the illusions belong to different representational strategies: Pierre's vision of Hélène's body brings her into the same mimetic sphere as Pierre himself, linking her with the need to represent what transcends typifying language.

Hélène's vividness lasts only long enough to lure Pierre into a marriage coded as an existential mismatch: "he felt that he was occupying someone else's place here beside Hélène. 'This happiness is not for you, some inner voice whispered to him. This happiness is for those who have not in them what there is in you'" (226; 9:259–60). Indeed, faced with the consequences of this marriage, Pierre tries to beat Hélène back into the material of which she was originally made: "'I'll kill you!' he shouted, and seizing the marble top of a table . . . he made a step towards her brandishing the slab" (343; 10:32).

Hélène's conversion back into marble and the distant space of mock epic, however, is not accomplished so easily. Indeed, she returns so persistently that some readers have seen her as one of the novel's heroines. She establishes a salon that rivals Anna Pavlovna Scherer's own; Boris Drubetskoy courts her, Napoleon takes notice of her beauty (470; 10:178), and Natasha falls under her "shadow" (608; 10:333). After she has played her secondary role in Natasha's seduction, her place in the novel grows: she ends by anchoring several caustically narrated scenes in her own right, as she converts to Catholicism and divorces Pierre. The classical marble impassivity of her beauty has by now been reimagined novelistically—as the "lacquer from all the thousand gazes that have slid over her body" (492; 10:204). This "lacquer" of gazes suggests a compromise between the vivid physicality Hélène garners when she is seen through Pierre's eyes, and her actual distance from the heart of life as the novel represents it.

It might be argued that Tolstoy lends Hélène a vividly sensuous body precisely so that he can show this sensuality to be self-vanquishing: early in book 4, she falls ill with "an inconvenience resulting from marrying two husbands at the same time" (1006; 12:4)—an apparent euphemism for the abortion of her first, illegitimate pregnancy—and she kills herself soon after. But the very moralization of this death points up the work the narrative has to do to get rid of Hélène's body, some thousand pages after her physical presence has played its most important role—to return it to conventional literary form once Pierre has seen it as real.

The representation of Boris Drubetskoy follows an opposite trajectory. He begins the novel as an explicitly embodied character, who blushes when the thirteen-year-old Natasha asks if he wants to kiss her (47; 9:54), and who smiles "the happy smile seen on the faces of young men who have been under fire for the first time" at the Battle of Austerlitz (302; 9:347). But over the course of the novel, this physicality wavers and eventually disappears.[64] Just as Hélène's brief physical "life" springs from Pierre's realization of her sensuality, Boris's transparency follows from Natasha's diminishing perception of his body.

The last mention of Boris after he has kissed Natasha, before a two hundred–page disappearance, is Natasha's summons to sing his part in a quartet at the name day party—which we know that he joins only because it *was* a quartet (70; 9:79). We do not hear his name again until Natasha confesses that she can no longer picture him when she closes her eyes (249; 9:287). Almost immediately afterward, the Rostovs begin to discuss Boris in a purely functional role as a broker of connections: "it was decided to send the letters and money by the Grand Duke's courier to Boris, and Boris was to forward them to Nikolushka" (252; 9:290).

This functionality spreads from the Rostovs' perception of Boris to his representation in the omniscient narrative. When the narrator finds him immediately after this scene, Boris is embedded in a chain of messages and purposeful links: "Boris during the campaign had made the acquaintance of many persons who might prove useful to him, and through [*cherez*] a letter of recommendation he had brought from Pierre, had become acquainted with Prince Andrei Bolkonsky through whom [*cherez kotorogo*] he hoped to receive a post" (254; 9:291). Tied to a thematic function (ambition) and a narrative task (linking) that send him *through* the novel's other characters, Boris no longer has a consistent physical presence in *War and Peace*. Not even his "white hands" (254; 9:291) recur as a metonymic bodily marker, in the way that Napoleon's and Speransky's famously do.

Boris's very ghostliness is useful to the novel. He observes the meeting of Alexander and Napoleon at Tilsit, timing it to precisely one hour and fifty-three minutes (436; 10:139).[65] He finds a way, too, to observe the conversation at the June 1812 ball where Alexander learns that Napoleon has resumed hostilities (656; 11:14). His perspective thus inserts the political pivots of Russia's war with Napoleon into *War and Peace*, even as his nose for historical significance alienates him from the core of its represented world. Similarly, Boris intersects with all the major fictional characters—as Nikolai's friend, Andrei's protégé, Pierre's rival, and a suitor to Natasha and Marya—but the connections turn out to be arid: Nikolai and Boris part ways at Tilsit, Andrei's patronage comes to nothing, Pierre never duels with Boris, and Boris does not propose to Marya or Natasha.

It is Boris's final, brief attraction back toward Natasha that best sums up this hybrid place in the narrative, the palpable use that narrator and protagonists make of his transparency. When he returns to the Rostovs' house, three years after the novel began, Natasha sums up Boris's intervening transformation, which mirrors our memory of him timing the Emperors' meeting at Tilsit: "he is so narrow, like the dining-room clock. . . . Narrow, you know, gray, light" (483; 10:194). Like Natasha's subsequent attempt to describe herself through the eyes of "some very wise man," her image of Boris as a gray clock reinforces her connection with the omniscient narrative—a connection that runs both through Boris and over his head. He provides the occasion for a new stage in her erotic awareness of herself, although his own fictional body is by now invisible.[66]

By the end of book 2, Boris has been safely and satirically married off to Julie Karagina. After the Battle of Borodino, he disappears from the novel, and his very absence can be taken as the sign of its solidifying central circle—the decisive end of the emperors' political negotiations, the major characters' clustering toward their final configurations. In his time-keeping grayness, the vanishing Boris might be taken for a phantom of his initial self. Boris's example, then, pushes the question of minorness further: What discourages or preserves the impulse to experience a character's mimetic life in *War and Peace*? How long does the illusion last?

In Lise Bolkonskaya, Prince Andrei's wife, the problem of the minor character's body meets this problem of its longevity, the span of the minor character's mimetic life.

Lise's raised, downy upper lip is an iconic metonym in nineteenth-century Russian literature—in Dmitrii Merezhkovsky's words, a trait referenced so often that it is "engraved on our memory, stamped onto it with indelible clarity, so that we cannot remember the little princess without also imagining the raised upper lip with the little moustache."[67] Merezhkovsky compares this technique to the layering on of paint, "stroke upon stroke, thickening it more and more," the device that makes Tolstoy a master of "representing the human body by means of the word." But he also notes that a repeated trope like Lise's lip can seem eerily detached: "it acts on its own and lives its own separate, strange, almost supernatural life."[68]

Merezhkovsky's observations capture something fundamental about the minor characters of *War and Peace*. The repetition that links appearance and moral character throughout the novel—Hélène's shoulders and her animal sensuality, Julie Karagina's powdered chin and her false sentiment, Marya's luminous eyes and her spiritual depth, Pierre's massivity and his social clumsiness—"thickens" the details that make its world feel physically real. But in the case of most minor characters, these physical fragments do not correspond to a sustained mimetic life in the novel. Reminded of these bodies while immersed in the stability of the novel's character-system, we may begin to feel that something is living that ought not to be.[69]

Lise's case is most revealing because the impulse to compare her to the novel's central protagonists comes with her placement in the narrative. Unlike Hélène and Boris, who bring their family spheres into collision with those of the major protagonists, Lise has been annexed to a family in which she evidently does not belong. Evoked primarily by her raised upper lip, her character is overwhelmed and (eventually) destroyed by the proportions of the scenes in which she is placed: faced with the same door between life and death that defines Marya and Andrei, Lise dies in the throes of an offstage childbirth.

But Merezhkovsky's description of Lise's upper lip as "engraved on our memory, stamped onto it with indelible clarity" suggests that another, still broader device is also at stake. He evokes not just the thinness, but also the power attached to typifying characterization (stamping, engraving) as a literary device—to the containment of a figure in traits or words that can be broken off from the whole of the novel.

The heart of the problem and of the rhetorical potential presented in Lise, Boris Drubetskoy, and Hélène Kuragina is the fictional body made not just legible, but *over*-legible. When Natasha's reflection speaks to her in the mirror, it says, "There, that's me! [Vot ona ia!]" When the dead Lise

Bolkonskaya's expression speaks to Andrei, it says: "I love you all, and have done no harm to anyone; and what have you done to me? [chto vy so mnoi sdelali?]" (351; 10:41). Lise's "What have you done to me?" is Natasha's "There, that's me!" turned inside out. Where Natasha's face signifies the illusion of irreducible, extralinguistic presence, Lise's suggests the conversion of presence into word. She thus distills the device by which Hélène's vivid body asks Pierre, "You had not noticed that I am a woman?" and by which Boris appears, to Natasha, to be as "narrow as a dining room clock": the character reduced to a speaking characteristic. A character who can be so consistently read, however, also invites rewriting. With Lise, as with Dolokhov and Sonya, Tolstoy risks having created a character who becomes more alluring the more we imagine her as she was *not* written in *War and Peace*.[70]

In the case of the almost thoroughly idealized character Platon Karataev, Tolstoy makes an attempt to mobilize this strategy in another way: to write a character who can be detached from the whole of the novel just as he was written within it. Platon's body is as "round" as the water drop which, in Pierre's allegorical dream, reflects the whole of creation (1146; 12:158)—an image evoking a part that can separate from the whole while still being of it, a complete and perfect copy in itself. However, this very description of Platon demonstrates the obstacles that the realist representation of "life" poses to fulfilling Tolstoy's didactic vision. It separates the idea of Platon's organic life in the story from the technical components of mimetic life in the discourse, in a summary packaged for export: "Every word and action of [Platon's] was the manifestation of an activity unknown to him, which was his life. But his life, as he regarded it, had no meaning as a separate thing. It had meaning only as part of a whole of which he was always conscious. His words and actions flowed from him as evenly, inevitably, and spontaneously as fragrance exhales from a flower" (1048; 12:51). In Platon's case, content and technique clash: the difference the novel itself makes between a character drawn in typifying language, and one made to "live" in excess of overt characterization, turns this *description* of life into an oxymoron.[71] As I argue in the following chapters, the dream of writing a Platon Karataev—not just a vivid "positive hero," but a reliably portable one—continued to haunt both Tolstoy's and Dostoevsky's major novels.

MARGINAL CHARACTERS: STRETCHING THE ILLUSION OF MIMETIC LIFE

I have described how the illusion of the major protagonists' lives is woven into the main omniscient narrative of *War and Peace*, and I have discussed the minor characters that show what it means not, or not always, to have mimetic life in Tolstoy's novel. In the Kuragins, Karagins, Drubetskoys, and Dolokhovs, in Sonya and in Lise Bolkonskaya, Tolstoy creates figures whose fictional lives are explicitly tangential to *War and Peace*'s represented world. By collecting the traces of these "lives" that the novel does incorporate—contained interiority and diffused physicality, whether concentrated in the repetition of a single "speaking" body part or dissipated in the imagination of a body that fades throughout the text—we can imagine what the sustained illusion of their physical presence and the space of their minds would be like. But it is not an act of imagination that this novel's structure encourages.

In this respect, the character-system of *War and Peace* adopts and relies on the constraints of the European novel from which Tolstoy was anxious to distinguish his "book." To the extent that *War and Peace* needs a fictional plot, the Kuragins and Dolokhov provide it with one. When letters or secret notes must be transmitted, Sonya and Boris hand them on. This kind of functionality, which confines minor characters to their effect on the development of a story focused around major ones, does not stop with "negative" figures, or with the most prominent fictional families. The lisping Denisov spends large swaths of the novel offstage, but he always returns to pay tribute to the Rostovs. Agrafena Ivanovna Belova, the Rostovs' country neighbor, materializes to take Natasha to church after she has broken her engagement with Andrei and reappears as Countess Rostova's companion in the epilogue. The French drummer boy Vincent Bosse awakens Petya's compassion; the provincial governor's wife suggests that Nikolai should marry Marya; during the Moscow fires, the flamboyant French officer Captain Ramballe shows Pierre his love for Natasha in a new romantic light.

Ramballe, however, leads such an analysis into difficulties. Why should the novel find him again near the end of book 4, captured by the Fifth Regiment at Krasnoe? And why should we watch as his drunken servant Morel sings to the Russian soldiers and one of them tries to imitate his French (1179–80; 12:196)? Ramballe and Morel are the only familiar characters to appear in the scene of the camp at Krasnoe, which extends over three vivid chapters. The echo with a scene in book 1, where Andrei watches a Russian soldier address the enemy in French-like gibberish (187–88; 9:214–15), makes us feel how far the narrative has come from home. It is no longer always the case that scenes enter the novel through the network of its known fictional characters' gazes, or even that they are passed directly from familiar eyes to unfamiliar ones. If so minor a character as Ramballe can link us to the regiment at Krasnoe, the network of fictional characters has begun to grow exponentially: coincidence is no longer in the service of coherence. The novel has changed the ground beneath our feet.

The climactic developments in the fictional plot halfway through *War and Peace* mark a new stage in its narrative. After Natasha's seduction, the burden of movement and event gets transferred from families like the Drubetskoys and the Kuragins to historical actors like Kutuzov and Napoleon. At the same time, the light of representation increasingly falls on the characters I have called "marginal," located at the fringes of the fictional plot and so also, conventionally, of the reader's attention. These are collective groups or crowds, like the Polish Uhlans who struggle across the Viliya river in the "cold and uncanny" midst of the current under Napoleon's gaze (653; 11:10); as well as anonymous figures, like the weeping French cook with red sideburns whom Pierre sees being flogged as a suspected spy (806–7; 11:182–83). Focalized through the eyes of major characters or entirely dissociated from their stories, a growing cast of marginal characters occupies more and more narrative space as the novel continues.

I will focus on a single remarkable example of this shift, an eight-chapter sequence in book 3 (III.3.19–26) in which no known fictional characters are mentioned. Instead, there is Napoleon's internal monologue as he waits in vain for a deputation from surrendered Moscow—a bounded passage of interior representation that, like the scene of his plump body being brushed on the eve of the Battle of Borodino (834; 11:213), polemically cuts him down to the size of any other individual character. There are looting troops and hapless shopkeepers crowding onto the city's squares and bridges. In the first half of the novel, marginal characters most often bracket the named characters' experiences—the "humming infantry" that surrounds Tushin's guns "like a frame" after Schön Grabern (208; 9:238), or the troops (including Boris and Nikolai) in the review at Olmütz, each "aware of being but a drop in that ocean of men, and yet at the same time . . . conscious of his strength as part of that enormous whole" (260; 9:299). But in the scene of the traitor Vereshchagin's massacre, at the climax of this historical sequence, the collective "ocean of men" erupts from its frame and framing function:

> The crowd remained silent and only pressed closer and closer to one another. To keep one another back, to breathe in that stifling atmosphere, to be unable to stir, and to await something unknown, uncomprehended, and terrible, was becoming unbearable. Those standing in front . . . all stood with wide open eyes and mouths, straining with all their strength, and held back the crowd that was pushing behind them. . . . But after the exclamation of surprise that had escaped from Vereshchagin he uttered a plaintive cry of pain, and that cry was fatal. The barrier of human feeling, strained to the utmost, that had held the crowd in check, suddenly broke. . . . Like the seventh and last wave that shatters a ship, that last irresistible wave burst from the rear and reached the front ranks, carrying them off their feet and engulfing them all. (955)[72]

Multiplicity has taken on agency as well as interiority, the crowd realized briefly as a collective character in its own right.

A final scene, interposed between the humiliation of Napoleon and the lynching of Vereshchagin, shows how the thematic organization of the novel's fictional character-system stretches to the scale of the historical mimetic project in its second half. The Rostovs have left Moscow, but their housekeeper, Mavra Kuzmyshina, offers hospitality and money to a stranded officer who claims to be their distant relative; as she repeatedly says, "If the count had been at home . . . [Kak by graf doma byli . . .]" (944; 11:336). In the Rostovs' literal absence, their generosity comes to stand for a general (national) trait, even as it is still expressed by their servant with reference to their name.[73] As Tolstoy has Andrei comment still more directly in one early draft outline: "Our success is the soldiers' success, the success of the *muzhik* . . . I've remembered about Dolokhov. His success is Bonap[arte's]. It is intrigue, it cannot alter, as character [*kharakter*] cannot alter, whatever war brings" (13:36).[74] What links Napoleon and Dolokhov is their reliance on plotting—their belief in their own capacity to influence and direct others' actions, which for Tolstoy results in minorness: the subordination of one's own fate to the outcome of others'. The outline fragment encourages us to see the Russian citizens resisting Napoleon as extensions of the "living" Rostovs and Bolkonskys, and to see Napoleon himself as subject, like Dolokhov or any minor character, to the demands of plot.

Classically, this expansion from the scale of fiction to the scale of history has been understood as a split between family novel and national epic, which preserves Tolstoy's evolving "stages of composition" in the published text of *War and Peace*.[75] However, there is a single formal and conceptual thread running across this divide: the problem of how to represent human lives. Much though Tolstoy would have resented the suggestion, his digressive reflections on historical agency, causality, and free will may thus be most salient to *War and Peace*'s readers as a guide to the ongoing transformation of the novel's own character-system.[76]

The second half of the novel poses an insoluble question about converting individual narratives into collective ones. Its terms are articulated in an early theoretical digression: "Napoleon began the war with Russia because he could not resist going to Dresden . . . Rostov charged the French because he could not restrain his wish for a gallop across a level field; and in the same way the innumerable people who took part in the war [neperechislimye litsa, uchastniki etoi voiny] acted in accord with their personal characteristics, habits, circumstances, and aims" (732; 11:99). This passage highlights an ontological hierarchy that my discussion of *War and Peace*'s character-system has largely bracketed. Fictional protagonists like Nikolai Rostov live in a world created by the novel's own language, whose only authority is the text itself. The same cannot be said of named historical characters like Napoleon, whose lives in the novel remain linked to the biographies of their real-world referents.[77] In the case of the historical *crowd* and its anonymous members, however, it is hard to choose between these two modes of reading. We know where to look for the lives of "Napoleon" and "Nikolai Rostov," but where are the lives of the "innumerable people" that their behavior exemplifies?

This mystery impels the skepticism about historical narrative worked out in part 2 of the epilogue: "History is the life of nations and of humanity. To directly seize and encompass in words, to describe the life of humanity or even of a single nation, appears impossible" (1270; 12:296). "Life" is a term charged in *War and Peace* with spiritual and philosophical meaning, but here as throughout my discussion, I want to stress its significance as a representational ideal.[78] Tolstoy confronts the sphere of historical writing with the impasse behind a fictional character-system: the problem of evoking the independent lives of many people within a single narrative. He rejects the traditional model, where individual heroes bend multitudes of others to their will: "So long as histories are written of separate individuals . . . and not the history of *all*, without a single exception *all*, the people who take part in an event, it is quite impossible to avoid ascribing to individuals a force compelling other people to direct their activity towards a single end" (1278; 12:305). However, the "history of *all*" is manifestly unwritable. The only truthful alternative is to go to the other extreme: a narrative focused on the events themselves, and not on any of the people involved. But to narrate in terms of the accomplished event is to leave out the consciousness of free will that "forms the essence of . . . life" (1294; 12:324)—and so again to fall short of the ideal of capturing many lives in text.

Tolstoy thus arrives at a divide between the essential sense of freedom that lies at the heart of any individual's conscious experience, and the absolute laws of cause and effect that objectively determine the course of historical events. Anyone who is alive, and conscious of being able to direct her own actions, cannot believe that she is really subject to absolute laws. Conversely, anyone who asserts that groups of people are acting according to the necessity of these laws cannot account for the sense of freedom that the living individuals who make up these groups must feel. Here is Tolstoy's own conception of the representational problem of one and many: true history is a "history of *all*," but it is governed by laws so absolute that no living individual, conscious of her own sense of open-ended freedom, could believe in them.

It follows that historians have to compromise between two equally flawed alternatives: either to relate the subjective experience that *every* participant in an event has of himself as free, or to present the event in terms of impersonal laws. The better we know the circumstances in which an action was performed, the less present in time it is to us, and the more clearly we see the chain of causation that produced it, the more necessary that action seems. Conversely, the less fully and objectively we can define an action and an acting subject, the freer they seem to be (1301; 12:332–33). Focusing on freedom's manifestations in world events, historians asymptotically approach the laws of which, in order to experience life, individuals must remain ignorant.[79]

Tolstoy thus offers no conclusive solution to the riddle of capturing "the life of nations and humanity"—whether in a fictional book like *War and Peace* or in more traditional historical chronicles.[80] But part 2 of the epilogue does explain how he himself negotiates it. Keeping in mind the two *kinds* of truth that Tolstoy argues a historical narrative can honor—the sense of freedom that defines individual "life" from within and the laws of necessity to which events are really subject—I can rewrite my account of *War and Peace*'s character-system.

At the core of *War and Peace* is a group of figures whose minds and characters are seen as complex, whose actions and decisions are often represented from the inside as ongoing and undetermined. This group includes not just the novel's protagonists but also its "potential protagonists": Pierre and Natasha; Petya Rostov and the artillery captain Tushin. Their consciousnesses appear to be subjectively present within, and inextricably from, a surrounding narrative that also represents their external boundaries as figures or characters, boundaries that they themselves cannot perceive. There is, indeed, a kind of allegory about Tolstoyan freedom and necessity in such mimetic life: a life embedded in text and thus absolutely determined, and yet felt as free each time we read that text, in the persons of the "live" protagonists themselves.

Contiguous with this core is a larger but still bounded group of characters who appear to be less complicated, more subject to the laws of the social world around them, and thus easier to represent in terms of typifying language. But this representational method tends to obscure the imagined indeterminate life of these minor characters, even though their *felt* sense of freedom must (in theory) be just as vivid as those of the protagonists. I have offered an account of some ways the novel uses its major characters' centrality—as any fiction does—to construct an absorbing, thematically organized world in which minor characters appear to exist less fully. Reading part 2 of the epilogue as a reflection on narrative characterization, we find a final move to motivate such distortion mimetically rather than formally, with Tolstoy's assertion that our understanding of an action as determined depends partly on the nature of the historical actor—that is, on the complexity of "the character and mind of the man in question" (1300; 12:331).

Finally—and here is where we must account for the idiosyncrasy of Tolstoy's approach—there is an innumerable group of marginal characters about whom we know so little that almost anything might be true of them. Part 2 of the epilogue suggests that this ignorance too produces an impression of free and indeterminate life: not because we have access to the characters' subjective sense of their own freedom but because we know almost nothing about the forces, of character and of situation, that determine their actions. Precisely by preserving its marginal characters on the edge between representation and referentiality, *War and Peace* undercuts the novelistic assumption that central figures "live" while all others cluster around their lives.

In other words, the novel juxtaposes two perspectives on what I have called mimetic life. It points at two kinds of fictional figures who appear to have entered the distorting artifice of text from elsewhere and to retain their own lives within it: at protagonists like Natasha, and at marginal characters like the members of the crowd that lynches Vereshchagin. Able to construct only a limited number of indeterminate historically placed lives from within, the novel indicates others from without, just by barely representing them at all.

Interpreted in the limited context of the relationship between a text and the people whose lives it sets out to capture, Tolstoy's theory of history helps explain the peculiarity of *War and Peace*'s stable-but-shifting character-system: it is performing two different jobs at once. It is divided not just between the living (major) and the artificial (minor) but also between two kinds of mimetic life; not just between characters represented as central and those deliberately placed off-center in the construction of a fictional world, but also between the characters we happen to experience from the inside and those we happen to experience from without.

This doubled character-system's chief innovation is the aesthetic emphasis it can place on characters who are continually poised to disappear from the novel—the French cook being flogged in Moscow, the throng of bare-headed soldiers avidly gazing at the Smolensk Mother of God before the Battle of Borodino (818; 11:196), or the two little girls whom Andrei glimpses stealing green plums at Bald Hills (755; 11:124). It is their readiness to disappear, without so much as a proper name to tie them back to the text, that seems to emancipate such characters from the artifice of fictional narrative. Many readers remember the scene where Pierre and Andrei watch the sinking sun from the Bogucharovo ferry, immersed in their talk about God and the purpose of life. Fewer likely remember the scene at Krasnoe where some soldiers of the Eighth Company join the soldiers of the Fifth to enjoy the antics of Ramballe's servant Morel, and pause to look up at the stars:

> All the young soldiers smiled merrily as they watched him. The older men, who thought it undignified . . . continued to lie at the opposite side of the fire, but one would occasionally raise himself on an elbow and glance at Morel with a smile.
>
> "They are men, too," said one of them as he wrapped himself up in his coat. "Even wormwood grows on its own root."

"O Lord, O Lord! How starry it is! Tremendous! That means a hard frost . . ."

They all grew silent. The stars, as if knowing that no one would see them now, began to play in the dark sky. Now flaring up, now vanishing, now trembling, they were busy whispering something joyful, but mysterious, to one another. (1180; second ellipsis in original)[81]

Equated with "no one," the soldiers disappear from the discourse in a different way from Boris Drubetskoy. They vanish not into the psyche of a protagonist but into the vision of a world. We never find out what the stars "whispered" or whether the soldiers were still watching them, just as we never find out what Natasha dreamt. Common to the soldiers, the stars, and Natasha is the illusion that they lead a life beyond narrative, capable of playing "as if knowing that no one would see them now." If the ineluctable impression of Natasha's life comes from the multitude of words that outline her space within the narrative, the barely experienced impression of the soldiers' life comes from the near infinity of what the novel will not tell us about them.

The distinctions among its fully realized protagonists, its partially realized minor characters, and its almost fully unrealized marginal characters remeasure the distance between *War and Peace* as a novel about heroes and *War and Peace* as an "epic" about national events. The first half of the novel establishes a relatively conventional character-system, a relationship between the representation of major and the representation of minor characters that makes us feel what mimetic life is and what it is not. But in its second half, the projection of nonfictional life in the many begins to overwhelm the realization of fictional life in the few. This encroaching marginality marks a final narrative limit, the upper horizon that is a "history of all": unlike the lives of the Rostovs, Bolkonskys, Kuragins, and Dolokhovs, the mimetic life of every person in this multitude could not be written by any human hand.

As the marginal characters of *War and Peace* limn its most ambitious representational horizon, its protagonists are left at the core of a narrative that swells larger and larger around them. Tolstoy illustrates this dynamic graphically—as Marya facing the unfathomable body of the peasants in revolt at Bogucharovo, as Pierre trying to out-shout his fellow noblemen while they debate how many conscripts to give Alexander, as Petya being physically suffocated by a crowd of fellow adorers at Alexander I's balcony. Approaching the end of the novel, we readers may feel a parallel threat. The character-spaces we have grown to recognize are overwhelmed by others we cannot even place: a form of life illegible by design threatens to displace a form of life native to the fictional text.

There is, however, another way to understand this asymmetry, with recourse to the terms established by *War and Peace* itself. Tolstoy cannot show us that a life narrated in terms of necessity yearns for a life narrated in terms of freedom: seeing some characters purely from the outside, we can only presuppose the infinity of each one's subjective experience. But he can reveal the opposite: a protagonist's desire to see *himself* clearly from the outside, written into the inevitable structure of a story whose meaning and outcome are beyond his view. More than any other character, Pierre Bezukhov makes us see this desire. To explore it, I will turn now—after this very lengthy interval—to the novel's fourth and final narration of dinner at the English Club.

Just after the Battle of Borodino, three soldiers Pierre meets on the road guide him to Mozhaisk. Falling asleep, Pierre begins to remember the battle and the people he saw there, whom he calls "they": "*They*, in Pierre's mind, were the soldiers, those who had been at the battery, those who had given him food, and those who had prayed before the icon. *They*, those strange men he had not previously known, stood out clearly and sharply from everyone else" (904; 11:293). Pierre's thoughts merge into a vivid dream:

> "To be a soldier, just a soldier!" thought Pierre as he fell asleep. "To enter that life-in-common completely, to be imbued with what makes them what they are. But how to cast off all this superfluous, devilish—all the burden of this outer man? . . . I might have been sent to serve as a soldier after the duel with Dolokhov." And the memory of the dinner at the English Club when he had challenged Dolokhov flashed through Pierre's mind, and then he remembered his benefactor at Torzhok. And now a solemn meeting of the Lodge presented itself to his mind. It was taking place at the English Club. . . . On one side of the table sat Anatole, Dolokhov, Nesvitsky, Denisov, and others like them (in his dream the category to which these men belonged was as clearly defined in his mind as the category of those he termed *they*), and he heard those people, Anatole and Dolokhov, shouting and singing loudly; yet through their shouting the voice of his benefactor was heard. . . . Pierre did not understand what his benefactor was saying, but he knew (the categories of thoughts were also quite distinct in his dream) that he was talking of goodness and the possibility of being what *they* were. And *they* with their simple, kind, firm faces surrounded his benefactor on all sides. But though they were kindly they did not look at Pierre and did not know him. Pierre wanted to attract their attention and speak. (904)[82]

Pierre's categories of figures—imported into his dream like "the categories of thoughts"—follow the lines of the character-system proposed in this analysis. His dream confronts us, further, with the shock of a protagonist who *sees* the system near the center of which he lies. Pierre finds himself caught between the force of the minor characters and that of the marginal; his dilemma is that of a central protagonist who longs both to step outside his own novel and to attract its attention. This desire both to be and not be at the subjective center of one's own story is unfulfillable, but it makes poignantly clear Pierre's envy for the social, economic, and (not least) narrative condition represented in the pronoun *they*. And Pierre's discontent mirrors the novel's own. This scene springs from the representation of Pierre's "living" consciousness, but what the scene shows is his desire to leave behind the center of the fictional text whose center is the only place that consciousness exists.

Pierre's dream gives shape to the antinomy that Tolstoy cannot solve. Even in a novel as expansive as *War and Peace*, one character's mimetic life is defined in relation to that of others: it is the economies of bounded narrative attention themselves that make possible the illusion of a boundlessly living world. In this sense, the undetermined consciousness that is key to an impression of life—both in Tolstoy's theory of history and in his fictional technique—requires the textual bounds of a novel for its representation. But such representation, achieving its fullest form, can only ever be asymmetrical. Pierre's envy for the "they" of his dream points to the dynamic discontent at the heart of the character-system of *War and Peace*. Even as the novel reaches away from the limits of its own narrative, toward the mimetic horizon of a "history of all," its protagonists reach for the utopian condition of marginality—of barely being narrated at all. Conversely, the novel's powerful gesture at the lives of its marginal characters remains a gesture, a tug toward stories that seem vivid precisely because they are never told.

"TWO, TWO!": THE DISCONTENTS OF CHARACTER IN *WAR AND PEACE*

Midway through part 1 of *War and Peace*'s epilogue, an otherwise unidentified minor character, Anna Makarovna, finishes knitting a pair of stockings. By some "secret process known only to herself," she is able to knit two stockings on the same needles, one inside the other. When she is finished, she "triumphantly" draws the inner stocking from the outer one, to the Rostov and Bezukhov children's ecstatic cries of "'Two, two!'" (1255–56; 12:280–81).

This episode stands out as an enigma within a narrative that by now has become relentlessly declarative. A range of prominent issues with contemporary resonances—the "woman question," the wrong of physical violence, and the moral education of children—assert themselves from within the description of the Rostovs' and Bezukhovs' idyllic family life. Moreover, a direct continuity links the narrator's pronouncements and the characters' illustration—most jarringly, Natasha's conversion into "an exemplary [*primernoiu*] wife and mother" (1243; 12:266):

> She had grown stouter and broader, so that it was difficult to recognize the slim lively Natasha of former days in this robust mother. Her features were more defined and had a calm, soft and serene expression. In her face now there was not, as before, the ever-burning flame of animation that had constituted its charm. Now her face and body were often all that one saw, and her soul was not visible at all. All that struck the eye was a strong, handsome and fertile female [*samka*]. The old fire very rarely kindled in her now. (1242)[83]

This description both narrates Natasha's transformation and enacts a transformation in her relationship to the narrative. Not only are her soul and fluid consciousness no longer "visible" to the external observer; even a reader's view cannot now glimpse the "flame of animation" that helps define Natasha. Her former refrain "There, that's me!" ("Vot ona ia!") has been absorbed into the face of her baby Petya, which tells her, "Here am I, and he is in me!" ("A ia vot on, a ia vot on!")—where the Russian pronoun *on* ("he") can stand for both Petya and his father and namesake Pierre (1247; 12:271).

At the novel's end, a new generality of pronoun and name thus blurs the narrated outline of each individual figure. Displacing the heroes "themselves" and prioritizing the subjects of their conversations, which their lives exemplify, long passages of part 1 of the epilogue resemble didactic fiction in their redundant clarity.[84] Here at the fringes of *War and Peace*, we see yet another potential transformation: one that makes every figural character minor, in comparison with the message from author to reader.

But it is also possible to ignore this experiment. Indeed, it may be closer to the experience of many readers to say that part 1 of the epilogue is like a shadow of the text before it—a somewhat ethereal repetition of the fictional world we have come to know. This repetition recapitulates the character-system, following the structure of generations established in the main body of the text. There is another dog Milka, the daughter of the first; another little Natasha, who dances; and another Andrei (called Nikolenka), who dreams. As the glimpse of them in the epilogue suggests, the protagonists of this second novel stand poised to displace the old ones, moving Nikolai and Natasha to the distanced representational space their own parents occupied throughout the main body of *War and Peace*. In this reading, the epilogue serves not to transcend the novel's fictionality but to reaffirm its mimetic pattern: the illusion stops just where we can see it begin to extend into infinite generational succession, unbounded as the world.

In other words, *War and Peace*'s epilogue is lit by the intentional gleam of a reality from two sources—one inside, one outside of the fictional text. Passages in part 1 draw our attention to the reality outside by attempting to make fictional characters into bridges: exemplary types or clear conduits for moral and political problems. Part 2 of the epilogue, a never-closed digression, resoundingly completes this departure from self-contained novelistic illusion. But over and around that experiment wind the threads that encircle Tolstoy's characters in a text facing inward, into the bounded and asymmetrical world of *War and Peace* itself. What, then, were the figures that unfolded within this narrative? What do we carry away of them when our reading is done?

In a well-known passage from his essay "The Image of Proust" (1934), Walter Benjamin offers a metaphor for the dream logic of Proust's fictional world that encapsulates this problem:

> The similarity of one thing to another which we are used to, which occupies us in a wakeful state, reflects only vaguely the deeper similarity of the dream world in which everything that happens appears not in identical but in similar guise, opaquely similar to itself. Children know a symbol of this world: the stocking which has the structure of this dream world when, rolled up in a laundry hamper, it is a "bag" and a "present" at the same time. And just as children do not tire of quickly changing the bag and its contents into a third thing—namely, a stocking—Proust could not get his fill of emptying the dummy, his self, at one stroke in order to keep garnering that third thing, the image which satisfied his curiosity—indeed, assuaged his homesickness.[85]

One stocking—the fictive image elaborated in the gap between what was once real and what is now narrated—is enough to symbolize the stakes of the world that "detaches itself from the sentences" of Proust's narrative. But Tolstoy dreamed of "two!" Figuring a near-magical relationship between a container and its contents, Anna Makarovna's stockings draw attention to the ideal that haunts the end of Tolstoy's novel: one stocking drawn triumphantly from the other, the sense of history from the structure of fiction.

The two-part epilogue of *War and Peace*—half fictional and didactic, half philosophical—offers evidence of this desire, and the interleaving of mimetic, didactic, and overtly nonfictional discourses suggests that their juxtaposition here is itself important. It calls our attention, in the midst of this departure from a fictional world, to the fiction that is poised to lure us back. What is the power of the asymmetrical illusion that made Pierre, Natasha, and all Tolstoy's anonymous crowds seem to live, and what is its price? How far outside the bounds of a fictional world can the "truths" constructible *only* through its narrative extend?

The stability of the novel's fictional world, and of the character-system through which Tolstoy elaborates it, is the necessary condition for these destabilizing questions about the purposeful value of the "lives" of realist characters and the experience of reading novels. No less firmly motivated division among major, minor, and marginal characters could anchor such a shift in its own underlying narrative terms. But no novel less preoccupied with that division's artificiality could so keenly show the problem of two worlds that appear to be one: a likeness between real and written life whose vitality depends on their inner separation.

Chapter Two

"A Novel Needs a Hero . . .": Dostoevsky's Realist Character-Systems

IN 1918, GEORG Lukács published an essay on his friend Béla Balázs that includes the following credo: "Dostoevsky's people live, without distance, the essence of their souls. Meanwhile the problem of other writers, including even Tolstoy, consists in how a soul can overcome those obstacles by which it is prevented from an attainment, even a glimpse, of itself. Dostoevsky begins where the others end: he describes how the soul lives its own life."[1]

This comment draws on the notes Lukács made for his abandoned book on Dostoevsky, to which *The Theory of the Novel* (1916) was intended as a preface.[2] Together with the notes, it sheds light on Lukács's often-quoted pronouncement that "Dostoevsky did not write novels."[3] For Dostoevsky's characters, he writes, thought is action; they have no professions or marriage plots, and their behavior cannot be traced back to family or environment. Their "adventures" take place exclusively "in the soul."[4] This continuity between action and idea places the fictional sphere of action beside the point. Relinquishing the novel's simulacrum of a "rounded world" ideally fitted for its hero, Dostoevsky transcended what might be called the foundling plot of the novel genre as Lukács defines it: its status as an expression of "transcendental homelessness," as the "epic of a world . . . abandoned by God."[5] In other words, Dostoevsky gave up the artifice of divinely adequate creation that severs the novel, in a secular age, from the terms of reality itself.

A vital strand of twentieth-century criticism and theory extends both backward and forward from Lukács's reading of Dostoevsky's characters. It begins with the Symbolist critic Dmitrii Merezhkovsky (*L. Tolstoy and Dostoevsky*, 1900–1902), who wrote that Dostoevsky builds his heroes primarily from speech and thought—utterances so characteristic that they make the character seem "*too* live . . . so that it is almost frightening to look at him; it seems that he is ready at any minute to stir and step out of the frame like a ghost."[6] It continues through Viacheslav I. Ivanov's image of Dostoevsky's characters as "living ghosts": "they knock at our doors in dark and in white nights, they can be recognized on the streets in murky patches of Petersburg fog and they settle in to talk with us in insomniac hours in our own underground" ("Dostoevsky and the Novel-Tragedy" ["Dostoevskii i roman-tragediia," 1911/1916]).[7] The eerie vividness of characters created by their "own" speech frees Dostoevsky, as Merezhkovsky and Ivanov suggest, from the novel's limitations as a genre, transposing his works into the communal realms of tragedy and prophetic myth. In his *Problems of Dostoevsky's Poetics* (*Problemy tvorchestva Dostoevskogo*, 1929; *Problemy poetiki Dostoevskogo*, 1963), Mikhail Bakhtin extended the idea that Dostoevsky's characters are created by their "own" words, and he later made it the foundation for his theory of the novel as an unfinalizable genre, uniquely active within "the ongoing event of current life."[8]

For all these theorists, Dostoevsky's characters represent the point where the realist novel comes closest to crossing into its reader's world, overstepping the limits of fiction and text. His characters arrest us because they seem to author their own being; through them, as many readers have contended, Dostoevsky acknowledged the end of communal religious faith. This idea still defines Dostoevsky's place in (particularly) the Western popular imagination—answered by a reverse trend, in much post-Soviet Russian scholarship, toward reading Dostoevsky as a devoutly Christian writer. However, the most plausible position lies between these extremes. Could there be a better summary of the ambivalence of Dostoevsky's novels than (in Lukács's own iconic précis of the novel genre) "the epic of an age in which the extensive totality of life is no longer given . . . yet which still thinks in terms of totality"?[9]

In this chapter, I will show how a nostalgia for totality is written into the structure of Dostoevsky's novels and how it contributes to the mimetic effect produced by his characters—near invisibly, because what is new about Dostoevsky's mimetic techniques is so much more obvious than what is conventional about them. Dostoevsky's "Copernican revolution" in characterization, as Bakhtin described it, consists in the devices he coined for granting his characters a narrative authority that seems to rival the narrator's own.[10] At the same time, Dostoevsky strove to give a shape and an image to what he called "the real man of the Russian majority" (16:329): to fit fragmented contemporary figures for the very kind of vivid, all-enfolding fictional representation from which he was later seen to have liberated the novel genre. For Dostoevsky, the struggle toward spiritual and psychological wholeness is thus also a literary problem—specifically, a problem of characterization. His innovative dialogic techniques sever characters from author, but his characters reach for the coherent figural outlines that only an author could give them. The result is a hybrid approach to realist characterization, where the authored image both anchors and eludes the personality projected by the character's "own" voice. Dostoevsky's Symbolist critics and their successors envisioned this dissociation from the author as a form of freedom. But Dostoevsky himself (I will argue) understood it as a condition of *narrative illegitimacy*: the characters' felt estrangement from their rightful origins and name.

Although this chapter discusses writings from throughout Dostoevsky's mature career, I propose his enigmatic and underappreciated late novel *The Adolescent* (*Podrostok*, 1875) as a key to the problem of realist characterization in his novels. It is no coincidence that *The Adolescent* itself coheres around the trope of illegitimacy, and so also the fantasy of relegitimation. *The Adolescent* offers an unfamiliar vision of Dostoevsky as tormented by the limitations of his own novels, and of the novel genre as such. It suggests a Dostoevsky both more and less conventional than central twentieth-century critics presented him—aspiring *toward* a standard of mimetic characterization that later readers thought he had surpassed, but revealing a faith nothing short of radical in the spiritual power that such mimetic images might hold.

DOSTOEVSKY AND REALIST CHARACTER-SYSTEMS

In 1846, Dostoevsky made his debut with *Poor Folk* (*Bednye liudi*), a novella comprising a series of letters between the clerk Makar Devushkin and his beloved seamstress neighbor Varvara Dobroselova. At its high point, Varvara lends Makar a copy of Nikolai Gogol's story "The Overcoat" ("Shinel'," 1842), which tells the story of an impoverished clerk like Makar himself, holding Makar's own civil service rank of titular councilor (in 1846, just below the level of hereditary nobility). Makar castigates Gogol for unsympathetically turning the figure of the titular councilor into a text for others to read: "I'm sometimes afraid to show my face anywhere, because I tremble at the thought of what wicked tongues may be saying about me, because people can concoct a lampoon about one out of anything at all, anything, and then one's entire public and private life is held up for inspection in the form of literature."[11] With this passage, Dostoevsky's first protagonist throws down a gauntlet: an objection to being characterized without his knowledge and against his will. In Bakhtin's seminal analysis, what Gogol presented as information *about* or definition *of* the character now becomes a component of the character's self-consciousness: what captivates us is no longer the figure of a titular councilor but the question of how this figure might see and present his own worldview. The mimetic force of such a character is unprecedented, because he seems not only to exist beyond his literary characterization but actually to assume his own relationship toward it.[12]

To put it more soberly, Dostoevsky had a strong preference for indirect characterization—that is, the indication of a character through the "evidence" of a speech, emotion, action, or thought, rather than through authoritative description.[13] During his lifetime, readers were less likely to see this technique as preternaturally true to life. His contemporaries habitually (with aesthetic as well as ideological motivations) objected to the "phantasmagoria" and hyperbole of his criminal, diseased, "underground" characters, particularly in comparison with the sunlit and solid realist fictions of Tolstoy.[14] By the time *The Adolescent* was published in 1875, the hostile critic V. G. Avseenko could plausibly treat the unreality of Dostoevsky's characters as an acknowledged fact, seamlessly linking the charge of liminal abnormality with the language of the insubstantial: "It has often been said that Mr. Dostoevsky succeeds best with the representation of phenomena of life that stand on the boundary separating reality from the world of ghosts. . . . It is *not people* acting, but some degenerates of the human race, some *underground shadows*."[15]

It is striking that Dostoevsky's Symbolist admirers and his nineteenth-century detractors converge on the image of ghostliness to describe the effect that his characters create. This image points to a puzzle about Dostoevskian mimesis. His characters' "reality" depends on the sustained illusion that they are painted by their own thoughts and words, exceeding their characterization as given in the text. But to achieve this illusion, Dostoevsky sacrifices the solidity epitomized by realist characters like Tolstoy's: the imaginary physical presence established by extensive, systematically distributed narrative detail and description.[16] The illusion is compelling *because* it is ghostly—but its very ghostliness entails the loss, or the rejection, of key aspects of the quality I am calling "mimetic life": the reader's sense of the character's autonomous and embodied existence.[17] To account for these competing instincts, we need to define Dostoevsky's transformation of realist characterization more sharply.

By transferring the weight of characterization to quoted thought or speech, Dostoevsky subverts the conventional underpinning of realist character-systems, the idea that more narrative space and attention mean a more fully realized mimetic illusion. In his novels, a character does not always seem less "herself" for occupying a small space in the narrative, and a fictional self does not always appear warped for having less narrative attention devoted to it.[18] *Crime and Punishment* (*Prestuplenie i nakazanie*, 1866) is overwhelmingly focalized through Raskolnikov, alternating between the character's partial and the narrator's total field of vision.[19] But the narrator uses the same kind of focalization to make other characters emerge equally clearly, across the novel's ideological range. Thus, we learn of the vilified Luzhin (in his own vocabulary and register) that "until the very last minute, such an outcome was the last thing he'd ever expected. He had blustered [*kurazhilsia*] all the way to the end, never even recognizing the possibility that two penniless and defenseless women could escape from under his thumb."[20] Of the angelic Sonya, and with her characteristic breathlessness, Dostoevsky writes: "She was terribly relieved to get away at last. She walked off head down, hurrying along, anything so as to get out of sight as quickly as possible, to put these twenty paces behind her, turn right, and be alone at last, and then, walking along quickly, not seeing anyone, not noticing anything, to think, recall, consider every spoken word, every circumstance. Never, never before had she felt anything like it. A whole new world—obscurely, out of nowhere—had entered her soul" (226).[21] Such moments signal that a character can take comprehensive shape in whatever passage the narrative turns a particular mode of attention upon her—articulating the language so specific to her that it makes her "stir and step out of the frame like a ghost."

This is not to say, however, that Dostoevsky does not systematically manipulate narrative space and attention in constructing his characters. Some (like the paired blatherers of *The Idiot*, Lebedev and General Ivolgin) are constitutionally minor; the more they "speak," the more the reader learns to ignore them. Others vainly strive to catch both the protagonists' and the reader's attention.[22] What is more, the structure of Dostoevsky's character-systems tends to repeat from novel to novel, like the recurring casts of commedia dell'arte plays.[23] Sometimes, as in Balzac, a figure at the center of one novel will appear (renamed) on the sidelines of another.[24] Just as often, however, Dostoevsky's players maintain their relative positions across novels. The descant of the Marmeladov family theme in *Crime and Punishment* becomes the descant of the Snegirev family theme in *The Brothers Karamazov*—with recognizable roots in the impoverished Pokrovskys of *Poor Folk*. It takes a forceful effort to unsettle such patterns. The dandyish lackey Vidopliasov has no path to the center of "The Village of Stepanchikovo and Its Inhabitants" (1859), just as the dandyish hanger-on Ferdyshenko has no path to the center of *The Idiot* (1868–69); this intertextual history lurks behind the dandy and lackey Smerdyakov's uncanny suppression throughout *The Brothers Karamazov* (1879–80). The minorness and eccentricity of the figure exemplified by Katerina Ivanovna Marmeladova (*Crime and Punishment*), Katerina Nikolaevna Akhmakova (*The Adolescent*), and Katerina Ivanovna Verkhovtseva (*The Brothers Karamazov*) are so ingrained that even a related figure far more central to her narrative, *The Idiot*'s Nastasya Filippovna, must "script" the plot largely from offstage.[25] As the later part of this chapter will show, Dostoevsky upends his entire narrative aesthetic to bring the minor character realized in Ganya Ivolgin (*The Idiot*) to the center of his plans for "The Life of a Great Sinner" and then of the completed novel *The Adolescent*.

As with much else in Dostoevsky's novels, his character-systems thus juxtapose formula with subversion. Characters and relations between characters are set into preexisting patterns: generic, historical, personal to Dostoevsky's past and worldview, and other. At the same time, Dostoevsky challenges and relativizes systematic contrasts among major, minor, and marginal characters, as they are reflected in the distribution of narrative attention. Extending Bakhtin's framework, we might say that in Dostoevsky's novels, the character-system itself acquires a subjective and self-conscious component. By letting characterization depend on thought and speech, he makes the reader shift from center to center of each character's self-conscious view of her position in the story world—in relation to others, and also to her own idealized or formulaic image of herself. The difference between major and minor characters, which Tolstoy makes absolute, in Dostoevsky becomes the dynamic of many characters' self-narratives.

In other words, for readers of Dostoevsky, two visible kinds of character-system run simultaneously: the one each character constructs in her self-consciousness (of which she is the center and from which she "speaks"), and the one of which she is a part, which makes her a protagonist or minor character of this (and often of other linked) narratives. More narrative still tends to mean more mimesis, but Dostoevsky also exercises his power to align our attention with many different characters' subjective sense of centrality, such that simply being central is no longer enough to guarantee mimetic plenitude. Oddly, there is no better example for exploring this variation on the conventional realist character-system than a novella dominated by a single unnamed character: Dostoevsky's *Notes from Underground* (*Zapiski iz podpol'ia*, 1864).

THE EXPERIMENTAL CHARACTER-SYSTEM OF *NOTES FROM UNDERGROUND*

The Underground Man sums up his own soliloquy in an evocative (although swiftly disavowed) sentence: "'But I am one person, and they are *everybody*,' I thought, and—became lost in thought."[26] One conclusion that can be drawn from this complaint is that the Underground Man's self-narrative is largely about its own character-system. He is telling the story of his position in relation to the others in his narrative, and to the conventional heroic models (literary and otherwise) against which he judges himself. Both in part 1 of the novella, where he attempts to present his ideas and forestall the responses of his imaginary audience, and in part 2, where he remembers actual encounters with others, the question of where he stands within his own story often overshadows its content. He is "one" and "they are *everybody*," and he is tormented both by the solitude of this singularity, and by the fact that it does not seem to make him (in the words of Dickens's David Copperfield) "the hero of [his] own life."[27]

As Michael Holquist has argued, the master plot of *Notes from Underground* is the Underground Man's loss of faith in the defining power of plot itself. Constructing a series of "ready-made" (51; 5:133) literary or philosophical roles in his own imagination (from the despairing philosopher-hero of part 1 to the romantic benefactor of part 2), the Underground Man abandons each one as soon as it clashes with the chaos of reality and of his actual individual self. He emerges as tragic, but not for the reasons he thinks: he has no faith in plot understood broadly as "the possibility of a meaningfully coherent series," and yet he cannot do without the attempt to imagine a plot for himself.[28]

A similar conclusion can be expressed in terms of character—in the Underground Man's own word, "kharakter," which can refer both to a collection of traits and to a figure who exemplifies them. Like any "intelligent man of the nineteenth century," as the Underground Man claims, he finds the idea of particular characterization unacceptably limiting (5; 5:100). He does not want to be an easily summed-up minor character, and so, with his exquisite sensitivity to the workings of narrative character-systems, he is drawn instead to the unlimited, indefinite territory of a central hero (*geroi*). But he can imagine "no middle ground" between his subjective fantasy of himself as a "hero" and the humiliating lived experience that fails to match it: "I couldn't imagine myself playing a secondary role and this was exactly why in reality, I quite happily adopted the last. Either a hero or filth—there was nothing in between" (51; 5:133).

Accordingly, the Underground Man is consistently unsettled and enraged by evidence that others too experience this absolute dichotomy between "hero" and "filth," that they too can only envision themselves either as major or as marginal characters—at either the actual or the potential centers of their own narrative worlds. It is bitter to realize that the discourteous officer who (literally) displaces him in a crowded billiards room, or his former schoolmates at the party to which he disastrously invites himself, did not even notice many of the events that stand at the core of his narrative (71–72; 5:147). Still worse, however, is the memory of his "ulcer" (*iazva*), "scourge" (*bich*), or "executioner" (*palach*), his servant Apollon, who despises and looks down on the Underground Man and seems to have been exempted from all self-doubt (102; 5:167). Like the Underground Man, Apollon sees himself as a protagonist, and he continually places his claim to this position before the Underground Man's eyes. As the Underground Man gradually realizes—at first thrillingly, and then to his horror—the prostitute Liza also imagines herself as the singular thinker at the center of her own, and later their, story (84; 5:155). Part of the problem is that if she is this story's heroine (*geroinia*), then he cannot be the hero, but it is equally problematic that any doubt about the question could arise.

In other words, the Underground Man is tortured (among other things) by the suspicion that his sense of injured singularity might come not from any particular quality or "idea," but rather only, in the early Bakhtin's terms, from the *universal* state of knowing oneself as an ever-fluid "author" and not as a perfected "hero" (character), definable from the outside.[29] If protagonicity is entirely common and circumstantial—just what results from being conscious at the center of one's own life—then the state of being a protagonist becomes both inevitable and terrifying: an inability to achieve any stable identity because one's uncontainable, unconventional consciousness is the only content of one's narrative. *Notes from Underground* plays out mimetic life as the protagonist's private nightmare. It asks, in terms both philosophical and metafictional, what it would mean to be living if a seemingly irreducible consciousness—rather than a place at the center of a given biographical plot—were the sole ingredient of life.

The "notes" (*zapiski*) of which the Underground Man is the hero end with the acknowledgment—forced by his retelling of his own story—that his sense of centrality is indeed relative. But far from the moral awakening that an author less adventurous than Dostoevsky might have staged, this acknowledgment becomes an act of revenge; the Underground Man means to inflict his own sense of relativity and indefiniteness on his readers. The younger Underground Man was romantically aggrieved to feel that "I am one person, and they are *everybody*." Now he has lost the grounds for this consolatory romance, but at least he knows that his grievance ought to be universal:

> A novel needs a hero, but here *deliberately* all the features of an anti-hero have been gathered together and the main thing is, all this will produce a most unpleasant impression, since all of us have lost touch with real life . . . I know that you will perhaps be angry with me because of this, you'll start to scream and stamp your feet: "You are speaking," you say, "about yourself alone and your underground misery, so don't you dare say *all of us*." But excuse me, gentlemen, I'm not trying to justify myself by this *all of us*-ness. Strictly speaking, as far as I'm concerned, I've merely carried to extremes in my life things that you've never had the courage even to take halfway, and what's more, you've interpreted your cowardice as common sense and found comfort in deceiving yourselves. So I, if you like, come out still more "more alive" than you. Just take a closer look! (117–18)[30]

Everyone should, like the Underground Man, recognize the split between his idealization of himself as a romantic literary hero, and the irreducibly free authorial consciousness that resists such neat narrativization. To wish for a merger between these levels is to resist the labor of being "people with real, with *our own* flesh and blood" (118; 5:179). For the Underground Man then, the price of narrative "reality" is agreeing to be nothing *but* real. He takes the logic of realist character-systems (as of all other systems) to an extreme, such that the mimetic power of protagonicity threatens to undo the defining power of characterization itself.

Of course, the Underground Man cannot know the most salient fact about himself: that he *is* a formulizable character (kharakter) and also (objectively and even supremely) a fictional protagonist (*litso, geroi*). Dostoevsky brings this other, wider angle of vision to the reader's attention with a signed footnote on the story's first page, in which the Underground Man appears both as an authentic kharakter distilling a contemporary trend and as a kind of puppet created in order to demonstrate this trend to Dostoevsky's readers:

> The author of these notes and the *Notes* themselves are, of course, fictitious. Nevertheless, such figures [*litsa*] as the writer of these notes not only can, but even must exist in our society—taking into account the circumstances under which our society in general was formed. I wanted to bring before the face of the public, more distinctly than usual, one of the characters [*kharakterov*] of the recent past. . . . In this fragment, entitled "The Underground," this figure [*litso*] introduces itself, its worldview, and as if wants to explain the reasons why it [*ono*] appeared and *must* have appeared in our environment. In the next fragment will come the real "notes" of this figure, about certain events in its life.—Fedor Dostoevsky. (3)[31]

In the cordoned-off narrative space of the footnote, the author explains his responsibility for composing the character and "bringing him before the public" and also depersonalizes him, referring to him most often with the neuter noun *litso* (character/figure) and neuter pronoun *ono* (it).[32] The result is a split between character's and author's "planes" that is not separate from or prior to the work of mimetic characterization but rather continuously essential to it.[33] On the author's and reader's plane, the character is presented explicitly as a mimetic creation—produced by the author, and cut off at the author's conclusive imperative word. On his own plane, he is freed from the visible signs of authorial control, but he is also stripped of all the most ordinary intersections between being a character and being a person. The Underground Man is indeed aesthetically "embodied," but unlike the Tolstoyan biographical hero, his embodiment (all the way down to his name) remains beyond his field of vision.[34] He is trapped within the lack of any protagonizing narrative beyond the absolutely common one of consciousness itself.

The interaction between the mode of realist characterization represented in the footnote, and that represented in the Underground Man's monologue, is thus more complex than acknowledged by readers who pose an inherent conflict between characterological "freedom" and systematic narrative design.[35] In fact, *Notes from Underground* suggests a dual source for the mimetic life of Dostoevsky's characters, in keeping with the two levels of Dostoevskian character-systems. On the one hand, there is the irreducible "consciousness" from which the Underground Man suffers—the "voice" that seems to weave around and slip from under any attempt to pin the character down in generalization, epithet, narrative description, or even a proper name. On the other hand, there is his status (which he cannot possibly know about) *as* "the Underground Man": a figure shaped by the very authorial presence that the character, who is cut off from any intimation of it, craves and imperfectly mimics in the inadequate roles and conventional patterns that he serially adopts and discards.[36] The illusion of the character's life comes not just from a unusually sharp separation between the plane on which he exists as a fictional character (the discourse) and the plane on which he exists as an implied and conscious person (the story), but also from the narrative reenactment of this separation on the level of the character's discourse about himself.

If the Underground Man is an extreme distillation of many of Dostoevsky's protagonists—a lapidary match between the form of representation and the subject of characterization[37]—then this *felt* separation is key to what he models. Just as Dostoevsky's characters are cut off in the discourse from the present authority of omniscient narrative, their stories tend to document a lapse in authorized identity. The illusion of embodied, self-sufficient life here depends neither on authorial fiat nor on "unmediated" transcription of the character's self-consciousness, but on the staged gap between these two poles: the characters' desire for the external contours and given selves of which they have been made so radically unaware.

Bakhtin's preferred metaphor for the status of characters like the Underground Man, who emerge primarily from their own words about themselves, is "freedom" or "autonomy" (*samostoiatel'nost'*). But as Bakhtin also acknowledges, the severance from omniscient narrative produces an essential poverty or lack, which he calls a "longing for embodiment": a break in the genealogical link between fictional character and "world-creating word," between the character and the one who has the authority to name him.[38] Moreover, as the novella itself implies, the Underground Man's unmoored first-person voice reflects a divorce from the traditional religious, moral, and social foundations of life, which Dostoevsky saw as endemic to postreform Russia. To capture the ambivalence of this position, we need a metaphor less optimistic than "freedom." Over the course of his 1860s–70s novels, Dostoevsky developed his own master trope for exploring the pervasive condition of exile from one's origins—encompassing the literary techniques that he himself used to sever character from implied author—which I would like to call *narrative illegitimacy*. He came to imagine both the historical condition of what he called the "real man of the Russian majority," and the narrative condition of his own characters, by analogy with the condition of an illegitimate child.

While Dostoevsky's approach to characterization remains constant throughout his career, the metaphor of illegitimacy moves to the self-reflexive center of his novels only with time. Thus, *Crime and Punishment* (1866) repeats the configuration of *Notes from Underground*: a split between the author's and reader's clear vision of Raskolnikov as protagonist and character, and Raskolnikov's search for his own figural outlines. Raskolnikov commits a murder in order to become "extraordinary"—to define himself as the hero of his own life—but until late in the epilogue, he understands only that he "did not have the right" to this project, not that the project itself (at least for a Dostoevskian character) is doomed. Raskolnikov senses but does not fathom the absence of defining traits and circumstances that distances him (like the Underground Man) from even an ordinarily definite character or person. Dostoevsky so widens this distance that only an authorial intervention incredible within the framework of realism—the divine force that "sweeps up" Raskolnikov and throws him at Sonya's feet (516; 6:421)—can mold his narrative into the shape of a plotted biography and his character into the shape of a palpable self.[39]

Beginning with his 1867–68 notebooks for *The Idiot*, however, Dostoevsky was captivated by the idea of a novel with an illegitimately born protagonist—where the lack of a clearly authored identity and sanctioned plot would become part of what the character "knows" about his own situation from the first. Running through the background of *The Idiot* and *Demons* (*Besy*, 1871–72), and through plans for Dostoevsky's never-written novel "Atheism/The Life of a Great Sinner" ("Ateizm/Zhitie velikogo greshnika," 1868–70), the figure of the illegitimate protagonist comes to fruition in Dostoevsky's second-to-last novel *The Adolescent*.[40] Tracing the intensifying dialogue between illegitimacy as historical and narrative condition, and illegitimacy as plot device and theme, we see not just what is new about Dostoevsky's characters but also their complex relationship with established novelistic convention. By thematizing his own assault on conventional realist characterization and the social, historical, and spiritual situation that motivated it, Dostoevsky nurtured the salvific vision of mimesis itself that drives his final novels.

"NARRATIVE ILLEGITIMACY" IN DOSTOEVSKY'S NOTEBOOKS (1867–75)

According to notebook plans that date from mid-September 1867, Dostoevsky's thinking about *The Idiot* began with a "ruined noble family (of a decent name)," which has "fetched up" in Saint Petersburg (9:140). Dostoevsky fills this household with a dense and motley tangle of relatives: a mother, a father who has abandoned the family and then returned; a son and his fiancée; a daughter and her fiancé; the fiancé's cousin; the stepdaughter of the mother's sister ("Mignon"); and a third son who singlehandedly supports the family, but whom the mother has dubbed "the Idiot." The family is on the verge of a moral collapse that stems directly from their financial ruin: "As long as these people have money, they are . . . at least presentable; they count as human beings. Without money they are falling fast" (9:141). It is tempting to connect Dostoevsky's immediate focus on a tottering noble household, as he began to plan his novel in the fall of 1867, with the recent serialization of book 1, parts 1 and 2, of Tolstoy's *War and Peace* (*Russian Herald*, January 1865–April 1866).[41] Whether or not Tolstoy's example was on Dostoevsky's mind at this point—as it certainly would be after he recorded reading *War and Peace* the following year—his challenge to the genre of the "noble family novel" is already in evidence in his plans for *The Idiot*.[42] What rifts and sources of decay in families "of a decent name" does money serve to patch, and what violations—of both lineage and virtue—lie beneath the shell of "nobility"? The closely interconnected set of Dostoevsky's later novels unfolds from the doubts he cast on nobility and the family as a stable base, for social mores and realist representation alike.

It is thus unsurprising that Dostoevsky's early deliberations about his protagonist ("the Idiot") congeal around the problem of his legitimacy—his relationship to and status within the already fragmented noble family at the center of the projected narrative.[43] The idea that the Idiot could be an illegitimate son is first floated on October 18, in one of many entries labeled "Final Plan of the Novel" (9:158). Illegitimacy appears not as a cause but as a possible motivation for what has been the Idiot's character from the beginning: "He became known as 'an idiot' because of his mother, who hates him. He feeds the family, but everyone thinks he does nothing. He has epilepsy and nervous attacks . . . *The Idiot*'s passions are strong, his demand for love is burning, his pride measureless, out of pride he wants to master himself and conquer himself. He finds sensuous pleasure in his humiliations. Those who do not know him laugh at him" (9:141). In this section of the notebooks, illegitimacy competes with epilepsy, holy-foolishness, stepchildhood, poverty, and sheer unmotivated resentment for prominence in Dostoevsky's thinking about how to account for the character of his intended protagonist.

Despite this shifting landscape, the "CAPITAL QUESTION" (November 3, 1867; 9:187) associated for Dostoevsky at this point with the Idiot—will he be legitimately or illegitimately born?—does seem to have consistent bearing on the possibility of his redemption. The November 6 revelation that the Idiot is a "*prince*" (9:200) opens the way for the emergence of what would become Prince Myshkin's defining positive traits: his love for children (9:202), his meekness and simplicity (9:202), and his endearing oddness (9:205). It is at this point, too, that Dostoevsky starts to assign the dangerous traits of "grandiose magnanimity [*velikodushie*], malice, pride and envy" to other figures (9:204). Once Dostoevsky had conclusively rejected the possibility of illegitimacy, the Idiot seems to have drawn sufficiently close to a positive hero that Dostoevsky could jettison his former plan and begin conceiving his novel about "Prince Christ" (9:253).

So what potential character did Dostoevsky exorcise along with the possibility of the Idiot's illegitimate birth, consequent lack of noble rank, and estrangement from his family? That protocharacter was to resurface frequently in later novels and novel drafts. Its elements are most evocatively described in notes from November 2, 1867, when the question of the Idiot's birth and status was still in doubt:

> THE MAIN AND FOUNDATIONAL THOUGHT OF THE NOVEL, FOR THE SAKE OF WHICH EVERYTHING ELSE IS THERE: the thought that he [the Idiot] is proud to such an unhealthy extent that he cannot *not* consider himself a god, and *at the same time*, so little respects himself (so clearly analyzes himself), that he cannot *not* endlessly despise himself, so forcefully as to be unfair. (He feels that dull revenge on everyone for his own sake would be a degradation, and at the same time he does this, he acts villainously and takes revenge.) He feels that he has nothing to take revenge for, that he is *like everyone*, and ought to be content. But since he demands more than everyone else, because of measureless vanity and self-love and at the same time a thirst for truth, all this is insufficient for him. In his development and his environment he has soaked up all these poisons and origins, which have entered into his blood. In a thoroughly insulted heart, grandiose magnanimity and the demand for love are without measure. *He has not had them*, and because of this he acts villainously towards and takes revenge on those whom he would like to love infinitely and give his blood for, on all those who are dear to him. . . . For the future—calculation; I will be a banker, the king of the Jews, and I will hold everyone in chains under my feet. "Either I will rule tyrannically, or I will die for everyone on the cross—I believe that this is all that's possible, according to my nature. But just simply to fade out—that is what I do not want."[44]

This portrait compiles an exhaustive list of the feelings and self-perceptions that Dostoevsky, when beginning work on *The Idiot*, suspected could best be motivated and emblematized by the condition of illegitimacy. It contains clear echoes of the emotional contradictions resulting from the Underground Man's isolation and wounded pride, and also of the Underground Man's obsession with "heroism," his claim to protagonicity within his own self-narrative. Nevertheless, this nascent portrait of an illegitimate protagonist hints at a question not yet posed in the tightly focused novella *Notes from Underground*: how might such a figure be placed at the center of a world of other characters, in the complex system of a full-length realist novel?

When Dostoevsky abandoned the idea of the Idiot as illegitimate and instead began to imagine him as a "perfectly beautiful man" or "Prince Christ,"[45] the traits of the figure I am calling the "illegitimate protagonist" came to rest in the minor character Ganya Ivolgin—an eldest son humiliated, desperate for social and economic power, and cripplingly ashamed of his family.[46] The common origin of Ganya and Myshkin in the Idiot of Dostoevsky's notebooks suggests that he saw the problem of representing Prince Christ and the problem of representing the illegitimate protagonist or "king of the Jews" (9:180) as two sides of the same coin. Neither figure fits into the existing conventions of Russian realism; the novel genre must be remade for both, and each represents a different approach to the task of transforming the novel for the spiritual demands of a disordered and chaotic postreform Russia. Accordingly, after completing *The Idiot*, Dostoevsky returned to his attempt to shape a realist novel around the figure of the illegitimate protagonist. The result was a brief but saturated set of notes for a projected epic entitled "The Life of a Great Sinner"—in Dostoevsky's shorthand, "the underground idea for the *Russian Herald*" (November 2, 1869; 9:125).

As Dostoevsky commented both in his own notes and in his letters, he hoped that the "Life" in its final form would rival Tolstoy's *War and Peace*: an epic not of historical but of contemporary Russian life.[47] The Great Sinner seems to have been illegitimately born (although this is never directly explained), and because of this, he has been raised apart from his family, and separated even from his guardians' children to avoid contaminating them (9:126, 132, 135). Thus, unlike with Tolstoy's hero Pierre Bezukhov—who begins the novel bearing his natural father's name and quickly also inherits his title and fortune—illegitimacy tells on the Great Sinner as the single most salient fact about him:

> A type completely opposed to the sprig of that noble count's house, shallow to the point of swinishness, that T[olstoy] represented in *Childhood* and *Boyhood*. This will just be a type from the root, unconsciously disturbed by his very own typical strength, which is completely unmediated and does not know what to found itself upon. . . . He rests at last upon Christ, but his whole life is tempest and disorder.[48]

Through the condition of illegitimacy, Dostoevsky reaches for a character who is the opposite of Tolstoy's noble-born "sprig"—a character consumed by a force that "does not know what to found itself upon," who may thus turn at last to the foundation of Christ.

By the time of the "Great Sinner" notes, then, illegitimacy had emerged as Dostoevsky's master trope for representing both the loss and the spiritual potential of the *absent foundation*, which opens a character to "tempest and disorder" on the one hand and to Christ on the other. Dostoevsky's drawn-out struggle to decide the question of the Idiot's legitimacy appears in retrospect as a struggle to decide whether he was yet writing the novel of this absent foundation. That potential novel is the germ for both the hapless Ganya Ivolgin and the proud Stavrogin; for both the nobleman Versilov and Arkady, his illegitimate son.[49] In a series reaching back toward the Underground Man, all these characters share in the illegitimate child's condition of divorce from his name and origins, whether or not they are literally illegitimate themselves.

For Dostoevsky and his readers, the trope of illegitimacy had longstanding cultural resonance. The image of Russia as the illegitimate child of East and West traces back as far as Petr Chaadaev's "First Philosophical Letter" (1829): "We others [Russians], like illegitimate children, come to this world without patrimony. . . . Each one of us must himself once again seek to tie the broken thread of the family line [le fil rompu de la famille]."[50] This idea of Russia's interrupted ancestry—its "isolation in the European family of peoples," as Dostoevsky puts it in the 1873 *Diary of a Writer* (21:70)—was compounded in his eyes after the additional rupture of the 1861–64 Great Reforms. The illegitimate protagonist's sense of rancor and exclusion signals the bitter national bind of postreform Russia as Dostoevsky saw it, faced with the task of *re*constructing foundations that it had never fully owned.

At the same time, as I have suggested, the figure of the illegitimate protagonist did no more than make explicit, on the level of plot and theme, what had always been the premise of Dostoevsky's unconventional techniques of characterization. From his first published fiction onward, he used a projection of the character's "own" speech, cut off from the foundational authority of omniscient narrative, to represent figures whose inner lives had not yet found a place within artistic literature. After Makar Devushkin (who rejects Gogol's stock characterization of the impoverished titular councilor) and the Underground Man and Raskolnikov (who reject any limiting external characterization at all), this challenge extended to representing figures for whom there is putatively nothing to characterize. As the narrator of *The Idiot* puts it, these are the "people who are usually called 'ordinary people'": Ganya Ivolgin, Arkady Dolgoruky, and behind them, the drafted figures of the original Idiot and the Great Sinner, accumulating wealth in order to compensate for the lack of any inherited position, identity, or name.[51] Progressing from *Makar* Alekseevich Devushkin to Arkady *Makar*ovich Dolgoruky, Dostoevsky paints ever more broadly the problem of a contemporary character that lies outside the line of Russian realist narrative. In the absence of any established template for representing such "ordinary people," he increasingly resorted to the strategy of letting the character seem to spring unsanctioned from his own words—a narrative alienation from origins that reproduces both the plight and the potential of illegitimacy as Dostoevsky describes it.

In this respect, Dostoevsky's long internal debate over the Idiot's legitimacy in 1867 parallels his equally lengthy deliberations over whether *The Adolescent* should be narrated from the hero's own first-person perspective in 1874 (16:47–151). Indeed, it is the same debate, played out first on the level of story, and then on the level of discourse. The notebooks for *The Adolescent* record a competition between two potential protagonists: a prototype of Arkady's father, the landowner Andrei Petrovich Versilov—a narrative as well as literal aristocrat, "a genuine heroic type" (February [?] 1874; 16:7)—and Arkady, the "Youth" or "boy," whom Dostoevsky was explicitly determined to make the novel's "hero" (July 1874; 16:24) and who would eventually settle as Versilov's illegitimate son. After numerous reminders to himself to provide "a larger role for the Youth," Dostoevsky recorded "AN IMPORTANT SOLUTION OF THE PROBLEM. Write *in the first person*. Start with the word: *I*. 'Confessions of a great sinner, for himself'" (August 12, 1874; 16:47).[52] But he then equivocated over this formal "solution" for another six weeks. Having at last decided to tackle the novel of an illegitimate and "ordinary" protagonist, Dostoevsky was reluctant to admit that such a figure could be created only through the labor of his own first-person narration. Since Dostoevsky's narrators had become less omniscient and authoritative with every novel since *Crime and Punishment*, his long resistance to adopting a first-person narrative is striking. What exactly did Dostoevsky fear Arkady would lose that the protagonists of his other major novels have?

This question, emerging at the height of Dostoevsky's exploration of his characters' narrative illegitimacy, should return us with new urgency to their insecure status as realist creations. In a March 1875 draft preface to *The Adolescent*, written soon after the novel had begun publication and received largely negative reviews, Dostoevsky tried to defend his characters against his critics' charges of both excessive naturalism and shadowy unreality. Where some critics accused him of transgressing the proper sphere of art by making readers feel rather than contemplate his characters' deranged emotions, others (as we have seen) condemned his "pathological" fascination with "the boundary that separates reality from the world of ghosts."[53] As A. S. Dolinin argues, both accusations stung for the same reason, because both implied that Dostoevsky had failed to create compelling literary "types": the characters of *The Adolescent* were not vivid syntheses of common human experience but monstrous exceptions.[54] Dostoevsky's drafted self-defense is cryptic, but suggestive:

> Facts. They pass by. They don't notice. *There are no citizens*, and no one wants to make an effort and force himself to think and notice. I could not tear myself away, and all the cries of critics that I am representing an unreal life have not deterred me. . . . Our talented writers, who have been representing, with high art, the life of our mid-upper-class (family) circle—Tolstoy, Goncharov—thought that they were representing the life of the majority—I think it was they who were representing the life of exceptions. On the contrary, their life is the life of exceptions, and mine is the life of the general rule. Future generations who are less partial will recognize this; the truth will be on my side. They say that I have been representing real thunder and real rain, as if on the stage. Where? Do Raskolnikov, Stepan Trofimovich (the main heroes of my novels) really give rise to such rumors? . . . From this (civic) feeling, I was ready to go over to the Slavophiles, thinking to resurrect the dreams of childhood. But the underground and "Notes from Underground." I am proud that I was the first to depict the real man of the *Russian majority* and the first to lay bare his monstrous and tragic side. The tragic element lies in his consciousness of monstrosity. . . . Only I alone depicted the tragic element of the underground, consisting in suffering, in self-condemning, in the consciousness of something better and the inability to achieve it and mainly, in the clear conviction of these unfortunates that everyone is the same way, and so there is no use in reforming![55]

Dostoevsky answers the accusation of "representing an unreal life" by claiming that he, rather than Tolstoy or Goncharov, has captured the "real man of the Russian majority"—and that this unconventional subject dictates his unconventional techniques. Raskolnikov, Stepan Trofimovich, and the Underground Man become fit ("tragic") matter for literature not because of their monstrosity, but because of their *consciousness* of monstrosity. As Dostoevsky suggests, a focus on capturing the character's self-perception was the only way the "real man of the Russian majority" could be represented at all. He answers the charge of naturalism ("real thunder and real rain") by defensively presenting these same characters as examples of compelling realist images. But do his "main heroes" already possess aesthetic coherence and distance from the reader, or do these qualities belong together with his idealistic "dreams of childhood," which his consciousness of the "underground" will not yet let him "resurrect"? Is Dostoevsky speaking positively for his methods of characterization, or defending them as a necessary last resort? And if some of his readers, and perhaps even Dostoevsky himself, did see his evolving protagonists as inadequate by the standards of nineteenth-century Russian realism, what made them so?

The last of these questions is the most pressing, because it reaches beyond Dostoevsky's time to address a set of expectations that may still be relevant to readers of realist novels today. In my discussion of *Notes from Underground*, I have emphasized the interdependence between authorial framing and characterological "freedom," or illegitimacy, in the Underground Man's characterization. The deliberately separated presence of the author provides a foundation for the character's forced autonomy, throughout the character's failed story-world attempts to create an equally coherent figure for himself. I now want to ask what Dostoevsky feared losing and what he hoped to gain as he wrote novelistic characters that depart still further from their solidifying foundation in omniscient narrative. The biographical Dostoevsky's ideas about conventional realist representation illuminate the play with convention that we find in his novels and the transformational aspirations that propel it. To clarify these ideas, we have to digress briefly into the literary-critical debates about mimetic characterization that surrounded the writing and publication of Dostoevsky's fiction.

"NARRATIVE ILLEGITIMACY" AND THE PROBLEM OF TYPE

Among the most central categories within Dostoevsky's aesthetics, inherited from the earlier (1840s–60s) Russian realist tradition from which he worked, were the ideally mimetic characters designated as "types."[56] For Dostoevsky and his predecessors (foremost among them Vissarion Belinsky), the type's mimetic power was equal parts documentary and artistic—a matter both of identifying an aspect of human life and of crystallizing it in vivid, "ideal" fictional form. Both these senses (and more) are contained within the German idealist notion of the type as a manifestation of the universal within the particular, which Belinsky assimilated from Schelling and later Hegel.[57] This ambiguity, which allows invocations of type to slide freely between "world-reflecting" and "world-creating" mimesis, is precisely what made the concept useful for a wide variety of Russian realist writers.[58] Ivan Turgenev could present his character Bazarov as a fictional distillation of the 1860s nihilist (the label that he himself invented), and the radical critic Dmitrii Pisarev then considered himself free to rewrite the nihilist type Bazarov as an example for others to follow, moving far beyond his original portrait in Turgenev's novel.

In Dostoevsky's own 1860s–70s literary criticism, the noun "type" (*tip*) and adjective "typical" (*tipicheskii*) denote a complex of prized artistic qualities that likewise mediate between novels and the lives of their readers. "Type" implies a character that synthesizes and models an aspect of the real. Unlike such critics as Pisarev, however, Dostoevsky suggests that readers recognize types not by their clear connection to everyday reality but by their qualities within the text. "Typical" characters strike us as self-sufficient and autonomous—and this internal coherence guarantees that neither they nor the works in which they take shape have been governed by an author's overt polemical purposes. Once read and aesthetically recognized, the type becomes a portable image that the reader will remember and use to organize her own worldview. Types thus serve *both* as the most visible sign of the aesthetic unity and self-sufficient autonomy of the texts in which they appear, *and* as a two-way passage between that self-sufficient textual world and the real world it is understood to represent.

This Janus-faced conception of the ideally mimetic character is particularly clear in Dostoevsky's programmatic essay "Mr.—bov and the Question of Art" (1861), although he does not use the term type there. In this essay, the failure of the Ukrainian writer Marko Vovchok's characters to emerge as "people" becomes a measure of her work's aesthetic failure or "monstrosity," and also a sign that she has neglected to depict the real "Russian person" clearly under the sway of her polemical convictions.[59] Ten years later, in an unsigned review in the journal the *Citizen* (which Dostoevsky then edited), the mimetic type more explicitly performs a Ricoeurian triple duty.[60] A paucity of types signifies the aesthetic poverty of contemporary literature, that literature's failure to adequately represent the world, and its failure to serve the reader:

> "Types [*Tipov*], give us types, our literature has no types,"—these are the words that one is obliged to say and hear almost every day. . . . And indeed, the absence of types in literature is one of the many illnesses of our epoch. Our journals now abound with novels, stories, tales; but with the exception of such capital works as the novel of Count Tolstoy, Dostoevsky's *The Devils*, and Leskov-Stebnitsky's *Cathedral Folk*, are there many types in them? All these characters are statues, cast in the most ingenious poses, where one thing is lacking: a central living thought [glavnoi zhivoi mysli] which permeates the whole work and unites all its constituent parts.[61]

Over and above their classificatory social function, vividly typical characters signify the presence of the "central living thought" that unifies the novel as a whole.

In Dostoevsky's writings about literature, the type thus forms a unique bridge between aesthetic and lived experience, and the creation of "ordinary" and "contemporary" types becomes a social and spiritual as well as a literary mission.[62] Smuggled within this idealized process of authoring types, there is a crucial claim about the resemblance between art and life. The work's aesthetic autonomy guarantees the type's fidelity to reality and vice versa: the most relevant *mimetic* standard is the author's success in yielding to the inner *aesthetic* logic of the work. The invocation of type thus anchors the idea that a created text could be the faithful model of a (divinely) created world—for Dostoevsky, perhaps, the essential promise of realism itself.

It is hard to hold together in a single concept all the aesthetic and spiritual work—the totalizing synthesis of world creation and world reflection—that Dostoevsky hoped types could perform. It proved even more difficult to realize this concept in practice. *Notes from Underground* approaches such a synthesis, but at the expense of devoting an entire text to the rigorous representation of a single typical character—and one (moreover) presented and defined as such by an author who hovers only halfway in the wings, ready to push the character onstage and pull him off when required.

Dostoevsky's 1860s–70s novels, in a progression that culminates in *The Adolescent*, attempt a riskier task: the representation of typical characters in and through character-systems that are increasingly framed as if under a character's (a narrator-chronicler's or narrator-hero's) imperfect control. As their reception histories attest, these experimental narratives turned out to ideally privilege the *portable* side of Dostoevskian "type": the creation of characters who draw vividness from their social or political recognizability. Such characters were widely understood, in the tradition of Turgenev's "nihilist" Bazarov, as giving figures and names to the developments of modernity, which could then be passed along and transformed for future readers and in future texts.[63] Ever more uncertain, however, was the question of whether such decentralized character-systems could produce types in Dostoevsky's fullest sense—characters who organize experience *because* their vividness seems to spring from and bespeak a coherent aesthetic vision or a "central living thought." In *Notes from Underground*, readers know that the character is an authored type, although the character himself does not. In later novels, readers and characters alike sense omniscient authorship only as a distant possibility. Can a genuine type (in Dostoevsky's idealized triple conception) take shape under such complete conditions of what I have called narrative illegitimacy—where the characters obscure the level of the creating omniscient author from even the reader's view?

Of course, to ask this question is to put aside the biographical evidence that Dostoevsky was anything but omniscient throughout the process of writing and serially publishing *The Idiot, Demons, The Adolescent*, and *The Brothers Karamazov*; indeed, he did not yet know the end of the plot at the time each of these novels began to appear in print. More consequentially, I am also posing an alternative to Gary Saul Morson's argument that the inherent openness and contingency of serialization entered into the design of Dostoevsky's fiction, doing away with the standards of omniscient, omnipotent authorship and neat poetic structure themselves.[64] I want instead to emphasize Dostoevsky's lingering attachment, as reflected in his works, to the theological affinities of authorship, which are associated with the author's capacity to write what Barthes calls the "Proper Name," the fully realized individual mimetic character.[65] Dostoevsky equated the writing of such Proper Names (in his own shorthand, types) with the greatest directed power that realist fiction can exert upon its readers—power modeled on the performative force that the word of the Bible holds for some religious believers. The failure to write the Proper Name, and to create the vivid embodiedness that underlies it, then also means sacrificing the compellingly seductive force of a novel populated by "living" types. Dostoevsky describes this seduction in "Mr.—bov and the Question of Art":

> But we believe that art has its own, integral, organic life [sobstvennaia, tsel'naia, organicheskaia zhizn'] and, consequently, foundational and immutable laws for this life. Art is as much a requirement for man as eating and drinking. The demand for beauty and for creative art that embodies it is inseparable from man, and without it man, perhaps, would not wish to live on earth. Man longs for beauty, and finds and accepts it *without any conditions*, but just so, simply because it is beauty, and he bows down before it with awe, not asking, what is it good for and what can I use it to buy? And perhaps, in this lies the greatest secret of artistic creation, that the image of beauty produced by it immediately becomes an idol, *without any conditions*. And why does it become an idol? Because the demand for beauty develops most fully when man is at odds with reality, in disharmony, in struggle; that is, when he is most alive [kogda on naibolee zhivet]. (18:94)

The shift in the meaning of the word "life" between the beginning and the end of this passage points to the problem with Dostoevskian character: life is both the closed-off, purposive illusion cast by an organically beautiful work of art, and the open, contingent state in which artistic beauty becomes most necessary to the spectator or reader. Art threatens to be absolutely different from real life, but it inspires credence and worship by reproducing life's indeterminate quality, within a form that ultimately guarantees a resolution. The rhetorical power of this illusion of life was a potential that Dostoevsky saw built into the realist novel and was passionately interested in using. And mimetic life becomes an especially strong source of power if produced in concert with the conditions of real life, rather than as an idyllic fantasy or escape. Indeed, an "illegitimate" contemporary character who also bore the vivid stamp of his own authoredness—that is, a contemporary type in Dostoevsky's fullest sense—would model the advent of heaven on earth. To write characters that could name and organize the quality of the reader's experience was not enough. Again, at its most ambitious, Dostoevsky's conception of type promises to envelop the reader in his cherished analogy between the created world of the novel and a real world created by God.

It may be wrong to suggest that this essentially conservative aspect of Dostoevsky's aesthetic and religious philosophy is reflected in his revolutionary techniques of characterization. Perhaps what his novels and characters *do* do should be read as the opposite of what he thought art *should* do. Generations of readers' responses to his novels, as well as the doubts about God's existence woven into their very fabric, suggest that on some level this is true. However, the impulse toward a different, more closely coordinated aesthetic and spiritual response is also present in the texts themselves, and it too clusters, in ways we often do not recognize while reading, around our experience of Dostoevsky's characters as real. In later works as in *Notes from Underground*, the combination of offstage authorial shaping and onstage characterological formlessness is key to Dostoevsky's mimetic technique. The difference is that in later novels, the typifying author's presence becomes ever less evident, even as the task of giving form to the illegitimate, chaotically decentered protagonist remains at the heart of the narrative.

In support of this argument, let me turn now in detail to what most readers agree is Dostoevsky's most chaotic mature novel, *The Adolescent*. Frequently (although ever less) sidelined in studies of Dostoevsky's fiction, *The Adolescent* illuminates the tension at the heart of his artistic project, insofar as that project is concentrated in acts of characterization. It marks the outer pole of what I have called the illegitimacy of the Dostoevskian protagonist, but it also points to Dostoevsky's most utopian ambitions for the realist novel and type, for which this excessive illegitimacy offers a kind of negative sign. *The Adolescent* clarifies one of the basic operations of Dostoevsky's mimesis by writing it large. Dismantling the conventional terms of realist characterization, Dostoevsky used the resulting void as a space in which to imagine a convergence between the real world and the realist novel as authored wholes.

ILLEGITIMACY AND CHARACTERIZATION IN DOSTOEVSKY'S *THE ADOLESCENT*

The Adolescent recounts the first year that Arkady Makarovich Dolgoruky spends in Saint Petersburg with his natural father, the dissolute landowner Andrei Petrovich Versilov, and his mother, born a peasant on Versilov's estate. While Arkady arrives intending to discover the truth about Versilov's moral character, he soon becomes infatuated with Katerina Nikolaevna Akhmakova, who is also an object of Versilov's affection. Arkady's "notes" tell the increasingly sordid story of the rivalry between himself and Versilov, juxtaposed with his idyllic encounter with his legal peasant father, Makar Ivanovich Dolgoruky, just before the latter's death. An elaborate blackmail plot, revolving around a document in Arkady's possession that could give him power over Katerina Nikolaevna, runs through the novel and culminates in a crisis, averted by chance, in which Katerina Nikolaevna is almost raped by Arkady's former schoolmate Lambert and almost murdered by Versilov. The story ends, inconclusively, with the implication of a future relationship between Arkady and Katerina Nikolaevna and Versilov's reunion with (although not marriage to) Arkady's mother. The novel's last section is the comments of Arkady's former tutor, Nikolai Semyonovich, on the manuscript of Arkady's "notes" (the main text of the novel).

This summary gives only a bare impression of the multitude of figures and events that crowd Arkady's narrative. Digressions and repetitious subplots hang from the basic plotline—suicides, other blackmails, gambling episodes, several other rumored rapes, a host of abandoned or illegitimate children. Nevertheless, Arkady's notes follow a coherent pattern: they are structured as a *Bildungsroman*, a series of tests meant to illuminate Versilov's true character, and so to establish the chief model available for Arkady to define his future path on or against.[66] From the beginning, we know that Arkady's portrait of Versilov—whom he calls "even now . . . in a great many ways a complete riddle to me" (6; 13:6)—will remain inconclusive.[67] But the task of describing Versilov is the impetus from which the narrative unfolds.

It is notable, then, that Arkady's weaknesses as a narrator cluster around the introduction of new characters into his story. The description of an incidental character, Olimpiada, is symptomatic:

> I looked at her quite closely and found nothing special: not a very tall girl, plump, and with extremely ruddy cheeks. Her face, however, was rather pleasant, the kind that the materialists like. Her expression was kind, perhaps, but with a wrinkle. She could not have been especially brilliant intellectually, at least not in a higher sense, but one could see cunning in her eyes. No more than nineteen years old. In short, nothing remarkable. We'd have called her a "pillow" in high school. (If I describe her in such detail, it's solely because I'll need it in the future.) By the way, everything I've been describing so far, with such apparently unnecessary detail, all leads to the future and will be needed there. (39)[68]

This passage is a parody of a realist character portrait. Arkady qualifies each feature he mentions, blurring it even as it meets the page. More importantly, although he is putatively writing a year after the events he recounts, he misleads the reader about Olimpiada's significance—the *size* of the character-space she will occupy in his narrative. Olimpiada demands close attention, but she turns out to be "nothing special." The details of her appearance will be necessary "in the future," but as it happens, she returns only once. Arkady begins by signaling the conventions of omniscient realist characterization, but in the same breath, he disrupts them.

The same trend continues throughout the narrative. Arkady introduces almost every new character with a portrait like Olimpiada's, offering concrete physical details (as Dostoevsky dubbed them in notebook plans) "à la L[eo] T[olstoy]" (16:73, 87). But a reader attempting to associate these details with a stably recurring figure in a stably sized space (à la Leo Tolstoy) will be disappointed: Arkady's technical difficulties with characterization reflect and exacerbate the convolution of the story he is trying to tell. His frequent confusion at the changeability of faces culminates in the suspicion (as he writes of the blackmailer Stebel'kov) that individual physical traits "not only did not personalize his character, but seemed precisely to endow it with something general, like everyone else. . . . He passes quickly from a laughing to a grave look, from a grave to a playful or winking one, but it is all somehow scattered and pointless" (142; 13:118). The mobile face is a standard feature of physiognomic character portraits in Dostoevsky's novels.[69] But in *The Adolescent*, this mobility infects the entire project of characterization; the narrative, like a kaleidoscope, shifts among constellations of minor figures without specifying the connections between them.[70] There are two Princes Sokolsky, no relation to one another. Stebel'kov, whose schemes dominate the middle third of the novel, is eclipsed without notice by a second blackmailer, Lambert. Bit characters unfurl from their functional roles to give speeches that touch on the novel's most central preoccupations, and then vanish for good. Even Makar Dolgoruky, the legal father who, late in the novel, offers Arkady a "seemly" alternative to the disorder around Versilov, dies before his influence can crystallize. Names too are unstable: the suicide Olia's mother, called Daria Onisimovna in part 1, becomes Nastasia Egorovna in part 3.

The novel's minor characters thus fail to meet one of the most basic definitions of realist character ever formulated (again by Barthes), as that which results "when identical semes traverse the same proper name several times and appear to settle upon it."[71] Some of this chaos is due to the circumstances of serial publication, but its effect on a reader's ability to construct a coherent fictional world is none the weaker for being unintentional. In a *Bildungsroman* built around two central projects of characterization—Versilov and Arkady himself—Arkady tells a story in which almost *all* the figures struggle to take shape. Indeed, Versilov's hiddenness remains the clearest preoccupation of Arkady's narrative, emblematized by the recurring "wrinkle" that conceals whether Versilov is sincere or mocking, sane or mad (209, 244, 463; 13:171, 223, 372). He ends as the most elusive of the novel's shifting points—still unmarried to Arkady's mother, still an uncertain Christian, and still in the shadow of Arkady's attempts at explanation: "In my opinion, Versilov, in those moments . . . could not have had any firm aim, and I don't think he even reasoned at all here, but was under the influence of some whirlwind of feelings. However, I do not admit of any genuine madness, the less so as he is not at all mad now. . . . But all this is only my guess; to decide for certain is difficult" (552; 13:446).[72]

The chaos of "Arkady's" characterizations may simply suggest that Dostoevsky's approach to the novel's structure, as laid out in his notebooks, was successful. The narrator Arkady emerges as protagonist, characterized primarily by his own first-person "notes." In turn, the other characters (especially Versilov) are screened by the very text that pursues them, revealing the teller at the expense of the tale. In *Poor Folk*, Dostoevsky brought new life to the Gogolian titular councilor Makar Devushkin by making him responsible for his "own" epistolary narration. In *The Adolescent* he takes this technique a step further, by making Arkady (Makarovich) responsible for the cast of an entire novel. The result is *hyperbolically* dialogic, a concatenation of voices cut off from fictional selves that Arkady can only fleetingly make cohere.[73] But by the very act of composing his narrative, as some readers have argued, Arkady conveys his own characterization or identity, and in the process, he discovers his future path.[74]

However, there is a key aspect of the novel that this relatively optimistic reading does not capture: *The Adolescent*'s orientation (beginning with its title) on its own present inadequacy, on the condition of not yet being fully instated or grown. Age is the hopeful metaphor for this condition. It is shadowed throughout by the more insidious trope of illegitimacy: a suggestion that the lack may never be fully remedied, the gap between "desire and possession" never entirely bridged.[75] First attached to Arkady's birth, the condition of illegitimacy shades into his compensatory idea of becoming "as rich as Rothschild," accumulating the capital that will turn him into an extraordinary (if not a noble) man. He quickly becomes distracted from his "idea," but its logic does not end with him; it is mirrored in the theories of the intellectual Kraft, who kills himself because he has concluded that "the Russian people are a second-rate people . . . whose fate is to serve *merely as material for a more noble race*" (51; 13:44 [my italics]). Surprisingly, Versilov's paean to his own nobility reflects a similar pattern of thought:

> I repeat to you that I can't help respecting my nobility. Over the centuries we have developed a high cultural type never seen before . . . the type of universal suffering for all. . . . It preserves in itself the future of Russia. There are

> perhaps only a thousand of us . . . but the whole of Russia has lived up to now only to produce this thousand. . . . Only the Russian . . . is capable of becoming most Russian precisely only when he is most European. (468–69)[76]

A distortion of Dostoevsky's treasured notion of Russian "panhumanism" (*vsechelovechestvo*), Versilov's submissive vision of an elite "thousand" who are "most Russian" precisely when they are "most European" recalls the image of Versilov's own illegitimate son Arkady, kissing the hands of the French tutor who used to beat him to remind him of his lowly origins. Arkady, Kraft, and Versilov are united by the dream of accumulation, the desire to *live into* something better with time. In representing an "accidental family," Dostoevsky shows the sense of illegitimacy spreading outward, from the narrator-hero's birth to the historical moment that he portrays.

In the novel's enigmatic epilogue, Arkady's former teacher Nikolai Semyonovich invites us to extend the same logic of illegitimacy and accumulation to its central narrative, the text of Arkady's first-person notes:

> Yes, Arkady Makarovich, you are *a member of an accidental family*, as opposed to our still-recent hereditary types, who had a childhood and youth so different from yours. I confess, I would not wish to be a novelist whose hero comes from an accidental family! Thankless work and lacking in beautiful forms. And these types in any case are still a current matter, and therefore cannot be artistically finished. . . . What, though, is the writer to do who has no wish to write only in the historical genre and is possessed by a yearning for what is current? To guess . . . and be mistaken. But "Notes" such as yours could, it seems to me, serve as material for a future artistic work, for a future picture—of a disorderly but already bygone epoch . . . the future artist will find beautiful forms even for portraying the past disorder and chaos. It is then that "Notes" like yours will be needed and will provide material—as long as they are sincere, even despite all that is chaotic and accidental about them . . . (563–64; second and fourth ellipses in original)[77]

With this implicit comparison to the "beautiful forms" of the Tolstoyan family novel, Nikolai Semyonovich frames Arkady's notes as "material for a future artistic work." Subtitled "A Novel" ("*Roman*"), *The Adolescent* dares us to read this future artistic work as a reference to its own text. With equal daring, however, it challenges us to justify this reading. If Arkady's notes on their own are not (yet) a novel, then perhaps it is the self-reflexive epilogue that creates the work of art. Notes become novel with the very move that *de*legitimizes them by the standard of beautiful form—insisting on what they are not yet and what they could become.

There is another way to conceive of this structure that clarifies its essential consistency with Dostoevsky's earlier works. In Arkady's notes, the mirage-like succession of "heroic" identities that haunted *Notes from Underground* has been externalized as a crowd of tantalizingly incomplete secondary characters. In *The Adolescent* as in *Notes from Underground*, solidity remains out of reach: Arkady can neither consistently conjure it in his portraits of others nor define it from within his (necessarily unfinished) portrait of himself. In the rare case where Arkady does manage to portray a stably recurring secondary character—such as the blackmailer Lambert—this very stability seems to give that character demonic power to tyrannize over the unformed Arkady.[78] Nevertheless, in *The Adolescent* as in *Notes from Underground*, an authorially given container offers us (the readers) the option of experiencing the unfinalizable narrator-protagonist as a coherent mimetic figure, fixed in text. Mimetic life results from the "stereoscopic" technique of superimposing the character's unfinalizable voice upon his authored outlines, and both these images are essential parts of the illusion.[79] The innovation in *The Adolescent*, which has made so many readers dismiss the novel, is that the very authorial container placed around Arkady's notes looks *toward* completion rather than asserting a claim for it. The authored structure that composes Arkady is in fact as complete and bounded as any novel, but unlike most conventional novels, it pretends not to be.

Dostoevsky's boldest move in *The Adolescent*, as a novelist and writer of mimetic types, thus depends on compounding the sense of inadequacy figured in his protagonist's illegitimate birth and reflected in the "accidental" form of his notes. With zealous self-abasement, *The Adolescent* trumpets its own distance from the ordered solidity of a Tolstoyan fictional world. But in the process, I think Dostoevsky grasps beyond *both* the finished beauty of Tolstoyan mimetic form *and* the techniques by which he himself was attempting to capture contemporary disorder, for a still bigger prize: the reclamation of the divinely "given" world of what pre-Marxist Lukács calls the epic. As Dostoevsky has Arkady's father Versilov lament in a revealing notebook draft of the final pages of *The Adolescent*,

> I have, my dear, one favorite Russian writer. He is a novelist, but for me he's almost a historiographer of our nobility. . . . He takes a nobleman from his childhood and youth, he draws him in his family . . . and all so poetically, so unshakably and inarguably. He is a psychologist of the nobleman's soul. But the main thing is that this is given as inarguable, and of course, you agree. You agree and you envy. Oh, how they envy! There are children who from childhood already fall to thinking about their families . . . , and, the main thing, already in childhood are beginning to understand the disorder and accidentalness of the foundations of their life, the absence of established forms and inherited wisdom. These should envy my writer, envy [my] his characters and, perhaps,

> dislike them. Oh, these are not characters, they are sweet children, who have wonderful, sweet fathers, eating at the club, entertaining around Moscow.[80]

Conceived in the generic setting of Arkady's notes, Versilov looks covetously over to the characters narrated "so unshakably and inarguably" in Tolstoy's novels, and he sees "not characters, but sweet children, who have wonderful sweet fathers." Versilov's envy implies a mimetic standard that even Tolstoy could not meet: in the idyll he imagines, to be narrated authoritatively is to be not just vivid, but real. I suggest that the desire he voices coincides with Dostoevsky's own: that a "future novel," filled with mimetically embodied contemporary types, could restore a vision of reality as equally susceptible to benevolent divine creation. Much as (in Derrida's famous variation on Plato's *Phaedrus*) all claims to the legitimacy of speech hinge on the space that is opened by the illegitimacy of writing, so here, this extravagant hope for future transcendence springs from the ostentatiously chaotic narrative of an "accidental family."[81]

On this interpretation, mimetic characterization in Dostoevsky traces the same dialectic between earthly, living struggle and immortal perfection that lies at the center of his religious philosophy, articulated most directly in the well-known 1864 notebook passage written while Dostoevsky was keeping vigil with the body of his first wife, Maria Isaeva ("Masha is lying on the table"; 20:171–74). Earthly life presupposes a state of development and struggle toward the ideal of Christ-like "love for another as oneself"; immortality in paradise must be imagined as the state where this ideal has been achieved (20:172–73). A similarly absolute split between present imperfection and future transformation structures Dostoevsky's thought about characterization and the novel. Although the novelist can realize "the real men of the Russian majority" only partially—as voices or ghosts rather than vividly embodied types—he is then free to envision the future, fully typical representation of these characters as leading to the actual redemption of the fallen world that he represents. Crucial to this vision is an insistence on what is missing from the Dostoevskian character. In the space opened by this lack, Dostoevsky imagines overleaping the bounds of fiction and the novel genre themselves.

The Adolescent is unique among Dostoevsky's novels in laying bare this ambition, placing the growing metaphorical illegitimacy of *all* his characters at the visible center of its narrative. Although Dostoevsky's "real men of the Russian majority" project the condition of illegitimacy in both story and discourse, their narratives tend toward rediscovery of their true "legitimate" origins as created beings—and in a utopian scenario, the reader who receives these characters as authored types may learn to see her own world as divinely authored too.

When *The Adolescent* is read as an aesthetic credo rather than an aberration, a failure, or even an innovative departure, it brings this larger project into focus. Precisely because Dostoevsky's transformation of "real men" into realist characters remains so incomplete, an aura of fantastic historical consequence gathers around it. The obvious problem confronting Dostoevsky is that an Arkady Dolgoruky will never be a Pierre Bezukhov. But the blatant divide between Dostoevsky's "contemporary" hero and Tolstoy's "historical" one serves to distract the reader from a problem that lies much deeper: *The Adolescent*—no less than *War and Peace* or any realist novel—deploys a character-system whose mimetic power depends on its boundedness; in Lukács's phrase, a "totality comprised between the beginning and the end."[82] In a risky response to this conundrum, *The Adolescent* compounds the character's narrative illegitimacy so thoroughly that it begins to deconstruct the illegitimacy of the novel genre, its tormenting separation from the terms of secular modern life. Writing a novel that masquerades as material for a future novel—with a hero who masquerades as the seed of a future, more typical hero—Dostoevsky presents that future novel and type as transforming the world they capture and, in turn, the world in which they are read. I suggest that this utopian fantasy was a response to the inherently limited aesthetic and narrative tools that Dostoevsky knew he was using—tools that (as he also knew) could only seal his novels off from the contemporary reality that they purport to (re)create.

At its most experimental, then, Dostoevsky's approach to character in the novel meant replacing the imitation of embodiment with the longing for it. If we use this slanted lens to imagine a Dostoevsky who *did* write novels—novels as early Lukács would have them, and not later Bakhtin—we come to a new account of realist characterization itself as it underlies the novel genre's imaginative and intellectual work.

Realist characters emerge not as the novel's most detachable elements, but rather as that which will always reach toward a "body," the stable textual presence that springs from the correspondence between authored hero and authored world. Characters at their most seductively embodied are thus woven into the act of reading—an act that cannot help separating them from the rest of what Bakhtin calls the "ongoing event of current life." To the extent that Dostoevsky's characters draw upon and invoke this tradition, they cannot also signify its rupture. The world-creating power that they hold to absorb us as realist novel readers is not the same as the world-reflecting power that they might also hold as categories in which to perceive our everyday lives. And the appeal to the aesthetic power of absorption reemerges where we least expect it: just at the point where we imagine Dostoevsky's characters as a bridge between the nostalgic realist novel and the secular modern world. The compelling mimesis of characters like the Underground Man rests to an unexpected degree on the *gesture* of authorship, the invitation to enter into fiction that attends the experience of reading. By eliding this gesture, Dostoevsky made his later novels more closely reflect the conditions he was representing, but he did not change the fundamental contract of the novel genre. Much though Dostoevsky deplored the absence of established forms in his chronicles of "real men of the Russian majority," many of his novels—when compared with *The Adolescent*—turn out to rely more heavily on conventions of realist characterization than is usually acknowledged. When, as in *The Adolescent*, the "rounded world" of the novelistic hero truly does begin to erode, the prevailing mood is not triumph at an illusion overcome but hope for its eventual restoration as reality.[83]

It would be fruitless to hold that only one of these sides of Dostoevsky's approach to characterization and the novel is relevant—either the adventure of seemingly authorless fictional being, or the fantasy of the author's redemptive rediscovery. The Dostoevsky who hopes to merge authored novel and created world challenges the Dostoevsky who makes characters look autonomous from their texts. Perhaps neither impulse triumphs, but equally, neither vanishes. Instead, they ensure one another's perpetual homelessness: the foundling plot of the novel, whose dimensions Dostoevsky ingeniously and anxiously explored.

Chapter Three

"A Living Matter": The Doubled Character-System of *Anna Karenina*

THERE ARE NO characters in the first sentence of Tolstoy's *Anna Karenina* (1875–77). "All happy families are alike, each unhappy family is unhappy in its own way" (1).[1] In this iconic opening, difference and individuation—the conversion from "all" (*vse*) to "each" (*kazhdaia*)—appear as a fall from grace. The "happy" is that about which nothing particular can be narrated or said; it is only in being unhappy that a family develops the capacity to exist "in its own way," with its own discrete story and identity. In other words, *Anna Karenina*'s first sentence links "unhappiness" with the qualities that are generally considered foundational to the realism of the realist novel: in Ian Watt's classic summation, the stories of "particular people in particular circumstances," rather than the formulas of older narrative genres.[2] The "unhappy" descent from the general to the particular reads as a descent into realism's (and its scientific age's) approach to understanding the world.

For many readers, the relationship Tolstoy's novel bears to its opening aphorism—no less than to its biblical epigraph—has been a source of bewilderment. Does *Anna Karenina* tell the story of any happy families? If so, in what sense are they all alike? If it tells only the stories of unhappy families, then why are there so many similarities among them? The enigma lifts if we read the opening, more generally, as a claim about the happiness of likeness and the unhappiness of individuation. The process of individual character emerging from general category runs just beneath the narrative of the novel's first unhappy family:

> Everything was confusion in the Oblonskys' house. The wife had found out that the husband was having an affair with their former French governess, and had announced to the husband that she could not live in the same house with him. . . . The wife would not leave her rooms, the husband was away for the third day. The children were running all over the house as if lost; the

> English governess quarreled with the housekeeper . . . ; the cook had already left the premises the day before, at dinner-time; the kitchen-maid and coachman had given notice. (1)[3]

The fictional players introduced here—"wife," "husband," "children," "coachman"—take on specific identities only by their association with another collective, "the Oblonskys." Their roles, so insistently repeated, propel the novel's claim to authority outward from this husband and this wife, toward husbands and wives as such. Appropriately, however, it is the philanderer Stiva Oblonsky who chains Tolstoy's family narrative to the realist particularity of time, place, social sphere, and (above all) physical experience:

> On the third day after the quarrel Prince Stepan Arkadyich Oblonsky—Stiva, as he was called in society—woke up at his usual hour, that is, at eight o'clock in the morning, not in his wife's bedroom but in his study, on a morocco sofa. He rolled his full, well-tended body over on the springs of the sofa, as if wishing to fall asleep again for a long time, tightly hugged the pillow from the other side and pressed his cheek to it; but suddenly he gave a start, sat up on the sofa and opened his eyes.[4]

The stream of individuals that follows on Stiva's awakening—his wife Dolly, his valet Matvei—thus originates in perceptions already mired in a "pampered" (*kholenoe*) body and self (6; 18:8). Almost from the start, reality in this novel bears the flush of individuation, and the result is a hyperrealist aesthetic: a narrative not just of "particular people in particular circumstances," but *only* as seen in particular ways.[5] As often noted, the progression from the biblical epigraph to the "confusion" of the Oblonsky household carries the reader from the divine realm of absolute law to the prosaic, morally relative conditions of the novel.[6] Just as strikingly, the progression from the generality of the epigraph to the opening of Stiva's eyes mirrors the descent from "all" to "each" outlined in the novel's first sentence. Governed by a hypothesis that associates happiness with uniform likeness and unhappiness with particular difference, by the end of its first page *Anna Karenina* has become the unhappiest of all fictional worlds.

In this economical opening, Tolstoy sets up a new shift in the terms of the novelistic character-system, qualitatively different from the one that (as I argued in chapter 1) structures his earlier novel *War and Peace*. At issue in *War and Peace* was the fundamental falsehood produced by a sense of individual narrative centrality—reflected uneasily within a form that cannot help but direct the reader to distribute attention unequally among major, minor, and marginal characters. Novelistic narrative reproduces a rich individual sense of consciousness and freedom, which Tolstoy ends by striving, rigorously but regretfully, to unmask as illusion. In *Anna Karenina*, by contrast, individual existence appears from the first as inherently deceptive, violent, and diminished. By linking unhappiness with differentiated individuality, *Anna Karenina* challenges the good of being a realist character—and still more, a realist protagonist—in the same way that philosophical pessimism challenges the good of being born. The spirit of the novel's opening, like that of its epigraph, is Schopenhauerian.

It is well known that Tolstoy's work on *Anna Karenina* ran in parallel with his effort to escape the basic tenets of Schopenhauerian pessimism that he had encountered while writing the epilogue to *War and Peace*, a process that came to fruition three years after the completion of *Anna Karenina*, with Tolstoy's conversion and avowed turn away from novel writing itself.[7] *Anna Karenina* is thus a kind of laboratory for exploring a pessimistic premise: that the embodied drive toward individuation—so natural to the formal terms of the realist novel—is an endlessly antagonistic fight to maintain an ultimately unsatisfying mode of being.

In this chapter, I offer a reading of *Anna Karenina* as Tolstoy's attempt to solve the problems that he understood realist representation to share with Schopenhauer's "world as will," by using and remaking the medium of the realist novel. I will argue that the rancorous Schopenhauerian realm of the conventional novelistic character-system, as modeled in the narrative to which Anna is most central, becomes the backdrop to a Platonic and Christian ascent out of this realm that is modeled by the novel's other protagonist, Konstantin Levin. Anna's half of *Anna Karenina* works to surfeit the reader's taste for conventional realist representation, while Levin's works to elevate and transform it—and so in turn, to challenge the novel reader's conception of reality itself as a condition that conventional realist representation can capture.

The uncertain success of this project points, still more clearly than the vexed ending of *War and Peace*, to the practical limits of mimetic characterization in the novel. Tolstoy's failure to write what I will call a "marginal protagonist"—a character who is central to the novel's action and narrative but whose lure compels us beyond the bounds of the novel itself—exposes the persistent dependence of mimetic life on the system that supports it.[8] Thus, Tolstoy's turn away from novelistic realism during and after the completion of *Anna Karenina* can be understood as an acknowledgment that the marginal protagonist constitutes a paradox, an irresistible but unrealizable dream. As it takes shape in the narrative of *Anna Karenina*, this paradox clarifies the interdependency between the mimetic illusion of character in the novel and the absorbed aesthetic moment of reading.

The two-way pull that my discussion explores—Anna, toward the realist illusion attached to the center of the novel; Levin, toward the realist illusion straining against its margins—emerges most plainly in the only scene where the two protagonists meet:

> Another lamp with a reflector burned on the wall, throwing its light on to a large, full-length portrait of a woman, to which Levin involuntarily turned his attention. This was the portrait of Anna painted in Italy by Mikhailov. While Stepan Arkadyich went behind a trellis-work screen and the male voice that had been speaking fell silent, Levin gazed at the portrait, standing out from its frame in the dazzling light, and could not tear himself away from it. He even forgot where he was and, not listening to what was said around him, gazed without taking his eyes from the astonishing portrait. It was not a painting but a living, lovely woman with dark curling hair, bare shoulders and arms, and a pensive half-smile on lips that were covered with tender down, looking at him triumphantly and tenderly with eyes that bewildered him. The only reason why she was not alive was that she was more beautiful than a living woman can be. "I'm very glad," he suddenly heard a voice beside him, evidently addressing him, the voice of the same woman he was admiring in the portrait. Anna came to meet him from behind the trellis, and Levin saw in the half light of the study the same woman from the portrait, in a dark dress of varying shades of blue, not in the same position, and not with the same expression, but at the same height of beauty on which she had been captured by the artist in the portrait. She was less dazzling in reality, but in the living woman, there was instead some new element of attraction that was not there in the portrait. (696–97)[9]

Levin's intricately staged act of viewing resembles a conjuring trick or moment of demonic enchantment. Stiva vanishes behind the screen and re-emerges in the guise of Anna, the "same woman from the portrait" brought magically to life. Her "real" body has been substituted for Stiva's, her speaking voice substituted for that of the male voice in the study. At the same time, even as Tolstoy trains such ostentatious narrative power on the act of representing Anna, he invites the reader to sink *unconsciously* into the equally fictional perspective of Levin's gaze. The illuminated portrait that compels Levin's absorption thus reflects two opposing fantasies about mimetic representation. The first is of a novel that could direct the entire animating force of the reader's attention to a single figure who occupies its frame—such that Levin's impression of a "living" Anna, the sole subject of Mikhailov's portrait, could be transferred to the "living" Anna of Tolstoy's narrative. The second is that in watching Anna and her portrait through Levin's eyes, the reader will forget that Levin is a fictional character too. In both cases, Tolstoy entertains the seductive vision of a character whose vividness exists independently of the system that supports it. But only in Anna's case is this vision marked as seductive, as if to flag the illusory quality of all mimetic life (whether painted or in prose). One protagonist's mimetic life obviously rests in a deceptive aesthetic experience; the other, constructed by contrast, silently claims the right to transgress aesthetic bounds.

In his own labyrinthine portrait *Anna Karenina*, Tolstoy thus created (as one scholar puts it) "an enclosure that by its very artifice reminds us we are enclosed and thus points our vision to what is not or cannot be contained, and to the means of entrance and exit traversing the frame."[10] I think the primary agent of this transcendence is the technical contrast between Anna and Levin as characters, which suffuses the scene of their meeting and also the narrative as a whole. Levin is a realist protagonist meant to be realized away from the center of *Anna Karenina*'s attention. As such, he represents Tolstoy's strongest bid to transform the reader by repurposing (rather than rejecting) the conventional techniques of psychological realism. The uncertain success of this move points us toward the boundaries of novelistic characterization itself.

ANNA, VRONSKY, AND THE SCHOPENHAUERIAN CHARACTER-SYSTEM

A premise of my reading is that *Anna Karenina* has two protagonists—two figures at the center of its narrative attention, and so also at the center of its character-system, the set of interrelationships among characters that unfolds over the course of an entire narrative.[11] Among their many other functions, characters like Stiva, Dolly, Vronsky, Karenin, and Kitty are there in order to set off and signal Anna and Levin's positions at the narrative center. In the narrative as focused on Anna, Tolstoy reveals and underscores a forbidding analogy between the pessimistic vision of the world as described by Schopenhauer and the traditionally protagonist-centered character-systems of European realist novels. Its terms emerge in two parallel scenes.

The first is Vronsky's initial glimpse of Anna at the Moscow train station, which is also her first appearance in the novel. Anna draws Vronsky's eye, and they look at each other in passing:

> In that brief glance Vronsky had time to notice the restrained animation [*sderzhannuiu ozhivlennost'*] that played over her face and fluttered between her shining eyes and the barely noticeable smile that curved her red lips. It was as if a surplus of something so overflowed her being that it expressed itself beyond her will, now in the brightness of her glance, now in her smile. She deliberately extinguished the light in her eyes, but it shone against her will in a barely noticeable smile. (61)[12]

Vronsky's first sight of Anna recalls the narrator's first description of Natasha Rostova in *War and Peace*: "This black-eyed, wide-mouthed girl, not pretty but full of life [nekrasivaia, no zhivaia]."[13] However, where Natasha's life is established by an omniscient narrator, in explicit contrast to the superficial social scene that her entrance interrupts, Anna's animation appears through the eyes of a character who is himself manufactured on the "machine" of this social world (55; 18:60), and it places her extraordinary charm squarely within it. Vronsky's gaze initiates Anna as a "living" protagonist in the story of their adultery. The spark of her irrepressibly attractive, "surplus" physical being—the trope of restraint creating the vitality that is there to be restrained—brightens or flickers throughout the first parts of the novel depending on whether Vronsky is looking at her (62, 103, 106, 112, 127; 18:67, 18:109, 18:112–13, 18:119, 18:135). But referenced so often, it becomes (along with her "light step" and unruly curls) part of the matrix of qualities attached to Anna's name. The reader cannot imagine Anna without seeing the sexualized mimetic life that places her at the center of her plot.[14]

The second scene, a few chapters later in part 1, takes us to the opposite end of the character-system of *Anna Karenina*. Here Vronsky, who has followed Anna onto the Petersburg train to confess his love, unwittingly discomfits one of his fellow passengers:

> [Vronsky] sat in his seat, now staring straight ahead of him, now looking over the people going in and out, and if he had struck and troubled strangers before by his air of imperturbable calm, he now seemed still more proud and self-sufficient. He looked at people as if they were things. A nervous young man across from him, who served on the circuit court, began to hate him for that look. The young man lit a cigarette from his, tried to begin a conversation with him, and even jostled him, to let [Vronsky] feel that he was not a thing but a person, but Vronsky went on looking at him in just as the same way as he looked at the lantern, and the young man grimaced, feeling that he was losing his self-possession under the pressure of this non-recognition of himself as a person. (104)[15]

The "nervous young man" never appears in the novel again, and he is rarely highlighted in the voluminous commentary on this section of *Anna Karenina*. But it would be hard to imagine a fuller dramatization of a minor character's disappearance. Shown trying to kindle both his cigarette and his own existence from Vronsky, the nervous young man gets extinguished in the very next sentence by a narrative that chooses to follow Vronsky instead of him. The reader is not asked to remember him, any more than is Vronsky himself. Tolstoy's satire extends to both characters: to Vronsky for neglecting to recognize the nervous young man as a person, and to the nervous young man for craving this recognition so strongly that his self-possession (like his fictional being) depends on it.[16] Still more basically on trial, however, is the Schopenhauerian tenor of the protagonist-centered realist character-system, the narrative environment in which both Anna's entrance and the nervous young man's disappearance take place.

In his major 1819/1844 treatise, Schopenhauer describes the world's deceptive nature as "representation" (*Vorstellung*), a veil distorting the true nature of reality by individuating it according to the limits of human perception; and its true nature as "will" (*Wille*), a perpetually seething impulse that has no goal and so can never be satisfied. His notorious pessimism is rooted in this vision of the world's two aspects—a pervasive illusion that once recognized, turns out to conceal limitless, purposeless, and antagonistic desire. Driven to embody the will in what appears to us to be different ways, the levels of natural being (from minerals on up to humans) engage in continual struggle: "Every grade of the will's objectification fights for the matter, the space, and the time of another . . . mechanical, physical, chemical, and organic phenomena, eagerly striving to appear, snatch the matter from one another, for each wishes to reveal its own Idea," its own particular form of the will.[17]

Close to the surface in *Anna Karenina* is an inherent resemblance between Schopenhauer's "world as will" and the structure of realist character-systems. Just as in Schopenhauer's account each life form, as we perceive it, competes for "the matter, the space, and the time of another," so in the European realist novel, characters "jostle for limited space within the same fictive universe."[18] This systematic jostling is a narrative principle of *Anna Karenina* as well, but with a Schopenhauerian caveat: if each character's embodied individuality depends on the amount of attention paid to it, then embodied fictional individuality is a pernicious illusion that also requires ceaseless, corrosive competition to maintain. Vronsky—who habitually divides his world between the "real people" (*nastoiashchie liudi*) who socially matter and all others who do not (114; 18:121), and who refers to his and Anna's servants as "our parasites" (757; 19:337)—encapsulates the spirit of this asymmetrical perception. But what Vronsky embodies is also the spirit of the genre, the expectations that encourage the nervous young man to disappear so quickly from the reader's memory, and Anna to linger so vividly and long. If she unreflectively follows the lines of attention laid down by the narrative, the reader reads through the eyes of Vronsky, and this mode of reading is flawed not so much in a moral sense, as in an epistemological one. The narrative creates an illusory reality where our limited attention is the sole index and source of the characters' existence. In scenes like the nervous young man's disappearance, Tolstoy holds this *essentially* superficial world up for our contemplation, but in a gesture that any reader absorbed by plots of erotic desire will miss.

In *Anna Karenina*, the novel reader's imagination thus often works against her—precisely because the narrative is so expertly directed toward making her see and sense the fleshy "living" characters produced on these unhappy novelistic terms. Tolstoy distributes the capacity to act as a center of consciousness unusually widely among the novel's actual and potential protagonists, ranging from Konstantin Levin to Dolly Oblonskaya and from Seryozha Karenin to Laska the dog. However, he divorces this capacity from animating, sensuous bodily description, which is linked rather—and with marked consistency—to participation in plots of erotic love.

We have already seen how Anna's sensuous "animation" emerges from her initial portrait, focalized through Vronsky's sexualizing gaze. Not only is Anna's life in the novel tied up with the beginning of her and Vronsky's affair, but it is also the quality that both she and the narrator suggest has been "stifled" by her marriage to Karenin (292; 18:308). In marrying Anna, the narrator explains, Karenin gave her "all the feeling he was capable of," and this "attachment . . . excluded from his soul the last need for heartfelt [*serdechnykh*] relationships with people" (507; 19:77). This judgment lends weight to Anna's derision of Karenin—"He's not a man, not a person, he's a puppet . . . He's not a person, he's an administrative machine" (360; 18:379). In a parodic inversion of Anna's novel reading in the train car, Karenin takes up a paper knife and dreams over his book, but what briefly lends *his* cheeks the "flush of animation" (*kraska ozhivleniia*) is bureaucratic wrangling over the irrigation of fields in the Zaraisk province (285; 18:300–302). The heroine's and the narrator's matching treatment of Karenin as mechanical or dead thus strengthens the tie between novelistic mimetic life and a romanticized (and sexualized) vision of personhood that excludes him.

Kitty Shcherbatskaya anchors a parallel hierarchy of sensuous "animation" and physicalization adjacent to the center of the novel's other romance plot. (As Nabokov noted, Tolstoy is especially attentive to her gestures.[19]) Although Tolstoy rigorously distinguishes the narrative of Kitty and Levin's marriage from the narrative of Anna and Vronsky's adultery, Kitty is nevertheless linked with Anna and Stiva's characteristic "light step" at its romantic climax, when Levin arrives to propose: "As soon as [Mlle. Linon] went out, there came the sound of quick, quick light steps over the parquet, and his happiness, his life, he himself—better than his own self, that which he had sought and desired for so long—was quickly approaching him" (404; 18:425).[20] Meanwhile Kitty's placid friend Varenka, who "lacked what Kitty had in over-abundance—the restrained fire of life [*sderzhannogo ognia zhizni*] and an awareness of her attractiveness" (215), shares in the illusion of fully fleshed life at precisely the moment when she thinks that Levin's brother Koznyshev is about to make her a proposal: "Varenka . . . quickly came up to [Kitty] with a light step. Her quickness of movement, the flush (*kraska*) that covered her animated (*ozhivlennoe*) face—all showed that something extraordinary was taking place within her" (553; 19:125).[21] Physical life, again, attaches to romance and sexuality—equally in Anna's demonized case and in the case of Kitty or Varenka, where sexuality is contained and sanctioned by the prospect of marriage.

Conversely, as Gary Saul Morson has argued, Kitty's sister Dolly Oblonskaya becomes the novel's moral heroine largely because her life does *not* lend itself to the center of a romantic plot.[22] This distance from the romantic center is marked in the narrative's instructions about how to imagine Dolly's body. Associated in rare physical descriptions with her thinning (vanishing) hair, hands, and face (10, 613; 18:12, 19:187), Dolly garners explicit "animation," tellingly, only once—in the moment when she recounts her visit to Anna and Vronsky's adulterous household (642; 19:219). Tolstoy thus steers not only the reader's narrative attention but also her sensuous imagination away from Dolly as moral heroine. While other mimetic effects help realize Dolly as a sharply delineated individual consciousness, the narrative designations of life and physical solidity elude her. Tolstoy thus presents mimetic life as an illusion reinforcible only through the kind of descriptive and narrative attention systematically drawn to romanticized, sexualized characters like Kitty and (especially) Anna.

One more variation on this theme is too striking to pass without comment. At the opposite pole from the virtuously unromantic Dolly stand the jaded society women Liza Merkalova and Sappho Stoltz, for whom infidelity is no more consequential than "some details of the toilette" (18:314). Such a dissolution of the moral stakes of adultery makes Liza and Sappho as unfit as Dolly or Karenin to occupy the living center of this novel; as Liza herself complains to Anna: "You live, but I'm just bored [Vy zhivete, a ia skuchaiu]" (300; 18:317). But where Dolly and Karenin become faded or machine-like in the novel reader's vision, Liza and Sappho briefly lacerate it. Indeed, Sappho, who enters Princess Betsy's salon trailing two lovers, seems to have been introduced *only* for the sake of her grotesquely eye-catching description:

> Anna had not met this new celebrity before and was struck both by her beauty, and by how extremely far her costume went and the boldness of her manner. On her head, such an edifice of a coiffure had been made from her own and other women's delicately golden-colored hair, that her head equaled in size her sveltely rounded bust, much exposed from the front. She headed so decisively forward that at every movement the forms of her knees and upper

> legs were outlined beneath her dress, and the question involuntarily arose as to where, at the back of this built-up, undulating mountain, really *ended* her actual, small and svelte, so bare above and so concealed behind and below, body. (299; I have adjusted the translation to preserve the strained syntax of the Russian original. Italics added for clarity.)[23]

In Tolstoy's near-Cubist portrait (focalized through Anna), Sappho's "actual body" appears as an accessory to her elaborate costume. It seems that when adultery becomes a "detail of the toilette" in *Anna Karenina*, mimetic physicality does too: moral distortion finds a mirror in the distortion of characterization. An inversion of the nervous young man losing his self-possession under the pressure of Vronsky's indifference, Sappho falls apart in the wake of her own promiscuous demand for attention, which her narrative position cannot sustain.

Not for nothing, then, does Stiva repeatedly refer to the railroad—crossroads for all demonic forces in *Anna Karenina*—as a "living matter" (*zhivoe delo*; 721–22, 729; 19:299–300, 307). Through these major and minor characters, Tolstoy sets up an argument: the novel reader's misguided tendency to focus on romance plots is reflected in the omniscient narrator's cues about who is most physically alive. Like Vronsky and Anna, we are punished for our lopsided mimetic vision by Anna's suicide and its drably gruesome aftermath: a "bloodied corpse sprawled shamelessly among strangers, still filled with recent life"; a vindictive judgment from Vronsky's mother; and the gnawing toothache that keeps Vronsky from playing the bereaved lover (780; 19:362). Read in this way, Anna's death and Vronsky's devastation are designed to dispel not just one well-wrought illusion of mimetic life in a novel, but the desire for romance (and for mimesis) that draws us to novels themselves.

On this moralistic reading, however, it is hard to account for the sheer saturation of life in Anna as a novelistic character.[24] If Tolstoy's only purpose is to reform readers, then why start by enchanting us so thoroughly? The novel's wealth of sensuous detail points toward a more complex design: a repurposing of novelistic mimesis, rather than an outright rejection. The seductive but poisonous illusion of Anna's physical life throws doubt not on mimesis itself, but on vivid physical presence as a reliable *measure* of the mimetic. It is Anna who exemplifies the novel genre's capacity for painting life, but it is also Anna who models this skeptical stance. Succumbing to the terms that place her at the vivid center of the fictional plot, we lay ourselves open to the (Schopenhauerian) questions she asks about her own reality and that of the world around her. Tolstoy thus sets up a double move, on the levels of story and discourse: as Anna begins to doubt the validity and worth of earthly life and sensory perception, her plot prepares us to doubt that sensuous mimetic illusion is the limit of what realist narrative can bring about.

In a progression that many readers have traced, Anna's awakening to her desire for Vronsky entails a dissociation from the world and self she has known before, and a newly uncertain relationship to her own reality. These doubts overtake her as she tries to read on the return train to Saint Petersburg: "She kept having moments of doubt whether the carriage was moving backwards or forwards, or standing still. Was that Annushka beside her, or some stranger? 'What is that on the armrest—a fur coat or some animal? And what am I? Am I myself, or someone else?'" (101; 18:107). Later in their affair, she watches her own eyes "shining" in the darkness (148; 18:156) and raves about "the other one" who has invaded her soul (412; 18:434); close to the end of the novel, she kisses her own hand (755; 19:335). Desire makes her undergo a fragmentation that is also a multiplication of selves—a still more horrifying descent into the unhappiness of individual, embodied particularity, because individuality itself has broken into pieces.

And yet, precisely because Anna sinks ever deeper into the fruitless struggle to satisfy this individual will, she comes close to exposing bounded, mortal individuality as the realm of deception. Near the end of the novel, her terrified vision of the shadow of her own death invokes Plato's iconic allegory of the cave, as well as the Platonic tenet that Schopenhauer adopted—the provisional ("representational") quality of individual physical objects as such:

> She lay in bed with her eyes open, looking by the light of a single burnt-down candle at the molded cornice of the ceiling and the shadow of a screen spread over part of it, and she vividly pictured to herself what he would feel when she was no more and had become only a memory for him. "How could I have said those cruel words to her? . . . But now she's no more. She's gone from us forever. She's there . . ." Suddenly the shadow of the screen wavered, spread over the whole cornice, over the whole ceiling; other shadows from the other side rushed to meet it; for a moment the shadows left, but then with renewed swiftness moved in again, wavered, merged, and everything became dark. "Death!" she thought. (752; second ellipsis in original)[25]

It is a folding screen (*shirma*) that casts the shadow Anna associates with death, and in this way, Tolstoy's scene both condenses and revises Plato's allegory. Socrates describes the shadows cast by objects carried along a low wall between the prisoners in the cave and the fire, "like the screen in front of puppeteers above which they show their puppets" (*Republic* 7.514b).[26] Tolstoy has the deceptive shadow cast not by individual "puppets" but by the screen itself. Death (to extend Anna's explication of Tolstoy's allegory) is a product of the master illusion that makes our vision faulty—a shadow that spreads in proportion to the flaring-up of an earthly (and novelistic) attachment to individual embodied life. The more Anna splinters into vividly concrete particularity, the more inevitable becomes her death; indeed, one crucial function of her character is to expose this relationship. As we watch Anna's characterization and her plot unfold in tandem, we are also invited to identify the assumptions—about novelistic realism and about mortal human being—that determine her ever-narrowing path.[27]

The astonishing narrative of Anna's final journey to the Obiralovka station, an extended stream of consciousness that weaves the crowds around Anna together with her thoughts, realizes the unhappiness of this supreme state of realist particularity, as predicted in the novel's opening lines. The objects and passersby surrounding Anna, from the boys eating "dirty ice cream" to the self-pitying beggar with her baby, become (in Vronsky's image) "parasitic" on her perception. The scene's experimental narrative form thus comes close to realizing the fantasy of identity between text and protagonist, as figured in Mikhailov's portrait of Anna and as projected by the novel's title. It magnifies the conventional relationship between protagonists and minor characters, who fall into the narrative's view only when and because the protagonist's story touches theirs. By the time Anna arrives at the station, the reader has been invited to share her solipsistic sense that her mind knows and contains the minds of all others, that there is nothing in them that exists beyond her: for example, when she encounters a pretentious man and woman on the train, "It was as if Anna could see their story and all the hidden corners of their souls, turning a light on them" (766; 19:346). The novel's entire fictional world has temporarily been intertwined with her perception.

Anna's death is the high point of this exaggerated convergence between her fictional being and the illusion of life inherent in the novel's text, as animated by the absorbed reader's attentive imagination. As I have already suggested, the candle that flares up here can be imagined (among other things) as the light of Anna's own individual protagonicity, by which she has been reading and living her story all along. In the moment of her death, the emblem of the candle reveals the drawback of being a novelistic character so hyperbolically "protagonized" as Anna. The problem turns out to be, precisely, the perfect continuity between character and text:

> And suddenly, remembering the man who was run over the day she first met Vronsky, she realized what she must do. With a quick, light step she went down the stairs that led from the water pump to the rails and stopped by the train that was passing close by her. . . . And just at the moment when the midpoint between the two wheels came even with her, she threw the red handbag

> aside and, drawing her head down between her shoulders, fell on her hands under the carriage and with a light movement, as if preparing to get up again at once, sank to her knees. But in that same instant she was horrified at what she was doing. "Where am I? What am I doing? Why?" She wanted to rise, to throw herself back; but something huge, implacable struck her head and dragged her by the spine. "Lord, forgive me for everything!" she said, feeling the impossibility of any struggle. A little muzhik, muttering something to himself, was working over some iron. And the candle by which she had been reading that book filled with anxieties, deceptions, grief and evil, flared up with a brighter light than ever, lit up for her all that had once been in darkness, sputtered, began to grow dim, and went out forever. (768)[28]

Tolstoy ends Anna's narrative by explicitly driving home what he wants us to recognize about it: her life—in the senses of both fictional biography and mimetic characterization—can be entirely reduced to a "book." Because every resource of the novelistic character-system has been concentrated on Anna in order to animate and embody her as protagonist, Anna *as read* ought to differ more than any other character in the novel from Anna as remembered, described, or paraphrased after reading. Her narrative ends with a surprising lesson: the inexorable limitations of being so realized, by text and body alike. In this passage as in Anna's own earlier vision, the candle is there to reveal the shadow: an analogy between the limits of a mimetic life that belongs only to the moment of reading, and the limits of a human life that depends only on mortal flesh. Anna's death thus offers a point of departure: what would it mean for either character or reader to be realized differently? What would it mean for the character *not* to end with her body in the novel and for the reader not to end with his body in the flesh?

Posing these questions with visceral force, the dénouement of Anna's narrative prepares the reader for the dénouement of Levin's. We can again borrow Vronsky's metaphor to call Levin's plot "parasitic" on Anna's—in this case, a parasite not just nourished but also transported and delivered by its host.[29] With its romantic center so sensuously and completely occupied by Anna, *Anna Karenina* gains a less rigid space in which to construct Levin as an alternative model of fictional existence. Just as Levin's plot models a different kind of love from Anna's—love of the immortal soul, and not the mortal body—so his characterization models the possibility of metafictional immortality. Where Anna provides a paradigmatic example of the powerful mutual interdependence between realist character and realist text, Levin embodies the dream of a character who could not just remain but also transmit himself, in fully compelling realist detail, even after the book of *Anna Karenina* is closed.

LEVIN AND THE DREAM OF THE MARGINAL PROTAGONIST

Levin's character in *Anna Karenina* takes shape reluctantly. Where Anna's entrance ties her (in the space of a single passage) to a specific fictional body and specific fictional plot, Levin's entrance is strangely indefinite: "It was not yet two when the big glass door of the office suddenly opened, and someone came in. All the members, from under the imperial portrait and behind the zertsalo, turned toward the door, glad of the diversion; but the porter at once banished the intruder and closed the glass door behind him" (16; 18:17). Levin begins as an anonymous apparition: the working corps of the novel (as concentrated in the form-bound bureaucracy of Stiva's office) looks up at him, momentarily distracted, and then returns to its work. It is several paragraphs before Levin receives a physical description, and a paragraph more before he has a name. Like the title *Anna Karenina*, Levin's entrance primes us to accept the oxymoron of a protagonist who avoids attracting his own novel's attention.

When we do first "see" Levin—"'That's the one,' the porter said, pointing to a strongly built, broad-shouldered man with a curly beard, who, without taking off his lambskin hat, was quickly and lightly running up the worn steps of the stone stairway" (16; 18:18)—it is no accident that he is climbing stairs. Anna's narrative ends with her "quick, light step" descending toward suicide: the final stage (I have argued) of her descent into the fallen state of sensuous realist protagonicity. Levin's begins by asking what an ascent *out* of this state—for a character who is also and equally a protagonist of the novel's action—might mean.[30]

The image of the steps Levin climbs, correspondingly, might serve to orient us away from Schopenhauerian pessimism and toward another major philosophical intertext of *Anna Karenina*, Plato's *Symposium*.[31] As Socrates's teacher Diotima explains, all lovers crave "birth in beauty, whether of body or soul." A ladder or stairway thus leads from the pseudoimmortality of procreation, up to the more perfect forms that issue from "pregnancy in the soul"—poetry, civic virtue, science, and at last philosophy, which teaches the love of virtue itself, beyond the bounds of any single embodiment in time and space.

> This is what it is to go aright, or be led by another, into the mystery of Love: one goes always upwards for the sake of this Beauty, starting out from beautiful things and using them like rising stairs: from one body to two and from two to all beautiful bodies, then from beautiful bodies to beautiful customs, and from customs to learning beautiful things, and from these lessons he arrives in the end at this lesson, which is learning of this very Beauty. . . . The

> love of the gods belongs to anyone who has given birth to true virtue and nourished it, and if any human being could become immortal, it would be he. (*Symposium* 211c–212a)[32]

Diotima's stairway suggests a more hopeful view of the question of how to reach beyond the suffering of embodied being and its eternally unsatisfied desires, which is reflected in the difference between Anna and Levin as protagonists. Shaped to climb upward, Levin uncovers the possibility that the realist novel might use its generic embroilment in the particular to represent a different kind of being—still rooted in physical existence and sensation, but no longer bounded by time, death, or individual selfhood. But what kind of fictional body could anchor this transformation?

We can begin to answer this question by noting that there is no equivalent in Levin's narrative to Vronsky's sustained gaze at Anna, or to the repeated descriptive phrases associated with her (Anna's "light step," round arms, escaping curls, etc.). As a rule, Levin's body is more perceiving than perceived. Gender contributes to this difference, but it cannot alone account for the frequent moments when Levin's gaze itself becomes a physical presence. Indeed, our sense of Levin's "body" and of his narrative centrality is most often continuous with the tangible world conveyed to us by his perceptions. When Levin goes to hunt snipe, his "quick, light step" carries him to an erotic experience of a completely different kind from Anna's, a walk through the marsh at dawn. But unlike Anna and Vronsky's elided liaison, Levin's walk is represented as a full set of specific physical sensations: "The moon . . . now merely gleamed like a bit of quicksilver. . . . Still invisible without the sun's light, the dew on the fragrant tall hemp, from which the heads had already been plucked, wetted Levin's legs and his blouse above the waist" (592).[33] Levin's body is as central to these passages as Anna's body is to her affair with Vronsky—but here, rather than watching this body, we have been asked to inhabit it.

The result is an unexpected division of labor between the novel's two protagonists. Both Anna and Levin possess (in Dorrit Cohn's term) "transparent minds"; both are sites for the exploration of psychological experience. However, despite the sensuous particularity of Anna's fictional presence, it is Levin who more often has the "transparent body." Second only to (and often collaborating with) omniscient narration, Levin's senses act as Tolstoy's instrument for drawing the reader into his representation of the physical world.

The two major plots of *Anna Karenina* thus model two different ways of being a novelistic protagonist, and correspondingly, two different modes of minorness.[34] Anna's narrative encourages an understanding of the protagonist as the vivid fictional object at the heart of a romantic plot. The dissolving nervous young man, the fractured Sappho Stoltz, and the threadbare Dolly Oblonskaya all exemplify the distorting mode of minorness that attends this conventional mode of centrality. So do many other characters: the "famous Petersburg lawyer"—perhaps Tolstoy's closest approach to Dickens—who catches the moths flying around his office with his small hairy hands and hopes to reupholster his furniture with the proceeds from the Karenins' divorce (366; 18:386); Stiva and Dolly's rotating cast of children (Tanya, Grisha, and others invented as required);[35] the consumptive artist Petrov who dashes Kitty's hopes of blameless philanthropy; the foreign prince "as fresh as a big, green, waxy Dutch cucumber" who enters the novel in order to show Vronsky an uncomfortable mirror image of himself (354; 18:373).[36] Although it occurs across all the novel's plots, this minorness finds its counterpart in Anna's fantasies of romantic heroinism, which turn life into an individualistic Schopenhauerian struggle and the novel into a competition for the reader's limited image-making attention.

Levin embodies a different view of the novelistic protagonist, as the *lens* for narrative rather than its object, and this mode of protagonicity suggests its own corresponding minorness. While Anna's centrality is set off by characters whose fictional presence is less vivid, less emphasized, and less ample than hers, Levin's is set off by characters less apt to last vividly outside the purview of the romance plot. His narrative often courts not the novel reader's attention, but her boredom—averted or softened only by the promise of an eventual connection to Levin himself. It thus repeats in miniature the idiosyncratic narrative structure of *War and Peace*: lengthening passages limning the outlines of historical marginal characters, held only tenuously within the network of the named fictional characters' stories. The hope now, however, is that not the narrative but the protagonist himself might turn out to exceed fictional bounds. Levin's mobile gaze constructs him as a "living" thread that leads now toward, now away from, the central narratives of *Anna Karenina*.

Some of the alternative models for being toward which Levin pulls us are tantalizingly inaccessible and self-sufficient. A clear example is the line of mostly unnamed peasant workers whom he joins to mow a meadow:

> Already from the top of the hill there came into view, at the foot of the hill, the shady, already mowed part of the meadow, with graying rows and the black heaps of caftans, which the mowers had taken off at the place where they started the first row. As he approached nearer, the muzhiks came into view, following each other in a strung-out line and swinging their scythes variedly, some in caftans, some in only their shirts. He counted forty-two men. (249)[37]

Levin sees the muzhiks first through the landscape marked by their labor, melded strikingly with their bodies through the equivalency between "graying rows and the black heaps of caftans"—where discarded clothing presages finished work. In Russian, they are a singular collective noun (*vere-nitsa* [line]) before they are plural (*muzhiki*), and they are numbered, also collectively, before any individual is named. Levin's consuming desire "not to fall behind [ne otstat' ot]" the line of muzhiks (251; 18:265) represents identity with this collective as the highest possible good. And yet Levin's narrative position as focalizer underscores the rift between a protagonist, realized by a set of marked novelistic techniques, and marginal characters whose virtue lies in their *exemption* from individual narrative attention.

Most often, however, Levin's covetous idealization of more minor characters' lives makes them look functional, subordinated to his plot. For example, when Levin watches the peasant Ivan Parmenov and his wife at work, his envy for their intertwined love and labor turns his sensuous vision of both characters into a didactic object:

> Ivan Parmenov stood on the cart, receiving, spreading and stamping down the enormous loads of hay that his young beauty of a wife deftly heaved up to him, first in armfuls and then by the fork. The young woman worked easily, cheerfully, and deftly. The thick, packed-down hay did not immediately go onto the fork. She first loosened it up, stuck the fork in, then leaned the whole weight of her body onto it with a supple and quick movement and at once, bending her back tightly girded with a red sash, straightened up and, sticking her chest out beneath her white smock, shifted her grip on the fork in her deft manner and heaved the load high up on to the cart. Ivan hastily, obviously trying to spare her every moment of extra work, picked up with widespread arms the load pitched to him and spread it on the cart. After pitching him the last of the hay with a rake, the woman shook off the hay dust that had gotten on her neck and, having straightened the red kerchief that had gone askew on her white, untanned forehead, crawled under the cart to tie down the load. . . . In the expressions on both their faces showed strong, young, recently awakened love. (274)[38]

Physical and existential desire are closely tangled in Levin's idealized image of the Parmenovs. This desire climaxes, a few sentences later, in the "thundercloud" of the song sung by a group of peasant women, which envelops Levin so that "the haystack on which he lay, and all the other haystacks and carts, and the whole meadow with the distant fields all started moving and heaving to the rhythm of this wild, rollicking song with its shouts, whistles and whoops [vse zakhodilo i zakolykhalos' pod razmery etoi dikoi razveseloi pesni s vskrikami, prisvistami i iokan'iami]." For a moment, the world that Levin perceives is suffused with the collective anonymity he longs for. Nevertheless, the song that transports him then leaves him "enviously" (*zavidno*) behind; "he could do nothing and had to lie there and look and listen" (275; 18:290). Relegated to the "looking and listening" functions of a focalizing novelistic protagonist, Levin gets reabsorbed, along with the reader, into the protagonist's inherent isolation.

Several scenes later, when Levin encounters yet another happy peasant family, Tolstoy tells us that "something in this impression called for his special attention" (324; 18:344). *Our* attention, however, remains filtered through Levin himself. Other characters, like the reserved *zemstvo* activist Sviyazhsky, appear in digression after digression—debating with Levin about agriculture, instructing him at the provincial elections, dining with his father-in-law at their club in Moscow. But like Levin, we have no way of moving beyond the "reception rooms of Sviyazhsky's mind" (327; 18:346). No matter how far Levin's gaze travels from the central plot of his narrative, it makes auxiliary the marginal and minor others whom it tries to put on display—and this contrast inevitably sets off Levin's own centralized consciousness and senses.

Thus, although Anna and Levin are equally privileged as focal points of the narrative, they inhabit the function of the protagonist differently, making two different kinds of appeal to the reader's attention. Where Anna's vivid body pulls us toward her as the magnetic center of her plot, Levin's vivid gaze urges us to follow him for the sake of a captivating way of seeing the world. The contrast between minor or marginal characters and protagonist becomes a way of nudging us further, and more firmly, into Levin's persistent point of view.

Indeed, the high points of Levin's plot are themselves often moments of vision, which take Levin's perspective for their explicit subject. On the morning when Levin goes to propose to Kitty, Tolstoy mirrors his ecstatic sensation that his physical being has melted away with a narrative "melting" into free indirect discourse:

> All that night and morning Levin had lived completely unconsciously and had felt himself completely removed from the conditions of material life. He had not eaten for a whole day, had not slept for two nights, had spent several hours undressed in the freezing cold, yet felt not only fresh and healthy as never before but completely independent of his body: he moved without any muscular effort and felt he could do anything. . . . And what he saw then, he afterwards never saw again. He was especially touched by children going to school, the gray-blue pigeons that flew down from the roof to the pavement, and the white bread rolls sprinkled with flour that some invisible hand

> had set out. These bread rolls, pigeons and the two boys were unearthly beings. All this happened at the same time: a boy ran up to a pigeon and, smiling, looked at Levin; the pigeon flapped its wings and fluttered off, sparkling in the sun amidst the snow-dust trembling in the air; and the smell of baked bread wafted from the window and the bread rolls were set out in it. All this together was so extraordinarily good that Levin laughed and wept from joy. (403)[39]

The repeated *chuvstvoval* (felt) in the first paragraph gives way to the *videl* (saw) that introduces the second, and the sensation of escaping the desiring individual body gives way to the scene that this sensation produces. The narrative models first the experience of a love that leads beyond the mortal body and then the vision of a world in "unearthly" and timeless guise, as it appears through such a body's senses (although in the form of narrative, Tolstoy cannot reproduce the eradication of sequential time). Levin's "feeling" is thus converted from an aspect of his characterization into an aspect of the novel's reality. Both story and discourse register the impulse from the particular and individual toward the shared—from embodiment to expansive and "unearthly" happiness; from Levin's characterizing experience to a scene focalized through and beyond him, for the reader to experience for herself.

This scene, which occurs near the novel's exact midpoint, prepares the ground for Levin's last and most significant shared moral sensation: his epiphany that he has always known what it is to live "for the soul" and not "for the belly," and that everyone else has always known it too. In part 8, as Levin lies with the beetles "in the succulent, broad-bladed forest grass," he looks up at the sky and realizes that he is right to see it as a "firm blue arch," even though he knows that it is really infinite space. He suddenly becomes aware of "mysterious voices speaking joyfully and anxiously about something among themselves [tainstvennym golosam, o chem-to radostno i ozabochenno peregovarivavshimsia mezhdu soboi]" (800; 19:382). This moment parallels a mimetic high point of *War and Peace*, in which not just the individual protagonists but the narrator himself seem to recede from a fictional world caught miraculously unawares: "The stars, as if knowing that no one would see them now, began to play in the dark sky. Now flaring up, now vanishing, now trembling, they were busily whispering something joyful, but mysterious, to one another."[40] In *Anna Karenina*, however, the "mysterious voices" point not outward to a world but inward to a character—in the sense of both a fictional figure, and a mode of thought and behavior—that Tolstoy hopes can exist beyond the bounds of novelistic narrative itself.

The final feeling into which Levin's fictional body invites the novel's readers is thus this revelation of a common foundation for virtue. Christianizing the Platonic structure of knowledge as the soul's recollection, Levin's conversion also carries the trace of Diotima's metaphor in the *Symposium*: a "birth in beauty" midwifed by the example of the principled peasant Platon Fokanych:[41]

> "This new feeling hasn't changed me, hasn't made me happy or suddenly enlightened, as I dreamed—just like the feeling for my son. Nor was there any surprise. And faith—not faith—I don't know what it is—but this feeling has entered into me just as imperceptibly through pangs of suffering and has firmly lodged itself in my soul. I'll get angry in the same way with the coachman Ivan, argue in the same way, speak my mind inappropriately, there will be the same wall between my soul's holy of holies and other people . . .—but my life now, my whole life, independently of everything that may happen to me, every minute of it, is not only not meaningless, as it was before, but has the unquestionable meaning of the good which it is in my power to put into it!"
>
> The End (817)[42]

What Levin discovers is "not faith"; it is a "new feeling" (*chuvstvo*) that enters into his soul with spiritual pangs parallel to the physical ones Kitty experienced when bearing their son. Like the physical senses, his feeling for the good is understood as a common ground for experience, independent of particular circumstances at any moment of any one life: "And not I alone, but everybody, the whole world, fully understands this one thing, and this one thing they do not doubt and always agree on" (795; 19:377). Levin's moral sense transcends individuality and time to unify all who "feel" it—in a body that is common and therefore abstract, but with the same immediacy as sensation itself.

With this passage, Levin's monologue and Tolstoy's novel come to a joint conclusion, the character's voice separated from the reader only by the boundary of a closing quotation mark and the word *Konets* (The End). Anna's narrative ends with her realization that she has all along been inhabiting a book; Levin's, with an invocation of life that opens a conduit into the world of *any* reader who feels the difference between living for the belly and living for the soul. His perspective tugs toward the margins of text and reading, away from the fictional body to which it has been attached. Just as Levin has found a conception of the good that does not depend on the "artificial construction" of philosophical argument (788; 19:369–70), Tolstoy hopes to have written a protagonist whose compelling vividness no longer depends on the intricate verbal mimesis of the realist novel.

But the *Konets* that bisects the common ground between reader and text threatens the practical outcome of this project. The only difference between "belly" and "soul" that *Anna Karenina* can be sure of constructing hangs on the differences between Anna's and Levin's narrated lives, accumulating as the narrative alternates in steady rhythm between their plots. Without the system that confines and solidifies it—and in particular, the continual shaping contrast provided by Anna—how "real" can Levin's unmoored voice seem? Cut off from this differentiated particularity and from the vividness of the fictional world so often filtered through his senses, does Levin remain a compelling mimetic lure? No absorbed reader of *Anna Karenina* could end the novel doubting that its characters live under stars "thrown by some unerring hand" (815; 19:398). Whether the reader draws the same conclusion about her own world lies entirely beyond the author's control.

In the real-time responses to *Anna Karenina* recorded in his published writings, Dostoevsky made no secret of his dislike for Tolstoy's character Levin. The epilogue to Dostoevsky's novel *The Adolescent* (*Podrostok*), published in December 1875 when *Anna Karenina* had appeared through the first half of part 3, alludes to Levin in barbed terms as the solitary "misanthropic grandson" of the characters of *War and Peace*. As Dostoevsky writes, Levin "should even appear as a sort of eccentric [*chudak*], whom the reader could recognize at first glance as someone who has quit the field, and be convinced that the field is no longer his."[43] In this guise of a defeated "eccentric," Levin supports Dostoevsky's idea of the Tolstoyan family novel as a mirage with no real relationship to contemporary reality. At best, he is isolated; at worst, as Dostoevsky would later argue in his July/August 1877 *Diary of a Writer*, Levin is irretrievably sunk in his own narrow self-interest. Dostoevsky predicts that Levin's "idle wavering" (*prazdnoshataistvo*), an inheritance of Westernized rational thinking, will keep him from standing by his hard-won conversion, just as it keeps him from supporting the Russian volunteers headed off to join the struggle for Serbian liberation. Because the primary concerns in Levin's life remain his wife's appetite and his infant son's bath, it is obvious to Dostoevsky that he has not truly achieved the clear and lasting "feeling" for God that would unite him with the common collective of the Russian people (25:205).

Dostoevsky's criticism of Levin may have sprung partly from the affinity that he sensed between Tolstoy's hopes for *Anna Karenina* and his own lifelong novelistic project. Levin registers an aspiration (standard for Dostoevsky's novels, but more unusual in Tolstoy's) toward realist typicality, which Dostoevsky endowed with messianic spiritual force.[44] By definition, typical characters bridge the gap between reader and text. But where Dostoevsky saw types as seizing and crystallizing particular aspects of human life—whether fully formed, or in the process of formation—Tolstoy offers Levin as the articulation of a voice that each reader might discover in *herself*.

Where Dostoevsky hoped that novelistic characters could give a name and shape to contemporary reality and so infuse it with the novel's own created harmonious order, Tolstoy hoped that characters could dissolve in the process of guiding the reader toward new forms of life. Dostoevsky thus mistrusted Levin not only because he disagreed with Tolstoy about pan-Slavicism and the Serbian War, but also because he found characters like Levin to be an insufficient basis for creating the universal spiritual community that Tolstoy invokes. Unlike Tolstoy, Dostoevsky did not trust that most contemporary readers instinctively "felt" the difference between life for the belly and life for the soul—and if this unanimity does not already exist, then Tolstoy may be too quick to imagine that an "idly wavering" Levin is a compelling enough example to bring it about. To recast this doubt in my own terms, Tolstoy is too sanguine in thinking that Levin can be absolutely separated from Anna, mimesis as portable model from mimesis as immersion in a fictional world. If our vivid experience of Levin's belief is no more universal than our vivid vision of Anna's body, then both are equally dependent on the temporary aesthetic communion of reading.

As I have argued in this chapter, the alternating double plot of *Anna Karenina* fills much the same role as the overt theoretical digressions in *War and Peace*, raising a similar set of questions about the multiple possible approaches to narrating and evoking human lives. Anna's narrative asks us to recognize how conventional novelistic mimesis distorts both narrative and reality by centering them on individual embodied persons. Levin's asks us instead to imagine a novel that would direct attention outward—away from the unhappiness and mortality of any individual person, toward a collective vision of humanity as always already united by a common moral code. But just as, in *War and Peace*, the protagonist-centered form of the European novel undermines Tolstoy's antiheroic view of history, so in *Anna Karenina*, the context that *produces* realist illusion blocks the purpose to which Tolstoy wants to turn it. The fragmentation of Anna's world seems to oppose the unity of Levin's, but both modes of protagonicity rely on similar methods—at the heart of which lie the differences between major and minor characters and the persistent opposition between Anna and Levin themselves. Tolstoy instructs us to remember Anna's life as a book and Levin's as a life, but do these instructions bear weight once the book of *Anna Karenina* is closed?

By staging an absolute split between his two protagonists, Tolstoy tries to overcome the link that Walter Benjamin has made between the novel reader's isolation and the conventional novelistic character, whose meaning springs from the consummating moment of his death:

> Actually, there is no story for which the question "How does it continue?" would not be legitimate. The novelist, on the other hand, cannot hope to take

> the smallest step beyond the limit at which he writes "Finis," and in so doing invites the reader to a divinatory realization of the meaning of life. A man listening to a story is in the company of the storyteller; even a man reading one shares this companionship. The reader of a novel, however, is isolated, more so than any other reader . . . "A man who dies at the age of thirty-five," Moritz Heimann once said, "is at every point in his life a man who dies at the age of thirty-five." . . . The nature of characters in a novel cannot be presented any better than it is in this statement, which says that the "meaning" of their life is revealed only in their death. But the reader of a novel in fact looks for human beings, from whom he derives the "meaning of life." . . . The novel is significant, therefore, not because it presents someone's fate to us, perhaps didactically, but because this stranger's fate, by virtue of the flame which consumes it, yields to us the warmth which we never draw from our own fate. What draws the reader to a novel is the hope of warming his shivering life with a death he reads about.[45]

Because novel readers read alone, the "warmth" and "companionship" they draw from the novel comes from the death that lies outside the characters—the only visible mark of the novelist who wrote the book that "invites the reader to a divinatory realization of the meaning of life." The novelist's "Finis" completes this death, in the discourse if not the story, and so it marks the end of the "divinatory" power that the reader has invited the novelist to exercise. If the novel's significance comes precisely from the shaping closure it exercises on the biographies of characters, the companionship it offers the reader will always be a ghostly one—the trace of a *vanished* author, left by the *ending* of a fictional character's plot.

Levin's ending, like his narrative as a whole, looks outside of the enchanted novelistic circle formed between the title (which excludes him) and the closing "Finis." In the last passages of his final monologue, Levin comes within a hair's breadth of merging with the novel's omniscient narrator. Tolstoy thus imagines combining the novel genre's controlled image-making power with the open-ended shared significance of a Benjaminian "story"—as if the character could anchor an ongoing spiritual community with his example, rather than a temporary community of readers with his narrative death. Distinguished on the one hand from the incidental quality of the minor characters we instantly forget and on the other hand, from the pull of a protagonist like Anna who draws our attention toward her romantic plot, Levin charts the longed-for middle ground of what might be called a "marginal protagonist": a character who remains vividly concrete even as he slips off the edge of fiction and into reality. The ideal reader of *Anna Karenina* would find that the very act of interpreting the novel has bound her to a community of others who share the ineluctable sense that Levin's "life for the soul" is virtuous and Anna's "life for the belly" is flawed. In a metafictional parallel to Levin, she would move from reading the novel to discovering that she already lives by its principles—and so has no need to look in fiction for the meanings she finds herself given in life.[46]

Decades of interpretation attest that *Anna Karenina* has never received such a homogeneous response. Indeed, more than any of Tolstoy's other works, it seems to fail the test that he articulated in the later treatise *What Is Art?* (1898): "*Art is a human activity consisting in this: that one man consciously, by means of certain external signs, hands on to others feelings he has lived through; and that others are infected by these feelings and also experience them.*"[47] Although *Anna Karenina* does "infect" most of its readers with feelings, it lacks the control and commonality that mark Tolstoy's ideal process of infection—the artist "conscious" of the feelings he is handing on, the whole audience infected precisely by "these feelings," and not by any others. As Tolstoy himself commented in an often-quoted letter to Nikolai Strakhov, when *Anna Karenina*'s serial publication had reached the middle of part 5:

> But if I were to try to say in words everything that I intended to express in my novel, I would have to write the same novel I wrote from the beginning. And if the short-sighted critics think that I only wanted to describe the things that I like, what Oblonsky has for dinner or what Karenina's shoulders are like, they are mistaken. In everything, or nearly everything I have written, I have been guided by the need to gather together ideas, linked among themselves for the purpose of self-expression [myslei, stseplennykh mezhdu soboiu, dlia vyrazheniia sebia]; but every idea expressed separately in words loses its meaning and is terribly impoverished when taken by itself out of the linkage in which it is found. The linkage [*stseplenie*] itself is made up, I think, not by the idea, but by something else, and it is impossible to express the basis of this linkage directly in words. It can only be expressed indirectly—in words describing characters, actions, and situations. . . . For me, one of the most manifest proofs of this was Vronsky's suicide. . . . The chapter about how Vronsky accepted his role after meeting the husband had been written by me a long time ago. I began to correct it, and quite unexpectedly for me, but unmistakably, Vronsky went and shot himself [Vr. stal streliat'sia]. And now it turns out that this was organically necessary for what came afterwards. (April 23 and 26, 1876)[48]

It is telling that Tolstoy links the character's lifelike autonomy to the novel's "organic" complexity, and to the impossibility of paraphrasing its contents. For Tolstoy, *Anna Karenina*'s self-contained mimetic illusion opposes its powers of direct communication.[49] Nevertheless, the end of the novel entertains the hope that illusion and infection could be combined. What if every reader did close the book to find a new character within herself, defined by a shared perception of Levin's "feeling" for the good?

With his self-proclaimed turn away from artistic literature in the second half of his life, and his disavowal of *War and Peace* and *Anna Karenina* in particular, Tolstoy seems to have abandoned this hope as a false promise. I suggest that a key locus of the deception is the nature of mimetic characterization in the realist novel. While the perfection of the character's life lies at the heart of the difference between novels and what Benjamin calls "stories," it is also at the heart of what makes novels *feel* like stories while we are caught up in them. Characters are both the gateway into a sharable authored world and a reminder of that world's artificiality, its absolute dependence on the text and the reader's engagement with it. Tolstoy throws these competing faces of mimetic character into relief by trying to split them between two protagonists—one carried undiminished beyond the end of the novel, the other bound up with the bounded act of reading. Tolstoy's own metaphor, the systematic "linkage" reflected in the mimetic integrity of his protagonists, predicts that this separation will fail. His identity as a spiritual and social teacher provided a surer platform for the synthesis of narrative and message.

Tolstoy's later fiction, accordingly, reflects a concerted effort to bypass the inward face of the character's mimetic life, an aesthetic program first and most clearly laid out in "The Death of Ivan Ilyich" ("Smert' Ivana Il'icha," 1886). Ivan Ilyich is dead even before we begin to read; there is no compelling illusion of an open-ended physical presence within his predetermined biography to draw us into the text. Rather, Tolstoy builds his protagonist around the novella's central idea that the self outlasts the body, whether physical or made of words. For a reader who grasps this moral, Ivan Ilyich not only *could* be anybody, but *is*. We read not in order to experience a life that has been shaped or authored to its conclusion but in order to realize that death "is no more," precisely in the sense that it no longer matters whose life death closes off. In turn, Tolstoy's posthumously published *Hadji-Murat* (1912), his last substantial work of fiction, perfects this vision in Hadji-Murat's death scene, which is also an allegorical dismantling of realist characterization itself:

> The wound in the side was fatal, and he felt that he was dying. Memories and images replaced one another with extraordinary swiftness in his imagination. . . . And all these memories ran through his imagination without calling up any feeling in him: no pity, no anger, no desire of any sort. It all seemed so insignificant compared with what was beginning and had already begun for him. But meanwhile his strong body went on doing what had already been

> started . . . what had seemed to them a dead body suddenly stirred. First the bloodied, shaven head, without a papakha, rose, then the body rose, and then, catching hold of a tree, he rose up entirely. He looked so terrible that the men running at him stopped. But he suddenly shuddered, staggered away from the tree, and, like a mowed-down thistle, fell full-length on his face and no longer moved. . . . After that he no longer felt anything, and his enemies trampled and hacked at what no longer had anything in common with him. Ghadi Aga, placing his foot on the back of the body, cut the head off with two strokes, and carefully, so as not to stain his chuviaki with blood, rolled it aside with his foot. Scarlet blood gushed from the neck arteries and black blood from the head, flowing over the grass.[50]

Receiving his mortal wound, Hadji-Murat (unnamed throughout this passage) loses first his memories, images from the story that has just been told; then his body as it gets fragmented into parts; and finally, his capacity for sensation. The elements of narrative being recede until they have nothing more "in common" with Hadji-Murat, leaving impersonal traces (scarlet blood, black blood) just vivid enough to mark his sudden but total narrative absence.[51] If Tolstoy despaired of realist fiction when he found that readers cannot be "infected" with a character carried away from the text, he ended by discovering the next best alternative: how to capture the ineffable process by which a protagonist leaves his body in the text behind.

It was Dostoevsky, however, who more fully embraced the challenge posed at the end of *Anna Karenina*, the goal of writing realist "types" that could (as one scholar puts it) "deepen and strengthen the very fact of individual consciousness and being in Russia."[52]

The first half of Dostoevsky's 1877 *Diary of a Writer*, including his responses to *Anna Karenina*, has long been recognized as a formative ground for ideas and motifs that would become central to *The Brothers Karamazov* (*Bratia Karamazovy*, 1879–80). It has been argued, for example, that the damning portrait of Stiva Oblonsky in the February 1877 *Diary* serves as a rough draft of Ivan Karamazov's devil, and that the extended discussion of Levin and the "Eastern question" in the July/August 1877 installment rehearses Ivan's "rebellion" against the unjust suffering in God's world.[53] Let me carry this line of thought a step further. Whether consciously or unconsciously, Dostoevsky—an avid but dissatisfied reader of *Anna Karenina* throughout its serial publication—*rewrote* the "eccentric" (chudak) Konstantin Levin, his full brother Nikolai Dmitrievich Levin, and his half-brother Sergei Ivanovich Koznyshev as his own "chudak" Alyosha Karamazov, Alyosha's half-brother Dmitri, and his full brother Ivan.

The structural similarities between Levin and his brothers and Dostoevsky's Karamazovs have so far (to my knowledge) escaped commentary.

This is probably because Tolstoy and Dostoevsky put their sets of brothers to such patently different uses. Levin's older full brother Nikolai Dmitrievich at one time lived "like a monk," but he then "fell into company with the most repulsive people and descended into the most wayward debauchery" (84; 18:90). Arrested for beating first a young serf who was his ward, and then his superior in the civil service, Nikolai has become a "lost man"—living with a former prostitute and fatally ill with consumption. He has run through his inheritance and broken with both his brothers, especially his elder half-brother Sergei Ivanovich Koznyshev, a leading Moscow intellectual, with whom he is involved in a bitter legal battle over his share of their mother's inheritance (85; 18:91). Adjusting the lines of kinship brings us close to the opening scenario of *The Brothers Karamazov*: Dmitri Fyodorovich arrives in Skotoprigonevsk to settle a dispute with his father over his mother's inheritance and meets his two half-brothers, the former novice Alyosha and the educated intellectual Ivan. (Notably, Dmitri and Ivan Karamazov are linked to their counterparts in *Anna Karenina* not by name but by patronymic.) Like Nikolai Dmitrievich, Dmitri Fyodorovich is intemperate and violent. He too is involved with a kept woman, and he too causes a scandal by beating the hapless Captain Snegirev, to the outrage of Snegirev's consumptive young son.[54] Like Sergei Ivanovich, Ivan Fyodorovich is a writer and rational thinker, connected to the world of scholarship and science. And like Levin, Alyosha is a chudak and spiritual seeker, poised at the threshold of finding his path in life. Adding, crucially, the repulsive common father who unites them under a single family "breed" and name—and mobilizing Tolstoy's characterizing details as elements of plot—Dostoevsky brought Tolstoy's three brothers from the periphery to the center, and he found in the tensions and affinities among them the foundations of his final novel's narrative.

However, as Dostoevsky's published responses to *Anna Karenina* suggest, more is at stake in this transformation than the chance to mine untapped potentials within the story of Levin and his brothers. I believe that Dostoevsky and Tolstoy also shared the common rhetorical aim of creating around a novel and its characters a durable moral and spiritual community; in Levin's phrase, an "everyone" (*ves' mir*) (19:377) that would last beyond the literal moment of reading. By reimagining Levin, Nikolai, and Koznyshev as Alyosha, Dmitri, and Ivan Karamazov, Dostoevsky implies that similar characters *differently made* can be used to to tell this more vital and urgent kind of story, which would transcend the insularity and "idle wavering" of Tolstoy's Levin as Dostoevsky read him. In Dostoevsky's revision, the three brothers were to provide not the aesthetic framework for a European psychological novel, but the stabilizing matrix for a new Russian myth.

The following chapter will explore this metamorphosis of realist character and characterization in Dostoevsky's final novel, which functioned at once as a rebuke to Tolstoy and as a kind of belated apprenticeship. In *The Brothers Karamazov*, Dostoevsky carried to new heights the experimental mimetic techniques both of Tolstoy's *Anna Karenina* and of his own earlier novels. In this sense, *The Brothers Karamazov* and *Anna Karenina* stand facing one another at the outer limit of narrative mimesis that the Russian realist novel helps expose. Tolstoy's turn away from the novel after writing *Anna Karenina* bears witness to this limit: a realism so fallen into vivid particularity that it resists its longed-for dissolution in the real.

Chapter Four

The Eccentric and the Contemplator: Family Character in *The Brothers Karamazov*

DOSTOEVSKY'S "THE DREAM of a Ridiculous Man: A Fantastic Story" ("Son smeshnogo cheloveka: Fantasticheskii rasskaz"), published in the April 1877 issue of the *Diary of a Writer*, begins from a question that has long been an impetus to narrative: What would it mean to live in paradise? The story's narrator-hero is tempted toward suicide as a false answer to this question. Walking home on the night when he plans to shoot himself, the "Ridiculous Man" is interrupted by an encounter with a crying child, which makes him think about what will happen to everything around him once he is gone: "It seemed clear that life and the world were now as if dependent on me. One might even say that the world was now as if made for me alone: I'd shoot myself and there would be no more world, at least for me."[1] Suicide presents itself to the Ridiculous Man as the ultimate act of self-fashioning, but also as a way of imagining a world ideally built around such a self—a way of weaving the illusion that the world is made "for him alone," if only by solipsistically envisioning its instant disappearance after his death. With this vision in mind, he falls asleep and dreams that he has indeed committed suicide, only to encounter an external author, the "master of all that was happening with me" (328; 25:110). The "master" carries him to a true paradise: a planet Eden made expressly for its inhabitants, the blessed "children of their own sun." At the end of his dream, he corrupts the sun children and cannot restore their innocence. But when he awakens, he has lost the desire to die; he now knows what a genuine harmony between self and world looks like, and he is no longer tempted by the false simulacrum of suicide. His only tragedy lies, he tells us, in his inability to communicate his vision of harmony between self and world: "But how to set up paradise—I don't know, because I'm unable to convey it in words. I lost the words after my dream" (341; 25:118).

In this story, Dostoevsky makes a parable out of the inherent unnarratability of dreams: the Ridiculous Man's vision of paradise cannot be shared, just as any dream becomes impossible to recount upon waking.[2] For similar reasons, this parable can also be read as metafictional. In his dream journey to the new star, the Ridiculous Man glimpses the conditions of his own being as the authored protagonist of a written narrative, woven entirely around him and for the sake of his portrayal. Unlike the Underground Man, he is capable of having faith in such an idyllic condition, but "The Dream of a Ridiculous Man"—no less than *Notes from Underground*—is powerless to extend it beyond the bounds of the narrative itself. The Ridiculous Man already exists within the paradise of having been authored, but the reader finds herself exiled from this Eden as soon as she has finished the story's closing sentence.

In chapter 2, I suggested that Dostoevsky's 1860s–70s fiction dwells increasingly consciously on the gap between novelistic representation as he idealized and indeed practiced it, and the rootlessness and displacement that he saw as the specific condition of his contemporaries and their world. Dostoevsky represented this gap through the trope of illegitimacy. In a sequence of works that begins with *The Idiot* (*Idiot*, 1868) and culminates in *The Adolescent* (*Podrostok*, 1875), he experimented with augmenting what I have called the narrative illegitimacy of his protagonists, who exist ever more distantly from the authority of omniscience. By underscoring this vision of chaos, Dostoevsky constructed a contrasting, utopian vision of mimetic art—a mimesis so renewed that its formative power could reach beyond the bounds of text and fiction.

In the riddling preface to his final novel *The Brothers Karamazov* (*Bratia Karamazovy*, 1879–80), Dostoevsky takes a more direct approach to this complex mimetic project: "the trouble is that I have one biography [*zhizneopisanie*], but two novels. The main novel is the second—that is the activity of my hero already in our time, precisely in our present current moment. The first of the novels took place already thirteen years ago, and it is even almost *not* a novel, but rather just one moment from my hero's first youth."[3] Biographical evidence suggests that Dostoevsky was indeed planning a sequel, in which Alyosha Karamazov might have become a political revolutionary involved in a plot to assassinate the tsar.[4] But his invocation of this sequel in the preface serves a rhetorical purpose as well: it instructs us to receive his retrospective novel's own meticulously structured narrative as a "moment," and to imagine the events of the "present current moment" as the contents of a novel. With this inversion, Dostoevsky lays his cards on the table. Where *The Adolescent* took to its furthest extreme the gap between chaotic contemporary "moment" and idealized "historical novel," in order to imagine a future act of mimesis that could make them converge, *The Brothers Karamazov* asserts from the start that such a convergence is possible. If we can forget the difference between created novel and experienced moment not just while reading, but afterward—living now as if already between the covers of the "second novel"—then *The Brothers Karamazov* will have realized Dostoevsky's vision of a parity between retrospective fiction and contemporary world. The novel (in Lukács's phrase) "comprises the essence of its totality between the beginning and the end" of its protagonist's biography, but Dostoevsky projects this perfection forward into an indefinite future.[5] The space of the novel thus becomes potentially synonymous with the space of the world, and realist technique makes a bid to shape reality.

Unfolding together with the initial introduction of Alyosha as protagonist, this move suggests that Dostoevsky is at once occupying the territory of conventional realist representation, and self-consciously raising its stakes. In the epilogue to *The Adolescent*, Dostoevsky had dismissed Tolstoy's character Levin as a misanthropic eccentric (chudak), who has lost any claim he might have once had to anchor Russia's literary and historical future.[6] He uses the preface to *The Brothers Karamazov* to explain why his own "chudak" protagonist, Alyosha Karamazov, has a better right to the reader's time and attention—why he might "bear within himself the heart of the whole, while the other people of his epoch have all for some reason been torn away from it for a time by some kind of flooding wind" (3; 14:5). As Dostoevsky had argued, both in *The Adolescent* and in the July/August 1877 issue of his *Diary of a Writer*, a nobleman as thoroughly infected as Levin with the habit of Westernized philosophical reasoning was incapable of lighting the way toward a reunification of the Russian people and a restoration of their common spiritual and national roots. So what would it mean to write a different kind of protagonist, who could not just encapsulate but also disseminate the quality that Dostoevsky calls "wholeness"? This challenge pivots on Dostoevsky's extension of the framework of characterization itself into the reader's own time and space—spreading the conditions of aesthetic representation over the field of contemporary life.[7] In other words, it calls for a hybrid between the new realist techniques that Dostoevsky had been developing and the more conventional ones that by the late 1870s, he associated above all with Tolstoy.

The preparatory notebooks for *The Adolescent* are punctuated with admiring invocations of other authors—most frequently, of Pushkin's graceful economy and precision, and of Tolstoy's clarity and gift for physically concrete detail.[8] To be sure, when the theme of realist detail enters into the text of *The Brothers Karamazov* itself, it comes through the derisive lips of Ivan Karamazov's devil: "Listen: in dreams and especially in nightmares, well, let's say as a result of indigestion or whatever, a man sometimes sees such artistic dreams, such complex and real actuality, such events, or even a whole world [*tselyi mir*] of events, woven into such a plot, with such unexpected details, beginning from your highest manifestations down to the last shirt button, as I swear even Leo Tolstoy couldn't write" (639; 15:74).[9] This jibe is in keeping with Dostoevsky's resentment of what he called "landowner literature," but any reader of *The Adolescent*—or for that matter, "The Dream of a Ridiculous Man"—should at the same time detect a note of envy. Anxious as Dostoevsky was to prove (as he put it in a famous 1868 letter to Apollon Maikov) that "our idealism is realer than their [realism]" (28.II:329), he was just as eager to recapture the vividly realized solidity that he believed permeates the historical novel and eludes the contemporary one. Could the reader's own "present current moment" be ensconced within the kind of "artistic dream" that Ivan's devil invokes—compelling enough to let Ivan believe in the devil and so also in God?

In pursuit of this goal, Dostoevsky developed a different set of mimetic techniques for *The Brothers Karamazov* than he had used in any of his earlier novels. The most basic difference lies in his construction of his novel's character-system around a family whose very name stands—as the Rostovs and Bolkonskys stand in *War and Peace*—for the foundational force of life itself. Elaborating this centripetal system with Tolstoyan rigor, Dostoevsky worked at the same time to give it a new flexibility and openness—to hollow out a space within his evocation of life for the reader to inhabit, and to give this space of mimetic characterization an outline that she might carry with her even after the book is closed.

Although the aesthetic form of the novel stands behind this dream, the novel's conventional limitations *as* bounded aesthetic experience pose an obstacle to its realization. This paradox motivates a final twist in Dostoevsky's use of the trope of illegitimacy (as discussed in chapter 2)—now applied not to his own genre-challenging novels but to the limits of the novel genre itself, which he hoped they might overcome.

With the composition of his novel around the Karamazov family and the "breed force" of Karamazovism, Dostoevsky set out to endow his own rootless characters with the fleshy stability of a Tolstoyan realist hero, without sacrificing their special claim to address the contemporary reader and to represent his world.[10] I will suggest that throughout the narrative, the suppression of Fyodor Pavlovich Karamazov's probable illegitimate fourth son, Smerdyakov, helps compensate for Dostoevsky's shift back toward more conventional techniques of realist characterization. Unable to do away with the bounds of the character-system in which realist characterizations most effectively unfold, Dostoevsky both concealed and reviled them in the figure of the shadow Karamazov brother Smerdyakov—without whom, nevertheless, the novel's mimetic and narrative architecture would collapse. Now using rather than deconstructing the realist novel's established resources for mimetic characterization, he tried to finesse the separation that they make inevitable—the difference between the realist novel's intentionally created dream world and the chaotically unauthored nature of reality.

By this point, it will come as no surprise that I argue this project remains incomplete. Nevertheless, *The Brothers Karamazov* shows—perhaps more clearly than any of Dostoevsky's other novels—how the encounter with a system of "living" characters gives way to the captivating experience of a set of ideas. Harnessing realism's rhetorical potential, Dostoevsky broke ground for later *theories* of the novel that would extend his own vision of transformational reading, beyond the aesthetic limits of which he himself remained keenly aware.

"YOUR WHOLE KARAMAZOV QUESTION": "KARAMAZOVISM" AND THE SPACE OF THE PROTAGONIST

For all the weighty problems it raises—of God and the good, the individual and the state, immortality and damnation—the plot of *The Brothers Karamazov* coheres around a surprisingly simple question: who gets to be a Karamazov? It turns on three possible marriages and a probable but unacknowledged illegitimate son's patricide. Even characters who are not trying to become Karamazovs are most often found talking about them, courting their favor, or envying them—conscious of being placed (as the narrator says of the Karamazovs' cousin by marriage Pyotr Alexandrovich Miusov) "evidently in the background [vidimo na vtorom plane]" (59; 14:55). The adjective Karamazovian (*karamazovskii*) itself designates one of the novel's basic (mostly negative) moral categories. The acerbic seminarian Misha Rakitin defines it most succinctly: "Your whole Karamazov question [ves' vash Karamazovskii vopros] comes down to this: sensualists, acquirers, and holy fools!" (80; 14:75).

What Rakitin calls the "Karamazov question" permeates Dostoevsky's novel from the center outward, anchoring a character-system in which narrative "space" and thematic architecture are obsessively aligned. Robert Belknap summarizes the thematic side of this system in his classic study *The Structure of "The Brothers Karamazov,"* where he posits two axes that define ways of believing and behaving throughout the novel (see fig. 1). The vertical ("metaphysical") axis extends from the nihilism and sensuous cruelty associated with Ivan's devil, up to the active love for other people and for God's world associated with Alyosha's revered elder Zosima. The horizontal ("existential") axis reaches from "buffoonery" and overblown shame at one end, to "strain" (*nadryv*) and excessive pride on the other. "Karamazovism" (*karamazovshchina*), in turn, becomes the novel's shorthand for all of these attributes—encompassing in its broadness both vileness and pride, sensuality and intellectual hunger, holy-foolishness and the spirit of political revolt, the thirst for life and the attraction to suicide.[11] Thus, on a Cartesian graph of

Fig. 1. Components of "Karamazovism"

this character-system as Belknap describes it, protagonicity would appear as both a narrative and a spiritual condition. The word "Karamazovism" characterizes the novel's protagonists, but it also defines existential and moral axes along which all its characters can be placed.

The close uniformity of this character-system—at once centered on the story of the Karamazovs and circumscribed by their traits—is clear at every juncture of the narrative, which rarely strays from scenes in which at least one Karamazov is present. Thus, the novel's constellation of prominent female characters (three young and one old) mirrors the central configuration of Karamazovs, and each reflects and recombines the traits of the individual Karamazov(s) with whom she is entangled.[12] Katerina Ivanovna blends Dmitri's (Mitya's) romanticism with Ivan's pride; Grushenka, Fyodor Pavlovich's erotic sensuality with Mitya's motif of folk religion. Lise Khokhlakova's laughter ties her sometimes to Alyosha's angelic gaiety and sometimes to Ivan's demonic wickedness, while her mother's absurd loquacity echoes the weightier buffoonery of Fyodor Pavlovich. Similarly, the trajectories of many minor male characters recombine the narrative possibilities available to the Karamazovs: the schoolboy Kolya Krasotkin's budding atheism, Pyotr Kalganov's projected marriage to Lise, Zosima's visitor's narrow escape from committing a second murder. As full as the novel is of fictional people, they all stand in necessary relation to Karamazovism and the Karamazovs, and few of their stories do not lead back toward the Karamazovs in the end.[13] At the novel's margins, this closure can become claustrophobic: in *The Adolescent*, characters continually slide out from under their designated names and traits, but in *The Brothers Karamazov*, names and situations return with uncanny persistence. Nazar Ivanovich, Grushenka's porter, forgets to tell his nephew Prokhor not to let Mitya into her house, and several hundred pages later Prokhor Ivanovich Nazaryev has been reabsorbed into the Karamazovs' plot, as a juror at Mitya's trial. Lizaveta Smerdyashchaya runs away from the widow Kondratiev's house to give birth to Smerdyakov in Fyodor Pavlovich's garden, and Smerdyakov later takes up with Maria Kondratievna, the daughter of Fyodor Pavlovich's impoverished next-door neighbor. In turn, the "lengthy train" (literally tail, *khvost*) of Maria Kondratievna's incongruously grand dress (102, 224, 226; 14:95, 14:204, 14:206) echoes the "fat tail" (*khvostishche*) of the demon glimpsed by Father Ferapont (169; 14:153), as well as the "little tails" (*khvostiki*) of the neurons that Mitya fears will replace the idea of the immortal soul (589; 15:28).[14] In this way, even the most minor of characters gets integrated into the novel's all-encompassing symbolic system.

The Brothers Karamazov thus takes place within a fictional world whose structure and mimetic resources are both dominated and circumscribed by the unfolding representation of its protagonists. Here Dostoevsky uses, and indeed intensifies, the correspondence between the size of a character's narrative "space" and the strength of the illusion that makes him seem to be an autonomous, conscious, and embodied person. Whether as "sensualists" (the narrator's and Rakitin's word) or as "insects" (Mitya's), the Karamazovs are united under what Ivan calls their "thirst" for earthly life:

> True, it's a feature of the Karamazovs, to some extent, this thirst for life despite all; it must be sitting in you, too; but why is it base [*podlaia*]? There is still an awful lot of centripetal force on our planet, Alyosha. I want to live, and I do live, even if it be against logic. Maybe I don't believe in the order of things, but the sticky little leaves that tumble out in the spring are dear to me. (230)[15]

"Living" and loving life become part of the definition of the family name at the novel's center. The Karamazovs' defining scenes are linked, in turn, with a sensuous experience of bodies and things that readers have seldom associated with Dostoevsky's writing, here moved into prominent focus. Fyodor Pavlovich holds court "over the cognac," and Mitya is tempted toward murder by the sight of his repulsively prominent Adam's apple; undressing for the investigators later on, Mitya is humiliated by his own "crude, flat, somehow curved-under toenail" (484; 14:435). Ivan orders fish soup and cherry jam for Alyosha before declaiming his "rebellion," and "the sticky little leaves that tumble out in the spring" are a repeated metonym for the earthly joy that holds him back from suicide. Constructed around a quality that also implies a set of literary techniques, the name "Karamazov" both places a thinking, feeling sensuality at the novel's center and formalizes the criteria for fullest participation in this central lived sensuality, encapsulating these criteria in a single name. As with the Rostovs in *War and Peace*, being a

Karamazov is associated with living "life" within *The Brothers Karamazov*, with vividness and amplitude of representation. But unlike *War and Peace*, which grows almost too large for its central families to anchor, *The Brothers Karamazov* is unremittingly focused on the small central group of the Karamazov family.

At the same time, Karamazovism is not only a stable mimetic and thematic anchor for the novel's narrative. It is also (in Rakitin's word) a "question"—the kind of question that could not be framed around the Rostovs or Oblonskys. The quality of Karamazovism is given, in the sense that characters who are not Karamazovs can only reflect it more palely than those who are. However, the breadth of this quality throws its consequences—for character, if not for mimetic characterization—into doubt. Tolstoy presents breed force as a destiny; Dostoevsky, as a challenge, a fixed range within which each Karamazov has the capacity to define himself. The fictional effect of sensuous life now also encompasses an illusion of the autonomy to determine what this life will mean.

The interdependent elements of Dostoevskian characterization—the framework of omniscient authorship and the framework of characterological "autonomy"—stand in especially delicate balance in *The Brothers Karamazov*, precisely because of Dostoevsky's reliance on the realist effects that a strongly centralized and vividly present character-system makes possible. In his radical previous novel *The Adolescent*, which sabotages the very foundations of a character-system, Dostoevsky embraced a swing toward disorder and illegitimacy that creates space for a utopian vision of what the ordered mimesis of a future novel might achieve. In *The Brothers Karamazov*, Dostoevsky's visible organization of the novel around the "living" Karamazov family at its center courts the opposite risk. The presence of this character-system threatens to become overbearing, subjecting the text to the felt aesthetic limits of any realist novel. Dostoevsky's technical innovations in his last novel aim to create a space within authoritative realist characterization where the character can nevertheless seem to slide out from under the narrative's defining word. This drama—the characters' negotiation with the identity imposed by the name "Karamazov," set within the illusion of autonomous physical life that this name carries with it—employs the tools of realist characterization against the limits of the novel genre itself.

Read in this light, *The Brothers Karamazov* has both a speaking and a silent plot.[16] Alongside the dialogues, actions, and collisions *among* characters in the novel's fictional world, Dostoevsky stages an encounter *within* each protagonist between name and still-indefinite self, between a "Karamazov" as seen from the outside and an "I" as seen from within. Rakitin gleefully draws attention to this equivocation: "You, Alyoshka, are the quiet type [*tikhonia*], you're a saint, I admit; but you're the quiet type, and the devil knows what hasn't gone through your head. . . . You are a Karamazov yourself, a full-fledged Karamazov—so race and selection do mean something. You're a sensualist after your father, and after your mother—a holy fool" (80; 14:74). In a later conversation with Dmitri, Alyosha imagines the distance between "sensualist" and "holy fool" as a ladder on which each Karamazov must find his position:

> "The steps are all the same. I'm on the lowest, and you are above, somewhere on the thirteenth. . . . Whoever steps on the lowest step will surely step on the highest."
>
> "So one had better not step at all."
>
> "Not if one can help it."
>
> "Can you?"
>
> "It seems not."
>
> "Quiet [*Molchi*], Alyosha, quiet, my dear, I want to kiss your hand, so, just out of tenderness. That rogue Grushenka has an eye for men; she once told me she'd eat you up some day. I'll be quiet, I'll be quiet! (110)[17]

Silence is a prerequisite for the character's steps along this ladder, which leads onto the inner stage where the drama of Karamazovism itself is set. If (in Alex Woloch's terms) the "character-space" of a Jane Austen protagonist is the portion of the narrative that constructs and gives play to her implied human personality, then *The Brothers Karamazov* turns the "space" of its protagonists inside out.[18] It focuses not on the character defined within a narrative space, but on the process of definition that occurs within the space accorded to some central characters.

One technical problem that confronts Dostoevsky in *The Brothers Karamazov*, then, is how the space of characterization can be represented as a landscape, available both for the author to shape and for the reader to inhabit. As Dostoevsky had found in *The Adolescent*, creating this space by having the contemporary character narrate his own formation destabilizes the basis for characterization itself. But it is clearly not enough to suggest—the move already perfected in *Notes from Underground*—that a fluid, indefinite fictional self is writhing on the hook of particular characterizing traits and utterances. This strategy results in its own kind of dead end, on display in the first extended portrait of Fyodor Pavlovich Karamazov:

> I have already mentioned that he had gone very flabby and fat. His physiognomy by that time presented something testifying acutely to the characteristics and essence of the whole life he had lived. Besides the long, fleshy bags under his eternally insolent, suspicious, and leering little eyes, besides the multitude of deep wrinkles on his fat little face, a big Adam's apple, fleshy and oblong like a purse, hung below his sharp chin, giving him a sort of repulsively sensual appearance. Add to that a long, carnivorous mouth with plump

> lips, behind which could be seen the little stumps of black, almost decayed teeth. He sprayed saliva whenever he spoke. However, even he himself liked to make jokes about his face, although he was apparently pleased with it. He pointed especially to his nose, which was not very big but was very thin and noticeably hooked. "A real Roman one," he used to say. (23)[19]

The narrator is fully aware of deploying the conventions of realism: as surely here as in Balzac or Dickens, Fyodor Pavlovich's "physiognomy . . . presented something testifying acutely to the characteristics and essence of the whole life he had lived."[20] The character, who "liked to make jokes about his face, although he was apparently pleased with it," is just as well positioned to deconstruct these realist conventions. Such moments in Fyodor Pavlovich's portrayal imply a self determined to escape its own "physiognomy." But for an underground Dostoevskian character like Fyodor Pavlovich, there is no intermediate narrative space in which the representation of that self could develop or unfold—in which steps up or down the "ladder" of Karamazovism could become a subject for narration. Any potential narrative of Fyodor Pavlovich's formation is frustrated by the rigidity of the narrator's portrait on one end and the character's resistance to definition on the other.

Before Dostoevsky can represent the three-part *Bildung* set in motion by Fyodor Pavlovich's murder, he thus has to write a narratable space into the Karamazov brothers as protagonists. In his recent study, Yuri Corrigan traces a "perilous journey inward" through *The Brothers Karamazov*, looking at how a transformative dream allows each brother to begin forging the interior space of the self or personality.[21] I will focus on how the same process becomes a model of literary character formation, undergirding the renewal of realist narrative in which Dostoevsky places his mimetic and mathetic hopes. The explosive question that Mitya asks about Fyodor Pavlovich—"Why is such a man alive? [Zachem zhivet takoi chelovek?]" (74; 14:69)—is a provocation addressed not just to the novel's other characters but to the narrative itself. What is the mimetic life of a Dostoevskian character for? Alyosha Karamazov's trajectory through the first half of the novel marks out an initial answer to this question.

"AS FIRM AND IMMOVABLE AS THIS HEAVENLY VAULT": THE MAKING OF AN IDEA-HERO IN *THE BROTHERS KARAMAZOV*

We can better understand the problem of narrating the silent drama of Karamazovism by linking it to Dostoevsky's affinity for the rhetorical trope of apophasis—telling by denying or by claiming it is unnecessary to tell—and its theological counterpart—the idea of coming to know God by denying that anything can be known about him, and describing him by naming what he is not.[22] Recent studies argue that apophatic narrative devices, often in the mouths of untrustworthy or incompetent narrators, indicate Dostoevsky's "basic distrust in the capacity of the word to express a person's essence" and his orientation on the nonverbal image of the divine.[23] The question of how to construct a silent landscape of character formation through verbal narrative—averting both the determinism of "physiognomy" and the shapelessness of infinite dialogue—is related to the question of how to wrest a true image from inherently misleading language or speech. This struggle coheres around Alyosha Karamazov, who begins as the novel's least definite and quietest protagonist.

From the first, the narrator-chronicler describes Alyosha in negative terms:

> In his childhood and youth he was not effusive, not even talkative, but not from distrust, not from shyness or sullen unsociability (even quite the opposite), but from something different, from some inner preoccupation, as it were, strictly personal, of no concern to others, but so important for him that because of it he would, as it were, forget others. But he did love people. . . . There was something in him that told one, that convinced one (and it was so all his life afterwards) that he did not want to be a judge of men, that he would not take judgment upon himself and would not condemn anyone for anything. (19)[24]

Alyosha is remarkable for his quiet pensiveness (the source of which is hidden) and for his reluctance to judge, formulated in three separate negative constructions. He has the gift of "awakening a special love for himself" as a reaction to his presence, with no positive action on his part. At school, he does not show off in front of his classmates; does not fear anyone, and never takes pride in his own fearlessness; does not remember or even take account of offenses; and covers his ears against classmates' lascivious talk, "not saying a word to them, not abusing them, silently bearing the offense" (20; 14:20). Nor does he audibly respond to what turns out to be the initial object of his visit to Skotoprigonevsk, his mother's grave.

Throughout the first half of the novel, Alyosha's silence becomes the ground for kinship with the reader. We follow him from scene to scene, often as he carries messages from one character to another, and the narrator's intermittent attention to him weaves his thoughts into the fabric of this narrative. But like us, he spends most of this time listening. His spoken lines are remarkable for their brevity; other characters talk to him or for his benefit, but he does not perform for them in return. Though the narrator often says that Alyosha has vividly relayed events to someone who did not see them, he summarizes Alyosha's accounts rather than quoting them. When Alyosha is most deeply touched by what he has heard from others, he responds in pantomime—as when he falls to the floor after Fyodor Pavlovich tells him about his mother the "shrieker" or kisses Ivan at the end of "The Grand Inquisitor." At key points when he does try to use words, they betray him, as when he stammers through his revelation about Katerina Ivanovna's strained love for Ivan (191–92; 14:174).[25]

Alyosha's opening narrative thus continues in the same line as the preface "From the Author," drawing us to him as "hero" on the strength of what he *refrains* from doing, or promises but has not yet done. This reluctance either to describe Alyosha or to have him speak leads us to expect a mimetic illusion that relies on neither of these techniques; at the same time, the filling up of Alyosha's silence with other characters' speech creates the implicit drama of his story. How will he be shaped by the onslaught of other characters' counsels, examples, and provocations—and how will the narrative carve out a space for the story of that formation? The question of Alyosha's characterization is an extension of the question posed by Karamazovism itself: is there a range of end points toward which sensuous and speaking "life" in this novel can lead? Again, where is the middle ground between finalizing description and endless dialogue?

The novel's commitment to discovering that mimetic middle ground is never seriously in doubt. The point where Zosima's devotion and Ivan's rebellion meet is their felt delight in living materiality: Zosima's exhortation to "love everything and grasp God's mystery in *things*" (319; 14:289) and Ivan's exultation in "the sticky little leaves that tumble out in the spring" (230; 14:209). In this context, the realist novelist's ability to evoke living sensuous solidity in contemporary fictional "types" becomes its own article of faith.[26] The crisis that begins for Alyosha with the decay and stink of Father Zosima's body, marked by the reverse Eucharist of Rakitin's sausage and vodka, sets the stage for the resurrection of realist characterization itself.

The sudden intrusions of the novel's first-person narrator create the crucial background for this renewal:

> Here again I will add, speaking for myself personally, that I find it almost loathsome to recall this frivolous and tempting occurrence [the decay of Zosima's body], essentially quite insignificant and natural, and I would, of course, omit all mention of it from my story, if it had not influenced in the strongest and most definite way the soul and heart of the main, *though future*, hero of my story, Alyosha, causing, as it were, a crisis and upheaval in his soul, which shook his mind but also ultimately strengthened it for the whole of his life, and towards a definite purpose. (329)

And then,

> I shall frankly admit that it would be very difficult for me now to convey clearly the precise meaning of this strange and uncertain moment in the life of the hero of my story, whom I love so much and who is still so young. To the rueful question Father Paissy addressed to Alyosha . . . I could, of course, answer firmly for Alyosha: "No, he is not with those of little faith." (338)[27]

In his eagerness to "answer for" Alyosha and explain his apparent lapse of faith, the narrator takes on the voice of a hagiographic chronicler.[28] These outbursts separate the narrator as an embodied chronicler from the words that produce the novel itself. One reason why the narrator thickens into visibility and personalized "voice" when launching the story of Alyosha's crisis is so that later, in his apparent absence, the act of narration can seem to become transparent, beyond language. The invisible authority of realist world making takes over from the marked act of "chronicling" as soon as the narrator appears to exit the novel's stage.

At first, Dostoevsky uses this world-making authority for the essentially familiar modes of dialogue and free indirect discourse. Alyosha marvels at Grushenka's folk parable of the onion and her redemptive capacity to forgive in an uncharacteristically long and eloquent speech, surprising Rakitin, "who had never expected such a tirade from the quiet Alyosha" (355; 14:322). And yet, to play out Alyosha's salvation in dialogue is not enough. The flood of speech exchanged between Alyosha and Grushenka is followed by another scene conducted almost entirely in silence: Alyosha's dream, which mingles with the parable of the wedding at Cana being read over Zosima's body, followed by the vision that he has after leaving Zosima's cell.

As Alyosha listens to the biblical reading, on the threshold between sleep and waking, his reverie is represented in the form of a virtual cosmos: "shards of thoughts flashed in [Alyosha's] soul, ignited like small stars, and immediately burnt out, replaced by others" (359; 14:325). When he leaves the cell, this metaphor for his fragmentary private thoughts swells to the proportions of the novel's own fictional landscape:

> Over him the heavenly dome, full of quiet, shining stars, hung boundlessly. From the zenith to the horizon the still-dim Milky Way stretched its double strand. . . . The silence of the earth seemed to merge with the silence of the heavens, the mystery of the earth touched the mystery of the stars . . . Alyosha stood gazing and suddenly, as if he had been cut down, threw himself to the earth. He did not know why he was embracing it, he did not try to understand why he longed so irresistibly to kiss it, to kiss all of it, but he was kissing it, weeping, sobbing, and watering it with his tears, and he vowed ecstatically

> to love it, to love it unto ages of ages. "Water the earth with the tears of your joy, and love those tears . . . ," rang in his soul. What was he weeping for? Oh, in his rapture he wept even for the stars that shone on him from the abyss, and "he was not ashamed of this ecstasy." It was as if threads from all those innumerable worlds of God all came together in his soul, and it was trembling all over, "touching other worlds." He wanted to forgive everyone and for everything, and to ask forgiveness, oh! not for himself! but for all and for everything, "as others are asking for me," rang again in his soul. But with each moment he felt clearly and almost tangibly something as firm and immovable as this heavenly vault descend into his soul. Some sort of idea, as it were, was coming to reign in his mind—now for the whole of his life and unto ages of ages. (362–63; second and third ellipses in original)[29]

In this passage, Zosima's quoted speech intersects anonymously with Alyosha's and with the narrator's about him, all gathered into Alyosha's "own" consciousness like the "threads from all those innumerable worlds of God." Many of Dostoevsky's works (from *The Double* on) rely on the technique of spreading out the protagonist's consciousness as a populated landscape, his fears and desires embodied in the form of separate characters who act in their own right in the fictional world, and whom all the other characters can see. Alyosha's vision pointedly reverses this technique—not dissolving the character's mind into a represented landscape but enfolding a landscape into the representation of the character's own mind.

Here, then, is what it means in practice to balance the "contemporary" realism that Dostoevsky saw as his unique representational territory with the "historical" realism that he had come to associate with his rival Tolstoy. The heavenly "vault" (*svod*) that becomes a visible sign of conversion may have reminded Dostoevsky's readers of a climactic moment at the end of Tolstoy's *Anna Karenina*, first published over two years earlier in summer 1877: "Lying on his back, [Levin] was now looking at the high, cloudless sky. 'Don't I know that this is infinite space and not a round vault? But no matter how I squint and strain my sight, I cannot help seeing if as round and limited, and despite my knowledge of infinite space, I am undoubtedly right when I see a firm blue vault, more right than when I strain to see beyond it. . . . Can this be faith?' he wondered, afraid to believe his happiness."[30] But where the vault remains outside and above Levin, here it "descends" into the private boundaries of Alyosha's "soul"—which in turn takes on, for a moment, the expansive concreteness of a realist fictional world.

It has been observed that Alyosha's embrace of the earth both takes the place of the sexual encounter with Grushenka that he escapes, and represents an unexpectedly sacred moment of intercourse with the "earthen force of the Karamazovs" (220; 14:201), which he has inherited from his father.[31]

The resulting birth is equally significant: "some sort of idea, as it were, was coming to reign in his mind." With this awakening to his own idea, Alyosha learns to speak the language of a Dostoevskian protagonist. His collision with his Karamazovian love for earthly life is at the same time a collision with his own centrality: a scene that allows us to watch the steps by which he is constructed as an autonomous ideological voice. After this epiphany, neither Alyosha's receptive silence nor his mirroring gestures are available to invite and crystallize the ideas of other characters, and he is no longer the primary internal focalizer for the novel's key scenes. The space of Alyosha's silence, widened in the novel's first half to encompass a number of worldviews, closes once it has served to model the process by which an idea-hero comes to be.

The idea that takes possession of Alyosha remains unspecified, although both Zosima's teachings as conveyed by Alyosha, and the advice that Alyosha offers other characters after Zosima's death, point toward its content. Alyosha begins to articulate this idea only in the novel's final pages, in his speech to the boys at Ilyusha's grave, where he describes a unifying resurrection that will mirror the meeting of "God's worlds" that he himself has experienced:

> You all are dear to me, gentlemen, from now on I shall keep you all in my heart, and I ask you to keep me in your hearts, too! Well, and who has united us in this good, kind feeling, which we will remember and intend to remember always, all our lives, who, if not Ilyushechka. . . . Let us never forget him, and may his memory be eternal and good in our hearts now and unto ages and ages! . . . "Karamazov!" cried Kolya, "can it really be true as religion says, that we shall all rise from the dead, and come to life, and see one another again, and everyone, and Ilyushechka?"
>
> "Certainly we shall rise, certainly we shall see and gladly, joyfully tell one another all that has been," Alyosha replied, half laughing, half in ecstasy. (775–76)[32]

In Alyosha's vision, his and the boys' hearts open, as Alyosha's soul did when he kissed the ground outside the monastery, to provide the space in which a reunion of the living and the dead could be imagined. There is a long gap between the dedication of Alyosha's "voice" to this ideal of resurrection and the speech in which he first articulates it fully.[33] But Dostoevsky's experiment with forging dialogic characterization from silence has already done the work of modeling the resurrected *realism* in which the story of Alyosha's "idea" could be told—a story centered on a fully and sensuously realized character, who offers at the same time an outline for the reader to inhabit. Through Alyosha, an ideally typical character, Dostoevsky projects the framework of authored personhood forward into the time and space of the reader herself.

"A SCOUNDREL, BUT NOT A THIEF, NOT A THIEF, ANYTHING YOU LIKE, BUT NOT A THIEF"—"IT WAS *NOT YOU* WHO KILLED FATHER": DMITRI, IVAN, AND THE HABITABLE SPACE OF THE IDEA-HERO

The Brothers Karamazov ends with a virtuosic exercise in realist illusion—four chapters "excerpted" from the prosecution's speech at Dmitri Karamazov's trial and four from the defense, offering characterizations of the novel's protagonists that we identify as false by comparing them with the "true" and "living" characters constructed in the rest of the novel. It is telling that Ippolit Kirillovich, the prosecutor, and Fetyukovich, the defense lawyer, make up only one complete proper name between them. Their opposed logic marks (among other things) the distorting extremes of two possible flawed approaches to characterization. Ippolit Kirillovich offers his portrait as if it were the only possible verbal likeness of Mitya, and Fetyukovich offers a multitude of "novels" about Mitya and the crime to show that no such likeness is definitive. Dostoevsky relies on the novel's peculiar generic authority to suggest that these approaches are equally wrong. There is exactly one verbal likeness of each Karamazov, and it unfolds in the novelistic space of mimetic life, a middle ground between direct and indirect characterization that only fictional world making can underwrite.[34] Fetyukovich invokes the novel's ability to "create a person" (*litso*) (731–32; 15:158–59), but because he is speaking in court and not writing a novel, he cannot mimic it.

In order to differentiate the novel's own way of characterizing from Ippolit Kirillovich's or Fetyukovich's, Dostoevsky mobilizes the techniques for making the space of formation tangible that he has developed throughout Alyosha's narrative in the first half of the novel. Can all the protagonists of *The Brothers Karamazov* occupy such landscapes of formation—so that these landscapes become indivisible from the space of realist protagonicity itself? In Alyosha's case, this task is easier, because he begins from negative (apophatic) description and silence, to arrive at a defining idea and "voice." Dmitri and Ivan, by contrast, are each tied up from the beginning of the novel with self-conscious images of who and what they are.

To create the fictional landscape in which formation can become a perceptible process, Dostoevsky thus begins by tearing open a gap between Dmitri's and Ivan's visions of their own identities, and the "actual" selves that the events of the plot begin to expose. In their cases as in Alyosha's, characterization involves an ordeal of negotiation with the meaning and implications of the name Karamazov. Forced to acknowledge their participation in crimes that they resist not just in personal but in family terms, Mitya and Ivan are temporarily emptied of the narrated identity contained in their family name, the set of traits associated with being a Karamazov. The forced moment of dissociation from that identity clears the path to the inner stage on which the drama of formation takes place.

From his first extended monologue, Dmitri embraces the seemingly infinite "broadness" of Karamazovism, which lets him plummet "head up and heels down into the abyss" of depravity, and from its very depths "begin a hymn" to divine beauty: "Let me be cursed, let me be base and vile [*podl*], but let me also kiss the hem of that garment in which my God is clothed" (107; 14:99). However, he makes a distinction between his vital and broad Karamazovian vileness and a type of crime that lies outside its parameters: "I tell you, Alexei: I can be a mean man [*nizkim chelovekom*], with passions mean and ruinous, but a thief, a pickpocket, a pilferer, that Dmitri Karamazov can never be!" (119; 14:110). Although he implies to Alyosha that he has stolen the three thousand rubles that he was meant to forward on Katerina Ivanovna's behalf, in fact he has kept half the money, sewing it up in a rag that he keeps around his neck "in place of an amulet" (490; 14:441).

As one recent reading has emphasized, Mitya's "amulet" becomes a concrete symbol for the indeterminate moral potentiality at the center of his story: if he returns the fifteen hundred rubles to Katerina Ivanovna, he is "a scoundrel [*podlets*], but not a thief, not a thief, anything you like, but not a thief" (492; 14:443).[35] However, it is equally true that the amulet preserves the stable identity to which he clings: "Dmitri Karamazov can never be" a thief—so if he is not yet a thief, then it is still possible for him to be "Dmitri Karamazov." His peculiar later exchange with the civil servant Pyotr Ilyich Perkhotin points to this fissure, a disconnect between the act of theft and the very foundation of Mitya's sense of himself:

> "Incidentally, Pyotr Ilyich, I wanted to ask you: have you ever stolen anything in your life? . . . From someone's pocket, you see, someone else's property? . . . someone else's property: right from their pocket or purse, eh?"
>
> "I once stole twenty kopecks from my mother, from the table, when I was nine years old. Took it on the sly and clutched it in my fist."
>
> "And then what?"
>
> "Then nothing. I kept it for three days, felt ashamed, confessed, and gave it back."
>
> "And then what?
>
> "Naturally I got a whipping. Why, you haven't stolen anything, have you?"
>
> "I have," Mitya winked slyly.
>
> "What have you stolen?" Pyotr Ilyich became curious.
>
> "Twenty kopecks from my mother, when I was nine, I gave it back in three days." Having said this, Mitya suddenly rose from his seat. (407; 14:367)

Mitya admits to his theft only by sliding away from it, adopting the narrative of a different thief. This dialogue reproduces the split between "I" and "Dmitri Karamazov" that appears already in his declaration to Alyosha—if "I" am a thief, then "I" cannot be Dmitri Karamazov. To acknowledge his theft of Katerina Ivanovna's money would be to lose his identity and name.

This moment of reckoning is the climax of Mitya's confession to the prosecutors, who do not recognize its genuine weight. Pressed to explain what was wrong with keeping back half of Katerina Ivanovna's money inside the amulet, Dmitri at last identifies his crime:

> That I stole, that's what! Oh, God, you horrify me with your lack of understanding! All the while I carried that fifteen hundred sewn up on my chest, I kept saying to myself every day and every hour: "You are a thief, you are a thief!" . . . But know that all the while I carried it, every day and every hour, I kept saying to myself at the same time: "No, Dmitri Fyodorovich, perhaps you're not yet a thief." And only yesterday did I decide to tear the amulet off my neck . . . and as soon as I tore it off, at that moment I became a final and inarguable thief, a thief and a dishonest man for the rest of my life. Why? Because along with the amulet, I also tore up [*razorval*] my dream of going to Katya and saying: "I am a scoundrel, but not a thief [podlets, a ne vor]!" (493–94)[36]

Mitya's later complaint emphasizes the depth of this split: "I have, so to speak, torn my soul in half [razorval popolam] before you, and you take advantage of it and go rummaging with your fingers in both halves of the torn spot" (496; 14:446). Having defined "Dmitri Karamazov" as "a scoundrel, but not a thief," by admitting to his theft he tears *himself* in two—becoming an "I" who can no longer be "Dmitri Karamazov."

Like the silence that lays Alyosha open to "threads from all of God's innumerable worlds," this fissure makes a space for Mitya's dream of the "wee one" (*dityo*), the vision that allows him to accept his undeserved suffering when he is later convicted of his father's murder. The white, black, and brown steppe sketched in his dream gives a tangible landscape to Mitya's temporary absence of identity. Unfolding in between the moment when Mitya gives his statement and the moment when he signs the transcript with his own name, the dream creates a vacant site for the slow rebirth that follows his arrest for Smerdyakov's crime. In his own words, "a new man has resurrected in me" (591; 15:30).

The resolution of Mitya's spiritual ordeal, like that of Alyosha's, thus depends on a new set of techniques: no longer either the Dostoevskian dispersal nor the Tolstoyan reflection of the character's interiority in fictional space, but the reconstruction of interiority as an outline that both character and reader can occupy. Through Mitya's "torments" and dream, he becomes a concrete realist character with something of a mythical archetype's inhabitable abstraction. Although he returns, when he answers the charges at his trial, to his old formula—"Dmitri Karamazov is a scoundrel, but not a thief!" (660; 15:94)—he has accepted the label of "thief" (and therefore, not–Dmitri Karamazov) for long enough to open a gap for conversion. The two poles encompassed in Karamazovism span the vertical range from damnation to salvation, but only through Mitya's temporary exile from his own Karamazovian nature can the reader follow him as he begins to travel from one to the other.

The vertical "broadness" of Mitya's Karamazovism finds an answer in the infectious dispersal of Ivan's. Figured in biblical terms as a "puff of dust" (175; 14:159), his character spreads outward through the idea that "everything is permitted," a distillation of the sensuous egoism that governs Fyodor Pavlovich Karamazov's life.[37] But like Mitya, Ivan takes refuge in the Karamazovian moral category of vileness (*podlost'*) to avoid association with Smerdyakov's crimes of murder and theft: "in the inmost part of his soul," he understands his silent acquiescence to Smerdyakov's intentions as "the vilest [*samym podlym*] action of his whole life," and after reporting to Smerdyakov that he is leaving for Chermashnya, he whispers to himself, "I am a scoundrel [Ia podlets]" (276; 14:251 and 280; 14:255). Here as with Mitya, the split between Karamazovian "scoundrel" (*podlets*) and Smerdyakovian "murderer" sets the stage for the lapse of identity that will occur when Ivan at last realizes that he may be "a murderer too" (617; 15:54). This contained gap in characterization transposes the story's spiritual stakes onto the level of discourse, and thus of the relationship between novel and reader. Dostoevsky asks how absorption in the biography of a realist character dissociated from his own specificity—the protagonist (Karamazov) who can be temporarily stripped of his given identity (Karamazovism)—might open up new possibilities for the reader's transformation.

This framework helps account for a mystifying lapse in the novel's religious and ethical message of shared responsibility for immorality and sin. Despite Father Zosima's insistence that salvation lies in recognizing one's guilt "on behalf of all and for all" (320; 14:290), Alyosha never wavers in his insistence that Ivan is not a murderer: "It was *not you* who killed father [Ubil otsa *ne ty*] . . . it was not you who killed him . . . the murderer was not you, do you hear, it was not you! God has sent me to tell you that" (601–2; 15:40).[38] Alyosha's "*not you*," which seems to erase Ivan's responsibility for their father's death, makes more sense if it is read as a single word: a pronoun that designates the open emptiness of Ivan's character once he has admitted his guilt, creating an outline around the fictional landscape of formation. Just as Dmitri must become a not-Karamazov in order to envision himself as a

Smerdyakovian thief, so Ivan must become a "not-you" to grapple with his role in Smerdyakov's murder. Just as Dmitri's salvific dream of the "wee one" arises in the space of the not-I, so the space of this not-you becomes the setting for Ivan's equally salvific nightmare, his interview with the devil.

As Ivan himself points out, the devil's goal "is precisely to convince me that you are in yourself and are not my nightmare" (639; 15:74). What Alyosha realizes is that the devil thus works for, and not against, Ivan's reformation: if Ivan imagines the devil as real, he can detach his own self from it.[39] The stakes of the scene, in turn, extend from fiction toward theology. The more compellingly Dostoevsky draws the reader into the space of Ivan's nightmare, where the devil exists, the more fully he or she entertains the possibility of an evil that is neither caused nor remedied by human agency and that therefore invites belief in God.

Last in the sequence of dream scenes that allow Dostoevsky to reimagine realist protagonicity as a space that can be occupied by both character and reader, Ivan's nightmare takes this technique to new levels of complexity. The gleefully precise physical and sociological detail of the devil's portrait is the more striking because Ivan himself never receives a physical description: "It was some nobleman or, rather, a Russian gentleman of a certain sort, no longer young, 'qui frisait la cinquaintaine' . . . with not too much gray in his dark, rather long, and still thick hair and with a beard shaved to a point. He was dressed in a sort of brown jacket, evidently from the best of tailors, but already shabby, made approximately three years ago . . . such as no well-to-do man of society had been seen in for at least two years" (635; 15:70–71). Similarly, a small set of concrete objects—the towel Ivan wets to soothe his headache, the glass he throws at the devil to stop him from talking—become crucial to the scene as "reality effects," in precisely the opposite of Barthes's well-known sense. There is no place in this scene for objects or details of characterization that signify "the real" through their superfluity, because narrative mimesis has become the main question at issue. By struggling to sustain his image of the devil as a concretely embodied figure and the dream room as a habitable landscape, Ivan takes on the task of his own salvation, and Dostoevsky (in turn) makes this task narratable.

In the case of many other authors, the interpretation of an act of mimesis as a metafictional path toward faith would seem glib. But as I have argued, it is Dostoevsky's ideal of mimetic characterization that does most to forge the link between his lifelong "quest for form" and his desire to believe in a created and perfectible universe.

Dostoevsky's often-quoted 1854 letter to Natalia Fonvizina places this juxtaposition in a more familiar light:

> For myself, I will tell you that I am a child of my century, a child of unbelief and doubt to this day. . . . And nevertheless, God sometimes sends me mo-

> ments in which I am perfectly at peace . . . and in such minutes I have composed within myself a symbol of faith [ia slozhil v sebe simvol very] in which everything for me is clear and holy . . . : to believe that there is nothing more beautiful, deeper, sweeter, more reasonable, more manly, and more perfect than Christ. . . . What is more, if someone were to prove to me that Christ is outside the truth, and if it *really* [*deistvitel'no*] were the case that the truth is outside Christ, then I would rather remain with Christ, rather than with the truth. (28.I:176; end of January to February 20, 1854)

Here the inner mental act of sustaining belief in Christ's beauty represents or, in a more radical interpretation, actually constitutes faith for Dostoevsky. On the one hand, it is a measure of Ivan Karamazov's blasphemy that at the end of his tirade in the chapter "Rebellion," a litany of sadism and undeserved suffering, he echoes Dostoevsky's own sentiment: "I don't want harmony, for love of mankind I don't want it. I want to remain with unrequited suffering. Better I remain with my unrequited suffering and my unquenchable indignation, *even if I were wrong*" (245; 14:223). On the other hand, this echo shows that Dostoevsky gave Ivan something like his own sense of the high spiritual stakes of image making itself.[40] Belief and atheism alike depend on figural construction. Whether the image constructed is of the beauty of Christ or of a devil who embodies and so also contains human unbelief and evil, the interior *scene* of construction thus holds equal potential for salvation.

Even if we are not willing to go so far, it is clear that the conversion of inner space into setting—where "God is struggling with the devil, and the battlefield is human hearts" (108; 14:100)—is crucial to the transformation of realist protagonicity that Dostoevsky stages in *The Brothers Karamazov*. The spectacle of Ivan fighting to sustain his detailed vision of the devil, in a fictional room that doubles as the stage set of his dream, serves to underscore the difference between Ivan and realist protagonists as they have been written before him. Dostoevsky asks us to accept Ivan's mind not as a reflection of narrated traits, but as a narrative place both capacious enough for this struggle and stable enough for its vivid representation. Without the competing claims that empty Ivan of his name and character—the "you are the most lawful murderer" that pulls him toward Smerdyakov and the "It was *not you* that killed father" that pulls him back toward the Karamazovs—there is no room in which his interview with the devil could be set. Without a self that can be temporarily stripped of its narrated identity, there are no characters fit to present the silent inner plot of Dostoevsky's novel. It may be important, as Bakhtin stressed, to recognize that each of Dostoevsky's protagonists is a *you*.[41] But the vital innovation of his hybrid technique in *The Brothers Karamazov* is to construct his protagonists as *not-yous*, held together by a common name even when the illusion of their ongoing formation exceeds it.[42]

Tied to a story of sin, salvation, and resurrection, this method of characterization offers a key to Dostoevsky's attempt in his final novel to remake realism itself. Placed at the novel's thematic cornerstones, his Karamazovs also support a mimetic illusion that depends both on thickening and on transcending the narrated textual details of a fictional world. They are designed as characters that can be temporarily abstracted from any kind of trait an omniscient narrator could assign, while still shaping and holding our imaginative attention. In the process of following such characters into the vivid outlines of protagonicity, the reader may absorb a form for her own struggle toward belief in a world and self whose createdness would mirror that of the authored realist novel and its heroes. *The Adolescent* draws attention to the chaotic absence of what is "unshakable and inarguable" in Dostoevsky's realist protagonists; *The Brothers Karamazov* shows the richness of the narrative arising in this newly emptied space.

Looking back from this point, the extent to which Dostoevsky's final novel relies upon (and indeed, embraces) the conventionally asymmetrical structure of realist character-systems becomes clear. Not only do unavoidable limitations of genre and narrative require that other characters receive less narrative attention than do the Karamazovs; Dostoevsky has constructed a literary model of being that hinges on this imbalance. The space of formation into which he invites the reader can be outlined *only* by a set of narrative protagonists, whose emptied vividness all the rest of the novel's character-system functions to center and hold in place.

Toward the end of the novel, in turn, Dostoevsky suggests how this "Karamazovian" space of formation might become more generalizable. Tempted by "egotistical vanity" and "vile [*podloe*] despotism," Alyosha's thirteen-year-old friend Kolya Krasotkin identifies himself as "a scoundrel in many ways [podlets vo mnogom]." Alyosha prophesies to him, echoing Zosima's prophecy to Ivan: "you are going to be a very unhappy man in your life. . . . But on the whole you will bless life all the same" (558; 14:504). Similarly, as she descends into her struggle with the same sadism and misanthropic despair that have gripped Ivan, Lise Khokhlakova chants to herself, "Mean, mean, mean, mean!" ("*Podlaia, podlaia, podlaia, podlaia!*"; 585; 15:25). In these passages, the hopeful space of presanctified moral struggle captured in the image of Karamazovism and its component qualities (such as vileness [*podlost'*]) begins to encompass characters like Lise and Kolya too. Adopting and applying to other characters this complexly typical image, which is made portable by its concentration in a single family name, the reader is primed to assimilate the conception of perfectible human nature that it implies.

Surprisingly then, to forge characters that model the process of coming to live by what Father Zosima calls "the idea of serving mankind, of the brotherhood and oneness of people" (314; 14:285), Dostoevsky intensifies the realist novel's orientation around a few individual protagonists, to the relative diminution of more minor characters that reflect or inflect their stories. In this particular novel, the idea that minor characters as implied persons deserve an equal claim on the reader's attention may yield something like the bargain of Ivan's Grand Inquisitor: sacrificing the most powerfully transformative potential of mimetic life in exchange for a mirage of equal distribution. Instead, we play *The Brothers Karamazov*'s weightiest game by accepting the ethical difference between characters and persons, to encounter a model of personhood that is built to outlast the bounds of reading.

"I AM [THE] MURDERER, NOT KARAMAZOV": SMERDYAKOV AND THE SPACE OF THE NOT-PROTAGONIST

Nevertheless, the bounded asymmetry of the novel's character-system remains an obstacle to Dostoevsky's furthest-reaching designs on the reader. This limitation emerges with a final turn: from the capacious not-you of the Dostoevskian protagonist to the unexplorable inner space of a character he defines as minor.

In my discussion of the named Karamazov brothers, I have suggested that the name "Karamazov" and the set of traits associated with it provide a central pillar with reference to which each Karamazov is made to define "himself." The initially unformed Alyosha's role as idea-hero is strengthened and sealed in his Karamazovian encounter with the earth, where his soul is imagined as a physical meeting point for "the threads of all God's innumerable worlds." From the opposite direction, Mitya and Ivan lose their firm identification with spiritually charged Karamazovian "vileness" (*podlost'*) in a dangerous approach to the literally "*podlyi*" (baseborn) Smerdyakov's crimes of theft and murder. Within this temporary lapse in identity, their selves too are constructed as landscapes where a narrative of formation can be set. Through these negotiations of the meaning of the family name "Karamazov," the novel creates a set of techniques for staging its silent or spiritual plot, the dramas of fall and resurrection that belong *within* the Karamazovs as Dostoevskian protagonists.

The ultimate promise of this new kind of realist protagonist, which combines Tolstoyan concreteness with Dostoevskian indeterminacy, is that it might draw the absorbed reader's imagination and memory toward the conditions of createdness and perfectibility themselves, divorced from any particular character's traits. While drawing on the techniques that produce the bewitching solidity of Tolstoy's protagonists, Dostoevsky attempts to transcend the complete and adequate writtenness on which they depend. But this project is threatened by the possibility that Dostoevsky's Karamazovs need the defining contrast with the minor characters in the novel's bounded system to make their "living" outlines clear. What if the Karamazovs become vivid templates or archetypes only when juxtaposed with the *not*-Karamazovs that help to hold their archetypal identities in place? I want to suggest that this anxiety stands behind Dostoevsky's suppression of the Karamazovs' probable illegitimate brother, Smerdyakov.

In arguing that Smerdyakov could not have been the murderer, the prosecutor Ippolit Kirillovich asks why he failed to add a sentence to his suicide note: "I am the murderer, not Karamazov [ubiitsa ia, a ne Karamazov]" (712; 15:141). In Russian, this sentence requires only a change of word order—and in English, of articles—to make "murderer" and "Karamazov" into mutually exclusive categories: "I am a murderer, not a Karamazov." Just as Ivan imagines a devil that might let him believe in a separation between human nature and absolute evil, so the novel itself needs a character that separates the Karamazovs from the acts of theft, murder, and (especially) suicide. At the moments when Ivan and Mitya recognize their proximity to Smerdyakov's crimes, they begin to be remade as Karamazovs (not as Smerdyakovs). Once Smerdyakov confesses to these crimes, by contrast, he can only destroy himself. Where, then, is the key characterological difference between a Karamazov and a Smerdyakov?

Both the narrator-chronicler and the other characters are apt to frame Smerdyakov as a misplaced object, unworthy of careful consideration and unwelcome when he demands it—a reticence that distracts us from his position at the very heart of the novel's plot. Finishing the story of how Stinking Lizaveta bore Smerdyakov in Fyodor Pavlovich's garden, the narrator puts this reticence in terms of class: "It really is necessary to say something more about him in particular, but I am ashamed to distract my reader's attention for such a long time to such ordinary lackeys, and therefore I shall go back to my narrative, trusting that with regard to Smerdyakov it will all somehow work itself out [o Smerdiakove kak-nibud' soidet samo soboiu] in the further course of the story" (100; 14:93). Ivan Karamazov feels Smerdyakov's unwanted presence more viscerally, as a mysterious source of "anguish" (*toska*):

> Above all, this anguish vexed and irritated him because it had some sort of accidental, completely external appearance; this he felt. Somewhere some being or object was standing and sticking up, just as when something sometimes sticks up in front of one's eye and one doesn't notice it for a long time . . . and meanwhile one is clearly irritated, almost suffering, and at last it dawns on one to remove the offending [*negodnyi*] object, often quite trifling and ridiculous, something left in the wrong place, a handkerchief dropped on the floor, a book not put back in the bookcase, or whatever. At last, in a very

> bad and irritated state of mind, Ivan Fyodorovich reached his father's house, and . . . he at once realized what was tormenting and worrying him so. On the bench by the gate, idly enjoying the cool of the evening, sat the lackey Smerdyakov, and Ivan Fyodorovich realized at the first sight of him that the lackey Smerdyakov was also sitting in his soul, and that it was precisely this man his soul could not bear. . . . "But can it be that this worthless villain [*negodiai*] troubles me so much!" (265–66)[43]

Ivan's reaction to the Smerdyakov "sitting in his soul" mirrors his reaction to the devil he later sees sitting in his room. In both cases, the repulsive figure functions to make Ivan aware of what he cannot tolerate in himself, and also to let him imagine the space of his self as separate from it. In the description of Smerdyakov, however, the narrative itself emphasizes the link between "offending" object and offensive person, *negodnyi* and *negodiai*. This echo implies that Smerdyakov has "accidentally" been left at the very crux of *The Brothers Karamazov*—carrying out the murder that spurs on each brother's transformation, while keeping the murderer from having to be a Karamazov by name.

For the reader then, as for Ivan, the act of excluding Smerdyakov from the central circle of Karamazovs is at least as important as the act of recognizing moral kinship with him.[44] The master figure that prompts us to look through Smerdyakov, as a minor character both necessary and "accidental," is his illegitimate birth, and the separation it motivates between "Smerdyakov" and "Karamazov."[45] As a literal podlets (bastard), Smerdyakov cannot use the word in its figurative moral sense of "scoundrel," as Dmitri and Ivan do, to ally himself with the redeemable vileness of Karamazovism rather than with the damning crimes he has committed. Unlike the named Karamazovs, Smerdyakov virulently rejects this label: "I'd kill in a duel with a pistol the man who said to me that I was baseborn [*podlets*] because I came from the Stinkess, without a father" (225; 14:204).

The most basic narrative consequence of this separation from the Karamazovs and their traits is Smerdyakov's suicide. Always a "squeamish" eater and a dandy (125–26; 14:115–16), he ends by turning his face away entirely from the deep and earthy life force that sustains the four so-named Karamazovs. This alliance with surfaces rather than depths is reflected, in turn, in the aspect of his characterization that *technically* curtails his participation in the Karamazovs' spiritual plot, the compounded opacity of his inner life:

> Only rarely did he speak. If at that time it had occurred to someone to ask, looking at him, what this fellow was interested in, and what was most often on his mind, it would really have been impossible to tell from looking at him. Yet he would sometimes stop . . . fall into thought, and stand like that even for ten minutes. A physiognomist, studying him, would have said that

> his face showed neither thought nor reflection, but just some sort of contemplation. The painter Kramskoy has a remarkable painting entitled *The Contemplator*: it depicts a forest in winter, and in the forest, standing all by himself on the road, in deepest solitude, a stray little peasant in a ragged caftan and bast shoes; he stands as if he were lost in thought, but he is not thinking, he is "contemplating" something. If you nudged him, he would give a start and look at you as if he had just woken up, but without understanding anything . . . perhaps suddenly, having stored up [*nakopiv*] his impressions over many years, he will drop everything and wander off to Jerusalem to save his soul, or perhaps he will suddenly burn down his native village, or perhaps he will do both. There are plenty of contemplators among the people. Most likely Smerdyakov, too, was such a contemplator, and most likely he, too, was greedily storing up his impressions, almost without knowing why himself. (127)[46]

"Contemplation," as the narrator describes it, is both an absolutely superficial and an absolutely closed process. There is no possible access to what the contemplator is thinking; even the contemplator, who remains on the surface level of his "impressions," does not know. Associating Smerdyakov with the figure of the contemplator and the painting that captures it, the narrator assembles his character with a single stroke, but one that preempts further narration. It is as if, for Smerdyakov, the entrance to the inner starlit vault where Alyosha senses the threads of all God's worlds, or to the hallucinated room where Ivan talks with his devil, has been covered over with the canvas of Kramskoy's painting.

We can link Smerdyakov's identification with Kramskoy's "Contemplator," finally, to his affinity for the surfaces of *texts*, for the letter of a given text rather than its spirit. His snide reaction to Gogol's *Dikanka* stories—"It's written all about lies" (125; 14:115)—prefigures his opportunistically unquestioning relationship to Ivan's "word," the dictum that if there is no immortality, "everything is permitted" (632; 15:67). Indeed, in this eagerness to be directed by just what is written or said, Smerdyakov resembles a character in search of a Tolstoyan omniscient narrator.[47] The only God he recognizes is an invisible and all-seeing eye: "That third one is God, sir, Providence itself, sir, it's right here with us now, sir, only don't look for it, you won't find it" (623; 15:60). While his crimes set the Karamazov brothers on a course of controlled liberation from authoritatively narrated traits, they confine Smerdyakov himself to the small corner of the novel's world in which he can sustain the fantasy of Ivan's omniscience, his perfect understanding of Smerdyakov's own secret thoughts and desires.[48]

Like Smerdyakov's illegitimate birth, the idea that he lives by "greedily storing up" or accumulating his impressions connects him with Arkady Dolgoruky, the protagonist of *The Adolescent*. "Arkady's" characters too, as I have argued, long for the authority of an omniscient narrator. But in *The Adolescent*, the drive to accumulate is a response to the anxiety of illegitimate birth, and in turn, its chaotic narrative is redemptively framed as "material" for a future, more stable and harmonious hero and novel. By contrast, illegitimacy and contemplation only compound Smerdyakov's essential poverty, cutting him in his superficial opacity off from the Karamazov brothers in their narratable depth; these qualities serve to suppress rather than to centralize him. This difference becomes necessary precisely because of the global shift in Dostoevsky's realist technique throughout *The Brothers Karamazov*. *The Adolescent* ostentatiously compounds the instability, or (as I have called it) the narrative illegitimacy of Dostoevsky's characters, in order to envision the contrasting idyll of a "future novel" that would remake reality in its own created image. *The Brothers Karamazov* turns, instead, to the stable scaffolding of a near-Tolstoyan character-system. The danger to counter is thus now not the chaotic "illegitimacy" of the Dostoevskian contemporary character but the larger illegitimacy of the novel genre itself: the specter of the novel as the epic of a world "abandoned by God," whose nostalgically "totalizing" form seals it off from fluid unauthored contemporaneity.[49] Suppressing Smerdyakov, Dostoevsky also suppresses the threat of a novel whose vivid fictions would not matter. By criminalizing and making repulsive Smerdyakov's affinity for authorial omniscience, Dostoevsky distracts us from *The Brothers Karamazov*'s own perilously close approach to the aestheticized forms of what he himself called "historical realism."

Smerdyakov thus crystallizes a doubt that the novel can neither fully exorcise nor fully contain. His craven response to the task of "storing up" his own character makes him a kind of parody not just of the dead Tolstoyan but also of the resurrected Dostoevskian protagonist.

Through the "stinking" Smerdyakov, Dostoevsky performatively reviles the temptation to seek out one's own mortal narrator. In spiritual terms, he is allied with earthly rather than heavenly bread; in metafictional terms, he embodies a characterological solidity confined to the text, rather than a "living" model that extends beyond its bounds. But Dostoevsky cannot keep Smerdyakov's crimes from appearing to unfold from what one critic calls "the fullness of his nature as a cockroach-crushing, cat-hanging, master-and-self-slaughtering fungus."[50] In other words, Smerdyakov too is subject to the pervasive mimetic illusion that characters act autonomously, according to what they are. This illusion is so strong that, as the voluminous and inventive critical literature on his character attests, it is possible to write about Smerdyakov as though he could have acted differently: as though by the time of his suicide, he too has found room in himself for a dialogue with the voice of Christ.[51] For some readers, he enters together with the Karamazov brothers into the novel's sweeping narrative of sin and salvation.

Here, I think, we find ourselves in a double bind. To accept Smerdyakov for what he is—that is, for the version of his character that this narrative prompts us to imagine—is also to follow the novel's representational logic: a character made as Smerdyakov is made is something *other* or *less* than an implied person. Ironically, Dostoevsky needs this demonic figure for the new kind of story he is telling about a new kind of protagonist—one whose open potential for perfectibility might transcend the particular written narrative of an artistic text. On the other hand, to extend Smerdyakov too into what he *could* be, venturing into the intellectual and moral inner space of his character that the narrative seals off, is to efface him: to dissolve Smerdyakov just by absorbing him into the brothers Karamazov. If we refrain from imagining Smerdyakov as an autonomous fictional person, we acknowledge the limitations of Dostoevsky's (or any) novel, which requires a complex character-system to make and sustain its vision of reality. But if we insist on imagining Smerdyakov as a person, the character as written in the novel melts away.

The problem that Smerdyakov creates for *The Brothers Karamazov* thus remains unsolved either by his suicide in the story or by his salvation at the hands of committed readers. In *The Brothers Karamazov*, Dostoevsky clarifies and mobilizes a set of techniques for writing a new kind of protagonist, one that can seem at the most intense moments of his life to stand alone without narrated traits, as an indeterminate but still embodied self. The space of this living self emerges through the persistent contrast between Karamazovs and not-Karamazovs; most starkly, between a Karamazov and a Smerdyakov. But Smerdyakov's intrusively minimized presence in the narrative points to the fragility of this solution. The example of Smerdyakov threatens to collapse the fiction of the Karamazovian unnarrated self, and to diffuse the anticontemplative mode of reading that such protagonists demand.

Both crucial to and exiled from *The Brothers Karamazov*'s narrative, Smerdyakov gives shape to the fear that the composed, written boundaries of the novelistic protagonist may not stretch to the mythical breadth of the genres hopefully signaled within *this* novel's text (legend, parable, saint's life). More precisely, his presence suggests that the novel can make this stretch only provisionally—by adapting the asymmetry of any bounded novelistic character-system to a different set of generic purposes. Defining themselves and their Karamazovian nature against Smerdyakov and his crimes, Alyosha, Mitya, and Ivan open the horizons of other genres; Smerdyakov stays behind to take care of the novel. In turn, he presents the problem of the novelistic character boiled down to its strongest concentration. How does the illusion of an implied person or consciousness interact with the text that fixes what he does and says? Does any realist character, even one as "autonomous" as Dostoevsky's protagonists, transcend the exact set of written characters that compose him?

The ending of *The Brothers Karamazov* energetically conceals the traces of this doubt. Not only is Smerdyakov dead, but his place in the novel's plot has been usurped by Mitya Karamazov, convicted of Smerdyakov's crimes and occupying his former room at the hospital (761; 15:183). By the final page, Smerdyakov's name has vanished beneath the boys' shout of "Hurrah for Karamazov! [Ura Karamazovu!]"—an exclamation that celebrates at once the novel's central individual hero, its central family name, and the narrative dance of family characterization in which most of its characters are engaged. But back at the beginning of every reading, Smerdyakov reemerges—inextricable from the material and textuality of narrative, misplaced into the heart of a novel bent on converting matter into spirit.

It is a measure of Dostoevsky's aesthetic achievement that a central line of twentieth-century theorists—from Dmitrii Merezhkovsky and Viacheslav Ivanov to Lukács and Bakhtin, and beyond—hailed his characters as a signal that the novel might transcend the bounds of modern literary fiction. With this claim, literary theory completed from the outside the work that no novel could have accomplished from within. Moved by their own demands and hopes for literary art, Bakhtin and his predecessors found in Dostoevsky's "unfinalized" characters the foundation for a vision of novels themselves as texts with open borders. No longer confined to the contemplation of an already-perfected object, novel reading in Bakhtin's account becomes as open-ended and contingent as life with people, and as consequential for the reader's understanding of her own relationship to others and the world.[52]

In Dostoevsky's *The Brothers Karamazov*—no less than in Tolstoy's *Anna Karenina*—we see how realist characterization challenges this vision of indeterminacy, even though the temptation to affirm it is integral to the illusion of characterization itself. The famously riddling passage on painting and writing in Plato's *Phaedrus* directs us to the deep roots of this problem.

Plato's Socrates complains that like a painted figure, the illegitimate written word "always needs its father's support"; alone, it "rolls about everywhere, reaching indiscriminately those with no understanding no less than those who have no business with it, and it doesn't know to whom it should speak and to whom it should not." By contrast, writing's "legitimate brother" speech is "written down, with knowledge, in the soul of the listener"; it is "the living, breathing discourse of the man who knows, of which the written one can fairly be called an image" (275d–276a).[53] In "Plato's Pharmacy" (1968), his seminal improvisation on this passage, Derrida turns Socrates's hierarchy on its head. The distanced, illegitimate written word becomes the essential ground on which the primacy of the "present" and "legitimate" spoken word arises. The "illegitimacy" inherent in writing, a divorce from clear and present origins, emerges as the precursor to all dialogue, even to assertions of the priority of speech.[54]

Dostoevsky's ambitions for his second-order characters—the images of living persons made up from the images of spoken words—fall somewhere in between these two extremes.

The *narrative illegitimacy* of Dostoevsky's characters—their apparent divorce from any originating omniscient authority—works to counter what Socrates calls the illegitimacy of the written word as such. At their most innovative, his characters seem to become living, breathing words spoken and authorized entirely by themselves. In his final novel, Dostoevsky made his closest approach to a set of protagonists whose characters can be *emptied* of what is written about them, and who yet preserve their designated places in their novel's ordering cosmology. Such protagonists begin to turn the literary, written novelistic text toward the oral generic sphere of national and religious myth, for which Dostoevsky nurtured messianic hopes. As realist types, the Karamazov brothers demand entrance into the minds and (crucially) the memories of readers—and with the word image of "Karamazovism," Dostoevsky draws a frame of created plenitude around their open-ended struggles. At the same time, a Derridean anxiety seeps into this project. Can the image of Karamazovism take on its redemptive form outside of the narrative system that defines it against its *ir*redeemable double? Perfecting the device of the free-standing but vivid protagonist in his Karamazovs, Dostoevsky acknowledged its ephemerality in the representation of Smerdyakov—a character whom we are all but ordered to ignore.

My approach to Dostoevsky's characters through the figure of illegitimacy, which connects the outer skin of *The Adolescent* to the hidden catch of *The Brothers Karamazov*, thus draws attention to the brittle power of his techniques of characterization. The limit that his characters encounter may, in the end, be the limit *of* technique: the complex composition that makes novels, like dreams, impossible to retell. In the absolute split between an Ivan Karamazov conversing with his nightmare devil and an illegibly "contemplating" Smerdyakov, this technical foundation—the hand performing the magic trick—flashes into view. Like the texts and paintings that Plato's Socrates describes, neither Ivan nor Smerdyakov ever say anything more than what is written on the page. But if some of Dostoevsky's characters invite a step beyond the boundary between novel and world, it is due to the very words that sever them from their authoritative generation in narrative. Realist illusion here lives so close to its own unmaking that it seems hardly to be made at all.

Afterword

AT THE BEGINNING of a pivotal scene in Dostoevsky's *The Idiot* (1868–69), the consumptive rebel Ippolit Terent'ev asks the idealistic hero Prince Myshkin, "Is it true, Prince, that you once said 'beauty' would save the world?"[1] A succession of Dostoevsky's readers—beginning soon after his death with the religious philosopher Vladimir Soloviev—have seized on the declarative form of this aphorism as a key to his work and worldview. In Soloviev's exegesis,

> for Dostoevsky [goodness, truth, and beauty] were three inseparable forms of one absolute Idea. The infinity of the human soul—as revealed in Christ, capable of encompassing within itself all the boundlessness of divinity—is at one and the same time the greatest good, and the highest truth, and the most perfect beauty. Truth is the good, as conceivable by the human mind; beauty is the same goodness and the same truth, corporeally embodied in a living concrete form. And beauty's full embodiment now in everything is the end, and the goal, and the perfection, and this is why Dostoevsky said that beauty would save the world.[2]

As mantra rather than question, "beauty will save the world" encapsulates the messianic hopes of Dostoevsky the thinker and journalist. An experience of beautiful objects or figures becomes a token for the perfectibility of people and life on earth; in turn, the analogy between aesthetic and divine creation makes itself felt as a sense of the beautiful object's "living concrete form."

This book began with the argument that the mimetic life of realist characters springs from a related, although secular, mode of aesthetic reception. The reader's impression of characters' independent "life," their physical solidity and self-determination, reflects her presupposition of the work's own organic coherence—the purposive "labyrinth of linkages" that the context of novel reading encourages us to think we will find. Within this narrative labyrinth, the illusion of any character's life can be heightened, accented, or suppressed. Realist novels thus frame ideas by narrating populated worlds.

Entering into such a world, readers enter too into the bounded narrative system that underlies the mimetic illusion—an experience imaginable, by the enduring organic metaphor of nineteenth-century European aesthetics, at once as "life" and as "beauty."

To anyone who accepts the role of realist novel reader, then, what Soloviev describes as the embodiment of "truth . . . in a living concrete form" should not sound overly foreign. The more radical move is Soloviev's insistence on a link between aesthetic and extra-aesthetic experience, and it is here that Dostoevsky the *novelist* was not always ready to follow him. What Soloviev takes as given enters into *The Idiot* not just as an unsolved question, but as an insoluble one: "Is it true, Prince," one fictional character asks another, "that you once said 'beauty' would save the world?" When beauty takes the novelistic shape of mimetic life, its power is embedded (like Ippolit's question) within the context of fictionality. The very conditions that support the illusion of the character's life set a boundary around the reader's encounter with him, which limits the novelist's power to turn this encounter toward lasting spiritual or social change.

Writing at the climax of the Russian realist tradition, Dostoevsky and his rival and contemporary Tolstoy threw this paradox into sharp relief. Historical, political, and institutional circumstances lent unusual weight and authority to the novel genre in mid-nineteenth-century Russia. But in mastering and extending the illusions that realist novels foster, Tolstoy and Dostoevsky each collided with the novel's conventional limitations. As both authors recognized, the novel's mathetic potential is often at odds with its mimetic power. Their novels draw readers into lifelike models of reality whose line of passage into reality itself remains uncertain. Along with Tolstoy's and Dostoevsky's social, political, and religious activity, the range of truth-claiming genres that they invoke within their novels—from philosophy and history to hagiography and myth—points to their shared ambivalence about the boundedness of fictionality and art. Pursuing a degree of authority on par with this range of genres, these novels at their most ambitious try to parlay the controlled vividness of novelistic realism into an equally controlled transformation of the reader's own worldview. The seductive, although only apparent, portability of realist character makes it a central locus for this project. Tolstoy ultimately rejected the rhetorical potential concentrated in characterization as a false promise. Dostoevsky continued to entertain that promise through the end of his life, and his novels became the foundation for a critical and theoretical tradition that would extend it still further. Nevertheless, his final novel *The Brothers Karamazov* underscores the tension that shadows any attempt to transcend the systematic nature of novelistic illusion. Where individual readers may accept individual characters, novels, or writers as sources of authority, the novelist's only direct realm of control begins and ends with the reader's absorption in the work that he has written.

Although it is grounded in the particular examples of Tolstoy's and Dostoevsky's lives and works, the argument I have pursued in this study has implications for the way we read and think about reading realist novels now.[3]

The mimetic life of individual characters is often understood as irrelevant to the complex question of how systems inside realist narratives correspond with those outside them. In different ways, Marxist, structuralist, semiotic, and psychoanalytic criticism all urge moving beyond the naive perception of characters as living people. I hope to have contributed to the case that in fact, the modulated illusion of characters' autonomous lives is near the heart of the realist novel's claim to reflect the workings of historically and socially placed human conditions.

However, by the same token, those who speak for the moral and social virtues of reading about "living" characters ignore the narrative systems controlling life effects at their peril. What is popularly called "relatability" is largely, I have argued, a function of relationality. The sense of empathizing or identifying with a character who seems especially true to life cannot be isolated from that character's position in the narrative where he appears.

The relationality of vividness has bearing on the widespread tenet that novels and novelists educate readers by placing them in contact with "voices" that they would not otherwise have had the chance to know, and thus giving them portable models for the perspectives of others. There is no doubt that realist novels have lasting meaning for readers who sink into them, or that often, both captivation and meaning begin with a reader's visceral impression of a novel's characters as real. But as Suzanne Keen convincingly argues, drawing on a range of disciplinary perspectives, the moral consequences of novel reading have proved elusive.[4] The systematic, self-contained nature of mimetic life helps account for the gap between readers' experiences of fictional characters and people's experiences with one another in the world. The "contract of fictionality" may, as Keen puts it, dispense with "the normal state of alert suspicion of others' motives that often acts as a barrier to empathy," and thus offer an occasion for "emotional transactions of great intensity," especially when activated by teaching or discussion with fellow readers.[5] But it is just as true that the "contract of fictionality" binds the Others for whom readers feel these emotions to the experience and moment of reading. If a character strikes a reader as compellingly realized, what narrative systems stand behind that impression, and how might this level of narrative organization filter the experience that *seems* directly analogous to a personal encounter while reading? Does the object of the reader's "emotional transaction" shift after the book is closed? And if so, when communities of readers talk about characters as vividly felt people, what exactly are they discussing? The reader's experience of living characters is not only not the most portable and communicable dimension of novel reading; on reflection (I have argued), it is one of the least. There is thus good reason to avoid presuming that dwelling with characters is like dwelling with people, or that when a reader imagines a character, that character's memorable human image is the only thing she absorbs.

For similar reasons, we should look twice at the arguments that story-level interactions between characters offer a straightforward arena for ethical reflection and inquiry or that in the irreducible particularity of the people and situations they represent, "great novels develop our ethical sense."[6] Although realist novelists like Tolstoy, Dostoevsky, Eliot, Trollope, and James are consummately subtle moral observers and thinkers, much else also goes on in their novels, and much of that *else* is itself bound up with the illusion of character. So when, for example, Martha Nussbaum describes James as a "high and fine mind concerning the tangled mysteries of [his characters'] imaginary lives"—such that the vividness of the characters helps bolster the novel(ist)'s claim to moral authority—I suspect that the reader she imagines is located in two places at once.[7] Whether a reader senses Maggie Verver's lifelikeness while he is absorbed in *The Golden Bowl* is one question, which has much to do with James's narrative; whether that same reader approaches *The Golden Bowl* as a site of moral education is another, which has much to do with his attitude toward James and his beliefs about novel reading. Equally, when Gary Saul Morson marvels that philosophers and economists do not turn to realist narratives to take advantage of "the most convincing portraits of people ever written," what he elides is the narrative and generic context in which these portraits come to look so three-dimensional.[8] Realist novels are indeed unsurpassed at evoking what Morson calls the "prosaic" detail, messiness, and contingency of human being, but they do so in the context of *poetic* narrative systems, without which readers would be unlikely to hail their worlds and characters as "real." It is for this reason, I think, that Chernyshevsky's *What Is to Be Done?* was so much better than Dostoevsky's *Crime and Punishment* at producing positive models of human behavior that 1860s Russian readers could actively use: one work is designed for practical dismemberment; the other, for aesthetic and mimetic coherence.

The question of how realist narratives and their characters are woven, then, is a significant dimension of the world models they construct—and in the classroom, the structures that produce mimetic illusion have a central place in conversations about the "possible people" that novelists create. Person-shaped though realist characters are, character-*systems* engender forms of thought that reach well beyond ethics. Tracing the mutual blindnesses that derail Anna Karenina's marriage to Karenin and romance with Vronsky, do we as readers entertain the Schopenhauerian pessimism and skepticism that underlie the very construction of these figures? Following the narrative of how the Karamazovs' "broad" potential and life force answer Ivan's denial of the world's essential goodness, how much of Dostoevsky's idiosyncratic Orthodoxy does an attentive reader temporarily take on board? Grappling with these questions means challenging any vision of Anna or Ivan that invokes the authority of their vividness without regard for the systems that foster and modulate their mimetic lives. Throughout my discussions of Tolstoy's and Dostoevsky's novels, I have focused on the impossibility of directly extending the terms of realist illusion to the reader's own worldview, and the traces that both authors' desire to do so leaves on narratives in which it cannot be realized. At the same time, absorbed engagement with realist novels shapes readers, as would any substantial encounter with a compelling artistic or intellectual system. When we start to think through the insights these novels provide about human thought and experience, we should think too about the construction of the authored texts in which those insights take such vivid form.

So what is to be done with the Russian realist novels that determinedly signal their own messiness, open-endedness, and contingency, their ostentatious subversion of aesthetic convention and textual bounds—a tradition that culminates in Dostoevsky's and Tolstoy's experiments with the bounds of mimetic characterization? We can begin by acknowledging these very signals as one of realism's calling cards—what Roman Jakobson called its "tendency toward the deformation of given artistic canons, conceived as a closer approach toward reality." And we can go on to delve beneath them for signs of the other mode of realism that Jakobson defines: "a conservative tendency within the boundaries of a given artistic tradition, conceived as faithfulness to reality."[9] Throughout their major novels, Tolstoy and Dostoevsky used Jakobson's modes of realism in masterful tandem. Even as they challenged the conventions that mark novel reading as an (only) aesthetic experience, they simultaneously drew on the novel's conventional resources to make absorbing fictional characters and worlds.

Poised on this border between biblical world reflection and Homeric world creation, Dostoevsky's and Tolstoy's novels at once unbalance the structure of novelistic character-systems and mobilize the character-system as a tool for the making of illusion. Their surest power is neither more nor less than to draw us, again and again, into the inexhaustible work of reading.

Notes

The following editions are cited parenthetically in the main text, by volume and page:

L. N. Tolstoi, *Polnoe sobranie sochinenii*, 90 vols., ed. V. G. Chertkov et al. (Moscow and Leningrad: Gosudarstvennoe izdatel'stvo, 1928–58). Accessed through the digitized edition published by the Tolstoy Museum at Iasnaia Poliana at http://tolstoy.ru/creativity/90-volume-collection-of-the-works/.

F. M. Dostoevskii, *Polnoe sobranie sochinenii*, 30 vols., ed. G. M. Fridlender et al. (Leningrad: Nauka, 1972–1990).

When I quote a novel in translation, corresponding Russian citations are given either after the Russian quotation in a footnote or in the text in the form (English citation; Russian citation). I regularly modify published English translations as necessary to bring out particular elements of the Russian text. I have followed the English translations I quote in the spelling of fictional characters' names.

INTRODUCTION

Epigraph: Virginia Woolf, "The Russian Point of View" (1925).

1. Aristotle, *Poetics* 1448a1. *The Basic Works of Aristotle*, ed. Richard McKeon (New York: Modern Library, 2001), 1456. On Aristotle's conception of mimesis as an act of fiction making, see Stephen Halliwell, *Aristotle's Poetics* (London: Duckworth, 1986), 22; Stephen Halliwell, *The Aesthetics of Mimesis* (Princeton, NJ: Princeton University Press, 2002), 171–76ff.; and Paul Ricoeur, *Time and Narrative*, trans. Kathleen McLaughlin and David Pellauer, vol. 1 (Chicago: University of Chicago Press, 1984), 34, 45.

2. I adopt Stephen Halliwell's distinction between the "world-reflecting" and the "world-creating" dimensions of mimetic art from *Aesthetics*, 5ff.

3. While using the terms "mimesis" and "mimetic" to invoke long-standing problems of representational art, I use "realism"/"realist" primarily as a period term, to describe norms of literary representation predominant in nineteenth-

century Europe, as suggested by René Wellek in "The Concept of Realism in Literary Scholarship," in *Concepts of Criticism* (New Haven, CT: Yale University Press, 1963), 222–55. It should be noted that both Tolstoy and Dostoevsky resisted the unqualified application of the label "realist" to their work.

4. Baruch Hochman, *Character in Literature* (Ithaca, NY: Cornell University Press, 1985), 72.

5. In his Dostoevsky book (1929/1963), Bakhtin describes Dostoevsky's genius for realizing the autonomous, unfinalized worldviews of his protagonists, rather than subordinating them to the "monologic" perspective of the author (Mikhail Bakhtin, *Problems of Dostoevsky's Poetics*, ed. and trans. Caryl Emerson [Minneapolis: University of Minnesota Press, 1984]; M. M. Bakhtin, *Sobranie sochinenii*, ed. S. G. Bocharov and N. I. Nikolaev, vol. 2 and 6 [Moscow: Russkie slovari, 2002]). In his foreword to the 1984 English translation, Wayne Booth extrapolates a vision of empathetic inclusivity from Bakhtin's ideas: "Polyphony, the miracle of our 'dialogical' lives together, is thus . . . a value to be pursued endlessly" (xxi). Gary Saul Morson has gone on to develop the ethical and pedagogical potential of Bakhtin's understanding of novelistic "unfinalizability"; see especially the essays collected in his *Prosaics and Other Provocations: Empathy, Open Time, and the Novel* (Boston: Academic Studies Press, 2013). Similarly, in the introduction to her book *Love's Knowledge: Essays on Philosophy and Literature* (Oxford: Oxford University Press, 1999), Martha Nussbaum describes "the imagination of the novel reader as one that is very valuable in the political (as well as the private) life, sympathetic to a wide range of concerns, averse to certain denials of humanity" (47–48). Dorothy Hale analyzes this deep-seated tendency to understand the novel, above all, as the form that models and makes room for autonomous persons, an ideology she calls the "novelistic aesthetics of alterity." See Dorothy Hale, "Aesthetics and the New Ethics: Theorizing the Novel in the Twenty-First Century," *PMLA* 124, no. 3 (2009): 896–903; and her earlier *Social Formalism: The Novel in Theory from Henry James to the Present* (Stanford, CA: Stanford University Press, 1998). See also her forthcoming *The Novel and the New Ethics* (Stanford, CA: Stanford University Press, 2020).

6. Obama's remarks read, in part, "When I think about how I understand my role as citizen . . . the most important stuff I think I've learned from reading novels. It has to do with empathy . . . the notion that it's possible to connect with some[one] else even though they're very different from you." "President Obama and Marilynne Robinson: A Conversation (II)," *New York Review of Books*, November 19, 2015.

7. For disparate but equally thorough accounts of this divide, see Alex Woloch, *The One vs. the Many: Minor Characters and the Space of the Protagonist in the Novel* (Princeton, NJ: Princeton University Press, 2003), 12–42; and John Frow, *Character and Person* (Oxford: Oxford University Press, 2014), 1–35.

8. Gérard Genette, *Narrative Discourse: An Essay in Method*, trans. Jane E. Lewin (Ithaca, NY: Cornell University Press, 1980), 30.

9. Seminal formalist writings that responded to a tradition of ethically and socially oriented criticism by analyzing artistic prose as experimentation in language and narrative, rather than as a representation of persons, include Boris Eikhenbaum's "How Gogol's 'Overcoat' Is Made," first published in 1918, and the essays in Viktor Shklovsky's *Theory of Prose*, first published together in 1925. The formalist approach to character was coded in B. V. Tomashevsky's *Theory of Literature* (1925), and in V. Ia. Propp's *Morphology of the Folktale* (1928).

10. Roland Barthes, *S/Z*, trans. Richard Miller (New York: Hill and Wang, 1974), 94–95.

11. On this aspect of structuralist theory generally, see Jonathan Culler, *Structuralist Poetics: Structuralism, Linguistics, and the Study of Literature* (Ithaca, NY: Cornell University Press, 1975), 131–60; and for the central original essays, Roland Barthes, "The Reality Effect" (1968); Gérard Genette, "Verisimilitude and Motivation" (1969); Hélène Cixous, "The Character of 'Character'" (1974); Jacques Derrida, "The Double Session" (1972); and Derrida, "Economimesis" (1975). For a revision and extension of structuralist and deconstructionist understandings of mimesis, see C. Prendergast, *The Order of Mimesis: Balzac, Stendhal, Nerval, Flaubert* (Cambridge: Cambridge University Press, 1986), 1–82.

12. Rita Felski gives an alternative summary of recent developments in Rita Felski, ed. "Character," special issue, *New Literary History* 42, no. 2 (Spring 2011): v–ix.

13. Foundational works in each of these categories include, for narratological approaches, Dorrit Cohn, *Transparent Minds: Narrative Modes for Presenting Consciousness in Fiction* (Princeton, NJ: Princeton University Press, 1978); Seymour Chatman, *Story and Discourse* (Ithaca, NY: Cornell University Press, 1978), 96–138; Shlomith Rimmon-Kennan, *Narrative Fiction: Contemporary Poetics* (London and New York: Routledge, 2002), 31–44; and Mieke Bal, *Narratology: Introduction to the Theory of Narrative*, 3rd ed. (Toronto: University of Toronto Press, 2009), 112–33. For approaches founded in possible world semantics, Uri Margolin, "Character," in *The Cambridge Companion to Narrative*, ed. David Herman (Cambridge: Cambridge University Press, 2007), 66–79; in cognitive science, Lisa Zunshine, *Why We Read Fiction: Theory of Mind and the Novel* (Columbus: Ohio State University Press, 2006); and Blakey Vermeule, *Why Do We Care about Literary Characters?* (Baltimore: Johns Hopkins University Press, 2010); and recently, in computational "distant reading," Andrew Piper, "The Constraints of Character: Introducing a Character Feature-Space Tool," https://txtlab.org/2016/01/the-constraints-of-character-introducing-a-character-feature-space-tool/. Prominent among the many accounts of how mimetic characters can address readers ethically and rhetorically are Martin Price, *Forms of Life: Character and Moral Imagination in the Novel* (New Haven, CT: Yale University Press, 1983); Wayne C. Booth, *The Company We Keep: An Ethics of Fiction* (Berkeley and Los Angeles: University of California Press, 1988), esp. 227–91; James Phelan, *Reading People, Reading Plots: Character, Progres-*

sion, and the Interpretation of Narrative (Chicago: University of Chicago Press, 1989), and Phelan, *Living to Tell about It: A Rhetoric and Ethics of Character Narration* (Ithaca, NY: Cornell University Press, 2005); Adam Zachary Newton, *Narrative Ethics* (Cambridge, MA: Harvard University Press, 1995); Shlomith Rimmon-Kennan, *A Glance beyond Doubt: Narration, Representation, Subjectivity* (Columbus: Ohio State University Press, 1996). Finally, a series of landmark studies rooted in reading cultures at specific points in time and space: Catherine Gallagher, *Nobody's Story: The Vanishing Acts of Women Writers in the Marketplace* (Berkeley and Los Angeles: University of California Press, 1994), 146–202, as well as later work (esp. "George Eliot: Immanent Victorian," *Representations* 90, no.1 [Spring 2005]); Deidre Shauna Lynch, *The Economy of Character: Novels, Market Culture, and the Business of Inner Meaning* (Chicago: University of Chicago Press, 1998); Elizabeth Fowler, *Literary Character: The Human Figure in Early English Writing* (Ithaca, NY: Cornell University Press, 2003); and Woloch, *The One vs. the Many*. Nicholas Paige tells a story parallel to Lynch's, about the gradual emergence of psychonarration and "round" characters alongside a particular conception of fictionality over the course of the eighteenth-century French tradition: *Before Fiction: The Ancien Régime of the Novel* (Philadelphia: University of Pennsylvania Press, 2011). See also a move to extend this history into twentieth-century English modernism in Julian Murphet, "The Mole and the Multiple: A Chiasmus of Character," *New Literary History* 42, no. 2 (Spring 2011): 255–76. Unfortunately, I became aware of Amanda Anderson, Rita Felski, and Toril Moi's recent study *Character*, which sets out to explore the phenomenon of character without censuring the impulse to treat characters as if they were persons, too late to take it into account in my own analysis. Anderson, Felski, and Moi, *Character: Three Inquiries in Literary Studies* (Chicago and London: University of Chicago Press, 2019).

14. Bal, *Narratology*, 113; Phelan, *Reading People*, 2ff.

15. Richard Walsh, *The Rhetoric of Fictionality: Narrative Theory and the Idea of Fiction* (Columbus: Ohio State University Press, 2007), 148–69.

16. Baruch Hochman anticipates this aesthetic explanation for the effect I am calling "mimetic life" (as well as a model of what Alex Woloch calls "character-space"): he writes of "the way the organization of the whole text creates a space—an area where converging perspectives meet—within which the character subsists . . . the vivifying context of the work as a whole and of the thoughts, feelings, and fantasies that are pulled into the vortex of our responsiveness to it" (*Character in Literature*, 68–69). On characterological life as an emergent quality in literary texts, see also Price, *Forms of Life*, 24–36. Unlike Hochman and Price, I focus on this "vivifying context" not from the reader's perspective but rather in terms of the textual instructions that create it.

17. Dorothy Hale has argued that Anglo-American theorists, readers, and authors tend to embrace the seeming self-sufficiency and autonomy of charac-

ters as an aesthetic standard specific to the novel, to which more traditional criteria of beauty do not comfortably apply. See Dorothy J. Hale, "The Art of English Fiction in the Twentieth Century," in *The Cambridge Companion to the Twentieth Century Novel*, ed. Robert L. Caserio (Cambridge: Cambridge University Press, 2009); Hale, "Aesthetics and the New Ethics"; and Hale, "*On Beauty* as Beautiful?: The Problem of Novelistic Aesthetics by Way of Zadie Smith," *Contemporary Literature* 53, no. 4 (Winter 2012): 814–44.

18. Kant's understanding of the beautiful as "purposive without purpose" encapsulates this idea of the beautiful object's autonomous logic. *Critique of Judgment*, trans. J. H. Bernard (New York: Hafner Press, 1951), 55. M. H. Abrams gives an intellectual history of "organic aesthetic" metaphors for artistic creation and reception in German and English Romanticism: *The Mirror and the Lamp: Romantic Theory and the Critical Tradition* (London, Oxford, New York: Oxford University Press, 1953), 184–225. Victor Terras traces the organic metaphor's extensive use across political camps in nineteenth-century Russian literary criticism, in his *Belinskij and Russian Literary Criticism: The Heritage of Organic Aesthetics* (Madison: University of Wisconsin Press, 1974).

19. Terry Eagleton, *The Ideology of the Aesthetic* (Oxford: Blackwell, 1990), 9.

20. On the many "a-psychological" literary works where characters function primarily as actants, see Tzvetan Todorov, "Narrative-Men," in *The Poetics of Prose*, trans. Richard Howard (Ithaca, NY: Cornell University Press, 1977), 66–79.

21. The phrase is from Tolstoy's much-quoted letter to his intellectual confidante, the philosopher and critic Nikolai Strakhov, April 23/26 1876 (62:269). I return to this letter below.

22. Georg Lukács, "Tolstoy and the Development of Realism," *Studies in European Realism*, trans. Edith Bone (New York: Grosset & Dunlap, 1964), 145 (translation slightly modified); Georg Lukács, *Werke*, ed. Frank Benseler and Gyorgy Markus (Neuwied and Berlin: Luchterhand, 1962–), 5:197–98. Written in German, 1936; first published in Russian, 1938. Lukács also uses the metaphor of "polyphony" in his pre-Marxist *The Theory of the Novel*, to describe how an aesthetic totality can be organized around a "dramatic problem." Georg Lukács, *The Theory of the Novel*, trans. Anna Bostock (Cambridge, MA: MIT Press, 1971), 54; *Die Theorie des Romans* (Neuwied am Rhein: Luchterhand, 1963), 50. I discuss Lukács's invocations of the "autonomy" of character more extensively in "Illusion and Instrument: Problems of Mimetic Characterization in Dostoevsky and Tolstoy" (PhD diss., University of California, Berkeley, 2016), 188–91.

23. On the romantic roots of the musical metaphor for reading sequences as wholes ("polyphony"), see Liisa Steinby, "Concepts of Novelistic Polyphony," in *Bakhtin and His Others: (Inter)subjectivity, Chronotope, Dialogism* (New York: Anthem Press, 2013), 42–45. Now most prominently associated with Bakhtin, this metaphor was in wide use in early twentieth-century Eastern and Central

European criticism and theory. It figures, for example, in Viacheslav Ivanov's 1911 essay "Dostoevsky and the Novel-Tragedy," *Sobranie sochinenii*, ed. D. V. Ivanov and O. Deshart (Brussels: Foyer Oriental Chrétien, 1971–87), 4:406; and in Roman Ingarden's 1931 *The Literary Work of Art*, trans. George Grabowicz (Evanston, IL: Northwestern University Press, 1973), lxii. While Bakhtin often resists systematic readings of novels and characters, the common metaphor of "polyphony" suggests that he shared Lukács's concern—not just for the number and diversity of a novel's "dramatis personae," but also for how the reader's experience of that diversity coheres to produce a unified aesthetic effect. On Bakhtin's affinity for complex formal wholes, see Michael Holquist, "Dialogism and Aesthetics," in *Late Soviet Culture: From Perestroika to Novostroika*, ed. Thomas Lahusen (Durham, NC: Duke University Press, 1993), esp. 165–73; and recently Caryl Emerson, "Bakhtin's Radiant Polyphonic Novel, Raskolnikov's Perverse Dialogic World," in *Dostoevsky's "Crime and Punishment": Philosophical Perspectives*, ed. Robert Guay (New York: Oxford University Press, 2019).

24. Philippe Hamon, "Pour un statut sémiologique du personnage," first published in 1972, then in *Poétique du recit*, ed. Gérard Genette and Tzvetan Todorov (Éditions du Seuil, 1977), 124–25ff.; and see his later works *Le personnel du roman: Le système des personnages dans les Rougon-Macquart d'Émile Zola* (Geneva: Librairie Droz S. A., 1983); and *Texte et ideologie* (Paris: PUF, 1984).

25. Jameson, "The Ideology of Form: Partial Systems in 'La Vieille Fille,'" first published in 1976, then in Fredric Jameson, *The Political Unconscious: Narrative as a Socially Symbolic Act* (Ithaca, NY: Cornell University Press, 1981), 151–84.

26. Woloch does not tie his concept of the character-system explicitly to that of his predecessors, but he liberally cites Hamon, Jameson, and Lukács. Jameson in turn has adopted Woloch's reinterpretation of the character-system in recent work. See Fredric Jameson, *The Antinomies of Realism* (London and New York: Verso, 2013), 96ff.

27. On the literary text as a set of instructions for imagining a fictional world, see Wolfgang Iser, *The Act of Reading: A Theory of Aesthetic Response* (Baltimore: Johns Hopkins University Press, 1978); he builds primarily on Ingarden's phenomenological account of reading fiction. See also Iser, *The Implied Reader: Patterns of Communication in Prose Fiction from Bunyan to Beckett* (Baltimore: Johns Hopkins University Press, 1974). Because I do not share Iser's emphasis on the reader's personal and individual ethical experience, I have tried to avoid his ingrained term "implied reader." On the character-system as a "distributed field of attention," see Woloch, *The One vs. the Many*, 17. Iser's highly formalized phenomenology of reading has been subject to revision, expansion, and elaboration. Work particularly relevant to my concern with literary mimesis in communication with the reader, and with narrative as a set of instructions for building fictional worlds, includes Garrett Stewart, *Dear Reader: The*

Conscripted Audience in Nineteenth-Century British Fiction (Baltimore: Johns Hopkins University Press, 1996), Elaine Scarry, *Dreaming by the Book* (New York: Farrar, Straus, and Giroux, 1999), Rita Felski, *Uses of Literature* (Malden, MA, and Oxford: Blackwell, 2008), and Marie-Laure Ryan, *Narrative as Virtual Reality: Immersion and Interactivity in Literature and Electronic Media* (Baltimore: Johns Hopkins University Press, 2001 and 2015). However, adopting Iser's basic formulation of narrative as instruction, and Woloch's basic construct of the "attentive reader," allows me to focus on the main subject of this book: mimetic characterization as a systematic effect created and modulated within fictional narratives. That there is an inherent gap between the reader figure toward whom the author directs this powerful set of effects, and actual readers in their everyday lives, is one of my recurring points. On this disjuncture, see Stewart, *Dear Reader*, 28–30 and Felski, *Uses*, 18.

28. Barthes, *S/Z*, 105.

29. On Bakhtin, see above, note 5. James's indictment of Tolstoy's *War and Peace* as "life" without "composition" is almost too well known to quote: "What do such large loose baggy monsters, with their queer elements of the accidental and the arbitrary, artistically *mean*?" Henry James, Preface to *The Tragic Muse* (1908), in *The Art of the Novel: Critical Prefaces*, ed. R. P. Blackmur (New York: Charles Scribner's Sons, 1934), 84. In turn, Lubbock compares Tolstoy to a sculptor shaping "ragged masses of life torn from their setting." P. Lubbock, *The Craft of Fiction* (New York: P. Smith, 1947), 18.

30. This reading of Dostoevsky as the forerunner of Symbolist "life-creation" stems primarily from D. S. Merezhkovsky's influential turn-of-the-century study *L. Tolstoy and Dostoevsky*. It is taken up and developed in Viacheslav I. Ivanov's later essays on Dostoevsky, especially "Dostoevsky and the Novel-Tragedy" and *Dostojewskij: Tragodie-Mythos-Mystik* (1932; translated as *Freedom and the Tragic Life: A Study in Dostoevsky*). For one especially enthusiastic extension, see L. V. Pumpianskii, *Dostoevskii i antichnost'* (Saint Petersburg, 1922. Repr., *Studien und texte*, no. 1, Bremen: K-Presse, 1973), 16–17. I discuss this critical tradition further in chapter 2.

31. On Woolf and her circle in particular, see Rebecca Rubenstein, *Virginia Woolf and the Russian Point of View* (New York: Palgrave, 2009).

32. L. Tolstoy, *War and Peace*, trans. Louise and Aylmer Maude, ed. Amy Mandelker (Oxford: Oxford University Press, 2010). The blurb is a free translation of Babel's original remark, in a 1937 interview with the periodical *Literaturnaia ucheba*: "When you read Tolstoy it's the world writing, the variety of the world." "O tvorcheskom puti pisatel'ia," in Isaak Babel', *Sobranie sochinenii*, ed. I. N. Sukhikh (Moscow: Vremia, 2006), 3:396.

33. On the institutional peculiarities of Russian realism, see especially William Mills Todd III, "The Ruse of the Russian Novel," in *The Novel*, ed. Franco Moretti (Princeton, NJ: Princeton University Press, 2006), 1:401–23. For

broader discussions of the extra-aesthetic orientation of Russian literature, see, e.g., Gary Saul Morson, "Introduction," in *Literature and History: Theoretical Problems and Russian Case-Studies*, ed. Gary Saul Morson (Stanford, CA: Stanford University Press, 1986), 14–27; Nicholas Rzhevsky, *Russian Literature and Ideology* (Urbana: University of Illinois Press, 1983), 16–17ff.; and recently—an account much in sympathy with my own—Molly Brunson, *Russian Realisms: Literature and Painting, 1840–1890* (DeKalb: Northern Illinois University Press, 2016), 11–25.

34. Boris Egorov offers a survey account of the literary and political polemics that took shape in "thick journals" of the 1860s: Boris Egorov, *Izbrannoe. Esteticheskie idei v Rossii XIX veka* (Saint Petersburg: Letnii sad, 2009). See also Charles A. Moser, *Esthetics as Nightmare: Russian Literary Theory, 1855–1870* (Princeton, NJ: Princeton University Press, 1989).

35. On the eve of emancipation in the 1860s, Jeffrey Brooks estimates the rate of literacy in the Russian rural population at around six percent. By 1897, census data suggest that it had risen to about twenty-one percent of the total population of the Russian Empire. Jeffrey Brooks, *When Russia Learned to Read: Literacy and Popular Literature, 1861–1917* (Princeton, NJ: Princeton University Press, 1985), 4.

36. See Richard D. Altick, *The English Common Reader* (Chicago: University of Chicago Press, 1957), 1–98.

37. Eikhenbaum describes this gradual approach to the long prose form of the novel in *Lermontov: Opyt istoriko-literaturnoi otsenki* (Leningrad: Gosizdat, 1924), 134–44, http://feb-web.ru/feb/lermont/critics/eich24/eich24.htm?cmd=p . For an illuminating much-expanded account, see Victoria Somoff, *The Imperative of Reliability: Russian Prose on the Eve of the Novel, 1820s–1850s* (Evanston, IL: Northwestern University Press, 2015).

38. Alexei Vdovin discusses the collaboration between critics and writers in the formation of the new Russian prose canon in his *Kontsept 'glava literatury' v russkoi kritike 1830–1860-kh godov* (Tartu: Dissertationes Philologiae Slavicae Universitatis Tartuensis 26, 2011), https://publications.hse.ru/mirror/pubs/share/folder/ut207e8849/direct/62727088.

39. Indeed, René Wellek suggests that an obsession with type is one of the few characteristics reliably distinguishing nineteenth-century Russian literary criticism from the European movements on which it drew. René Wellek, "The Essential Characteristics of Russian Literary Criticism," *Comparative Literature Studies* 29, no. 2 (1992): 137–38. On the quest for a "positive hero," see Egorov, *Izbrannoe*, 116–27; and Rufus Matthewson, *The Positive Hero in Russian Literature* (Stanford, CA: Stanford University Press, 1975), 13–112.

40. For a survey discussion of the realist "type" as negotiating between the categorizing "social type" and the archetypal (Hegelian) ideal, see Wellek, "Concept of Realism," 242–46; and more recently, Frow, *Character and Person*, 107–

48. See also Lidiia Ginzburg, *O literaturnom geroe* (Leningrad: Sovetskii pisatel', 1979), esp. 16–87. In the Russian context, Irina Paperno has traced in detail the "remarkable power" of characters understood as typical "to organize the actual life of a reader who, through familiar configurations of a social role that lies behind the text, recognizes himself in the world of a literary text." Irina Paperno, *Chernyshevsky and the Age of Realism: A Study in the Semiotics of Behavior* (Stanford, CA: Stanford University Press, 1988), 9.

41. Tolstoy's acclaimed *Childhood* (*Detstvo*) was published anonymously in 1852, in the *Contemporary* (*Sovremennik*). Despite swearing off literature (for the first of several times) in the late 1850s, he had begun work on *War and Peace* by 1863, the year Chernyshevsky's *What Is to Be Done?* was published. Dostoevsky, who had achieved fame with the novellas he wrote before his exile, returned to European Russia in 1858 and plunged into the literary-polemical fray with his journal *Time* (*Vremia*; 1861–63). His first postexile novels, *Notes from a Dead House* (*Zapiski iz mertvogo doma*) and *The Insulted and the Injured* (*Unizhennye i oskorblennye*), were serially published between 1860 and 1862.

42. For a summary account of the problem of "Tolstoy's aesthetics and his art" (Rimvydas Silbajoris's formulation), see Caryl Emerson, "Tolstoy's Aesthetics," in *The Cambridge Companion to Tolstoy*, ed. Donna Tussing Orwin (Cambridge: Cambridge University Press, 2002), 237–51. See also, for an especially relevant discussion, M. M. Odesskaia, "Traktat Tolstogo 'Chto takoe iskusstvo?' v kontekste krusheniia idealisticheskoi estetiki," *Filologicheskie nauki* 2 (2009): 20–29.

43. Partially quoted in Irina Paperno, *"Who, What Am I?": Tolstoy Struggles to Narrate the Self* (Ithaca, NY: Cornell University Press, 2014), 10.

44. Eikhenbaum recounts Tolstoy's scorn for these journals (and the *raznochinets* critics and editors associated with them) in his seminal biographical study, *Lev Tolstoi. I, 50-e gody* (Leningrad, 1928; repr. Munich: Wilhelm Fink Verlag, 1968), 184–235ff. On Tolstoy's split with Nekrasov's *Contemporary* and growing hostility to the liberal intelligentsia, see also Kathryn Feuer, *Tolstoy and the Genesis of "War and Peace,"* ed. Robin Feuer Miller and Donna Tussing Orwin (Ithaca, NY: Cornell University Press, 1996), esp. 158–67.

45. Leo Tolstoy, *Tolstoy's Letters*, trans. R. F. Christian (New York: Scribner, 1978), 1:196–97.

46. For a striking example, see Tolstoy's letter of January 18–23, 1865, shortly before the publication of the first parts of *War and Peace*, to his close friend and relative Aleksandra Tolstaia: "The materials from which [my] happiness is created are of the homeliest—the children, who (pardon me) soil themselves and scream; my wife, who is feeding one and walking the other, and reproaching me every minute for not seeing that they are both on the brink of the grave; and the paper and ink with which I describe the events and feelings of people who never existed. . . . I want you to love these children of mine. There

are marvelous people among them. I love them very much" (61:70; *Tolstoy's Letters*, 192).

47. From a letter to the poet A. A. Fet, at the time when Tolstoy thought he was drafting a novel about Peter the Great. November 17, 1870, 61:240; *Tolstoy's Letters*, 230.

48. Tolstoy to A. A. Tolstaia, October 26 (?), 1872; 61:332; *Tolstoy's Letters*, 252.

49. *Tolstoy's Letters*, 296–97. For fuller discussion and quotation of this letter, see chapter 3.

50. See, for example, Iu. M. Lotman, *Struktura khudozhestvennogo teksta* (Moscow: Iskusstvo, 1970), 18.

51. Paperno, "*Who, What Am I?*," 44–45.

52. Tolstoy would later attempt to fit the idea of the character's independent life into his expanded notion of artistic communication in his "Preface to the Works of Guy de Maupassant" (1893). Notably, even there, in his conception the "subject" and characters take shape independently of the novelist, whose task is to convey their vivid organic coherence through the visionary unity of his own "moral attitude" (30:18).

53. Dostoevsky's critique of Levin in his 1877 *Diary of a Writer* is discussed further in chapter 3. On Myshkin as the representation of a "fully" or "positively beautiful man," see Dostoevsky's letters to Apollon Maikov, December 31, 1867/January 12, 1868; and to his niece Sofia Ivanova, January 1/13, 1868; 28.II:241, 28.II:251. *Selected Letters of Fyodor Dostoevsky*, ed. Joseph Frank and David I. Goldstein, trans. Andrew MacAndrew (New Brunswick, NJ: Rutgers University Press, 1987), 260–72. In correspondence with his editors at the *Russian Herald* and with Konstantin Pobedonostsev in summer 1879, Dostoevsky frequently expressed the hope that Father Zosima as the concrete image of a "pure, ideal Christian" would counter Ivan Karamazov's "blasphemy." However, in the reading list he offered a correspondent who had asked for recommendations of literature suitable for his young daughter, his own novels are a notable absence. Letter to N. L. Ozmizdov, August 18, 1880; 30.I: 211–12; *Selected Letters* 509–11.

54. In post-Soviet Russian and also in some recent English-language criticism, the trend has now swung in the opposite direction, with a new emphasis on the biographical Dostoevsky's Christian thought as present in the texts of his novels. Carol Apollonio briefly surveys this development in her introduction to *The New Russian Dostoevsky: Readings for the Twenty-First Century*, ed. Carol Apollonio (Bloomington, IN: Slavica, 2010), 3–4. See especially Karen Stepanian, *Iavlenie i dialog v romanakh F. M. Dostoevskogo* (Saint Petersburg, Kriga, 2010), T. A. Kasatkina, *O tvoriashchei prirode slova: Ontologichnost' slova v tvorchestve F. M. Dostoevskogo kak osnova "realizma v vysshem smysle"* (Moscow: IMLI RAN, 2004), and V. N. Zakharov's programmatic essay "Khristianskii realizm v russkoi literature: Postanovka problemy," in *Evangel'skii tekst v russkoi*

literature XVIII-XX vekov, vyp. 3, ed. V. N. Zakharov (Petrozavodsk: PetrGU, 2001), 5–20.

55. For a fuller discussion of the importance of type to Dostoevsky's aesthetics, see Robert Louis Jackson, *Dostoevsky's Quest for Form: A Study of His Philosophy of Art*, 2nd ed. (Bloomington, IN: Physsardt, 1978), 92–123. I return to Dostoevsky's idiosyncratic understanding of "type" in chapter 2.

56. Friedrich Schiller, *On the Aesthetic Education of Man in a Series of Letters*, ed. and trans. Elizabeth M. Wilkinson and L. A. Willoughby (Oxford: Clarendon Press, 1967), 101. On Dostoevsky and Schiller, see D. I. Chizhevskii, "Shiller i *Bratia Karamazovy*," trans. S. P. Kratz et al., in *Dostoevskii: Materialy i issledovaniia* 19 (2010): 16–57; Edmund K. Kostka, *Schiller in Russian Literature* (Philadelphia: University of Pennsylvania Press, 1965); Joseph Frank, *Dostoevsky: The Seeds of Revolt* (Princeton, NJ: Princeton University Press, 1976), 60–61ff.

57. N. A. Dobroliubov, "Kogda zhe priidet nastoiashchii den'?," in *Sobranie sochinenii*, ed. B. I. Bursov et al. (Moscow: Gosizdat. Khudozhestvennoi literatury, 1963), 6:98. Ruth Lorenz also reflects on convergences between Dobroliubov and Dostoevsky in her "Realist Convictions and Revolutionary Impatience in the Criticism of N. A. Dobroliubov," *Slavic and East European Journal* 57, no. 1 (Spring 2013): 67–88.

58. Bakhtin, *Sobranie sochinenii*, 1:4; M. Bakhtin, *Art and Answerability: Early Philosophical Essays*, trans. V. Liapunov (Austin: University of Texas Press, 1990), 55.

59. Gary Saul Morson, *Narrative and Freedom: The Shadows of Time* (New Haven, CT: Yale University Press, 1994).

60. Rolf Hellebust, "Bakhtin and the 'Virtual Sequel' in Russian Literature," *Slavic and East European Journal* 44, no. 4 (Winter 2000): 603–22.

61. Woloch, *One vs. the Many*, 13.

62. For calling attention to minorness, see especially Woloch on Dickens, *One vs. the Many*, 125–243. Recently, Marta Figlerowicz has traced the figure of the "flat protagonist"—"characters who, given their limited capacities, seem to have been given too much narrative space"—from Aphra Behn on through to Proust. *Flat Protagonists: A Theory of Novel Character* (Oxford: Oxford University Press, 2016).

63. Woloch, *One vs. the Many*, 31.

64. For one discussion of radically transposed "democracy" focused on Dostoevsky's *Notes from a Dead House*, see Nancy Ruttenberg, *Dostoevsky's Democracy* (Princeton, NJ: Princeton University Press, 2008).

65. Woloch, *One vs. the Many*, 32.

66. Figlerowicz sketches a "countercurrent" in Western European realism that also experiments with deprivileging the center of the novelistic character-system. *Flat Protagonists*, 14. It is notable that she focuses on the chronological outer ends of the British and French traditions (the seventeenth to eighteenth

centuries and the late nineteenth to early twentieth centuries), rather than its mid-nineteenth-century heart—a mark of the difficulty of moving away from the model of a single, centralized individual protagonist from within European realism as conventionally conceived. However, for a recent study that turns decisively in this direction, see Emily Steinlight, *Populating the Novel: Literary Form and the Politics of Surplus Life* (Ithaca, NY: Cornell University Press, 2018).

67. Andrew Baruch Wachtel, *The Battle for Childhood: Creation of a Russian Myth* (Stanford, CA: Stanford University Press, 1990), 3ff.

68. See Tolstoy's indignant draft of a letter to Nekrasov and the more polite version he actually sent. November 18 and 27, 1852, 59:211–14; and *Tolstoy's Letters*, 33–35.

69. I draw this contrast assenting to J. Hillis Miller's caveat that the "language of the narrator is no stable base," but my focus remains on what happens when readers receive omniscient narrative as what Lubomir Doležel calls a "world-creating word," in accordance with the conventional contract of novel reading. See J. Hillis Miller, *Reading Narrative* (Norman: University of Oklahoma Press, 1998), 167; and Lubomir Doležel, *Heterocosmica: Fiction and Possible Worlds* (Baltimore: Johns Hopkins University Press, 1998), 149.

70. The distinction between "direct" and "indirect" characterization is outlined in B. V. Tomashevskii, *Teoriia literatury* (Moscow/Leningrad: Gosudarstvennoe izdatel'stvo, 1928), 153, and productively expanded by Shlomith Rimmon-Kenan and Joseph Ewan. Shlomith Rimmon-Kenan, *Narrative Fiction: Contemporary Poetics* (London and New York: Routledge, 2002), 61–69.

71. See Bakhtin's comparative analysis of Tolstoy's short story "Three Deaths," *Problems*, 71; *Problemy*, *Sobranie sochinenii*, 6:83.

72. Lydia Ginzburg does the most to develop the vision of the authoritative narrator as central to Tolstoy's incarnation of psychological realism, which lends to elusive inner experience the solidity of a vividly narrated landscape. Lydia Ginzburg, *On Psychological Prose*, trans. and ed. Judson Rosengrant (Princeton, NJ: Princeton University Press, 1991), 254 passim. V. V. Vinogradov describes in detail the overlap between authorial and characterological "spheres" in the narration of *War and Peace*. "O iazyke Tolstogo (50–60-e gody)," in *Iazyk i stil' russkikh pisatelei ot Gogolia do Akhmatovoi* (Moscow: Nauka, 2003), 218–28.

73. See especially V. B. Shklovskii, *Mater'ial i stil' v romane L'va Tolstogo "Voina i mir"* (Moscow: Federatsiia, 1928) and V. B. Shklovskii, *Za i protiv: Zametki o Dostoevskom* (Moscow: Sovetskii pisatel', 1957); Ginzburg, *On Psychological Prose*; Bakhtin, *Problems*; and Morson, *Narrative and Freedom*.

74. Lukács, *Theory of the Novel*, 83.

75. On the basis of Dostoevsky's novels, Tatiana Kasatkina has pursued this theologically inspired vision of the "ontological" fictional word that converts the reader to the novelist's worldview (*O tvoriashchei prirode slova*, 7, 70–87 passim). At one point, Kasatkina suggests without documentation that "those who

have read and loved Dostoevsky have in very, very great numbers, as a result of reading his novels, become not just people inclined toward some abstract 'spirituality,' but observant Orthodox believers" (224).

76. Eikhenbaum, *Molodoi Tolstoi* (Munich: Wilhelm Fink, 1968), 121.

77. Suzanne Keen, *Empathy and the Novel* (Oxford: Oxford University Press, 2007), vii.

78. Erich Auerbach, *Mimesis: The Representation of Reality in Western Literature*, trans. Willard R. Trask (Princeton, NJ: Princeton University Press, 1953), 13–15.

79. Auerbach, *Mimesis*, 202.

80. Auerbach, *Mimesis*, 480–81, 552–53.

81. Auerbach, *Mimesis*, 492.

82. Auerbach, *Mimesis*, 523.

CHAPTER ONE

1. Leo Tolstoy, *Collected Shorter Fiction*, vol. 1, trans. Louise and Aylmer Maude and Nigel J. Cooper (New York and Toronto: Knopf, 2001), 137; translation modified.

> Где выражение зла, которого должно избегать? Где выражение добра, которому должно подражать в этой повести? Кто злодей, кто герой его? Все хороши и все дурны. Ни Калугин . . . ни Праскухин . . . ни Михайлов . . . ни Пест . . . не могут быть ни злодеями, ни героями повести. Герой же моей повести, которого я люблю всеми силами души, которого старался воспроизвести во всей красоте его, и который всегда был, есть и будет прекрасен,—правда. (4:59)

2. "Geroi," *Slovar' tserkovno-slavianskago i russkago iazyka*, vol. 1 (Saint Petersburg: Imperatorskaia Akademiia Nauk, 1847), https://imwerden.de/publ-918.html.

3. On Tolstoy's lifelong struggle with the limitations of human narrative, see recently Paperno, *"Who, What Am I?"*

4. Tolstoy, *War and Peace*, 327; *Polnoe sobranie sochinenii*, 10:14. Subsequent references to these editions cited by page number parenthetically in the text. In quotations from the English translation, spelling has been changed throughout to conform to American English conventions, and I frequently modify the translation to correspond more closely to the Russian. I have followed this edition in the English spellings of characters' names.

5. "3-го марта во всех комнатах Английского клуба стоял стон разговаривающих голосов, и, как пчелы на весеннем пролете, сновали взад и вперед, сидели, стояли, сходились и расходились, в мундирах, фраках . . . члены и гости клуба. . . . Большинство присутствовавших были старые, почтенные

люди с широкими, самоуверенными лицами, толстыми пальцами, твердыми движениями и голосами" (10:16).

6. For a fuller discussion of character-systems, see my introduction.

7. Woloch, *One vs. the Many*, 14.

8. Both shorter lists of the novel's protagonists (typically, Pierre, Andrei, and Natasha) and longer ones (including, for example, Hélène Kuragina) are common. However, this list of five protagonists seems to me to be justified, for reasons I hope the ensuing discussion will clarify: briefly, it is these five figures to whom the novel most consistently returns as its narrative and thematic reference points, whose trajectories in the fictional plot prove to be most closely intertwined, and whose individual perspectives are (in turn) most often intertwined with that of the main omniscient narrative.

9. Evelina Zaidenshnur counts more than five hundred characters in *War and Peace*, about two hundred of which are historical. E. Ie. Zaidenshnur, *"Voina i mir" L. N. Tolstogo* (Moscow: Kniga, 1966), 328. The figure grows (necessarily, by an indeterminate amount) if one also counts the many unnamed characters and collective groups encompassed in the novel's narration.

10. Pavel Annenkov, "Historical and Aesthetic Questions in Count L. N. Tolstoy's Novel *War and Peace*," *Vestnik Evropy*, 1868, in *Tolstoy: The Critical Heritage*, ed. A. V. Knowles (London: Routledge and Kegan Paul, 1978), 104–5 (translation modified); in Russian, P. V. Annenkov, "Istoricheskie i esteticheskie voprosy v romane gr. L.N. Tolstogo *Voina i mir*," in *L. N. Tolstoi v russkoi kritike*, ed. S. P. Bychkov (Moscow: Khudozhestvennaia literatura, 1960), 240.

11. Emily Steinlight has documented a related impulse in the nineteenth-century British novel to "make masses and crowds not just perceptible but elemental to narrative" (*Populating the Novel*, 19). What she calls "masses and crowds" is both more and less concrete than what I mean by "marginal characters": rather than designating the sheer problem of social, (bio)political, and aesthetic superfluity, my term "marginal" refers to collective or individual characters whose experience lies beyond the named protagonists' stories and whose narrative representation is thus strictly minimal. Their defining quality is not so much multiplicity as anonymity.

12. In this sense, Tolstoy extends the project of the *Waverley* novels, where Scott enlisted a passive and "mediocre" central hero and the perspectives of many minor characters in an attempt "to create the illusion of historical reality without confining that reality to the illusion he created" (Iser, *Implied Reader*, 97–100). Iser's reading of Scott's character-system owes most to Georg Lukács, *The Historical Novel*, trans. Hannah and Stanley Mitchell (London: Merlin Press, 1962), 86–88. On Tolstoy and Scott, see also Dan Ungurianu, *Plotting History: The Russian Historical Novel in the Imperial Age* (Madison: University of Wisconsin Press, 2007), 97–124.

13. Shklovskii, *Mater'ial i stil'*, 110.

14. Ginzburg, *On Psychological Prose*, 246; in Russian, *O psikhologicheskoi proze* (Leningrad: Sovetskii pisatel', 1971), 317. On the conversion of hero into "process," see also Ginzburg, *O literaturnom geroe*, 130. Ginzburg elaborates on the representation of "life in general" in *War and Peace* in a revelatory article on *War and Peace*, published in January 1944, which anticipates a number of my observations about the novel's character-system: L. Ginzburg, "O romane Tolstogo *Voina i mir*," *Zvezda*, no. 1 (1944): 125–38.

15. G. S. Morson, *Hidden in Plain View: Narrative and Creative Potentials in "War and Peace"* (Stanford, CA: Stanford University Press, 1987), 130–89.

16. Only the section that is now book 1, parts 1 and 2, was serialized in the *Russian Herald* (*Russkii vestnik*, January and February 1865 and March, April, and May 1866, under the title *The Year 1805 [1805 god]*). Tolstoy began the process of publishing the books of the novel in their own edition in 1866, and both the complete first edition and a second edition appeared in 1868–69 (16:55–76, 97–131).

17. On this aspect of *War and Peace*, see Morson, chaps. 2 and 3 passim; Lina Steiner, "Tolstoy, Liberal and Pluralist: On 'Personality' and the Protagonist in *War and Peace*," *Russian Literature* 36 (2009), 424ff.

18. To speak of the "published novel" is itself controversial, since *War and Peace* existed in a number of editions and forms during Tolstoy's lifetime. My approach to the novel's character-system rests on the idea that for any reader, the published novel counts as the version she is reading and the particular set of instructions it gives for imagining a fictional world (see my introduction). While these instructions vary from edition to edition, the basic techniques I describe here exist across all of them.

19. The first chapter of *War and Peace* can be rewritten, with little rearrangement, as a dramatic script with extensive stage directions. See Kathleen Cameron Wiggins, "The Drama in Disguise: Dramatic Modes of Narration and Textual Structure in the Mid-Nineteenth-Century Russian Novel" (PhD diss., University of California, Berkeley, 2011), 88–97.

20. I am using the word "type" here in the common sense recently defined by John Frow: "schemata which generalize and simplify human being in conventional ways and make it available to understanding and action." *Character and Person*, 107. In chapter 2, I will discuss "type" in a different sense, specific to Dostoevsky's interpretation of realist aesthetics and shaped by the moral and social weight placed on fictional "types" in 1840s–60s Russian literature and criticism.

21. "Вскоре после маленькой княгини вошел массивный, толстый молодой человек с стриженою головой, в очках, светлых панталонах по тогдашней моде, с высоким жабо и в коричневом фраке. . . . Анна Павловна приветствовала его поклоном, относящимся к людям самой низшей иерархии в ее салоне. Но, несмотря на это низшее по своему сорту приветствие, при виде вошедшего Пьера в лице Анны Павловны изобразилось беспокойство и страх, подобно тому, который выражается при виде чего-нибудь слишком огром-

ного и несвойственного месту. Хотя, действительно, Пьер был несколько больше других мужчин в комнате, но этот страх мог относиться только к тому умному и вместе робкому, наблюдательному и естественному взгляду, отличавшему его от всех в этой гостиной" (9:11).

22. E. M. Forster, *Aspects of the Novel* (London: Penguin, 1974), 81. It can be taken as a measure of the success of the Russian realists' manipulations of the conventions of mimetic illusion that Forster himself found a paucity of flat characters in Russian novels, "where they would be a decided help" (74).

23. Many scholars comment on the central distinction that Tolstoy (following in the tradition of Rousseau) makes between social pretense and organic life and how this distinction helps organize his characters into "positive" and "negative," "living" and "dead." Particularly relevant here is Lydia Ginzburg's observation that "the opposition of the authentic [*podlinnogo*] to the spectral and the pretended [*prizrachnomu i minimomu*], so decisive for the whole construction of *War and Peace*, is realized in the very method of representing people and things" ("O romane Tolstogo" 131; my translation). See also John Bayley's suggestive analysis of "the thick, three-dimensional presence" of Pierre waiting at his father's deathbed, standing out conspicuously from "the tone of the surrounding novel." *Tolstoy and the Novel* (Chicago: University of Chicago Press, 1988), 159. For a recent account that classifies *War and Peace*'s characters by their thematic associations with "life" and "not life," see S. A. Nikol'skii, "Smysly i tsennosti russkogo mirovozzreniia v tvorchestve L. N. Tolstogo," *Voprosy filosofii* 9 (September 2010): 117–35.

24. "Наступило молчание. . . . Дочь гостьи уже оправляла платье, вопросительно глядя на мать, как вдруг из соседней комнаты послышался бег к двери нескольких мужских и женских ног, грохот зацепленного и поваленного стула, и в комнату вбежала тринадцатилетняя девочка, запахнув что-то короткою кисейною юбкою, и остановилась по средине комнаты. Очевидно было, она нечаянно, с нерассчитанного бега, заскочила так далеко. В дверях в ту же минуту показались студент с малиновым воротником, гвардейский офицер, пятнадцатилетняя девочка и толстый румяный мальчик в детской курточке" (9:46–47).

25. "С людьми, окружавшими его, от дочери до слуг, князь был резок и неизменно-требователен . . . каждый начальник той губернии, где было имение князя, считал своим долгом являться к нему и точно так же, как архитектор, садовник или княжна Марья, дожидался назначенного часа выхода князя в высокой официантской. И каждый в этой официантской испытывал то же чувство почтительности и даже страха. . . . В день приезда молодых, утром, по обыкновению, княжна Марья в урочный час входила для утреннего приветствия в официантскую и со страхом крестилась и читала внутренно молитву. Каждый день она входила и каждый день молилась о том, чтобы это ежедневное свидание сошло благополучно" (9:106–7).

26. For fuller discussion of this term, see my introduction.

27. On this family or "breed" force in *War and Peace*, see S. G. Bocharov, *Roman L. Tolstogo "Voina i mir"* (Moscow: Khudozhestvennaia literatura, 1963), 89–100; he focuses particularly on the system of families defined by the Rostovs, the Kuragins, and the Bolkonskys.

28. Anna Pavlovna Scherer and *"ma tante"* could be included as another named fictional family. There are also the three Mamontov sisters, Catiche, Olga, and Sophie (Count Bezukhov's nieces), and the Meliukovs, whom the Rostov children visit in the *sviatki* masquerades. Others appear, but still more fleetingly; for example, the Smolensk innkeeper Ferapontov and his wife.

29. I borrow the term "thematic function" from Phelan, *Reading People*, 9ff.

30. The famous image of the "doorway" is associated with Andrei long before the narration of his death (115; 9:132) and follows him and other Bolkonskys throughout the novel. See Ilya Vinitsky, "Behind the Door," *Tolstoy Studies Journal* 29 (2007): 80–86; and M. B. Pliukhanova, "Tvorchestvo Tolstogo," in *L. N. Tolstoi: pro et contra* (Saint Petersburg: Izdatel'stvo Russkogo Khristianskogo gumanitarnogo instituta, 2000), 837.

31. Discussed further in Morson, *Hidden*, 85–86.

32. On Pierre as *Bildungshero*, see Lina Steiner, *For Humanity's Sake: The Bildungsroman in Russian Culture* (Toronto: University of Toronto Press, 2011), 109ff.

33. On the structural importance of these brother-sister pairs in *War and Peace*, see Anna Berman, *Siblings in Tolstoy and Dostoevsky: The Path to Universal Brotherhood* (Evanston, IL: Northwestern University Press, 2015), 34–45.

34. It is notable, in this context, that Shklovsky suggests Vera is the only one of Tolstoy's "family heroes" who "apprehends life correctly, canonically" and thus cannot be used for *artistic* purposes of defamiliarization; she is thus technically as well as thematically superfluous. Shklovskii, *Mater'ial i stil'*, 109–10.

35. On Tolstoy's suspicion of sentimental conventions of friendship on the model of Rousseau's *Julie*, see Anne Eakin Moss, "Tolstoy's Politics of Love: 'That Passionate and Tender Friendship That Exists Only among Women,'" *Slavic and East European Journal* 53, no. 4 (Winter 2009): 566–86.

36. On Anatole's seduction of Natasha, in particular, as an inserted novella that follows the generic lines of Karamzin's "Poor Liza," see Galina Rylkova, "The History of Natasha Rostova's Affair with Anatole Kuragin," *Canadian-American Slavic Studies* 31, no. 1 (Spring 1997): 51–63.

37. Indeed, class itself distances Boris Drubetskoy from Tolstoy's conception of the heroic. Kathryn Feuer points out that none of the novel's "young men from the provinces"—among them Boris, Berg, and Dolokhov—is allowed to become a central protagonist or even a sympathetic character, because according to Tolstoy, "only hereditary privilege and fortune can put one outside 'the struggle between conscience and want.'" Feuer, *Genesis*, 165.

38. V. Propp, *Morphology of the Folktale*, trans. Laurence Scott and ed. Louis A. Wagner (Austin: University of Texas Press, 1968), 30.

39. Donna Orwin points out this connection, "the potential in the Rostovs to become like the Kuragins." Donna Tussing Orwin, *Tolstoy's Art and Thought, 1847–1880* (Princeton, NJ: Princeton University Press, 1993), 124–26; see also Bocharov, *Roman L. Tolstogo*, 89–100. The character Aline Kuragina, about whom we know almost nothing, functions to highlight their similarity. She makes the Kuragins the only prominent fictional family in the novel apart from the Rostovs to have both a husband/father and wife/mother represented in the discourse, and as Tolstoy's contemporary Konstantin Leont'ev complained, Aline Kuragina and Countess Rostova share an irrational feeling of jealousy toward their daughters' future married happiness. K. Leont'ev, *Analiz, stil' i veianie: o romanakh Gr. L. N. Tolstogo* (Moscow, 1911/1912; repr. Providence, RI: Brown University Press, 1965), 79–81.

40. For minor characters as "the proletariat of the novel . . . the subordinate beings who are delimited in themselves while performing a function for someone else," see Woloch, *One vs. the Many*, 27.

41. On the "fantasy" of omniscient narrative (in the context of Dickens's novels), see Audrey Jaffe, *Vanishing Points* (Berkeley: University of California Press, 1991).

42. "Она всё думала о том, что никто никак не может понять всего, что она понимает, и что в ней есть. «Соня?» подумала она, глядя на спящую, свернувшуюся кошечку с ее огромной косой. «Нет, куда ей! Она добродетельная. Она влюбилась в Николеньку и больше ничего знать не хочет. Мама, и та не понимает. Это удивительно, как я умна и как . . . она мила», продолжала она, говоря про себя в третьем лице и воображая, что это говорил про нее какой-то очень умный, самый умный и самый хороший мужчина . . . «Всё, всё в ней есть,—продолжал этот мужчина, умна необыкновенно, мила и потом хороша, необыкновенно хороша, ловка,—плавает, верхом ездит отлично, а голос! Можно сказать, удивительный голос!» Она пропела свою любимую музыкальную фразу из Херубиниевской оперы, бросилась на постель, засмеялась от радостной мысли, что она сейчас заснет, крикнула Дуняшу потушить свечку, и еще Дуняша не успела выйти из комнаты, как она уже перешла в другой, еще более счастливый мир сновидений, где всё было так же легко и прекрасно, как и в действительности, но только было еще лучше, потому что было по другому" (10:194–95; ellipses in original).

43. I quote from J. Hillis Miller's discussion of Wittgenstein's reflections on character in *The Brown Book*, in his *Ariadne's Thread* (New Haven, CT: Yale University Press, 1992), 83–94. For Miller, the loop undermines the construct both of fictional characters and of moral character or selfhood, but he discusses the novel as a safe space for "maintaining the fiction of selfhood in the teeth of a recognition that it is a fictive projection" (98).

44. "Kharakter," in M. Fasmer, *Etimologicheskii slovar' russkogo iazyka*, 2nd ed., trans. O. N. Trubacheva, vol. 4; "character, n.," *OED Online*, September 2013, Oxford University Press. "Kharakter" does not standardly refer to fictional personages; for its most common literary sense, see the fifth definition in the *Dictionary of the Modern Russian Literary Language*, vol. 17: "An artistic image that consolidates the typical traits of some group of people; a type."

45. See also Woloch on how Jane Austen defines "the interior realm of personality" within the narrative "space" of her protagonist Elizabeth Bennet (*One vs. the Many*, 56); and on the convergence between central protagonist and omniscient narrative (77–82). Bakhtin's idea of the "character zone" that can be outlined in free indirect discourse—irreducible to the character's direct, specific thoughts or speech—is also relevant here. "Discourse in the Novel," *The Dialogic Imagination*, ed. Michael Holquist, trans. Caryl Emerson and Michael Holquist (Austin: University of Texas Press, 1981), 316–20; "Slovo v romane," *Sobranie sochinenii* 3:70–74.

46. "Пьер, не переменяя своего положения задранных ног, смотрел на них через очки, и не понимал, что им может быть нужно и каким образом все они могли жить, не разрешив тех вопросов, которые занимали его. . . . О чем бы он ни начинал думать, он возвращался к одним и тем же вопросам, которых он не мог разрешить, и не мог перестать задавать себе. Как будто в голове его свернулся тот главный винт, на котором держалась вся его жизнь. Винт не входил дальше, не выходил вон, а вертелся, ничего не захватывая, всё на том же нарезе, и нельзя было перестать вертеть его. Вошел смотритель и униженно стал просить его сиятельство подождать только два часика. . . . Смотритель очевидно врал и хотел только получить с проезжего лишние деньги. «Дурно ли это было или хорошо?» спрашивал себя Пьер. « . . . Что дурно? Что хорошо? Что надо любить, что ненавидеть? Для чего жить, и что такое я? Что такое жизнь, что смерть? Какая сила управляет всем?» спрашивал он себя" (10:64–65).

47. V. V. Vinogradov analyzes the close interaction between omniscient narrative and the "prisms" of individual characters' perspectives in "O iazyke Tolstogo (50–60-e gody)," 218–28.

48. "Николай Ростов отвернулся и, как будто отыскивая чего-то, стал смотреть на даль, на воду Дуная, на небо, на солнце. Как хорошо показалось небо, как голубо, спокойно и глубоко! Как ярко и торжественно опускающееся солнце! . . . И еще лучше были далекие, голубеющие за Дунаем горы, монастырь, таинственные ущелья, залитые до макуш туманом сосновые леса. . . . «Ничего, ничего бы я не желал, ничего бы не желал, ежели бы я только был там,—думал Ростов.—Во мне одном и в этом солнце так много счастия»" (9:180; second ellipsis in original).

49. "Как бы со всего размаха крепкой палкой кто-то из ближайших солдат, как ему показалось, ударил его в голову. . . . Над ним не было ничего

уже, кроме неба—высокого неба, не ясного, но всё-таки неизмерно высокого, с тихо ползущими по нем серыми облаками. «Как тихо, спокойно и торжественно, совсем не так, как я бежал,—подумал князь Андрей,—не так, как мы бежали, кричали и дрались; совсем не так, как с озлобленными и испуганными лицами тащили друг у друга банник француз и артиллерист,—совсем не так ползут облака по этому высокому бесконечному небу»" (9:344).

50. On the differences reflected in these two landscapes, each fitted to the intellectual characters and desires of the protagonists who see them, see Patricia Carden, "The Expressive Self in *War and Peace*," *Canadian-American Slavic Studies* 12, no. 4 (Winter 1978), 528–29.

51. Genette, *Narrative Discourse*, 185. In these suggestive reflections on what he calls "the Balzacian model" of characterization, where each character gets "a recurrent linguistic characteristic" associated with a "personal and/or class marker," Genette notes that this technique draws the reader's attention to the shaky verbal basis of *all* realist characterization: "Here the strongest verbal existence is the sign and the beginning of disappearance."

52. "В дыму, оглушаемый беспрерывными выстрелами, заставлявшими его каждый раз вздрагивать, Тушин, не выпуская своей носогрейки, бегал от одного орудия к другому. . . . Вследствие этого страшного гула, шума, потребности внимания и деятельности, Тушин не испытывал ни малейшего неприятного чувства страха. . . . Ему казалось, что уже очень давно, едва ли не вчера, была та минута, когда он увидел неприятеля и сделал первый выстрел. . . . Неприятельские пушки в его воображении были не пушки, а трубки, из которых редкими клубами выпускал дым невидимый курильщик. . . . «Ну-ка, наша Матвевна», говорил он про себя" (9:234–35).

53. He might thus be described as a "card," W. J. Harvey's term for a striking character who combines "relative changelessness" with "a peculiar kind of freedom" to be "triumphantly himself"; or an "eccentric" (Alex Woloch's term for a "fragmentary character who plays a disruptive, oppositional role within the plot"). W. J. Harvey, *Character and the Novel* (London: Chatto & Windus, 1965), 61; *One vs. the Many*, 25. But it is notable how often Dolokhov's unrepresented life in the story gleams through the cracks of his represented life in the discourse: he is quite different in this sense from Bertha Mason, whom Woloch gives as the paradigmatic "eccentric" in nineteenth-century literature, and from Dickens's fragmentary minor characters.

54. "—Да, граф, он слишком благороден и чист душою,—говаривала она—для нашего нынешнего, развращенного света. Добродетели никто не любит, она всем глаза колет. Ну скажите, граф, справедливо это, честно это со стороны Безухова? . . . В Петербурге эти шалости с квартальным там что-то шутили, ведь они вместе делали? Что ж, Безухову ничего, а Федя все на своих плечах перенес! . . . Что ж теперь—эта дуэль! Есть ли чувство, честь у этих людей! Зная, что он единственный сын, вызвать на дуэль и стрелять так прямо!" (10:42).

55. Orwin, *Tolstoy's Art*, 120–21.

56. Morson, *Hidden*, 151.

57. See, for example, Svetlana Grenier, *Representing the Marginal Woman in Nineteenth-Century Russian Literature: Personalism, Feminism, and Polyphony* (Westport, CT, and London: Greenwood Press, 2001), 89–99; Brett Cooke, "Tolstoi i novyi Darvin(izm)," *Lev Tolstoi i mirovaia literatura* (Tula: Izdatel'skii dom Iasnaia Poliana, 2005), 198–201; Berman, *Siblings*, 45, 157.

58. Feuer notes that Sonya does have two potential last names in drafts of the novel, Cherboff and Niznova (*Genesis*, 261n95); in the final manuscript, both are absent.

59. Shklovsky sees in this inversion another potential novel, and a parable about the defamiliarizing power of realist art itself: "The Circassian is what Sonya could have been. . . . It is both Sonya, and not Sonya. Perception as if flickers, contradicts itself, doubles. . . . Art can, without touching things, change them, returning them to our consciousness." *Povesti o proze: Razmyshleniia i razbory* (Moscow: Khudozhestvennaia literatura, 1966), 2:208. But it seems significant that this inversion is temporary: even within the bounded artistic world of the novel, defamiliarization operates within an order that does not get permanently overturned.

60. This sentiment was already expressed in early reviews, perhaps most clearly by Tolstoy's later friend and collaborator Nikolai Strakhov (*Zaria*, no. 1, 1870): "Thousands of characters [*lits*], thousands of scenes, every conceivable scene of public and private life . . . everything is in the picture. And at the same time not a single figure pushes another into the background, not one scene, not one impression interferes with any other, everything is in its place, everything is clear, everything is distinct, everything is in harmony with itself and the whole." Knowles, *Critical Heritage*, 160 (translation modified); in Russian, *Roman L. N. Tolstogo "Voina i mir" v russkoi kritike*, ed. I. N. Sukhikh (Leningrad: Izdatel'stvo Leningradskogo universiteta, 1989), 257–58. Strakhov's observation reemerges, with similar hyperbole, in Isaiah Berlin: "The celebrated lifelikeness of every object and every person in [Tolstoy's] world derives from this astonishing capacity of presenting every ingredient of it in its fullest individual essence . . . always as a solid object, seen simultaneously from near and far, in natural, unaltering daylight, from all possible angles of vision, set in an absolutely specific context in time and space—an event fully present to the senses or the imagination in all its facets, with every nuance sharply and firmly articulated." *The Hedgehog and the Fox: An Essay on Tolstoy's View of History* (Chicago: Elephant Paperbacks, 1993), 41.

61. In this spirit, John Bayley describes *War and Peace* as "a massive feat of arbitration," where "all the characters . . . from the greatest to the least—get exactly what their natures require." *Tolstoy and the Novel*, 78.

62. The link, reflected in miniature here, between *War and Peace* and classical epic comes up in contemporary reviews of the novel, in Tolstoy's own di-

aries, and in his remark, quoted in Gorky's memoirs, that "*War and Peace* is like the *Iliad*." M. Gor'kii, *Vospominaniia*, excerpted in Bychkov, *L. N. Tolstoi v russkoi kritike*, 429. On Hélène as a transformation of Homer's Helen, see also B. M. Eikhenbaum, "Ocherednye problemy izucheniia L'va Tolstogo" in *Trudy iubileinoi sessii. Sektsiia filologicheskikh nauk* (Leningrad: Izdatel'stvo Leningradskogo gosudarstvennogo universiteta, 1946), 288; Laura Jepsen, *From Achilles to Christ: The Myth of the Hero in Tolstoy's* War and Peace (Author's copyright, 1978), 53–60.

63. "Ее бюст, казавшийся всегда мраморным Пьеру, находился в таком близком расстоянии от его глаз, что он своими близорукими глазами невольно различал живую прелесть ее плеч и шеи, и так близко от его губ, что ему стоило немного нагнуться, чтобы прикоснуться до нее. Он слышал тепло ее тела, запах духов и скрып ее корсета при движении. Он видел не ее мраморную красоту, составлявшую одно целое с ее платьем, он видел и чувствовал всю прелесть ее тела, которое было закрыто только одеждой. И, раз увидав это, он не мог видеть иначе, как мы не можем возвратиться к раз объясненному обману. «Так вы до сих пор не замечали, как я прекрасна?— как будто сказала Элен.—Вы не замечали, что я женщина?»" (9:251–52).

64. Boris's transformation might alternatively be mapped onto the novel's prehistory in drafts. Scholars have traced his passage from central to progressively more minor hero, as the novel's initial two protagonists were broken down into "negative and positive characteristics" and divided into four male characters (Feuer, *Genesis*, 23–24, 62–66, 114–15; see also Zaidenshnur, *Roman Tolstogo*, 158–59). Nevertheless, the traces of Boris's transformation from potentially major to definitively minor character remain in the final version of the novel.

65. Boris's observations closely follow the description of the Tilsit peace in A. I. Mikhailovskii-Danilevskii's *Opisanie vtoroi voiny imperatora Aleksandra s Napoleonom* (Saint Petersburg, 1846), one of the historical volumes on which Tolstoy relied (16:142). By having Boris time the meeting, Tolstoy places him in the position of a particular observer on the bank, Prince Mikhail Semenovich Vorontsov (Mikhailovskii-Danilevskii's source for the fact that the meeting lasted "one hour and fifty minutes"); Boris is still more pedantically accurate. *Opisanie vtoroi voiny*, 364–66.

66. In Woloch's terms, he has been recast as a "worker" (*One vs. the Many*, 25); in Henry James's and Harvey's, as a "ficelle," a character who "exists in the novel primarily to serve some function" (*Character and the Novel*, 58).

67. D. S. Merezhkovskii, *L. Tolstoi i Dostoevskii. Zhizn' i tvorchestvo* (Moscow: Nauka, 2000), 91–92.

68. Merezhkovskii, *L. Tolstoi i Dostoevskii*, 95, 96.

69. As Shklovsky points out, such "accenting" repetition is a device that makes up for the small *métrage* or "quantity of lines set aside for" characters like Lise (*Mater'ial i stil'*, 100–101), but Merezhkovsky's description emphasizes this

device's uncanniness. On the Gothic horror of his image, see Olga Matich, *Erotic Utopia* (Madison: University of Wisconsin Press, 2005), 35.

70. For this kind of reconstruction of Lise's life—closely following Tolstoy's text, but offering a narrative dissociated from the perspective of its central characters—see Natasha Sankovitch, *Creating and Recovering Experience: Repetition in Tolstoy* (Stanford, CA: Stanford University Press, 1998), 58–64.

71. Similarly, Jeff Love comments that for Pierre Bezukhov, Platon Karataev is an ideal "whose content contradicts its form": just by making him into an ideal, Pierre goes against the everyday, prosaic wisdom that he ought to have learned from Platon's example. Jeff Love, *The Overcoming of History in "War and Peace"* (Amsterdam: Rodopi, 2004), 177.

72. "Народ молчал и только всё теснее и теснее нажимал друг на друга. Держать друг друга, дышать в этой зараженной духоте, не иметь силы пошевелиться и ждать чего-то неизвестного, непонятного и страшного, становилось невыносимо. Люди, стоящие в передних рядах . . . все с испуганно-широко раскрытыми глазами и разинутыми ртами, напрягая все свои силы, удерживали на своих спинах напор задних. . . . Но вслед за восклицанием удивления, вырвавшимся у Верещагина, он жалобно вскрикнул от боли, и этот крик погубил его. Та натянутая до высшей степени преграда человеческого чувства, которая держала еще толпу, прорвалась мгновенно. . . . Как последний седьмой вал, разбивающий корабли, взмыла из задних рядов эта последняя неудержимая волна, донеслась до передних, сбила их и поглотила всё" (11:347–48).

73. Morson reads this episode as a "particularly telling example" of creation by potential in *War and Peace*, since it receives such narrative emphasis but has no repercussions on the fictional plot, the lives of the major characters, or the portrait of the abandoned city (*Hidden*, 148–49). A Russian reviewer countered that on the contrary, Mavra Kuzmyshina's donation of her twenty-five rubles speaks to the "general national sacrifice" and the unity inspired by Napoleon's invasion, one of the novel's most important thematic threads. A. G. Grodetskaia, "Vozvrashchenie k diskussii o zhanre *Voiny i mira*," *Russkaia literatura* 3 (1991), 185. My reading links these positions: the episode acts as a bridge between the lives of the major characters and the unbounded national events those lives must be made to illuminate and structure.

74. Partially cited in Feuer, *Genesis*, 165. As Feuer reads it, Tolstoy's point here is primarily political: Dolokhov's victory, like Napoleon's, would represent the triumph of a usurper over the natural socioeconomic order, based in the connection between landowner and peasant.

75. Boris Eikhenbaum gives the canonical version of this argument in his *Lev Tolstoi* (516ff.). Both Feuer and Evelina Zaidenshnur, after extensive work with Tolstoy's drafts, express skepticism about the novel's origin as an unmixed family chronicle; each identifies an initial political (Feuer) or national-historical

(Zaidenshnur) conception for the novel that influences all future drafts and layers (Feuer, *Genesis*, 44–53 and 200–206; Zaidenshnur, *Roman Tolstogo*, 5–10 and 391n2).

76. Among the surprisingly few prior critical accounts relating Tolstoy's theory of history to his practices of characterization are Michael Holquist, "Character Change as Language Change in *War and Peace*," in *Russianness: Studies on a Nation's Identity*, ed. Robert L. Belknap (Ann Arbor, MI: Ardis, 1990), 215ff.; Love, *Overcoming*, 157–81; and Lina Steiner, "Tolstoy, Liberal and Pluralist" and "The Ends of 'Personality': Tolstoy and the Problem of Modern Identity," in *From Petersburg to Bloomington: Studies Presented in Honor of Nina Perlina*, ed. John Bartle et al., 355–72. Bloomington, IN: Slavica, 2012. All these readings focus on named, central protagonists; here, I consider the epilogue's relevance to the novel's entire character-system.

77. Scholars of *War and Peace* differ widely about how its named historical characters fit into its fictional character-system. Shklovsky inaugurated the position that "if we see Napoleon and Kutuzov next to Natasha Rostova . . . we should consider them all in the writer's system of analysis, historical characters on the same footing as imaginary ones." V. Shklovskii, *Lev Tolstoi* (Moscow: Molodaia gvardiia, 1967), 291. For a similar treatment of historical characters, see Ruth Ronen, *Possible Worlds in Literary Theory* (Cambridge: Cambridge University Press, 1994), 122–30; and Doležel, *Heterocosmica*, 18; he reaffirms this position in his *Possible Worlds of Fiction and History* (Baltimore: Johns Hopkins University Press, 2010), 84–86. In the particular case of *War and Peace*, Dorrit Cohn argues for segregating the narrative portions of the novel, where Napoleon is treated like a fictional character, from the digressions, which remain "sharply separated" from the experience of fictional characters. Dorrit Cohn, *The Distinction of Fiction* (Baltimore: Johns Hopkins University Press, 1998), 153–60. Catherine Gallagher suggests a more flexible approach, which I adopt here: what is said about Napoleon in *War and Peace* may be fictional, but the referent of the name "Napoleon" is not. It is thus a generic requirement of the historical novel that its readers remain alert to shifts among fictional, historical, and counterfactual modes. See Catherine Gallagher, "What Would Napoleon Do?" *New Literary History* 42, no. 2 (Spring 2011): 315–36; and Gallagher, *Telling It Like It Wasn't: The Counterfactual Imagination in Fiction and History* (Chicago: University of Chicago Press, 2018), 72–75.

78. For a summary of this philosophical theme in *War and Peace*, see Orwin, *Tolstoy's Art*, chap. 5 (see esp. 123–40). Thomas Newlin offers an innovative perspective on the novel's "biological thinking" in his "'Swarm Life' and the Biology of *War and Peace*," *Slavic Review* 71, no. 2 (Summer 2012): 359–84.

79. This, as I understand it, is the essence of Jeff Love's conclusion in his detailed reconstruction of Tolstoy's philosophical argument in the digressions and part 2 of the epilogue. *Overcoming*, 72–95 and 123–56.

80. For readings that focus on pinpointing the relationship between *War and Peace* and historical narrative (beginning from Morson's claim that *War and Peace* is skeptical about *any* form of history; *Hidden*, 100–129), see Andrew Baruch Wachtel, *An Obsession with History: Russian Writers Confront the Past* (Stanford, CA: Stanford University Press, 1994), 88–122; Love, *Overcoming*, 156ff.; Ungurianu, *Plotting History*, 120ff.; and E. Tsimbaeva, "Istoricheskii kontekst v khudozhestvennom obraze: dvorianskoe obshchestvo v romane *Voina i mir*," *Voprosy literatury* 5 (October 2004): 175–215. In essentially dismissing Tolstoy's concern with history and historical accuracy, Morson and Tsimbaeva may go too far, but the collaboration in *War and Peace* between fictional and historical discourse demonstrated by Wachtel, Love, and Ungurianu is nevertheless unstable; as I argue, its terms are troubled from within the novel itself.

81. "Радостные улыбки стояли на всех лицах молодых солдат, смотревших на Мореля. Старые солдаты, считавшие неприличным заниматься такими пустяками, лежали с другой стороны костра, но изредка, приподнимаясь на локте, с улыбкой взглядывали на Мореля.—Тоже люди,—сказал один из них, уворачиваясь в шинель.—И полынь на своем кореню растет.—Оо! Господи, Господи! Как звездно, страсть! К морозу . . .—И всё затихло. Звезды, как будто зная, что теперь никто не увидит их, разыгрались в черном небе. То вспыхивая, то потухая, то вздрагивая, они хлопотливо о чем-то радостном, но таинственном, перешептывались между собою" (12:196; ellipsis in original).

82. "«Солдатом быть, просто солдатом!» думал Пьер, засыпая. «Войти в эту общую жизнь всем существом, проникнуться тем, что делает их такими. Но как скинуть с себя всё это лишнее, дьявольское, всё бремя этого внешнего человека? . . . Я мог еще после дуэли с Долоховым быть послан солдатом».—И в воображении Пьера мелькнул обед в клубе, на котором он вызвал Долохова, и благодетеля в Торжке. И вот Пьеру представляется торжественная столовая ложа. Ложа эта происходит в Английском клубе. . . . С одной стороны стола сидели Анатоль, Долохов, Несвицкой [*sic*], Денисов и другие такие же (категория этих людей так же ясно была во сне определена в душе Пьера, как и категория тех людей, которых он называл они), и эти люди, Анатоль, Долохов, громко кричали, пели; но из-за их крика слышен был голос благодетеля . . . Пьер не понимал того, что говорил благодетель, но он знал (категория мыслей так же ясна была во сне), что благодетель говорил о добре, о возможности быть тем, чем были они. И они со всех сторон, с своими простыми, добрыми, твердыми лицами, окружали благодетеля. Но они хотя и были добры, они не смотрели на Пьера, не знали его. Пьер захотел обратить на себя их внимание и сказать" (11:293).

83. "Она пополнела и поширела, так что трудно было узнать в этой сильной матери прежнюю тонкую, подвижную Наташу. Черты лица ее определились и имели выражение спокойной мягкости и ясности. В ее лице не было,

как прежде, этого непрестанно горевшего огня оживления, составлявшего ее прелесть. Теперь часто видно было одно ее лицо и тело, а душа вовсе не было видно. Видна была одна сильная, красивая и плодовитая самка. Очень редко теперь зажигался в ней прежний огонь" (12:265–66).

84. On the link between an "excessive" redundancy that eliminates ambiguity and the ideological novel genre, see Susan Rubin Suleiman, "Redundancy and the 'Readable' Text," *Poetics Today* 1, no. 3 (1980): 119–42.

85. Walter Benjamin, *Selected Writings*, trans. Rodney Livingstone et al., ed. Michael W. Jennings et al. (Cambridge, MA: Harvard University Press, 1999), 2:239–40. My reading of this passage is shaped by J. Hillis Miller's in his *Fiction and Repetition: Seven English Novels* (Cambridge, MA: Harvard University Press, 1982), 5–12. In his deconstruction of the mimetic relationship between model and copy, Miller in turn is following Deleuze: see Gilles Deleuze, *Difference and Repetition*, trans. Paul Patton (New York: Columbia University Press, 1994), 24–25ff.

CHAPTER TWO

1. "Béla Balázs and His Detractors" (1918). Quoted and translated from Hungarian into German in G. Lukács, *Dostojewski: Notizen und Entwürfe*, ed. J. C. Nyiri (Budapest: Akademiai Kiado, 1985), 27–28.

2. See the introductory note to the first journal publication of *The Theory of the Novel* in 1916, as discussed in Galin Tihanov, "Ethics and Revolution: Lukács's Responses to Dostoevskii," *Modern Language Review* 94, no. 3 (July 1999): 619; and Tihanov, *The Master and the Slave: Lukács, Bakhtin, and the Ideas of Their Time* (Oxford: Clarendon, 2000), 165–87. Lukács never completed a study of Dostoevsky, but after his conversion to Marxism, he continued to read Dostoevsky as the herald of a political and aesthetic utopia. He wrote several brief reviews on Dostoevsky in the early 1920s, casting him as a prophet of the classless society to come at the end of the revolution. Georg Lukács, *Reviews and Articles from "Die rote Fahne,"* trans. Peter Palmer (London: Merlin Press, 1983), 44–48ff. He abandoned this thesis in "On Dostoevsky's Legacy" ("Über den Dostojewski-Nachlaß," 1931), a notoriously expedient self-critique, but returned to it in softened form in a 1943 essay on Dostoevsky in *Dostoevsky: A Collection of Critical Essays*, ed. René Wellek (Englewood Cliffs, NJ: Prentice Hall, 1962), 146–58. On this evolution, see (in addition to Tihanov) Ferenc Fehér, "The Last Phase of Romantic Anti-Capitalism: Lukács' Response to the War," *New German Critique* 10 (Winter 1977): 140–44; and Zoltan Andor Feher, "Georg Lukács's Role in Dostoevsky's European Reception at the Turn of the Century" (PhD diss., University of California, Los Angeles, 1978), 106–237.

3. Lukács, *Theory of the Novel*, 152.

4. Lukács, *Dostojewski*, 42–62.

5. Lukács, *Theory of the Novel*, 41, 88.

6. Merezhkovskii, *L. Tolstoi i Dostoevskii*, 144.

7. Ivanov, *Sobranie sochinenii*, 4:400.

8. "Roman, kak literaturnyi zhanr," Bakhtin, *Sobranie sochinenii*, 3:634. In English, Mikhail Bakhtin, "Epic and Novel," in *The Dialogic Imagination*, 31.

9. Lukács, *Theory of the Novel*, 56.

10. Bakhtin, *Sobranie sochinenii*, 6:58; *Problems*, 49.

11. Fyodor Dostoevsky, *Poor Folk and Other Stories*, trans. David McDuff (New York and London: Penguin Books, 1988), 68; *Polnoe sobranie sochinenii* 1:63.

12. Bakhtin, *Sobranie sochinenii* 6:57–58 and 68; *Problems*, 48–49 and 58. Throughout chapter 2 of his Dostoevsky book, Bakhtin writes of the Dostoevskian hero's "non-coincidence with himself." *Sobranie sochinenii* 6:70; *Problems*, 59. In "Epic and Novel," he extended this "surplus of humanness" to all novelistic characters. *Sobranie sochinenii* 3:636–40; "Epic and Novel," 34–37.

13. On "direct" and "indirect" characterization, see Rimmon-Kenan, *Narrative Fiction*, 61–69; and note 70 to my introduction.

14. For a summary of this line of criticism, see V. A. Keldysh, "Nasledie Dostoevskogo i russkaia mysl' porubezhnoi epokhi," in *Sviaz' vremen: Problem preemstvennosti v russkoi literature kontsa XIX-nachala XX v.*, ed. Keldysh (Moscow: Nasledie, 1992), 77–88.

15. V. G. Avseenko, "Sketches of Current Literature," *Russkii mir*, no. 55 (1875). Quoted in A. S. Dolinin, *Poslednie romany Dostoevskogo* (Moscow: Sovetskii pisatel', 1963), 197–98.

16. As Vladimir Nabokov put it, "One feels that he does not see his characters physically, that they are merely puppets, remarkable, fascinating puppets plunged into the moving stream of the author's ideas." *Lectures on Russian Literature*, ed. Fredson Bowers (London: Picador, 1981), 129.

17. For further discussion of "mimetic life," see my introduction. Scholars who emphasize Dostoevsky's inheritance from the Gothic tradition have dwelt particularly on his departure from the model of literary characters as psychologically synthetic, physically embodied individuals; see, for example, Donald Fanger, *Dostoevsky and Romantic Realism: A Study of Dostoevsky in Relation to Balzac, Dickens, and Gogol* (Cambridge, MA: Harvard University Press, 1965), 264. Recently, Carol Apollonio and Yuri Corrigan pursue illuminating readings of Dostoevsky's characters as "facets of a *single, shared consciousness*." Carol Apollonio, *Dostoevsky's Secrets: Reading against the Grain* (Evanston, IL: Northwestern University Press, 2009), 9; Yuri Corrigan, *Dostoevsky and the Riddle of the Self* (Evanston, IL: Northwestern University Press, 2017).

18. On the conventional reduction or distortion of minor characters, see Woloch, *One vs. the Many*.

19. See Gary Rosenshield, *"Crime and Punishment": The Techniques of the Omniscient Author* (Lisse: Peter de Ridder Press, 1978), 26–85.

20. Fyodor Dostoevsky, *Crime and Punishment*, trans. Oliver Ready (New York: Penguin, 2014), 286; *Polnoe sobranie sochinenii* 6:234. Subsequent references to this edition are cited parenthetically in the text.

21. "Она ужасно рада была, что наконец ушла; пошла потупясь, торопясь, чтобы поскорей как-нибудь уйти у них из виду, чтобы пройти как-нибудь поскорей эти двадцать шагов до поворота направо в улицу и остаться наконец одной, и там, идя, спеша, ни на кого не глядя, ничего не замечая, думать, вспоминать, соображать каждое сказанное слово, каждое обстоятельство. Никогда, никогда она не ощущала ничего подобного. Целый новый мир неведомо и смутно сошел в ее душу" (6:187).

22. Greta Matzner-Gore, "Kicking Maksimov out of the Carriage: Minor Characters, Exclusion, and *The Brothers Karamazov*," *Slavic and East European Journal* 48, no. 3 (Fall 2014): 419–36.

23. On Dostoevsky's characters as "set dramatic types" moving among his novels, see L. P. Grossman, "Dostoevskii—khudozhnik," in *Tvorchestvo F. M. Dostoevskogo*, ed. N. L. Stepanov (Moscow: Izdatel'stvo akademii nauk SSSR, 1959), 368, 399.

24. A complex example, mediated by two different prototypes of real-life revolutionaries, is the echo of Stavrogin's conspiratory circle in *Demons* (1871–72) in the abortive subplot of Dergachev's circle in *The Adolescent* (1875; see 16:279). I am purposefully avoiding the term "type" to refer, as here, to the representative of a social or historical "species"; I return to Dostoevsky's idiosyncratic conception of realist type below.

25. See Sarah Young, *Dostoevsky's "The Idiot" and the Ethical Foundations of Narrative: Reading, Narrating, Scripting* (London: Anthem Press, 2004), 28–74; Olga Matich, "Time and Memory in Dostoevsky's Novels, or Nastasya Filippovna in Absentia," *Slavic and East European Journal* 60, no. 3 (Fall 2016): 397–421.

26. Fyodor Dostoevsky, *Notes from Underground and the Double*, trans. Ronald Wilks (New York and London: Penguin Classics, 2009), 40. Subsequent references to this edition are cited parenthetically in the text. I frequently modify the translation to correspond more closely to the Russian. "«Я-то один, а они-то все»,—думал я и—задумался" (5:125).

27. Charles Dickens, *David Copperfield*, ed. Nina Burgis (Oxford: Oxford University Press, 1997), 1.

28. Michael Holquist, *Dostoevsky and the Novel* (Princeton, NJ: Princeton University Press, 1977), 47–73.

29. Bakhtin, "Author and Hero in Aesthetic Activity," c. 1923–24. *Sobranie sochinenii* 1:89ff.; Mikhail Bakhtin, *Art and Answerability*, trans. Vadim Liapunov and Kenneth Brostrom (Austin: University of Texas Press, 1990), 5ff. For a broader interpretation of *author* and *hero* as temporal "functions" in Bakhtin, see Ilya Kliger, "Heroic Aesthetics and Modernist Critique: Extrapolations from

Bakhtin's 'Author and Hero in Aesthetic Activity,'" *Slavic Review* 67, no. 3 (Fall 2008): 551–66.

30. "в романе надо героя, а тут нарочно собраны все черты для антигероя, а главное, всё это произведет пренеприятное впечатление, потому что мы все отвыкли от жизни. . . . Знаю, что вы, может быть, на меня за это рассердитесь, закричите, ногами затопаете: «Говорите, дескать, про себя одного и про ваши мизеры в подполье, а не смейте говорить: «все мы». Позвольте, господа, ведь не оправдываюсь же я этим всемством. Что же собственно до меня касается, то ведь я только доводил в моей жизни до крайности то, что вы не осмеливались доводить и до половины, да еще трусость свою принимали за благоразумие, и тем утешались, обманывая сами себя. Так что я, пожалуй, еще «живее» вас выхожу. Да взгляните пристальнее!" (5:178).

31. "И автор записок и самые «Записки», разумеется, вымышлены. Тем не менее такие лица, как сочинитель таких записок, не только могут, но даже должны существовать в нашем обществе, взяв в соображение те обстоятельства, при которых вообще складывалось наше общество. Я хотел вывести перед лицо публики, повиднее обыкновенного, один из характеров протекшего недавнего времени. . . . В этом отрывке, озаглавленном «Подполье», это лицо рекомендует самого себя, свой взгляд и как бы хочет выяснить те причины, по которым оно явилось и должно было явиться в нашей среде. В следующем отрывке придут уже настоящие «записки» этого лица о некоторых событиях его жизни.—Федор Достоевский" (5:99).

32. On this objectifying move of "typification," see V. Kirpotin, *Dostoevskii v shestidesiatye gody* (Moscow: Khudozhestvennaia literatura, 1966), 469–79. In a reading that sharply differs from mine, Lewis Bagby makes a case for the footnote's parodic multivoicedness, arguing that Dostoevsky is not as committed to the framework of objective authorial characterization as it suggests. Lewis Bagby, *First Words: On Dostoevsky's Introductions* (Boston: Academic Studies Press, 2016), 69–90.

33. Bakhtin comments at length on this split between the author's view of the character and the character's view of himself; and more broadly, on the character's "freedom" as an inherent aspect of the author's "design." *Sobranie sochinenii* 6:76–77 and 6:254–64; *Problems*, 64–65 and 227–37. Gary Saul Morson and Caryl Emerson offer the following gloss on this seeming paradox: the polyphonic author "creates a world in which many disparate points of view enter into dialogue, and, in a quite distinct role, he himself participates in that dialogue." Emerson and Morson, *Mikhail Bakhtin: Creation of a Prosaics* (Stanford, CA: Stanford University Press, 1990), 239. However, Emerson and Morson downplay the necessary, *continuous* background that Dostoevsky's objectification of his characters provides for their "self-" expression. As I have discussed elsewhere, Bakhtin himself straddles between discussion of the hero's coherent and objective "image" in Dostoevsky, and discussion of Dostoevsky's techniques

for making the character's self-consciousness the "dominant" of that image. My account of how these two levels work simultaneously in the reader's imagination is in this sense consistent with Bakhtin's study. (For fuller discussion, see Kitzinger, "Illusion and Instrument," 166–82.)

34. Compare Bakhtin's discussion of the Underground Man's "longing for embodiment" (*zhazhda voploshcheniia*). *Sobranie sochinenii* 6:115; *Problems*, 101.

35. See especially Morson, *Narrative and Freedom*, 36–41.

36. The Underground Man's status as an aesthetic creation, which readers can see but he cannot, thus parallels the unvoiced religious solution to his struggle—the "fear of faith" that keeps him from understanding himself as *both* created and free. Carol Apollonio, "Fear of Faith: The Hidden Religious Message of *Notes from Underground*," *Slavic and East European Journal* 37, no. 4 (Winter 1993): 510–29.

37. Bakhtin, *Sobranie sochinenii* 6:61; *Problems*, 51.

38. See note 34 above. The phrase "world-creating word" is Doležel's. *Heterocosmica*, 149.

39. For one reading of the force that "sweeps up" Raskolnikov as divine (and Sonia herself as a verbally painted icon), see Kasatkina, *O tvoriashchei prirode slova*, 228–34. Recently, Ilya Kliger discusses this inexhaustibly problematic ending in his *The Narrative Shape of Truth: Veridiction in Modern European Literature* (University Park: Pennsylvania State University Press, 2011), 139–43.

40. Dostoevsky's first postexile novel, *The Insulted and the Injured* (*Unizhennye i oskorblennye*, 1861), also features an apparently illegitimate protagonist. While illegitimacy functions there primarily as a plot point, further research on the trope of illegitimacy throughout Dostoevsky's writings would enrich the thread that I trace partially in this chapter. Scholars have underscored the connection between *The Insulted and the Injured* and *The Adolescent*, esp. Susanne Fusso, *Discovering Sexuality in Dostoevsky* (Evanston, IL: Northwestern University Press, 2006), 56–68. See also Yuri Corrigan, who discusses both novels in relation to Dostoevsky's evolving account of past trauma and the problem of individual selfhood (*Riddle*, 51–67 and 104–19).

41. Indeed, in February–April 1866, parts of *Crime and Punishment* and of book 1, part 2 of *War and Peace* (then entitled *The Year 1805*) were published side by side in the *Russian Herald*. The editors of Dostoevsky's thirty-volume collected works see a reference to Tolstoy's description of General Mack's defeat (pt. 2, chap. 3 of *War and Peace*, pub. February 1866) in pt. 4, chap. 5 of *Crime and Punishment* (pub. July 1866), which suggests that Dostoevsky was reading at least some of the serialized installments of Tolstoy's novel. However, Dostoevsky's first explicit mention of *War and Peace* does not occur until February 18, 1868—already several months after the notebook entries in question—in a letter to A. N. Maikov (28.II:258–59). Robin Feuer Miller discusses the possible influence of *War and Peace* on Dostoevsky's initial plans for *The Idiot*, particularly on

his obsession with the "Idiot's" legitimacy. *Dostoevsky and "The Idiot": Author, Narrator, and Reader* (Cambridge, MA: Harvard University Press, 1981), 59–60.

42. On Dostoevsky's engagement with the legacy of the Russian novel as represented by his rival and contemporary Tolstoy, which culminates in *The Adolescent*, see A. L. Bem, "Khudozhestvennaia polemika s Tolstym (k ponimaniiu *Podrostka*)," *O Dostoevskom*, ed. A. L. Bem (Petropolis, 1936), 3:192–214; K. Mochul'skii, *Dostoevskii: Zhizn' i tvorchestvo* (Paris: YMCA Press, 1947), 409ff.; Nina Perlina, "Rethinking Adolescence," in *Celebrating Creativity: Essays in Honour of Jostein Børtnes*, ed. Knut Andreas Grimstad and Ingunn Lunde (Bergen: University of Bergen, 1997), esp. 221–23; and Kate Holland, *The Novel in the Age of Disintegration: Dostoevsky and the Problem of Genre in the 1870s* (Evanston, IL: Northwestern University Press, 2013), 103ff. I borrow the phrase "noble family novel" from Holland, and my understanding of the trope of illegitimacy in Dostoevsky's late 1860s–70s writings has been shaped throughout by her discussion of illegitimacy, narrative, and genre in *The Adolescent* (101–30).

43. Robin Feuer Miller first traced the theme of the Idiot's legitimacy through Dostoevsky's notebooks and pointed out its importance to the development of Myshkin's eventual character. *Dostoevsky and "The Idiot,"* 54–60.

44. "ГЛАВНАЯ И ОСНОВНАЯ МЫСЛЬ РОМАНА, ДЛЯ КОТОРОЙ ВСЕ: та, что он до такой степени болезненно горд, что не может не считать себя богом, и до того, вместе с тем, себя не уважает (до того ясно себя анализирует), что не может бесконечно и до неправды усиленно не презирать себя. (Он чувствует, что тупое мщение всем за себя—низость, и в то же время делает, злодействует и мстит.) Он чувствует, что ему не за что мстить, что он, как и все, и должен быть доволен. Но так как, из безмерного тщеславия и самолюбия и в то же время жажды правды, он требует больше всех, то ему всего этого мало. В развитии и в окружающей среде он почерпнул все эти яды и начала, которые в кровь вошли. Великодушие и требование любви у кругом оскорбленного сердца безмерные. Их он не имел, и потому он тем, которых бы он хотел бесконечно любить и за них кровь отдать, всем дорогим ему, он мстит и злодействует. . . . На будущее—расчет: буду банкиром, царем иудейским и буду всех держать под ногами в цепях. «Или властвовать тирански, или умереть за всех на кресте—вот что только и можно, по-моему, по моей натуре, а так, просто износиться я не хочу»" (9:180).

45. On Myshkin as the representation of a "fully" or "positively beautiful man" (polozhitel'no prekrasnogo cheloveka), see his letters to Apollon Maikov (December 31, 1867/January 12, 1868) and to his niece Sofia Ivanova (January 1/13, 1868). 28.II:241, 251; *Selected Letters*, 260–72.

46. Like Stendhal's Julien Sorel, Ganya can thus be considered figuratively, although not literally, illegitimate; see Peter Brooks, *Reading for the Plot* (New York: Knopf, 1984), 64.

47. See 9:128 and Dostoevsky's letters of March 24/April 5, 1870, to Nikolai Strakhov (29.I:111–12) and of March 25/April 6, 1870, to Apollon Maikov (29.I:117–18; *Selected Letters* 329–33). The *Polnoe sobranie sochinenii* editors describe and comment on these letters, 9:505–8.

48. "Совершенно обратный тип, чем измельчившийся до свинства отпрыск того благородного графского дома, которого изобразил Т[олстой] в «Детстве» и «Отрочестве». Это просто тип из коренника, бессознательно беспокойный собственною типическою своею силою, совершенно непосредственною и не знающею, на чем основаться. . . . Он уставляется наконец на Христе, но вся жизнь—буря и беспорядок" (9:128).

49. On the close links between "The Life of a Great Sinner" and Dostoevsky's 1870s novels, see Dolinin, *Poslednie romany*, 43–59; Joseph Frank, *Dostoevsky: The Mantle of the Prophet, 1871–1881* (Princeton, NJ: Princeton University Press, 2002), 149–55; and L. M. Rozenblium, "Tvorcheskaia laboratoriia Dostoevskogo romanista," in *Literaturnoe nasledstvo* 77 (Moscow: Nauka, 1965), 11–13; see also Jacques Catteau's theoretical analysis in his *Dostoevsky and the Process of Literary Creation*, trans. Audrey Littlewood (Cambridge: Cambridge University Press, 1989), 224–325.

50. P. Ia. Chaadaev, *Polnoe sobranie sochinenii i izbrannye pis'ma*, ed. Z. A. Kamenskii et al. (Moscow: Nauka, 1991), 1:92.

51. Fyodor Dostoevsky, *The Idiot*, trans. Richard Pevear and Larissa Volokhonsky (New York and Toronto: Knopf, 2002), 461; *Polnoe sobranie sochinenii* 8:383.

52. This formal "solution" to writing the illegitimate hero's biography is already presaged in Dostoevsky's fragmentary notes for "The Life of a Great Sinner," which include the query: "Shouldn't the story be told by [the sinner] himself? [Ne ot sebia li rasskaz?]" (January 24/12, 1870; 9:132).

53. The charge of excessive naturalism comes from A. M. Skabichevsky's review of *The Adolescent*, "*Mysli po povodu tekushchei literatury*," *Birzhevye vedomosti*, no. 35 (February 6, 1875). Dostoevsky's reference to "real thunder and real rain" is a direct quotation from Skabichevsky's review (quoted in Dolinin, *Poslednie romany*, 199; see also *Polnoe sobranie sochinenii* 17:347). On Avseenko and the charge of diseased abnormality, see above, note 15; and Frank, *Mantle*, 168.

54. Dolinin, *Poslednie romany*, 200.

55. "Факты. Проходят мимо. Не замечают. Нет граждан, и никто не хочет понатужиться и заставить себя думать и замечать. Я не мог оторваться, и все крики критиков, что я изображаю ненастоящую жизнь, не разубедили меня. . . . Талантливые писатели наши, высокохудожественно изображавшие жизнь средне-высшего круга (семейного),—Толстой, Гончаров думали, что изображали жизнь большинства,—по моему они-то и изображали жизнь исключений. Напротив, их жизнь есть жизнь исключений, а моя есть жизнь общего правила. В этом убедятся будущие поколения, которые будут беспри-

страстнее; правда будет за мною. Я верю в это. Говорили, что я изображал гром настоящий, дождь настоящий, как на сцене. Где же? Неужели Раскольников, Ст Трофимович (главные герои моих романов) подают к этому толки? . . . Из этого-то (гражданского чувства) я передался было к славянофилам, думая воскресить мечты детства. А подполье и «Записки из подполья». Я горжусь, что впервые вывел настоящего человека *русского большинства* и впервые разоблачил его уродливую и трагическую сторону. Трагизм состоит в сознании уродливости. . . . Только я один вывел трагизм подполья, состоящий в страдании, в самоказни, в сознании лучшего и в невозможности достичь его и, главное, в ярком убеждении этих несчастных, что и все таковы, а стало быть, не стоит и исправляться!" (March 22, 1875; 16:329).

56. Jackson, *Dostoevsky's Quest for Form*, 92–123. My understanding of the "type's" place in Russian realism has also been shaped by Paperno, *Chernyshevsky and the Age of Realism*, and by Ginzburg, *O literaturnom geroe*, 16–87.

57. As René Wellek points out, the equivocation has a prior history in the dual usage of "type" in 1830s–40s French criticism: both as in Balzac, to refer to an exemplary instance of a social group or class, and as in Schelling, to refer to literary characters (like Don Quixote or Hamlet) that distill "universal" aspects of the human condition and present them in vividly concrete form. What Victor Terras calls the tradition of "organic aesthetics" in Russian criticism, which flows from Belinsky to Dostoevsky and (equally) to his radical antagonists, ranged freely across this spectrum of meanings. See my introduction for references (note 40) and further discussion.

58. Halliwell, *Aesthetics of Mimesis*, 5ff.

59. For fuller discussion of this passage, see my introduction.

60. See Ricoeur, *Time and Narrative*, 1:45–87ff.

61. *Grazhdanin*, no. 1 (January 1, 1873). Quoted in V. V. Vinogradov, *Problema avtorstva i teoriia stilei* (Moscow: Gosizdat. khudozhestvennoi literatury, 1961), 510. Vinogradov makes a convincing case for Dostoevsky's authorship of the review. Translation adjusted from Jackson, *Dostoevsky's Quest*, 92.

62. Along with the passage on the problem of creating "ordinary types" in *The Idiot* (8:383), quoted above, and the epilogue to *The Adolescent*, Dostoevsky's struggle to conceptualize "contemporary type" is reflected in a February 1874 exchange with Ivan Goncharov, only one side of which has been preserved. I. A. Goncharov, *Sobranie sochinenii*, 8 vols. (Moscow: Gosizdat. khudozhestvennoi literatury, 1952–55), 8:456–61, http://feb-web.ru/feb/gonchar/default.asp?/feb/gonchar/texts/gs0/gs8/gs8.html. Frank comments on this exchange in *Mantle*, 115.

63. Michaela Bronstein tells one such transnational reception story, beginning with Dostoevsky's *Demons*, in her "Four Generations, One Crime," in *Crime Fiction as World Literature*, ed. Louise Nilsson et al. (New York and London: Bloomsbury, 2017), 59–74.

64. For this argument, see Gary Saul Morson, "Tempics and *The Idiot*,"

in Grimstad and Lunde, *Celebrating Creativity*, 108–34; and Morson, *Prosaics*, 15ff.

65. Barthes, *S/Z*, 68 and 94–95. In his earlier essay "The Death of the Author" (1968), Barthes links both authorship and mimetic representation to a hegemonic or "tyrannical" conception of literature, as opposed to the "antitheological activity" that refuses to fix the text's ultimate meaning. *Image, Music, Text*, trans. Stephen Heath (New York: Hill and Wang, 1977), 147.

66. On *The Adolescent* as *Bildungsroman*, see E. I. Semenov, *Roman Dostoevskogo "Podrostok": Problematika i zhanr* (Leningrad: Nauka, 1979). This argument has recently been renewed in Steiner, *For Humanity's Sake*, 135–73, and Holland, *Age of Disintegration*, 106ff.

67. F. Dostoevsky, *The Adolescent*, trans. Richard Pevear and Larissa Volokhonsky (New York: Knopf, 2003). Subsequent references to this edition are cited parenthetically in the text.

68. "Я глядел на нее довольно пристально и ничего особенного не находил: не так высокого роста девица, полная и с чрезвычайно румяными щеками. Лицо, впрочем, довольно приятное, из нравящихся материалистам. Может быть, выражение доброты, но со складкой. Особенной интеллекцией не могла блистать, но только в высшем смысле, потому что хитрость была видна по глазам. Лет не более девятнадцати. Одним словом, ничего замечательного. У нас в гимназии сказали бы: подушка. (Если я описываю в такой подробности, то единственно для того, что понадобится в будущем.) Впрочем, и всё, что описывал до сих пор, по-видимому с такой ненужной подробностью, всё это ведет в будущее и там понадобится" (13:33).

69. See Edmund Heier, *Literary Portraiture in Nineteenth-Century Russian Prose* (Cologne: Böhlau, 1993), 181–232.

70. The kaleidoscope image is developed in T. V. Tsiv'ian, "O strukture vremeni i prostranstva v romane Dostoevskogo *Podrostok*," *Russian Literature* 3 (1976), 243.

71. Barthes, *S/Z*, 67.

72. As Peter Jensen has pointed out, Arkady's relationship to Versilov parodies that of an omniscient narrator to his protagonist; we see Arkady "in pursuit of the scattered potential fragments" of Versilov's biography. P. A. Jensen, "Paradoksal'nost' avtorstva (u) Dostoevskogo," in *Paradoksy russkoi literatury*, ed. V. M. Markovich and Vol'f Shmid (St. Petersburg: Inapress, 2001), 231.

73. On this point, see also Liza Knapp, who notes that in his closing comments on "Arkady's" novel, the tutor Nikolai Semyonovich "seems to prefigure Bakhtin." *The Annihilation of Inertia: Dostoevsky and Metaphysics* (Evanston, IL: Northwestern University Press, 1996), 171.

74. For three different versions of this argument, see Iu. Kariakin, "*Besy* i *Podrostok*: Dva khronikera," in his *Dostoevskii i kanun XXI veka*, 269–83 (Moscow: Sovetskii pisatel', 1989); Holland, *Age of Disintegration*, 129–30; and T. A.

Kasatkina, "Roman F. M. Dostoevskogo *Podrostok*: 'Ideia' geroia i ideia avtora," *Voprosy literatury*, no. 1 (2004): 181–212.

75. On illegitimacy and the gap between "desire and possession," see J. Hillis Miller, *Charles Dickens: The World of His Novels* (Cambridge, MA: Harvard University Press, 1958), 251.

76. "я не могу не уважать моего дворянства. У нас создался веками какой-то еще нигде не виданный высший культурный тип . . . тип всемирного боления за всех. . . . Он хранит в себе будущее России. Нас, может быть, всего только тысяча человека . . . но вся Россия жила лишь пока для того, чтобы произвести эту тысячу. . . . Один лишь русский . . . получил уже способность становиться наиболее русским именно лишь тогда, когда он наиболее европеец" (13:376–77).

77. "Да, Аркадий Макарович, вы—член случайного семейства, в противоположность еще недавним родовым нашим типам, имевшим столь различные от ваших детство и отрочество. Признаюсь, не желал бы я быть романистом героя из случайного семейства! Работа неблагодарная и без красивых форм. Да и типы эти, во всяком случае,—еще дело текущее, а потому и не могут быть художественно законченными. . . . Но что делать, однако ж, писателю, не желающему писать лишь в одном историческом роде и одержимому тоской по текущему? Угадывать и . . . ошибаться. Но такие «Записки», как ваши, могли бы, кажется мне, послужить материалом для будущего художественного произведения, для будущей картины—беспорядочной, но уже прошедшей эпохи. . . . будущий художник отыщет прекрасные формы даже для изображения минувшего беспорядка и хаоса. Вот тогда-то и понадобятся подобные «Записки», как ваши, и дадут материал—были бы искренни, несмотря даже на всю их хаотичность и случайность . . ." (13:455; second and fourth ellipses in original).

78. Lambert's near-supernatural entrance, his transposition from Arkady's dream about his childhood into the novel's diegetic present, recalls the terror of waking from a dream and "finding it true." In Gothic novels, this device signals what Eve Kosofsky Sedgwick calls a "dangerously insoluble certainty about where to place the perimeters of the self." *The Coherence of Gothic Conventions* (New York and London: Methuen, 1980), 27–35.

79. The notion of the "stereoscopic character" is John Bayley's, quoted in Hochman, *Character in Literature*, 44.

80. "У меня, мой милый, есть один любимый русский писатель. Он романист, но для меня он почти историограф нашего дворянства. . . . Он берет дворянина с его детства и юношества, он рисует его в семье . . . и всё так поэтично, так незыблемо и неоспоримо. Он психолог дворянской души. Но главное в том, что это дано как неоспоримое, и, уж конечно, ты соглашаешься. Соглашаешься и завидуешь. О, сколько завидуют! Есть дети, с детства уже задумывающиеся над своей семьей, . . . а главное, уж в детстве начинающие

понимать беспорядочность и случайность основ всей их жизни, отсутствие установившихся форм и родового предания. Эти должны завидовать моему писателю, завидовать [моему] его героям и, пожалуй, не любить их. О, это не герои, это милые дети, у которых прекрасные, милые отцы, кушающие в клубе, хлебосольничающие по Москве" (17:142–43).

81. Jacques Derrida, "Plato's Pharmacy," in *Dissemination*, trans. Barbara Johnson (Chicago: University of Chicago Press, 1981), 63–171. I return to this essay in chapter 4.

82. Lukács, *Theory of the Novel*, 83.

83. Lukács, *Theory of the Novel*, 33.

CHAPTER THREE

1. "Все счастливые семьи похожи друг на друга, каждая несчастливая семья несчастлива по-своему" (18:3). All citations to *Anna Karenina* in English are from Leo Tolstoy, *Anna Karenina*, trans. Richard Pevear and Larissa Volokhonsky (New York: Penguin, 2000). Pevear and Volokhonsky follow the version of the text printed in M. V. Khrapchenko's twenty-two-volume edition of Tolstoy's collected works and in Zaidenshnur and Zhdanov's *Literaturnye pamiatniki* edition, which aims to free Tolstoy's text as far as possible from Strakhov's unauthorized edits and from copyists' errors. For the Russian text, I have followed (rather) the earlier Jubilee edition of Tolstoy's complete collected works, which reproduces the first corrected edition of the novel as serialized in the *Russian Herald*. For a partial account of the novel's complex textual history, see V. A. Zhdanov and E. Ie. Zaidenshnur, "Tekstologicheskie poiasneniia," in L. N. Tolstoi, *Anna Karenina: Roman v vos'mi chastiakh*, ed. V. A. Zhdanov and E. Ie. Zaidenshnur (Moscow: Nauka, 1970), 834–55. I have frequently modified Pevear and Volokhonsky's translation to bring it closer to the version of the Russian text I am using, or when I differed with the translators' rendering of key English words—sometimes in consultation with other published English translations.

2. Ian Watt writes of the novel's "primary criterion" as "truth to individual experience" in *The Rise of the Novel* (Berkeley and Los Angeles: University of California Press, 1964), 13, 15. With the Russian context more directly in mind, Lydia Ginzburg discusses the realism that developed "side by side with the development of the exact sciences," which "depicted concrete reality in terms of its causal conditionality, both social and historical" and so did away (as she argues) with the prevailing aesthetic regime of the beautiful. *On Psychological Prose*, 4.

3. "Все смешалось в доме Облонских. Жена узнала, что муж был в связи с бывшею в их доме француженкою-гувернанткой, и объявила мужу, что не может жить с ним в одном доме. Положение это продолжалось уже третий день и мучительно чувствовалось и самими супругами, и всеми членами

семьи, и домочадцами. Все члены семьи и домочадцы чувствовали, что нет смысла в их сожительстве и что на каждом постоялом дворе случайно сошедшиеся люди более связаны между собой, чем они, члены семьи и домочадцы Облонских. Жена не выходила из своих комнат, мужа третий день не было дома. Дети бегали по всему дому, как потерянные; англичанка поссорилась с экономкой и написала записку приятельнице, прося приискать ей новое место; повар ушел еще вчера со двора, во время обеда; черная кухарка и кучер просили расчета" (18:3).

4. "На третий день после ссоры князь Степан Аркадьич Облонский—Стива, как его звали в свете,—в обычный час, то есть в 8 часов утра, проснулся не в спальне жены, а в своем кабинете, на сафьянном диване. Он повернул свое полное, выхоленное тело на пружинах дивана, как бы желая опять заснуть надолго, с другой стороны крепко обнял подушку и прижался к ней щекой; но вдруг вскочил, сел на диван и открыл глаза" (18:3).

5. See Ol'ga Slivitskaia, who argues that the novel's strong "effect of lifelikeness" depends on the many different, equally valid perceptions of events available to its reader: "*Anna Karenina*: Effekt zhiznepodobiia," in *Istina v dvizhenii: O cheloveke v mire L'va Tolstogo* (Saint Petersburg: Amfora, 2009), 310. Vladimir Alexandrov also lays particular emphasis on the "relativity" of the novel's story world, although he reads it as a move away from literary and philosophical realism. Vladimir Alexandrov, *Limits to Interpretation: The Meanings of "Anna Karenina"* (Madison: University of Wisconsin Press, 2004), 134–232. Morson offers an ethical interpretation of relative vision in the novel, showing how characters enrich or disfigure their world by teaching themselves to see it in particular ways. Gary Saul Morson, *"Anna Karenina" in Our Time: Seeing More Wisely* (New Haven, CT: Yale University Press, 2007), 79–117.

6. The interplay between generality and particularity, in the progression from the novel's epigraph to its first sentence and paragraph, has been addressed throughout the voluminous scholarly literature on the opening of *Anna Karenina*. Commentators agree that the first sentence ("All happy families . . .") was originally intended as a second epigraph and only later joined to the main text (see Jubilee edition, 20:650). Chapter 1 in its final version thus has two beginnings, "philosophical" (*filosofskoe*) and "narrative" (*sobytiinoe*). E. G. Babaev, *Kommentarii*, in L. N. Tolstoi, *Sobranie sochinenii v 22 tomakh*, ed. M. B. Khrapchenko et al. (Moscow: Khudozhestvennaia literatura 1978–85), 9:424–25. For further commentary, see, for example, Orwin, *Tolstoy's Art and Thought*, 179–80; Robert Louis Jackson, "The Ambivalent Beginning of *Anna Karenina*," in *Semantic Analysis of Literary Texts*, ed. Eric de Haard et al. (Amsterdam: Elsevier, 1990), 345–52; and Kate Holland, "The Opening of *Anna Karenina*," in *Approaches to Teaching Tolstoy's "Anna Karenina,"* ed. Liza Knapp and Amy Mandelker (New York: Modern Language Association of America, 2003), 144–49. On the link Tolstoy draws between narrative ("story") and unhappiness, see Morson,

Seeing More Wisely, 35ff. Drawing together the themes of unhappiness and particularity, however, yields a conclusion that one would not expect from Morson's analysis: contingent individuality means unhappiness, no matter how unromantically it is understood. The "prosaic" world of the realist novel is the realm of narrative and individuation and thus partakes in the misery (as the first sentence suggests) of *any* story that privileges particular, individual life.

7. As Boris Eikhenbaum showed based on drafts of the novel, it is likely that Tolstoy initially translated the epigraph, "Vengeance is mine, I will repay [Mne otmshchenie, i Az vozdam]," from Arthur Schopenhauer's *The World as Will and Representation*—among his most intensive reading from late 1868 on. B. M. Eikhenbaum, *Lev Tolstoi: 70ye gody* (Leningrad: Khudozhestvennaia literatura, 1974), 160–73. On Tolstoy and Schopenhauer, I have been guided particularly by Eikhenbaum and by Sigrid McLaughlin, "Some Aspects of Tolstoy's Intellectual Development: Tolstoy and Schopenhauer," in *California Slavic Studies*, vol. 5, ed. Nicholas V. Riasanovsky and Gleb Struve (Berkeley and Los Angeles: University of California Press, 1970), 187–244. On the psychological necessity of Tolstoy's escape from Schopenhauer, see McLaughlin, "Some Aspects," 219–22; E. N. Kupreianova, *Estetika L. N. Tolstogo* (Leningrad: Nauka, 1966), 104–6; and Inessa Medzhibovskaya, *Tolstoy and the Religious Culture of His Time: A Biography of a Long Conversion* (Lanham, MD: Lexington Books, 2008), 131–90 passim, esp. 176.

8. I am reinvoking "mimetic life" as defined in my introduction: a character's "mimetic life" is the impression she gives the absorbed reader of autonomous, embodied existence, in and for herself, free from the bounds not just of authorial control but even of narrative language. For discussion of "marginal characters," see chapter 1.

9. "Другая лампа-рефрактор горела на стене и освещала большой во весь рост портрет женщины, на который Левин невольно обратил внимание. Это был портрет Анны, сделанный в Италии Михайловым. В то время как Степан Аркадьич заходил за трельяж и говоривший мужской голос замолк, Левин смотрел на портрет, в блестящем освещении выступавший из рамы, и не мог оторваться от него. Он даже забыл, где был, и не слушая того, что говорилось, не спускал глаз с удивительного портрета. Это была не картина, а живая прелестная женщина с черными вьющимися волосами, обнаженными плечами и руками и задумчивою полуулыбкой на покрытых нежным пушком губах, победительно и нежно смотревшая на него смущавшими его глазами. Только потому она была не живая, что она была красивее, чем может быть живая.—Я очень рада,—услыхал он вдруг подле себя голос, очевидно обращенный к нему, голос той самой женщины, которою он любовался на портрете. Анна вышла ему навстречу из-за трельяжа, и Левин увидел в полусвете кабинета ту самую женщину портрета в темном, разноцветно-синем платье, не в том положении, не с тем выражением, но на той самой высоте

красоты, на которой она была уловлена художником на портрете. Она была менее блестяща в действительности, но зато в живой было и что-то такое новое привлекательное, чего не было на портрете" (19: 273–74).

10. Amy Mandelker, *Framing "Anna Karenina": Tolstoy, the Woman Question, and the Victorian Novel* (Columbus: Ohio State University Press, 1993), 182. On the moral *Bildung* initiated by Levin's vision of Anna's portrait, see especially 104–21. I follow Mandelker in reading Anna's narrative as an impetus to the transcendence of artifice, from which both Levin and the reader are invited to learn. However, I believe Mandelker does not give sufficient weight to Levin's contrasting characterization as an engine of this transformation. My account of the rhetorical interaction between Anna's and Levin's narrative lines also differs from Liza Knapp's deconstructive conclusions in her recent *"Anna Karenina" and Others: Tolstoy's Labyrinth of Plots* (Madison: University of Wisconsin Press, 2016).

11. On character-systems, see my introduction and chapter 1. Sidney Schultz gives an instructive breakdown of the novel's three recurring plotlines (Anna/Vronsky/Karenin, Levin/Kitty, and Dolly/Stiva) by chapter and narrative "space" in *The Structure of "Anna Karenina"* (Ann Arbor, MI: Ardis, 1982), 18–20. He finds 113 chapters devoted to Anna's plot, 126 to Levin's, and a strict alternation between "segments" of their stories.

12. "В этом коротком взгляде Вронский успел заметить сдержанную оживленность, которая играла в ее лице и порхала между блестящими глазами и чуть заметной улыбкой, изгибавшею ее румяные губы. Как будто избыток чего-то так переполнял ее существо, что мимо ее воли выражался то в блеске взгляда, то в улыбке. Она потушила умышленно свет в глазах, но он светился против ее воли в чуть заметной улыбке" (18:66).

13. Tolstoy, *War and Peace*, 41; *Polnoe sobranie sochinenii* 9:47.

14. Barbara Lönnquvist offers an alternative reading of the "fire" or "spark" (*blesk*) that Vronsky awakens in Anna, connecting it to her seemingly supernatural physical power over him: Barbara Lennkvist, *Puteshestvie vglub' romana: Lev Tolstoi: "Anna Karenina"* (Moskva: Iazyki slavianskoi kul'tury, 2010), 20–32. The image of this virtual "spark" connects with one of the novel's core running motifs, the burning candle, traced by Elisabeth Stenbock-Fermor among many others. *The Architecture of "Anna Karenina"* (Lisse: Peter de Ridder Press, 1975), 41–51.

15. "Он сидел на своем кресле, то прямо устремив глаза вперед себя, то оглядывая входивших и выходивших, и если и прежде он поражал и волновал незнакомых ему людей своим видом непоколебимого спокойствия, то теперь он еще более казался горд и самодовлеющ. Он смотрел на людей, как на вещи. Молодой нервный человек, служащий в окружном суде, сидевший против него, возненавидел его за этот вид. Молодой человек и закуривал у него, и заговаривал с ним, и даже толкал его, чтобы дать ему почувствовать, что он не вещь, а человек, но Вронский смотрел на него все так же, как на фо-

нарь, и молодой человек гримасничал, чувствуя, что он теряет самообладание под давлением этого непризнавания его человеком" (18:111).

16. The "nervous young man's" lineage begins in *War and Peace*: he is a descendant of the Rostovs' German tutor, passed over at Natasha's name day party by the servant pouring wine (66; 9:75); and of the officer at Nesvitsky's impromptu picnic with the rear guard at Enns, who "would have dearly liked to take another pie but felt shy, and therefore pretended to be examining the countryside" (146; 9:166). The mildly contemptuous tone of this unmasking gaze turns interiority itself into a tool for making characters minor—most virtuosically developed in the case of the nervous young man, who actually can feel himself disintegrating beneath Vronsky's (and then the narrative's) lack of attention.

17. Arthur Schopenhauer, *The World as Will and Representation*, trans. E. F. J. Payne (New York: Dover, 1969), 1:147.

18. Woloch, *One vs. the Many*, 13.

19. Nabokov, *Lectures on Russian Literature*, 161ff.

20. A second passage emphasizing Kitty's "quick inaudible step" appears when she is attending on Nikolai Levin's deathbed (19:61)—a link between sexuality, femininity, and mortality that would become still more characteristic in Tolstoy's later work.

21. In this novel where no description vanishes once given, perhaps the best explanation for Koznyshev's failure to propose is Varenka's early appearance as "that girl in the mushroom hat [eta v shliape gribom]" to help the deranged and tubercular Nikolai Levin (218; 18:229). Later, instead of proposing as he had intended, Koznyshev finds himself asking Varenka a question about mushrooms. Just as the reader's first vision of Anna's irrepressible, sexualized "light" sets up the climax in which this candle is extinguished, so Varenka's sexless philanthropy, tied up with the initial image of her "mushroom hat," seals the anticlimax of her romantic plot.

22. Morson, *Seeing More Wisely*, 35–48.

23. "Анна ни разу не встречала еще этой новой знаменитости и была поражена и ее красотою, и крайностью, до которой был доведен ее туалет, и смелостью ее манер. На голове ее из своих и чужих нежно-золотистого цвета волос был сделан такой эшафодаж прически, что голова ее равнялась по величине стройно выпуклому и очень открытому спереди бюсту. Стремительность же вперед была такова, что при каждом движении обозначились из-под платья формы колен и верхней части ноги, и невольно представлялся вопрос о том, где сзади, в этой подстроенной колеблющейся горе, действительно кончается ее настоящее, маленькое и стройное, столь обнаженное сверху и столь спрятанное сзади и внизу тело" (18:315–16).

24. Indeed, in works of criticism Anna Karenina and *Anna Karenina* are often taken—even and perhaps especially by non-Slavists—as a paradigmatic high point of the novel's ability to create various aspects of the illusion of "life." For a

few examples, see Hochman, *Character in Literature*, 168–70; Scarry, *Dreaming by the Book*, 206–20; and Elaine Auyung, "Rethinking the Reality Effect: Detail and the Novel," in *The Oxford Handbook of Cognitive Literary Studies*, ed. Lisa Zunshine (Oxford Handbooks Online, 2015), DOI:0.1093/oxfordhb/9780199978069.013.0029.

25. "Она лежала в постели с открытыми глазами, глядя при свете одной догоравшей свечи на лепной карниз потолка и на захватывающую часть его тень от ширмы, и живо представляла себе, что он будет чувствовать, когда ее уже не будет и она будет для него только одно воспоминание. «Как мог я сказать ей эти жестокие слова? . . . Но теперь ее уже нет. Она навсегда ушла от нас. Она там . . . » Вдруг тень ширмы заколебалась, захватила весь карниз, весь потолок, другие тени с другой стороны рванулись ей навстречу; на мгновение тени сбежали, но потом с новой быстротой надвинулись, поколебались, слились, и всё стало темно. «Смерть!» подумала она" (19:331; second ellipsis in original).

26. Plato, *Republic*, trans. G. M. A. Grube (rev. C. D. C. Reeve) in *Plato: Complete Works*, ed. John M. Cooper (Indianapolis: Hackett, 1997), 1132.

27. Compare V. E. Vetlovskaia's analysis of the demonic "enchanted circle" of individualistic carnal desires that ties all the novel's characters, but especially Anna and Vronsky, to the realm of illusion and death—traced not with reference to philosophical intertexts, but entirely through the novel's interlaced motifs: V. E. Vetlovskaia, "Poetika '*Anny Kareninoi*': Sistema neodnoznachnykh motivov," *Russkaia literatura* 4 (1979): 17–37. Richard Gustafson also analyzes the novel from this perspective in his *Leo Tolstoy: Resident and Stranger* (Princeton, NJ: Princeton University Press, 1986), 118–32.

28. "И вдруг, вспомнив о раздавленном человеке в день ее первой встречи с Вронским, она поняла, что ей надо делать. Быстрым, легким шагом спустившись по ступенькам, которые шли от водокачки к рельсам, она остановилась подле вплоть мимо ее проходящего поезда. . . . И ровно в ту минуту, как середина между колесами поравнялась с нею, она откинула красный мешочек и, вжав в плечи голову, упала под вагон на руки и легким движением, как бы готовясь тотчас же встать, опустилась на колена. Но в то же мгновение она ужаснулась тому, что делала. «Где я? Что я делаю? Зачем?» Она хотела подняться, откинуться; но что-то огромное, неумолимое толкнуло ее в голову и потащило за спину. «Господи, прости мне всё!» проговорила она, чувствуя невозможность борьбы. Мужичок, приговаривая что-то, работал над железом. И свеча, при которой она читала исполненную тревог, обманов, горя и зла книгу, вспыхнула более ярким, чем когда-нибудь, светом, осветила ей всё то, что прежде было во мраке, затрещала, стала меркнуть и навсегда потухла" (19:348–50).

29. I am indebted here to James Ramey's explorations of literary "parasitism" and particularly his idea of the implied author as the parasite the text deliv-

ers to the reader, in his article "Parasitism and *Pale Fire*'s Camouflage: The King-Bot, the Crown Jewels, and the Man in the Brown Mackintosh," *Comparative Literature Studies* 41, no. 2 (2004): 185–213.

30. Ilya Kliger comments extensively on the difference between Levin's loose, "fabulaically" narrated storyline and Anna's storyline as caught in a "tight network of *siuzhet*." He too notes the sharp distinction between Anna's and Levin's entrances as a microcosm of this difference. *Narrative Shape of Truth*, 153–54.

31. At Levin and Stiva's dinner early in the novel, Levin recalls "both loves" defined in the *Symposium* (18:46)—as explained in the speech of Pausanias, "common" love, a craving for the body or flesh rather than the soul of the lover; and "heavenly" love, desire for the lover's intelligence and virtue. *Symposium* 180d–181e. At the end of the novel, this motif (recast as "life for the belly" and "life for the soul") returns in Levin's conversation with one of his peasant workers. Irina Gutkin has discussed Tolstoy's Christianization of the *Symposium* in his own treatment of "flesh and spirit." Irina Gutkin, "The Dichotomy between Flesh and Spirit: Plato's *Symposium* in *Anna Karenina*," in *In the Shade of the Giant*, ed. Hugh McLean (Berkeley and Los Angeles: University of California Press, 1989), 84–99.

32. Plato, Symposium, trans. Alexander Nehemas and Paul Woodruff, in *Plato: Complete Works*, 493–94.

33. "Месяц . . . теперь только блестел, как кусок ртути. . . . Невидная еще без солнечного света роса в душистой высокой конопле, из которой выбраны были уже замашки, мочила ноги и блузу Левина выше пояса" (19:166).

34. See also Greta Matzner-Gore, who similarly argues for two different types of minor character in *Anna Karenina*. She emphasizes the source of the difference in the protagonists' psychological and moral development: as Anna becomes further sunk in her own story, the minor characters around her become more functional and perfunctory. As Levin learns to see the others around him more clearly, his narrative becomes richer in nonfunctional, multidimensional minor characters who are superfluous to his plot. Greta Matzner-Gore, "From the Corners of the Russian Novel: Minor Characters in Gogol, Goncharov, Tolstoy, and Dostoevsky" (PhD diss., Columbia University, 2014), 97–101ff. While I will point out a similar distinction, I am inclined to see differences between minor characters in each narrative as reflecting different intended aesthetic and rhetorical effects on the reader, rather than as mirroring the progress of each protagonist's moral education or decline.

35. By my count, Tolstoy gives Stiva and Dolly ten children (living and dead) over the course of the novel. Considering how many of them he refers to as the "youngest," it is hard to argue that he was keeping track. I comment further on this point in my annotations to Vladimir Nabokov's lecture on Tolstoy, published at http://thenabokovian.org/annotations/Lectures_on_Russian_Literature/tolstoy.

36. On this character and the thematic thread of "pleasure and sophistication" in *Anna Karenina*, see Robert Belknap, "Tolstoy's Prince Who Resembles a Cucumber," in *Freedom and Responsibility: Essays on Russian Literature in Honor of Robert Louis Jackson*, ed. Elizabeth Cheresh Allen and Gary Saul Morson (Evanston, IL: Northwestern University Press, 1995), 153–58.

37. "Еще с горы открылась ему под горою тенистая, уже скошенная часть луга, с сереющими рядами и черными кучками кафтанов, снятых косцами на том месте, откуда они зашли первый ряд. По мере того как он подъезжал, ему открывались шедшие друг за другом растянутою вереницей и различно махавшие косами мужики, кто в кафтанах, кто в одних рубахах. Он насчитал их сорок два человека" (18:263).

38. "Иван Парменов стоял на возу, принимая, разравнивая и отаптывая огромные навилины сена, которые сначала охапками, а потом вилами ловко подавала ему его молодая красавица-хозяйка. Молодая баба работала легко, весело и ловко. Крупное, слежавшееся сено не бралось сразу на вилы. Она сначала расправляла его, всовывала вилы, потом упругим и быстрым движением налегала на них всею тяжестью своего тела и тотчас же, перегибая перетянутую красным кушаком спину, выпрямлялась и, выставляя полную грудь из-под белой занавески, с ловкой ухваткой перехватывала руками вилы и вскидывала навилину высоко на воз. Иван поспешно, видимо стараясь избавить ее от всякой минуты лишнего труда, подхватывал, широко раскрывая руки, подаваемую охапку и расправлял ее на возу. Подав последнее сено граблями, баба отряхнула засыпавшуюся ей за шею труху и, оправив сбившийся над белым, незагорелым лбом красный платок, полезла под телегу увязывать воз. . . . В выражениях обоих лиц была видна сильная, молодая, недавно проснувшаяся любовь" (18:289).

39. "Всю эту ночь и утро Левин жил совершенно бессознательно и чувствовал себя совершенно изъятым из условий материальной жизни. Он не ел целый день, не спал две ночи, провел несколько часов раздетый на морозе и чувствовал себя не только свежим и здоровым как никогда, но он чувствовал себя совершенно независимым от тела: он двигался без усилия мышц и чувствовал, что всё может сделать . . . И что он видел тогда, того после уже он никогда не видал. В особенности дети, шедшие в школу, голуби сизые, слетевшие с крыши на тротуар, и сайки, посыпанные мукой, которые выставила невидимая рука, тронули его. Эти сайки, голуби и два мальчика были неземные существа. Всё это случилось в одно время: мальчик подбежал к голубю и улыбаясь взглянул на Левина; голубь затрещал крыльями и отпорхнул, блестя на солнце между дрожащими в воздухе пылинками снега, а из окошка пахнуло духом печеного хлеба, и выставились сайки. Всё это вместе было так необычайно хорошо, что Левин засмеялся и заплакал от радости" (18:424).

40. Tolstoy, *War and Peace*, 1180; *Polnoe sobranie sochinenii* 12:196. See my fuller discussion of this passage in chapter 1.

41. Gutkin, "Flesh and Spirit," 98.

42. "Это новое чувство не изменило меня, не осчастливило, не просветило вдруг, как я мечтал,—так же как и чувство к сыну. Никакого сюрприза тоже не было. А вера—не вера—я не знаю, что это такое,—но чувство это так же незаметно вошло страданиями и твердо засело в душе. Так же буду сердиться на Ивана кучера, так же буду спорить, буду некстати высказывать свои мысли, так же будет стена между святая святых моей души и другими . . . но жизнь моя теперь, вся моя жизнь, независимо от всего, что может случиться со мной, каждая минута ее—не только не бессмысленна, как была прежде, но имеет несомненный смысл добра, который я властен вложить в нее!» Конец" (19:399).

43. Dostoevsky, *The Adolescent*, 562; *Polnoe sobranie sochinenii* 13:454.

44. I discuss Dostoevsky's conception of "type" further in chapter 2.

45. Benjamin, *Selected Writings*, 3:143, 166.

46. The reader would then be, to adapt Stanley Fish's famous title, "surprised by virtue"—and indeed, the ideal reception scenario I outline places Tolstoy in a similar position to Milton as Fish understands him, using orchestrated responses to the text to show readers "how they came to be the way they are." Stanley Fish, *Surprised by Sin: The Reader in "Paradise Lost,"* 2nd ed. (Cambridge, MA: Harvard University Press, 1997), x. My argument has been that in the context of a realist novel and (particularly) of his reliance on realist techniques of characterization, Tolstoy can engineer no such seamless transition from textual to extratextual authority.

47. Leo Tolstoy, *What Is Art? and Essays on Art*, trans. Aylmer Maude (London: Oxford University Press, 1930), 123; *Polnoe sobranie sochinenii* 30:65.

48. Tolstoy, *Tolstoy's Letters*, 296–97; *Polnoe sobranie sochinenii* 62:268–69.

49. See Paperno, *"Who, What Am I?,"* 44–45.

50. Leo Tolstoy, "Hadji-Murat," in *The Death of Ivan Ilyich and Other Stories*, trans. Richard Pevear and Larissa Volokhonsky (New York: Vintage Classics, 2009), 486–87.

> Рана в бок была смертельна, и он чувствовал, что умирает. Воспоминания и образы с необыкновенной быстротой сменялись в его воображении одно другим. . . . И все эти воспоминания пробегали в его воображении, не вызывая в нем никакого чувства: ни жалости, ни злобы, ни какого-либо желания. Все это казалось так ничтожно в сравнении с тем, что начиналось и уже началось для него. А между тем его сильное тело продолжало делать начатое. . . . то, что казалось им мертвым телом, вдруг зашевелилось. Сначала поднялась окровавленная, без папахи, бритая голова, потом поднялось туловище, и, ухватившись за дерево, он поднялся весь. Он так казался страшен, что подбегавшие остановились. Но вдруг он дрогнул, отшатнулся от дерева и со всего роста, как подкошенный репей, упал на лицо и уже не двигался. . . . Больше он уже ничего не чувствовал, и враги топтали и резали то, что не имело уже ничего общего с ним. Гаджи-Ага, наступив ногой

на спину тела, с двух ударов отсек голову и осторожно, чтобы не запачкать в кровь чувяки, откатил ее ногою. Алая кровь хлынула из артерий шеи и черная из головы и залила траву. (35:117)

51. On Hadji-Murat as an example of "atomized character" in Tolstoy, see Gustafson, *Resident and Stranger*, 278–79. David Herman reads the entire story as a challenge to realist narrative, an "inscription of silence," in his "Khadzhi-Murat's Silence," *Slavic Review* 64, no. 1 (Spring 2015): 1–23.

52. Robert Bird, "Refiguring the Russian Type: Dostoevsky and the Limits of Realism," in *A New Word on "The Brothers Karamazov,"* ed. Robert Louis Jackson (Evanston, IL: Northwestern University Press, 2004), 24.

53. I owe the metaphor of "translation" to Ellen Chances, "Links between *Brothers Karamazov* and *Anna Karenina*," *Dostoevsky Studies*, n.s., 15 (2011): 26. On the "Eastern question" and Ivan's rebellion, see I. L. Volgin, "Nravstvennye osnovy publitsistiki Dostoevskogo (Vostochnyi vopros v *Dnevnike pisatelia*)," *Izvestiia AN SSSR*, Serial literatury i iazyka, 1971, vol. 30, vyp. 4, 317–18, http://feb-web.ru/feb/izvest/1971/04/714–312.htm. On Dostoevsky's Stiva and Ivan's devil, see Morson, *Seeing More Wisely*, 48–50; see also his *The Boundaries of Genre: Dostoevsky's "Diary of a Writer" and the Traditions of Literary Utopia* (Evanston, IL: Northwestern University Press, 1981), 31–32ff. However, as Joseph Frank points out, Dostoevsky had actually introduced a figure similar to Ivan's devil before publication of *Anna Karenina* began, in the 1874 sketch "Little Pictures (on the Road)"—so in Stiva he perhaps recognized a type of his own creation (Frank, *Mantle*, 114–15).

54. Common notes sound, too, in the initial portraits of Nikolai Levin and Dmitri Karamazov—in particular, the unsettling combination of sickliness and imposing physical presence. See Tolstoy, *Anna Karenina*, 86; Tolstoi, *Polnoe sobranie sochinenii* 18:92; and F. Dostoevsky, *The Brothers Karamazov*, trans. Richard Pevear and Larissa Volokhonsky (New York: Farrar, Straus & Giroux, 1990), 67–68; Dostoevskii, *Polnoe sobranie sochinenii* 14:63.

CHAPTER FOUR

1. Fyodor Dostoevsky, "The Dream of a Ridiculous Man," in *The Eternal Husband and Other Stories*, trans. Richard Pevear and Larissa Volokhonsky (New York: Bantam Classics, 1997), 324. "Ясным представлялось, что жизнь и мир теперь как бы от меня зависят. Можно сказать даже так, что мир теперь как бы для меня одного и сделан: застрелюсь я, и мира не будет, по крайне мере для меня" (25:108).

2. Holquist, *Dostoevsky and the Novel*, 158–64.

3. Dostoevsky, *The Brothers Karamazov*, 3; *Polnoe sobranie sochinenii* 14:6. References to *The Brothers Karamazov* are cited parenthetically hereafter.

4. For two different considerations of the sequel's projected contents, see

James L. Rice, "Dostoevsky's Endgame: The Projected Sequel to *The Brothers Karamazov*," *Russian History/Histoire Russe* 33, no. 1 (Spring 2006): 45–62; and Igor' Volgin, *Poslednii god Dostoevskogo: Istoricheskie zapiski*, 4th ed. (Moscow: AST/Zebra E, 2010), 30–49; repr. in English translation in Apollonio, *The New Russian Dostoevsky*, 271–86. But as many critics discuss, this note "from the author" is also woven into the fictional narrating situation of *The Brothers Karamazov*: see, for example, N. Perlina, *Varieties of Poetic Utterance: Quotation in "The Brothers Karamazov"* (Lanham, MD: University Press of America, 1985), 6–7; Bagby, *First Words*, 144–63; and William Mills Todd III, "Storied Selves: Constructing Characters in *The Brothers Karamazov*," in *Self and Story in Russian History*, ed. Laura Engelstein and Stephanie Sandler (Ithaca, NY: Cornell University Press, 2000), 270–71.

5. Lukács, *Theory of the Novel*, 83. For an alternative reading—the device of the projected sequel as a bid to break out from aesthetic closure—see Hellebust, "Bakhtin and the 'Virtual Sequel' in Russian Literature."

6. Dostoevsky, *The Adolescent*, 562; *Polnoe sobranie sochinenii* 13:454.

7. On finishing Alyosha's character "beyond the novel," see Bird, "Refiguring the Russian Type," 27.

8. On Pushkin, see, for example, 16:47, 122, 156, 172, 260; on Tolstoyan "clarity" and "detail," 16:73, 87, 360.

9. Comparison with a similar passage in *Crime and Punishment* suggests that by the 1870s, Tolstoy had eclipsed Turgenev and perhaps even Pushkin in Dostoevsky's pantheon of mimetic writers. See 6:45–46 and the commentary to the *Brothers Karamazov* passage at 15:590–91.

10. On Tolstoy and "breed force," see Bocharov, *Roman L. Tolstogo*, 89–100.

11. Robert Belknap, *The Structure of "The Brothers Karamazov"* (The Hague and Paris: Mouton, 1967), 26–50.

12. On this doubling, and the subordination of the female characters' trajectories, see also Mochul'skii, *Dostoevskii*, 493. Lise Khokhlakova's ambivalent role has attracted particular scholarly attention. See Tatiana Kasatkina, *Kharakterologiia Dostoevskogo: Tipologiia emotsional'no-tsennostnykh orientatsii* (Moscow: Naslediie, 1996), 53–67; Nathan Rosen, "The Madness of Lise Khokhlakov," *Dostoevsky Studies* n.s., 6 (2002): 154–62. However, as Apollonio demonstrates, to escape the pervasive system defined by "Karamazovism," readers must turn to the novel's offstage female characters, the "mothers Karamazov" (*Dostoevsky's Secrets*, 144–65).

13. A partial list of about sixty of the novel's named (on- and offstage) characters can be found in Victor Terras, *A Karamazov Companion* (Madison: University of Wisconsin Press, 1981), 123–24. A full count, however, would yield a considerably larger cast: at least seventy named onstage characters, plus another sixty or so who are counted but not named, and at least a dozen significant named offstage characters.

14. In a notebook draft, Dostoevsky emphasized the attraction that Maria Kondratievna's train holds for Smerdyakov: "Smerdyakov very much liked two of her dresses, one with a train [*odno s khvostom*], and the way that she knew how to swing this train. At first the train awoke his indignation, but later he came to like it very much. Both of them discerned loftier people [*vysshikh liudei*] in one another" (15:214). The same demonic pride is echoed in another set of entirely marginal characters, the daughters of the rich peasant innkeeper Trifon Borisovich, who put on dresses "with three feet of train [*s arshinnym khvostom*]" to go out at night, but come home to sweep the inn's floor every morning (413; 14:373).

15. "Черта-то она отчасти карамазовская, это правда, жажда-то эта жизни, несмотря ни на что, в тебе она тоже непременно сидит, но почему ж она подлая? Центростремительной силы еще страшно много на нашей планете, Алеша. Жить хочется, и я живу, хотя бы и вопреки логике. Пусть я не верю в порядок вещей, но дороги мне клейкие, распускающиеся весной листочки" (14:209).

16. Diane Oenning Thompson writes of a "third plot" in *The Brothers Karamazov*, neither dramatic nor ideological, which is dedicated to "the artistic task of bringing [the] protagonists' voices into a dialogic relation with the voice of Christ, of making them aware of this voice within themselves." *"The Brothers Karamazov" and the Poetics of Memory* (Cambridge: Cambridge University Press, 1991), 64–65; for a similar formulation, see Stepanian, *Iavlenie i dialog*, 130. Although I focus on this "third plot" as the space of characterization rather than that of forming a relationship to Christ, I am arguing that for Dostoevsky, these two "artistic tasks" were linked.

17. "Всё одни и те же ступеньки. Я на самой низшей, а ты вверху, где-нибудь на тринадцатой. . . . Кто ступил на нижнюю ступеньку, тот всё равно непременно вступит и на верхнюю.

—Стало быть, совсем не вступать?

—Кому можно—совсем не вступать.

—А тебе—можно?

—Кажется, нет.

—Молчи, Алеша, молчи, милый, хочется мне ручку твою поцеловать, так, из умиления. Эта шельма Грушенька знаток в человеках, она мне говорила однажды, что она когда-нибудь тебя съест. Молчу, молчу!" (14:101)

18. Woloch, *One vs. the Many*, 14, 56ff.

19. "Я уже говорил, что он очень обрюзг. Физиономия его представляла к тому времени что-то резко свидетельствовавшее о характеристике и сущности всей прожитой им жизни. Кроме длинных и мясистых мешочков под маленькими его глазами, вечно наглыми, подозрительными и насмешливыми, кроме множества глубоких морщинок на его маленьком, но жирненьком личике, к острому подбородку его подвешивался еще большой кадык, мясистый и продолговатый, как кошелек, что придавало ему какой-то отвра-

тительно сладострастный вид. Прибавьте к тому плотоядный, длинный рот, с пухлыми губами, из-под которых виднелись маленькие обломки черных, почти истлевших зубов. Он брызгался слюной каждый раз, когда начинал говорить. Впрочем, и сам он любил шутить над своим лицом, хотя, кажется, оставался им доволен. Особенно указывал он на свой нос, не очень большой, но очень тонкий, с сильно выдающеюся горбиной: «Настоящий римский,— говорил он" (14:22).

20. Compare the famous portrait of Mme. Vauquer in Balzac's *Père Goriot*, analyzed by Erich Auerbach as a paradigmatic example of the kind of nineteenth-century realist description that links a character to his or her historical and social context: *Mimesis*, 468–73.

21. Corrigan, *Riddle*, 120–41.

22. Apophasis, the approach to comprehending God by negative description, was an especially important thread in Eastern mystical theology of the third to fifth centuries CE and has remained more prominent in Eastern Orthodoxy than in the Catholic and Protestant traditions. For a survey discussion, see Timothy Ware, *The Orthodox Church: An Introduction to Eastern Christianity* (New York: Penguin Books, 2015), 60–63. Studies arguing that a broader apophatic religious "dynamic" shapes the construction and style of Dostoevsky's novels include Grigorii Pomerants, "Otkrytost' bezdne," in *Otkrytost' bezdne: Etiudy o Dostoevskom* (New York: Liberty Publishing House, 1989), 239–62; Olga Meerson, *Dostoevsky's Taboos* (Dresden: Dresden University Press, 1998); Malcolm Jones, *Dostoevsky and the Dynamics of Religious Experience* (London: Anthem Press, 2005); and Apollonio, *Dostoevsky's Secrets*. For studies focused on apophatic rhetorical strategies in particular novels, see also Oge Hansen-Löve, "Diskursivnye protsessy v romane Dostoevskogo *Podrostok*," in *Avtor i tekst*, ed. V. M. Markovich and Vol'f Shmid (Saint Petersburg: Izdatel'stvo S.-Peterburgskogo universiteta, 1996), 229–67; Ingunn Lunde, "'Ia gorazdo umnee napisannogo': On Apophatic Strategies and Verbal Experiments in Dostoevskii's *A Raw Youth*," *Slavonic and East European Review* 79, no. 2 (April 2001): 264–89; and Robin Feuer Miller's study of *The Idiot*, which does not emphasize apophasis but traces Dostoevsky's implied vision of Myshkin as Christ-like from within the narrator's misleading, overt narrative about him.

23. Jensen, "Paradoksal'nost' avtorstva," 220. On Dostoevsky's orientation on the beautiful image, whose apex was the figure of Christ, see Jackson, *Dostoevsky's Quest for Form*; Caryl Emerson, "Word and Image in Dostoevsky's Worlds: Robert Louis Jackson on Readings that Bakhtin Could Not Do," in *Freedom and Responsibility: A Festschrift for Robert Louis Jackson*, ed. Elizabeth Cheresh Allen and Gary Saul Morson, 245–65 (Evanston, IL: Northwestern University Press, 1995); and Apollonio, *Dostoevsky's Secrets*, 3–12.

24. "В детстве и юности он был мало экспансивен и даже мало разговорчив, но не от недоверия, не от робости или угрюмой нелюдимости, вовсе

даже напротив, а от чего-то другого, от какой-то как бы внутренней заботы, собственно личной, до других не касавшейся, но столь для него важной, что он из-за нее как бы забывал других. Но людей он любил . . . Что-то было в нем, что говорило и внушало (да и всю жизнь потом), что он не хочет быть судьей людей, что он не захочет взять на себя осуждения и ни за что не осудит" (14:18–19).

25. L. G. Kashirina touches on this point in her very brief, though suggestive, discussion of Alyosha as a "captive voice" (*golos-podkhvat*) in the novel, a "counterpoint" to the voices of Ivan, Dmitri, and other characters. L. G. Kashirina, "Soderzhatel'naia sushchnost' obraza Aleshi Karamazova i ee reprezentatsiia v romane F. M. Dostoevskogo *Bratia Karamazovy* ," in *Dostoevskii i sovremennost'* (Novgorod, 1989), 52.

26. I discuss Dostoevsky's idiosyncratic notion of "type" and the particular problem posed by the "contemporary type" in chapter 2.

27. "Тут прибавлю еще раз от себя лично: мне почти противно вспоминать об этом суетном и соблазнительном событии, в сущности же самом пустом и естественном, и я, конечно, выпустил бы его в рассказе моем вовсе без упоминовения, если бы не повлияло оно сильнейшим и известным образом на душу и сердце главного, хотя и будущего героя рассказа моего, Алеши, составив в душе его как бы перелом и переворот, потрясший, но и укрепивший его разум уже окончательно, на всю жизнь и к известной цели. . . . Отец Паисий, конечно, не ошибся, решив, что его «милый мальчик» снова воротится. . . . Тем не менее признаюсь откровенно, что самому мне очень было бы трудно теперь передать ясно точный смысл этой странной и неопределённой минуты в жизни столь излюбленного мною и столь еще юного героя моего рассказа. На горестный вопрос отца Паисия . . . я, конечно, мог бы с твердостью ответить за Алешу: «Нет, он не с маловерными»" (14:297, 305).

28. See V. E. Vetlovskaia, *Poetika romana Dostoevskogo "Bratia Karamazovy"* (Leningrad: Nauka, 1977), 16 and 180–82. For further discussion of Alyosha's relation to the hagiographic model, see also Thompson, *Poetics of Memory*, 26–51; Perlina, *Varieties*, 70–82; and Jostein Børtnes, "The Function of Hagiography in Dostoevskij's Novels" (1978), repr. in *Critical Essays on Dostoevsky*, ed. Robin Feuer Miller, 188–93 (Boston: G. K. Hall, 1986).

29. "Над ним широко, необозримо опрокинулся небесный купол, полный тихих сияющих звезд. С зенита до горизонта двоился еще неясный Млечный Путь. . . . Тишина земная как бы сливалась с небесною, тайна земная соприкасалась со звездною . . . Алеша стоял, смотрел и вдруг как подкошенный повергся на землю. Он не знал, для чего обнимал ее, он не давал себе отчета, почему ему так неудержимо хотелось целовать ее, целовать ее всю, но он целовал ее плача, рыдая и обливая своими слезами, и исступленно клялся любить ее, любить во веки веков. «Облей землю слезами радости твоея и люби сии слезы твои . . . »—прозвенело в душе его. О чем пла-

кал он? О, он плакал в восторге своем даже и об этих звездах, которые сияли ему из бездны, и «не стыдился исступления сего». Как будто нити ото всех этих бесчисленных миров божиих сошлись разом в душе его, и она вся трепетала, «соприкасаясь мирам иным». Простить хотелось ему всех и за всё и просить прощения, о! не себе, а за всех, за всё и за вся, а «за меня и другие просят»,—прозвенело опять в душе его. Но с каждым мгновением он чувствовал явно и как бы осязательно, как что-то твердое и незыблемое, как этот свод небесный, сходило в душу его. Какая-то как бы идея воцарялась в уме его—и уже на всю жизнь и на веки веков" (14:328; second and third ellipses in original).

30. Tolstoy, *Anna Karenina*, 800; 19:381–82. Subscribers to the *Russian Herald*, in which *The Brothers Karamazov* was also serialized, had to read the end of *Anna Karenina* in a special pamphlet, published and distributed at Tolstoy's own expense when Mikhail Katkov, the editor of the *Russian Herald*, refused to print it because of political disagreements. Donna Orwin finds a common link for the image of the "heavenly vault" in Nikolai Strakhov's 1878 monograph *Ob osnovnykh poniatiiakh psikhologii*, which he had discussed with both Tolstoy and Dostoevsky while writing. Donna Orvin, "Psikhologiia very v *Anne Kareninoi* i v *Bratiakh Karamazovykh,*" in *Mir filologii: Posviashchaetsia Lidii Dmitrievne Gromovoi-Opul'skoi* (Moscow: Nasledie, 2000), 235–45. However, given Dostoevsky's close polemical engagement with *Anna Karenina*, it seems clear that he was also transforming Tolstoy's earlier scene.

31. See Fusso, *Discovering Sexuality*, 72–76, and Apollonio, *Dostoevsky's Secrets*, 163–64.

32. "Все вы, господа, милы мне отныне, всех вас заключу в мое сердце, а вас прошу заключить и меня в ваше сердце! Ну, а кто нас соединил в этом добром хорошем чувстве, об котором мы теперь всегда, всю жизнь вспоминать будем и вспоминать намерены, кто как не Илюшечка . . . Не забудем же его никогда, вечная ему и хорошая память в наших сердцах, отныне и во веки веков! . . . Карамазов!—крикнул Коля,—неужели и взаправду религия говорит, что мы все встанем из мертвых, и оживем, и увидим опять друг друга, и всех, и Илюшечку?—Непременно восстанем, непременно увидим и весело, радостно расскажем друг другу всё, что было,—полусмеясь, полу в восторге ответил Алеша" (15:196).

33. On this speech as Alyosha's "one and only monologic performance" in the novel, marking his final assimilation of Zosima's authoritative discourse, see also Perlina, *Varieties*, 44 and 192–94. As Robert Louis Jackson notes, specific verbal echoes serve to recall and oppose it to Ivan's "rebellion." Robert Louis Jackson, "Alyosha's Speech at the Stone: 'The Whole Picture,'" in *New Word*, 234–57.

34. Compare Mikhail Bakhtin's description of this effect, with an ethical rather than a formal emphasis: "The investigator, judges, prosecutor, defense at-

torney, and commission of experts are all equally incapable of approaching the unfinalized and undecided core of Dmitry's personality. . . . In place of this living core, bursting with new life, they substitute a sort of *ready-made definitiveness*, 'naturally' and 'normally' *predetermined* in all its words and acts by 'psychological laws.' All who judge Dmitry are devoid of a genuinely dialogic approach to him." *Problems*, 62; *Problemy, Sobranie sochinenii* 6:73.

35. Holland, *Age of Disintegration*, 175–88.

36. "Да то, что украл, вот что! О боже, вы меня ужасаете непониманием! Всё время, пока я носил эти полторы тысячи, зашитые на груди, я каждый день и каждый час говорил себе: «ты вор, ты вор!» Да и оттого и свирепствовал в этот месяц. . . . Я даже Алеше, брату моему, не решился и не посмел открыть про эти полторы тысячи: до того чувствовал, что подлец и мазурик! Но знайте, что пока я носил, я в то же время каждый день и каждый час мой говорил себе: «Нет, Дмитрий Федорович, ты, может быть, еще не вор.» . . . И вот вчера только я решился сорвать мою ладонку с шеи . . . и только что сорвал, в ту же минуту стал уже окончательный и бесспорный вор, вор и бесчестный человек на всю жизнь. Почему? Потому что вместе с ладонкой и мечту мою пойти к Кате и сказать: «Я подлец, а не вор»—разорвал!" (14:444).

37. The commentary cites a line in Psalm 1: "Not so the wicked, but like chaff that the wind drives away" (15:548). See Vladimir Kantor's discussion of "the theory 'all is permitted'" as "a chemically cleansed 'Karamazovism' . . . to the extent that 'Karamazovism' is the quintessence of the societal disintegration then underway." Vladimir Kantor, "Pavel Smerdyakov and Ivan Karamazov: The Problem of Temptation," trans. Caryl Emerson, in *Dostoevsky and the Christian Tradition*, ed. George Pattison and Diane Oenning Thompson (Cambridge: Cambridge University Press, 2001), 213. Originally published in Vladimir Kantor, *V poiskakh lichnosti: Opyt russkoi klassiki* (Moscow: Moskovskii filosofskii fond, 1994), 149–74.

38. Corrigan also comments on this anomaly: *Riddle*, 139.

39. On this point, see also Kantor, "Problem of Temptation," 193 and 211.

40. Boris Tikhomirov discusses Dostoevsky's "Christology" in two essays that give particular weight to Dostoevsky's letter to Fonvizina: "O 'khristologii' Dostoevskogo," in *Dostoevskii: Materialy i isledovaniia* 11 (1994): 102–21; and "Khristos i istina v poeme 'Velikii Inkvizitor,'" *Dostoevskii i mirovaia kul'tura* 13 (1999): 147–77. In the latter, he argues that Dostoevsky's own "creative process" gave him a form for overcoming the doubts of Ivan Karamazov, the character he was creating (176). For alternative takes, see Stepanian's claim that by the time of writing *The Brothers Karamazov*, Dostoevsky had outgrown and reformulated his 1854 profession of faith (*Iavlenie i dialog*, 299 and 317–22); and Wolf Schmid's reading of *The Brothers Karamazov* as "the author's strain" (*nadryv*), Dostoevsky's attempt to silence his own persistent ambivalence about the existence of a benevolent God. "*Bratia Karamazovy*, nadryv avtora, ili roman

o dvukh kontsakh" (1996), repr. in Vol'f Shmid, *Proza kak poeziia: Pushkin, Dostoevskii, Chekhov, avangard*, 171–93 (Saint Petersburg: Inapress, 1998).

41. *Problems*, 63; *Problemy, Sobranie sochinenii* 6:73.

42. In a different context, Leo Bersani traces the impulse to escape from a coherent notion of literary character and self, which would also mean an escape from the tyrannical patterns of suppressed or inhibited desires. Leo Bersani, *A Future for Astyanax: Character and Desire in Literature* (Boston and Toronto: Little, Brown, 1976). The transformative space of the "not-you," where Dostoevsky's Karamazov brothers are stripped of (and liberated from) their own identities, resembles the alternative state that Bersani calls the "clean blankness of being" (50), but crucially differs from it in being *temporary*—in *The Brothers Karamazov*, one self is emptied out so as to be arduously replaced with another, and the characters' name still preserves an outline for the "new man" (591; 15:30) that will arise in the old one's place.

43. "Главное, тем была она досадна, эта тоска, и тем раздражала, что имела какой-то случайный, совершенно внешний вид; это чувствовалось. Стояло и торчало где-то какое-то существо или предмет, вроде как торчит что-нибудь иногда пред глазом, и долго . . . не замечаешь его, а между тем видимо раздражаешься, почти мучаешься, и наконец-то догадаешься отстранить негодный предмет, часто очень пустой и смешной, какую-нибудь вещь, забытую не на своем месте, платок, упавший на пол, книгу, не убранную в шкаф, и проч., и проч. Наконец Иван Федорович в самом скверном и раздраженном состоянии духа достиг родительского дома и вдруг . . . разом догадался о том, что его так мучило и тревожило. На скамейке у ворот сидел и прохлаждался вечерним воздухом лакей Смердяков, и Иван Федорович с первого взгляда на него понял, что и в душе его сидел лакей Смердяков и что именно этого-то человека и не может вынести его душа. . . . «Да неужели же этот дрянной негодяй до такой степени может меня беспокоить!»" (14:242).

44. See Olga Meerson's argument that Smerdyakov's status as one of the brothers Karamazov is the novel's central "taboo," the truth that none of the novel's characters is willing to acknowledge. By overcoming this taboo, the reader learns to recognize Smerdyakov's claim to (literal and universal) brotherhood (*Dostoevsky's Taboos*, 183–209). The idea of the moral "test" associated with Smerdyakov's brotherhood has recently been expanded by A. Berman, "Siblings in *The Brothers Karamazov*," *Russian Review* 68 (April 2009): 263–82; and *Siblings in Tolstoy and Dostoevsky*, 124–28; and by Matzner-Gore, "Kicking Maksimov," 421–22. But this picture is complicated by the demonic uncertainty of Smerdyakov's birth—and much in the novel's structure depends on the fact that nominally, he is *not* a Karamazov. Folding him into the group of the "brothers Karamazov" may do as much to thwart Dostoevsky's narrative purposes as it does to serve them.

45. On the many valences of Smerdyakov's name, and its derivation from his

mother's epithet, see V. V. Ivanov, "O kompozitsionnoi roli familii geroev u Dostoevskogo. Smerdiakov," in *Miscellanea Slavica to Honour the Memory of Jan M. Meijer*, ed. B. J. Amsenga et al. (Amsterdam: Rodopi, 1983), 381–88.

46. "Редко, бывало, заговорит. Если бы в то время кому-нибудь вздумалось спросить, глядя на него: чем этот парень интересуется и что всего чаще у него на уме, то, право, невозможно было бы решить, на него глядя. А между тем он иногда . . . останавливался, задумывался и стоял так по десятку даже минут. Физиономист, вглядевшись в него, сказал бы, что тут ни думы, ни мысли нет, а так какое-то созерцание. У живописца Крамского есть одна замечательная картина под названием «Созерцатель»: изображен лес зимой, и в лесу, на дороге, в оборванном кафтанишке и лаптишках стоит один-одинешенек, в глубочайшем уединении забредший мужичонок, стоит и как бы задумался, но он не думает, а что-то «созерцает». Если б его толкнуть, он вздрогнул бы и посмотрел на вас, точно проснувшись, но ничего не понимая. Правда, сейчас бы и очнулся, а спросили бы его, о чем он это стоял и думал, то наверно бы ничего не припоминал, но зато наверно бы затаил в себе то впечатление, под которым находился во время своего созерцания. Впечатления же эти ему дороги, и он наверно их копит, неприметно и даже не сознавая,—для чего и зачем, конечно, тоже не знает: может, вдруг, накопив впечатлений за многие годы, бросит всё и уйдет в Иерусалим, скитаться и спасаться, а может, и село родно вдруг спалит, а может быть, случится и то, и другое вместе. Созерцателей в народе довольно. Вот одним из таких созерцателей был наверно и Смердяков, и наверно тоже копил впечатления свои с жадностью, почти сам еще на зная зачем" (14:116–17).

47. It is telling, in this respect, that Smerdyakov springs from a small matrix of parodic associations with *War and Peace*: his adoptive father, Grigory Vasilievich Kutuzov; and his adoptive mother, Marfa Ignatievna, whom Grigory once abused for performing "the 'Russian dance' in a special manner, not as village women did it, but as she used to dance when she was a servant of the wealthy Miusovs" (94–95; 14:88).

48. Curiously, as Bakhtin stresses in his analysis, Smerdyakov builds this fantasy of Ivan's omniscience on a dynamic of which Ivan is ignorant, his apprehension and appropriation of "that voice of Ivan's which Ivan is hiding from his own self" (*Problems*, 247–48, 258–60; *Problemy, Sobranie sochinenii* 6:276, 6:283–85). Whether Smerdyakov controls this voice, or simply collaborates with it, it is vital to his private narrative that the voice appear to come from Ivan himself, as an external authority.

49. Lukács, *Theory of the Novel*, 88.

50. Belknap, *The Structure of "The Brothers Karamazov,"* 71.

51. A number of critics have pursued the argument that Smerdyakov's character is redeemable. Lee Johnson ("The Struggle for Theosis: Smerdyakov as Would-Be Saint," in *New Word*, 74–89) finds evidence of Smerdyakov's quest to

partake in the divinity of God in his relationship to the scriptures and his last-minute association with a book of Isaac the Syrian's writings (a detail in which Olga Meerson also sees "a glimpse of redemption"; *Dostoevsky's Taboos*, 200). But Galina Galagan suggests that in Isaac the Syrian, Smerdyakov saw only a blasphemous challenge to elevate his will above all others'. "'Tsarstvo' razdora i sluga Pavel Smerdyakov," in *Dostoevskii: Materialy i issledovaniia* 16 (2001): 175–87. Vladimir Golstein and Natalia Rogova see in Smerdyakov a tragic, but preventable, failure of parenting and education. Vladimir Golstein, "Accidental Families and Surrogate Fathers: Richard, Grigory, and Smerdyakov," in *New Word*, 90–106; N. B. Rogova, "Ideia dukhovnogo 'otechestva' i 'bratstva' v romane *Brat'ia Karamazovy*: K osmysleniiu obraza Pavla Fedorovicha Smerdiakova," in *Dostoevskii i mirovaia kul'tura* 19 (2003): 189–99. Among the more adventurous attempts to vindicate Smerdyakov are V. V. Beliaev's suggestion that in a novel where food is so ideologically significant, the only chef could not possibly be evil; and V. G. Shevchenko's deliberately polemical argument that in the unwritten second novel, it must have emerged that a previously unknown or extremely marginal character committed the murder, on the basis of a number of logical implausibilities in the case against Smerdyakov. V. V. Beliaev, "Antinomiia zhivogo i mertvogo v *Brat'iakh Karamazovykh* Dostoevskogo i obraz Pavla Smerdiakova," in *Dostoevskii i sovremennost': Materialy VIII Mezhdunarodnykh 'Starorusskikh Chtenii' 1993 g.* (Novgorod, 1994), 42–49; V. G. Shevchenko, "Traktat o Smerdiakove," *Dostoevskii i mirovaia kul'tura* 10 (1998): 196–228. But Carol Apollonio uses the same implausibilities to suggest that Smerdyakov committed the murder in such unlikely circumstances that he cannot possibly be human (*Dostoevsky's Secrets*, 161–62). Such critical divergence gives credence to Morson's argument that Smerdyakov "embodies anomalies to all possible systems" ("Verbal Pollution in *The Brothers Karamazov*," repr. in Miller, *Critical Essays on Dostoevsky*, 234). But Smerdyakov's position is at least perfectly in line with the conventional contours of a realist character-system.

52. This link between the openness of novelistic character, the openness of novelistic texts, and "the ongoing event of current life" is particularly visible in Bakhtin's 1941 essay "Roman, kak literaturnyi zhanr" (*Sobranie sochinenii* 3:608–43; M. Bakhtin, "Epic and Novel," in *Dialogic Imagination*, 3–40). The longer, earlier study translated as "Discourse in the Novel" ("Slovo v romane," c. 1930–34) develops a more nuanced approach to the interplay between text and world by deemphasizing named characters in favor of the "images of speaking persons, dressed in concrete social and historical clothing," that "show through" (*skvoziat*) from behind each of a novel's diverse languages (*Sobranie sochinenii* 3:90; M. Bakhtin, "Discourse in the Novel," in *Dialogic Imagination*, 336).

53. Plato, *Phaedrus*, trans. Alexander Nehemas and Paul Woodruff, in *Plato: Complete Works*, 552–53.

54. Derrida, "Plato's Pharmacy," 63–171.

AFTERWORD

1. Dostoevsky, *The Idiot*, 382; 8:317.

2. V. S. Soloviev, "Three Addresses in Memory of Dostoevsky [Second Address]," in *The Heart of Reality: Essays on Beauty, Love, and Ethics*, ed. and trans. Vladimir Wozniuk (Notre Dame, IN: University of Notre Dame Press, 2003), 16 (translation modified); V. S. Solov'ev, *Sochineniia*, ed. A. V. Gulyga and A. F. Losev (Moscow: Mysl', 1988), 2:305–6.

3. My points in these concluding paragraphs inevitably stray into the territory of contemporary novels that evoke the legacy of realism, particularly as regards the creation of lifelike character. I do not aim to articulate these novels' relationship to the nineteenth-century realist tradition.

4. Suzanne Keen, *Empathy and the Novel* (Oxford: Oxford University Press, 2007). Compiling research in psychology, cognitive science, and moral philosophy, Keen argues that "the case for altruism stemming from novel reading [is] inconclusive at best and nearly always exaggerated in favor of the beneficial effects of novel reading" (vii), even though contemporary authors' and readers' invocations of literary empathy are "not an inconsiderable element of the creation and reception of fiction and . . . should be resituated to a central place in twenty-first century aesthetics" (xxv). She also finds widespread disagreement about whether literary empathy itself has positive moral, social, and political consequences or whether it more often results in complacency, self-centered "indulgence of feeling" (160), or overgeneralization. For a recent renewal of that case, see Namwali Serpell, "The Banality of Empathy," *NYR Daily*, March 2, 2019. https://www.nybooks.com/daily/2019/03/02/the-banality-of-empathy/.

5. Keen, *Empathy*, 168.

6. Morson, *Prosaics*, 28.

7. Nussbaum, *Love's Knowledge*, 154–55.

8. Morson, *Prosaics*, 207.

9. Roman Jakobson, "O khudozhestvennom realizme," in *Raboty po poetike*, ed. M. L. Gasparov (Moscow: Progress, 1987), 389.

Bibliography

Abrams, M. H. *The Mirror and the Lamp: Romantic Theory and the Critical Tradition*. London, Oxford, and New York: Oxford University Press, 1953.

Alexandrov, Vladimir E. *Limits to Interpretation: The Meanings of "Anna Karenina."* Madison: University of Wisconsin Press, 2004.

Altick, Richard D. *The English Common Reader*. Chicago: University of Chicago Press, 1957.

Anderson, Amanda, Rita Felski, and Toril Moi. *Character: Three Inquiries in Literary Studies*. Chicago: University of Chicago Press, 2019.

Andrushchenko, E. A. "Tainovedeniie Merezhkovskogo." In *L. Tolstoi i Dostoevskii*, edited by E. A. Andrushchenko, 490–506. Moscow: Nauka, 2000.

Apollonio, Carol. *Dostoevsky's Secrets: Reading against the Grain*. Evanston, IL: Northwestern University Press, 2011.

———. "Fear of Faith: The Hidden Religious Message of *Notes from Underground*." *Slavic and East European Journal* 37, no. 4 (Winter 1993): 510–29.

———. Introduction to *The New Russian Dostoevsky: Readings for the Twenty-First Century*, edited by Carol Apollonio, 1–6. Bloomington, IN: Slavica, 2010.

Aristotle. *The Basic Works of Aristotle*. Edited by Richard McKeon. New York: Modern Library, 2001.

Auerbach, Erich. *Mimesis: The Representation of Reality in Western Literature*. Translated by Willard R. Trask. Princeton, NJ: Princeton University Press, 1953.

Auyung, Elaine. "Rethinking the Reality Effect: Detail and the Novel." In *The Oxford Handbook of Cognitive Literary Studies*, edited by Lisa Zunshine. Oxford Handbooks Online, 2015. DOI:0.1093/oxfordhb/9780199978069.013.0029.

Babaev, E. G. *Kommentarii*. In L. N. Tolstoi, *Sobranie sochinenii*, edited by M. B. Khrapchenko et al., 9:417–88. Moscow: Khudozhestvennaia literatura, 1978–85. https://rvb.ru/tolstoy/02comm/introcomm_9.htm.

Babel', Isaak. *Sobranie sochinenii*. Edited by I. N. Sukhikh. 4 vols. Moscow: Vremia, 2006.

Bagby, Lewis. *First Words: On Dostoevsky's Introductions*. Boston: Academic Studies Press, 2016.

Bakhtin, M. M. "Author and Hero in Aesthetic Activity." In *Art and Answerability*, edited by Michael Holquist and Vadim Liapunov and translated by Vadim Liapunov and Kenneth Brostrom, 4–256. Austin: University of Texas Press, 1990.

———. "Discourse in the Novel." In *The Dialogic Imagination*, edited by Michael Holquist and translated by Caryl Emerson and Michael Holquist, 259–422. Austin: University of Texas Press, 1981.

———. "Epic and Novel." In *The Dialogic Imagination*, edited by Michael Holquist and translated by Caryl Emerson and Michael Holquist, 3–40. Austin: University of Texas Press, 1981.

———. *Sobranie sochinenii*. Edited by S. G. Bocharov and N. I. Nikolaev. 7 vols. Moscow: Russkie slovari, 1996–.

Bakhtin, Mikhail. *Problems of Dostoevsky's Poetics*. Edited and translated by Caryl Emerson. Minneapolis: University of Minnesota Press, 1984.

Bal, Mieke. *Narratology: Introduction to the Theory of Narrative*. 3rd ed. Toronto: University of Toronto Press, 2009.

Barthes, Roland. "The Death of the Author." In *Image, Music, Text*, translated by Stephen Heath, 142–48. New York: Hill and Wang, 1977.

———. "The Reality Effect." In *The Rustle of Language*, translated by Richard Howard, 141–48. Oxford: Basil Blackwell, 1986.

———. *S/Z*. Translated by Richard Miller. New York: Hill and Wang, 1974.

Bayley, John. *Tolstoy and the Novel*. 2nd ed. Chicago: University of Chicago Press, 1988.

Beliaev, V. V. "Antinomiia zhivogo i mertvogo v *Brat'iakh Karamazovykh* Dostoevskogo i obraz Pavla Smerdiakova." In *Dostoevskii i sovremennost': Materialy VIII Mezhdunarodnykh 'Starorusskikh Chtenii' 1993 g.*, 42–49. Novgorod, 1994.

Belknap, Robert. *The Structure of "The Brothers Karamazov."* The Hague and Paris: Mouton, 1967.

———. "Memory in *The Brothers Karamazov*." In *Dostoevsky: New Perspectives*, edited by Robert Louis Jackson, 227–42. Englewood Cliffs, NJ: Prentice Hall, 1984.

———. "Tolstoy's Prince Who Resembles a Cucumber." In *Freedom and Responsibility: Essays on Russian Literature in Honor of Robert Louis Jackson*, edited by Elizabeth Cheresh Allen and Gary Saul Morson, 153–58. Evanston, IL: Northwestern University Press, 1995.

Bem, A. L. "Khudozhestvennaia polemika s Tolstym (K ponimaniiu *Podrostka*)." In *O Dostoevskom*, edited by A. L. Bem, 3:192–214. Petropolis, 1936.

Benjamin, Walter. *Selected Writings*. Translated by Rodney Livingstone et al. and edited by Michael W. Jennings et al. 4 vols. Cambridge, MA: Harvard University Press, 1999.

Berlin, Isaiah. *The Hedgehog and the Fox: An Essay on Tolstoy's View of History*. Rev. ed. Chicago: Ivan R. Dee, 1993.

Berman, Anna. "The Sibling Bond: A Model for Romance and Motherhood in *War and Peace*." *Tolstoy Studies Journal* 18 (2006): 1–15.

———. "Siblings in *The Brothers Karamazov*." *Russian Review* 68 (April 2009): 263–82.

———. *Siblings in Tolstoy and Dostoevsky: The Path to Universal Brotherhood*. Evanston, IL: Northwestern University Press, 2015.

Bersani, Leo. *A Future for Astyanax: Character and Desire in Literature*. Boston and Toronto: Little, Brown, 1976.

Bird, Robert. "Refiguring the Russian Type: Dostoevsky and the Limits of Realism." In *A New Word on "The Brothers Karamazov,"* edited by Robert Louis Jackson, 17–30. Evanston, IL: Northwestern University Press, 2004.

Bocharov, S. G. *Roman L. Tolstogo "Voina i mir."* Moscow: Khudozhestvennaia literatura, 1963.

Booth, Wayne C. *The Company We Keep: An Ethics of Fiction*. Berkeley and Los Angeles: University of California Press, 1988.

Børtnes, Jostein. "The Function of Hagiography in Dostoevskij's Novels." *Scando-Slavica* 24 (1978): 27–33. Reprinted in *Critical Essays on Dostoevsky*, edited by Robin Feuer Miller, 188–93. Boston: G. K. Hall, 1986.

Bronstein, Michaela. "Four Generations, One Crime." In *Crime Fiction as World Literature*, edited by Louise Nilsson et al., 59–74. New York and London: Bloomsbury, 2017.

Brooks, Jeffrey. *When Russia Learned to Read: Literacy and Popular Literature, 1861–1917*. Princeton, NJ: Princeton University Press, 1985.

Brooks, Peter. *Reading for the Plot*. New York: Knopf, 1984.

Brunson, Molly. *Russian Realisms: Literature and Painting, 1840–1890*. DeKalb, IL: Northern Illinois University Press, 2016.

Bychkov, S. P., ed. *L. N. Tolstoi v russkoi kritike*. Moscow: Khudozhestvennaia literatura, 1960.

Carden, Patricia. "The Expressive Self in *War and Peace*." *Canadian-American Slavic Studies* 12, no. 4 (Winter 1978): 519–34.

Catteau, Jacques. *Dostoevsky and the Process of Literary Creation*. Translated by Audrey Littlewood. Cambridge: Cambridge University Press, 1989.

Chaadaev, P. Ia. *Polnoe sobranie sochinenii i izbrannye pis'ma*. Edited by T. I. Oizerman et al. 2 vols. Moscow: Nauka, 1991.

Chances, Ellen. "Links between *Brothers Karamazov* and *Anna Karenina*." *Dostoevsky Studies*, n.s., 15 (2011): 17–27.

Chatman, Seymour. *Story and Discourse*. Ithaca, NY: Cornell University Press, 1978.

Chizhevskii, D. I. "Shiller i *Bratia Karamazovy*." Translated by S. P. Kratz et al. *Dostoevskii: Materialy i issledovaniia* 19 (2010): 16–57.

Christian, R. F. *Tolstoy's "War and Peace": A Study*. Oxford: Clarendon Press, 1962.

Cixous, Hélène. "The Character of 'Character.'" *NLH* 5, no. 2 (Winter 1974): 383–402.

Cohn, Dorrit. *Transparent Minds: Narrative Modes for Presenting Consciousness in Fiction*. Princeton, NJ: Princeton University Press, 1978.

———. *The Distinction of Fiction*. Baltimore: Johns Hopkins University Press, 1998.

Corrigan, Yuri. *Dostoevsky and the Riddle of the Self*. Evanston, IL: Northwestern University Press, 2017.

Cooke, Brett. "Tolstoi i novyi Darvin(izm)." In *Lev Tolstoi i mirovaia literatura: Materialy III Mezhdunarodnoi konferentsii*, 195–202. Tula: Izdatel'skii dom Iasnaia Poliana, 2005.

Culler, Jonathan. *Structuralist Poetics: Structuralism, Linguistics, and the Study of Literature*. Ithaca, NY: Cornell University Press, 1975.

Deleuze, Gilles. *Difference and Repetition*. Translated by Paul Patton. New York: Columbia University Press, 1994.

Derrida, Jacques. *Dissemination*. Translated by Barbara Johnson. Chicago: University of Chicago Press, 1981.

———. "Economimesis." *Diacritics* 11, no. 2 (Summer 1981): 2–25.

Dickens, Charles. *David Copperfield*. Edited by Nina Burgis. Oxford: Oxford University Press, 1997.

Dobroliubov, N. A. "Kogda zhe priidet nastoiashchii den'?" In *Sobranie sochinenii*, edited by B. I. Bursov et al. 9 vols. Moscow: Gosizdat. khudozhestvennoi literatury, 1963.

Doležel, Lubomir. *Heterocosmica: Fiction and Possible Worlds*. Baltimore: Johns Hopkins University Press, 1998.

———. *Possible Worlds of Fiction and History*. Baltimore: Johns Hopkins University Press, 2010.

Dolinin, A. S. *Poslednie romany Dostoevskogo*. Moscow-Leningrad: Sovetskii pisatel', 1963.

Dostoevskii, F. M. *Polnoe sobranie sochinenii*. Edited by G. M. Fridlender et al. 30 vols. Leningrad: Nauka, 1972–1990.

Dostoevsky, Fyodor. *The Adolescent*. Translated by Richard Pevear and Larissa Volokhonsky. New York and London: Alfred A. Knopf, 2003.

———. *The Brothers Karamazov*. Translated by Richard Pevear and Larissa Volokhonsky. New York: Farrar, Straus, and Giroux, 1990.

———. *Crime and Punishment*. Translated by Oliver Ready. New York and London: Penguin Classics, 2014.

———. "The Dream of a Ridiculous Man." In *The Eternal Husband and Other Stories*, translated by Richard Pevear and Larissa Volokhonsky, 318–42. New York: Bantam Classics, 1997.

———. *The Idiot*. Translated by Richard Pevear and Larissa Volokhonsky. New York and Toronto: Knopf, 2002.

———. *The Notebooks for a Raw Youth*. Edited by Edward Wasiolek and translated by Victor Terras. Chicago: University of Chicago Press, 1969.

———. *Notes from Underground and The Double*. Translated by Ronald Wilks. New York and London: Penguin Classics, 2009.

———. *Poor Folk and Other Stories*. Translated by David McDuff. New York and London: Penguin Books, 1988.

———. *Selected Letters of Fyodor Dostoevsky*. Edited by Joseph Frank and David I. Goldstein, translated by Andrew R. MacAndrew. New Brunswick, NJ: Rutgers University Press, 1987.

Eagleton, Terry. *The Ideology of the Aesthetic*. Oxford: Blackwell, 1990.

Egorov, Boris. *Izbrannoe. Esteticheskie idei v Rossii XIX veka*. Saint Petersburg: Letnii sad, 2009.

Eikhenbaum, Boris. "How Gogol's Overcoat Is Made." In *Gogol from the Twentieth Century*, edited and translated by Robert A. Maguire, 267–91. Princeton, NJ: Princeton University Press, 1974.

Eikhenbaum, B. M. "Kak sdelana 'Shinel'' Gogolia." In *Skvoz' literaturu: sbornik stat'ei*, 171–95. Leningrad, 1924. Reprint, The Hague: Mouton, 1962.

———. *Lermontov: Opyt istoriko-literaturnoi otsenki*. Leningrad: Gosizdat, 1924. http://feb-web.ru/feb/lermont/critics/eich24/eich24.htm?cmd=p.

———. *Lev Tolstoi. I, 50-e gody*. Leningrad, 1928. Reprint, Munich: Wilhelm Fink Verlag, 1968.

———. *Lev Tolstoi. II, 60-e gody*. Leningrad, 1931. Reprint, Munich: Wilhelm Fink Verlag, 1968.

———. *Lev Tolstoi: 70ye gody*. Leningrad: Khudozhestvennaia literatura, 1974.

———. *Molodoi Tolstoi*. Petersburg and Berlin, 1922. Reprint, Munich: Wilhelm Fink, 1968.

———. "Ocherednye problemy izucheniia L'va Tolstogo." In *Trudy iubileinoi sessii. Sektsiia filologicheskikh nauk*, 279–93. Leningrad: Izdatel'stvo Leningradskogo gosudarstvennogo universiteta, 1946.

Emerson, Caryl. "Bakhtin's Radiant Polyphonic Novel, Raskolnikov's Perverse Dialogic World." In *Dostoevsky's "Crime and Punishment": Philosophical Perspectives*, edited by Robert Guay, 173–207. New York: Oxford University Press, 2019.

———. "Tolstoy's Aesthetics." In *The Cambridge Companion to Tolstoy*, edited by Donna Tussing Orwin, 237–51. Cambridge: Cambridge University Press, 2002.

———. "Word and Image in Dostoevsky's Worlds: Robert Louis Jackson on Readings That Bakhtin Could Not Do." In *Freedom and Responsibility: Essays on Russian Literature in Honor of Robert Louis Jackson*, edited by Elizabeth Cheresh Allen and Gary Saul Morson, 245–65. Evanston, IL: Northwestern University Press, 1995.

Emerson, Caryl, and Gary Saul Morson. *Mikhail Bakhtin: Creation of a Prosaics*. Stanford, CA: Stanford University Press, 1990.

Fanger, Donald. *Dostoevsky and Romantic Realism: A Study of Dostoevsky in Relation to Balzac, Dickens, and Gogol*. Cambridge, MA: Harvard University Press, 1965.

Fehér, Ferenc. "The Last Phase of Romantic Anti-Capitalism: Lukács' Response to the War." *New German Critique* 10 (Winter 1977): 139–54.

Feher, Zoltan Andor. "Georg Lukács's Role in Dostoevsky's European Reception at the Turn of the Century." PhD diss., University of California, Los Angeles, 1978.

Felski, Rita. ed. "Character." Special issue, *New Literary History* 42, no. 2 (Spring 2011).

———. *Uses of Literature*. Malden, MA, and Oxford: Blackwell, 2008.

Feuer, Kathryn. *Tolstoy and the Genesis of "War and Peace."* Ithaca, NY: Cornell University Press, 1996.

Figlerowicz, Marta. *Flat Protagonists: A Theory of Novel Character*. Oxford: Oxford University Press, 2016.

Fish, Stanley. *Surprised by Sin: The Reader in "Paradise Lost."* 2nd ed. Cambridge, MA: Harvard University Press, 1997.

Forster, E. M. *Aspects of the Novel*. London: Penguin, 1974.

Fowler, Elizabeth. *Literary Character: The Human Figure in Early English Writing*. Ithaca, NY: Cornell University Press, 2003.

Frank, Joseph. *Dostoevsky: The Mantle of the Prophet, 1871–1881*. Princeton, NJ: Princeton University Press, 2002.

———. *Dostoevsky: The Seeds of Revolt*. Princeton, NJ: Princeton University Press, 1976.

Frow, John. *Character and Person*. Oxford: Oxford University Press, 2014.

Fusso, Susanne. *Discovering Sexuality in Dostoevsky*. Evanston, IL: Northwestern University Press, 2006.

Galagan, G. Ia. "'Tsarstvo' razdora i sluga Pavel Smerdyakov." In *Dostoevskii: Materialy i issledovaniia* 16 (2001): 175–87.

Gallagher, Catherine. "George Eliot: Immanent Victorian." *Representations* 90, no. 1 (Spring 2005): 61–74.

———. *Nobody's Story: The Vanishing Acts of Women Writers in the Marketplace*. Berkeley and Los Angeles: University of California Press, 1994.

———. *Telling It Like It Wasn't: The Counterfactual Imagination in Fiction and History*. Chicago: University of Chicago Press, 2018.

———. "What Would Napoleon Do?" *New Literary History* 42, no. 2 (Spring 2011): 315–36.

Genette, Gérard. *Narrative Discourse: An Essay in Method*. Translated by Jane E. Lewin. Ithaca, NY: Cornell University Press, 1980.

———. "Vraisemblance et motivation." In *Figures II*. Paris: Éditions du Seuil, 1969.

Gerigk, Horst Jürgen. *Versuch über Dostoevskijs' Jüngling': Ein Beitrag zur Theorie des Romans*. Forum Slavicum 4. Munich: Wilhelm Fink Verlag, 1965.

Ginzburg, Lidiia. *O literaturnom geroe*. Leningrad: Sovetskii pisatel', 1979.
———. *O psikhologicheskoi proze*. Leningrad: Sovetskii pisatel', 1971.
———. "O romane L'va Tolstogo *Voina i mir*." *Zvezda*, no. 1 (1944): 125–38.
Ginzburg, Lydia. *On Psychological Prose*. Translated and edited by Judson Rosengrant. Princeton, NJ: Princeton University Press, 1991.
Golstein, Vladimir. "Accidental Families and Surrogate Fathers: Richard, Grigory, and Smerdyakov." In *A New Word on "The Brothers Karamazov,"* edited by Robert Louis Jackson, 90–106. Evanston, IL: Northwestern University Press, 2004.
Goncharov, I. A. *Sobranie sochinenii*. 8 vols. Moscow: Gosizdat. khudozhestvennoi literatury, 1952–55. http://feb-web.ru/feb/gonchar/default.asp?/feb/gonchar/texts/gs0/gs8/gs8.html.
Grenier, Svetlana. *Representing the Marginal Woman in Nineteenth-Century Russian Literature: Personalism, Feminism, and Polyphony*. Contributions in Women's Studies 185. Westport, CT, and London: Greenwood Press, 2001.
Grodetskaia, A. G. "Vozvrashchenie k diskussii o zhanre 'Voiny i mira.'" *Russkaia literatura* 3 (1991): 181–86.
Grossman, L. *Dostoevskii*. Moscow: Molodaia gvardiia, 1965.
Grossman, L. P. "Dostoevskii—khudozhnik." In *Tvorchestvo F. M. Dostoevskogo*, edited by N. L. Stepanov, 330–416. Moscow: Izdatel'stvo akademii nauk SSSR, 1959.
———. "Poslednii roman Dostoevskogo." In *Bratia Karamazovy: Roman v chetyrykh chastiakh s epilogom*, edited by L. P. Grossman, 1:3–51. Moscow: Khudozhestvennaia literatura, 1935.
Gustafson, Richard. *Leo Tolstoy: Resident and Stranger*. Princeton, NJ: Princeton University Press, 1986.
Gutkin, Irina. "The Dichotomy between Flesh and Spirit: Plato's *Symposium* in *Anna Karenina*." In *In the Shade of the Giant*, edited by H. McLean, 84–99. Berkeley and Los Angeles: University of California Press, 1989.
Hale, Dorothy J. "Aesthetics and the New Ethics: Theorizing the Novel in the Twenty-First Century." *PMLA* 124, no. 3 (2009): 896–903.
———. "The Art of English Fiction in the Twentieth Century." In *The Cambridge Companion to the Twentieth Century Novel*, edited by Robert L. Caserio, 10–22. Cambridge: Cambridge University Press, 2009.
———. *The Novel and the New Ethics*. Stanford, CA: Stanford University Press, 2020.
———. "*On Beauty* as Beautiful?: The Problem of Novelistic Aesthetics by Way of Zadie Smith." *Contemporary Literature* 53, no. 4 (Winter 2012): 814–44.
———. *Social Formalism: The Novel in Theory from Henry James to the Present*. Stanford, CA: Stanford University Press, 1998.
Halliwell, Stephen. *The Aesthetics of Mimesis*. Princeton, NJ: Princeton University Press, 2002.
———. *Aristotle's Poetics*. London: Duckworth, 1986.

Hamon, Philippe. *Le personnel du roman: Le système des personnages dans les Rougon-Macquart d'Émile Zola*. Geneva: Librairie Droz S. A., 1983.

———. "Pour un statut sémiologique du personnage." In *Poétique du recit*, edited by G. Genette and T. Todorov, 115–80. Éditions du Seuil, 1977.

———. *Texte et ideologie*. Paris: PUF, 1984.

Hansen-Löve, Oge. "Diskursivnye protsessy v romane Dostoevskogo *Podrostok*." In *Avtor i tekst*, edited by V. M. Markovich and Vol'f Shmid, 229–67. Saint Petersburg: Izdatel'stvo S.-Peterburgskogo universiteta, 1996.

Harvey, W. J. *Character and the Novel*. London: Chatto & Windus, 1965.

Heier, Edmund. *Literary Portraiture in Nineteenth-Century Russian Prose*. Cologne: Böhlau, 1993.

Hellebust, Rolf. "Bakhtin and the 'Virtual Sequel' in Russian Literature." *Slavic and East European Journal* 44, no. 4 (Winter, 2000): 603–22.

Herman, David. "Khadzhi-Murat's Silence." *Slavic Review* 64, no. 1 (Spring 2015): 1–23.

Hochman, Baruch. *Character in Literature*. Ithaca, NY: Cornell University Press, 1985.

Holland, Kate. *The Novel in the Age of Disintegration: Dostoevsky and the Problem of Genre in the 1870s*. Evanston, IL: Northwestern University Press, 2013.

———. "The Opening of *Anna Karenina*." In *Approaches to Teaching Tolstoy's "Anna Karenina,"* edited by Liza Knapp and Amy Mandelker, 144–49. New York: Modern Language Association of America, 2003.

Holquist, Michael. "Character Change as Language Change in *War and Peace*." In *Russianness: Studies on a Nation's Identity: In honor of Rufus Mathewson, 1918–1978*, edited by Robert L. Belknap, 210–26. Studies of the Harriman Institute. Ann Arbor, MI: Ardis, 1990.

———. "Dialogism and Aesthetics." In *Late Soviet Culture: From Perestroika to Novostroika*, edited by Thomas Lahusen, 155–76. Durham, NC: Duke University Press, 1993.

———. *Dostoevsky and the Novel*. Princeton, NJ: Princeton University Press, 1977.

Ingarden, Roman. *The Literary Work of Art*. Translated by George G. Grabowicz. Evanston, IL: Northwestern University Press, 1973.

Iser, Wolfgang. *The Act of Reading: A Theory of Aesthetic Response*. Baltimore: Johns Hopkins University Press, 1978.

———. *The Implied Reader: Patterns of Communication in Prose Fiction from Bunyan to Beckett*. Baltimore: Johns Hopkins University Press, 1974.

Ivanov, V. I. *Sobranie sochinenii*. 4 vols. Edited by D. V. Ivanov and O. Deshart. Brussels: Foyer Oriental Chrétien, 1971–87.

Ivanov, V. V. "O kompozitsionnoi roli familii geroev u Dostoevskogo. Smerdiakov." In *Miscellanea Slavica to Honour the Memory of Jan M. Meijer*, edited by B. J. Amsenga et al., 381–88. Amsterdam: Rodopi, 1983.

Ivanov, Vyacheslav. *Freedom and the Tragic Life: A Study in Dostoevsky*. Translated by Norman Cameron. New York: Noonday Press, 1952.

Jackson, Robert Louis "Alyosha's Speech at the Stone: 'The Whole Picture.'" In *A New Word on "The Brothers Karamazov,"* edited by Robert Louis Jackson, 234–57. Evanston, IL: Northwestern University Press, 2004.

———. "The Ambivalent Beginning of *Anna Karenina*." In *Semantic Analysis of Literary Texts*, edited by Eric de Haard et al., 345–52. Amsterdam: Elsevier, 1990.

———. "Dmitry Karamazov and the Legend of the Grand Inquisitor." In *The Art of Dostoevsky: Deliriums and Nocturnes*, 335–46. Princeton, NJ: Princeton University Press, 1981.

———. *Dostoevsky's Quest for Form: A Study of His Philosophy of Art*. 2nd ed. Bloomington, IN: Physsardt, 1978.

———. Introduction to *Freedom and the Tragic Life*, by Vyacheslav Ivanov. Translated by Norman Cameron, vii–xxxi. Wolfeboro, NH: Longwood Academic Press, 1989.

———. "The Sentencing of Fyodor Karamazov." In *The Art of Dostoevsky: Deliriums and Nocturnes*, 306–18. Princeton, NJ: Princeton University Press, 1981.

Jaffe, Audrey. *Vanishing Points: Dickens, Narrative, and the Subject of Omniscience*. Berkeley: University of California Press, 1991.

Jakobson, Roman. "O khudozhestvennom realizme. In *Raboty po poetike*, edited by M. L. Gasparov, 387–93. Moscow: Progress, 1987.

James, Henry. *The Art of the Novel: Critical Prefaces*. Edited by R. P. Blackmur. New York: Charles Scribner's Sons, 1934.

Jameson, Fredric. *The Antinomies of Realism*. London and New York: Verso, 2013.

———. *The Political Unconscious: Narrative as a Socially Symbolic Act*. Ithaca, NY: Cornell University Press, 1981.

Jensen, P. A. "Paradoksal'nost' avtorstva (u) Dostoevskogo." In *Paradoksy russkoi literatury*, edited by V. M. Markovich and Vol'f Shmid, 219–33. Saint Petersburg: Inapress, 2001.

Jepsen, Laura. *From Achilles to Christ: The Myth of the Hero in Tolstoy's "War and Peace."* Author's copyright, 1978.

Johnson, Lee. "Struggle for Theosis: Smerdyakov as Would-Be Saint." In *A New Word on "The Brothers Karamazov,"* edited by Robert Louis Jackson, 74–89. Evanston, IL: Northwestern University Press, 2004.

Jones, Malcolm. *Dostoevsky after Bakhtin: Readings in Dostoevsky's Fantastic Realism*. Cambridge: Cambridge University Press, 1990.

———. *Dostoevsky and the Dynamics of Religious Experience*. London: Anthem Press, 2005.

Kant, Immanuel. *Critique of Judgment*. Translated by J. H. Bernard. New York: Hafner Press, 1951.

Kantor, Vladimir. "The Problem of Temptation." In *Dostoevsky and the Christian Tradition*, edited by George Pattison and Diane Oenning Thompson, 189–225. Cambridge: Cambridge University Press, 2001.

———. *V poiskakh lichnosti: Opyt russkoi klassiki*. Moscow: Moskovskii filosofskii fund, 1994.

Kariakin, Iu. *Dostoevskii i kanun XXI veka*. Moscow: Sovetskii pisatel', 1989.

Kasatkina, T. A. *Khatakterologiia Dostoevskogo: Tipologiia emotsional'no-tsennostnykh orientatsii*. Moscow: Nasledie, 1996.

———. *O tvoriashchei prirode slova: Ontologichnost' slova v tvorchestve F. M. Dostoevskogo kak osnova 'realizma v vysshem smysle'*. Moscow: IMLI RAN, 2004.

———. "Roman F. M. Dostoevskogo *Podrostok*: 'Ideia' geroia i ideia avtora." *Voprosy literatury*, no. 1 (2004): 181–212.

Kashirina, L. G. "Soderzhatel'naia sushchnost' obraza Aleshi Karamazova i ee reprezentatsiia v romane F. M. Dostoevskogo *Bratia Karamazovy*." In *Dostoevskii i sovremennost': Tezisy vystuplenii na 'Starorusskikh chteniiakh,'* edited by L. I. Nikolaeva, 51–53. Novgorod, 1989.

Keen, Suzanne. *Empathy and the Novel*. Oxford: Oxford University Press, 2007.

Keldysh, V. A. "Nasledie Dostoevskogo i russkaia mysl' porubezhnoi epokhi." In *Sviaz' vremen: Problemy preemstvennosti v russkoi literature kontsa XIX-nachala XX v.*, edited by V. A. Keldysh, 76–115. Moscow: Nasledie, 1992.

Kirpotin, V. *Dostoevskii v shestidesiatye gody*. Moscow: Khudozhestvennaia literatura, 1966.

Kitzinger, Chloë. "Illusion and Instrument: Problems of Mimetic Characterization in Dostoevsky and Tolstoy." PhD diss., University of California, Berkeley, 2016.

———. "Tolstoy." In Annotations to Nabokov's *Lectures on Russian Literature*, http://thenabokovian.org/annotations/Lectures_on_Russian_Literature/tolstoy.

Kliger, Ilya. "Heroic Aesthetics and Modernist Critique: Extrapolations from Bakhtin's 'Author and Hero in Aesthetic Activity.'" *Slavic Review* 67, no. 3 (Fall 2008): 551–66.

———. *The Narrative Shape of Truth: Veridiction in Modern European Literature*. University Park: Pennsylvania State University Press, 2011.

Knapp, Liza. *"Anna Karenina" and Others: Tolstoy's Labyrinth of Plots*. Madison: University of Wisconsin Press, 2016.

———. *The Annihilation of Inertia: Dostoevsky and Metaphysics*. Evanston, IL: Northwestern University Press, 1996.

Knowles, A. V., ed. *Tolstoy: The Critical Heritage*. London: Routledge and Kegan Paul, 1978.

Kosofsky Sedgwick, Eve. *The Coherence of Gothic Conventions*. New York and London: Methuen, 1980.

Kostka, Edmund K. *Schiller in Russian Literature*. Philadelphia: University of Pennsylvania Press, 1965.

Kupreianova, E. N. *Estetika L. N. Tolstogo*. Leningrad: Nauka, 1966.

Lennkvist, Barbara. *Puteshestvie vglub' romana: Lev Tolstoi: 'Anna Karenina.'* Moscow: Iazyki slavianskoi kul'tury, 2010.

Leont'ev, K. *Analiz, stil' i veianie: o romanakh Gr. L. N. Tolstogo*. Moscow, 1911/1912. Reprint, Providence, RI: Brown University Press, 1965.

Lorenz, Ruth. "Realist Convictions and Revolutionary Impatience in the Criticism of N. A. Dobroliubov." *Slavic and East European Journal* 57, no. 1 (Spring 2013): 67–88.

Lotman, Iu. M. *Struktura khudozhestvennogo teksta*. Moscow: Iskusstvo, 1971.

Love, Jeff. *The Overcoming of History in "War and Peace."* Studies in Slavic Literature and Poetics 42. Amsterdam: Rodopi, 2004.

Lubbock, Percy. *The Craft of Fiction*. New York: Peter Smith, 1947.

Lukács, Georg. "Dostoevsky." In *Dostoevsky: A Collection of Critical Essays*, edited by René Wellek, 146–58. Englewood Cliffs, NJ: Prentice Hall, 1962.

———. *Dostojewski: Notizen und Entwürfe*. Edited by J. C. Nyiri. Budapest: Akademiai Kiado, 1985.

———. *The Historical Novel*. Translated by Hannah Mitchell and Stanley Mitchell. London: Merlin Press, 1962.

———. *Reviews and Articles from "Die rote Fahne."* Translated by Peter Palmer. London: Merlin Press, 1983.

———. *Studies in European Realism*. Translated by Edith Bone. New York: Grosset & Dunlap, 1964.

———. *Die Theorie des Romans*. Neuwied am Rhein: Luchterhand, 1963.

———. *The Theory of the Novel*. Translated by Anna Bostock. Cambridge, MA: MIT Press, 1971.

———. *Werke*. Edited by Frank Benseler and Gyorgy Markus. Neuwied and Berlin: Luchterhand, 1962–.

Lunde, Ingunn. "'Ia gorazdo umnee napisannogo': On Apophatic Strategies and Verbal Experiments in Dostoevskii's *A Raw Youth*." *Slavonic and East European Review* 79, no. 2 (April 2001): 264–89.

Lynch, Deidre Shauna. *The Economy of Character: Novels, Market Culture, and the Business of Inner Meaning*. Chicago: University of Chicago Press, 1998.

Mandelker, Amy. *Framing "Anna Karenina": Tolstoy, the Woman Question, and the Victorian Novel*. Columbus: Ohio State University Press, 1993.

Margolin, Uri. "Character." In *The Cambridge Companion to Narrative*, edited by David Herman, 66–79. Cambridge: Cambridge University Press, 2007.

Martinsen, Deborah. *Surprised by Shame: Dostoevsky's Liars and Narrative Exposure*. Columbus: Ohio State University Press, 2003.

Matich, Olga. *Erotic Utopia: The Decadent Imagination in Russia's Fin-de-siècle*. Madison: University of Wisconsin Press, 2005.

———. "Time and Memory in Dostoevsky's Novels, or Nastasya Filippovna in Absentia." *Slavic and East European Journal* 60, no. 3 (Fall 2016): 397–421.

Matthewson, Rufus. *The Positive Hero in Russian Literature*. Stanford, CA: Stanford University Press, 1975.

Matzner-Gore, Greta. "Kicking Maksimov out of the Carriage: Minor Characters, Exclusion and *The Brothers Karamazov*." *Slavic and East European Journal* 57, no. 3 (Fall 2014): 419–36.

———. "From the Corners of the Russian Novel: Minor Characters in Gogol, Goncharov, Tolstoy, and Dostoevsky." PhD diss., Columbia University, 2014.

McLaughlin, Sigrid. "Some Aspects of Tolstoy's Intellectual Development: Tolstoy and Schopenhauer." In *California Slavic Studies*, edited by Nicholas V. Riasanovsky and Gleb Struve, 5:187–244. Berkeley and Los Angeles: University of California Press, 1970.

Medzhibovskaya, Inessa. *Tolstoy and the Religious Culture of His Time: A Biography of a Long Conversion*. Lanham, MD.: Lexington Books, 2008.

Meerson, Olga. *Dostoevsky's Taboos*. Studies of the Harriman Institute. Dresden: Dresden University Press, 1998.

Merezhkovskii, D. S. *L. Tolstoi i Dostoevskii. Zhizn' i tvorchestvo*. Edited by E. A. Andrushchenko. Moscow: Nauka, 2000.

Mikhailovskii-Danilevskii, [A. I.] *Opisanie vtoroi voiny imperatora Aleksandra s Napoleonom*. Saint Petersburg, 1846. http://dlib.rsl.ru/viewer/01003542257#?page=1.

Miller, J. Hillis. *Ariadne's Thread*. New Haven, CT: Yale University Press, 1992.

———. *Charles Dickens: The World of His Novels*. Cambridge, MA: Harvard University Press, 1958.

———. *Fiction and Repetition: Seven English Novels*. Cambridge, MA: Harvard University Press, 1982.

———. *Reading Narrative*. Norman: University of Oklahoma Press, 1998.

Miller, Robin Feuer. *Dostoevsky and "The Idiot": Author, Narrator, and Reader*. Cambridge, MA: Harvard University Press, 1981.

Mochul'skii, K. *Dostoevskii: Zhizn' i tvorchestvo*. Paris: YMCA Press, 1947.

Mochulsky, Konstantin. *Dostoevsky: His Life and Work*. Translated by Michael A. Minihan. Princeton, NJ: Princeton University Press, 1967.

Morson, Gary Saul. *"Anna Karenina" in Our Time: Seeing More Wisely*. New Haven, CT: Yale University Press, 2007.

———. *The Boundaries of Genre: Dostoevsky's "Diary of a Writer" and the Traditions of Literary Utopia*. Evanston, IL: Northwestern University Press, 1981.

———. *Hidden in Plain View: Narrative and Creative Potentials in "War and Peace."* Stanford, CA: Stanford University Press, 1987.

———. Introduction to *Literature and History: Theoretical Problems and Rus-*

sian Case-Studies, edited by Gary Saul Morson, 1–30. Stanford, CA: Stanford University Press, 1986.

———. *Narrative and Freedom: The Shadows of Time*. New Haven, CT: Yale University Press, 1994.

———. *Prosaics and Other Provocations: Empathy, Open Time, and the Novel*. Boston: Academic Studies Press, 2013.

———. "Tempics and *The Idiot*." In *Celebrating Creativity: Essays in Honour of Jostein Børtnes*, edited by Knut Andreas Grimstad and Ingunn Lunde, 108–34. Bergen: University of Bergen, 1997.

———. "Verbal Pollution in *The Brothers Karamazov*." *PTL* 3 (1978): 223–33. Reprinted in *Critical Essays on Dostoevsky*, edited by Robin Feuer Miller, 234–42. Boston: G. K. Hall, 1986.

Moser, Charles A. *Esthetics as Nightmare: Russian Literary Theory, 1855–1870*. Princeton, NJ: Princeton University Press, 1989.

Moss, Anne Eakin "Tolstoy's Politics of Love: 'That Passionate and Tender Friendship That Exists Only among Women.'" *Slavic and East European Journal* 53, no. 4 (Winter 2009): 566–86.

Murav, Harriet. *Holy Foolishness: Dostoevsky's Novels and the Poetics of Cultural Critique*. Stanford, CA: Stanford University Press, 1992.

Murphet, Julian. "The Mole and the Multiple: A Chiasmus of Character." *New Literary History* 42, no. 2 (Spring 2011): 255–76.

Nabokov, Vladimir. *Lectures on Russian Literature*. Edited by Fredson Bowers. London: Picador, 1981.

Naiman, Eric. "Kalganov." *Slavic and East European Journal* 57, no. 3 (Fall 2014): 294–318.

Newlin, Thomas. "'Swarm Life' and the Biology of *War and Peace*." *Slavic Review* 71, no. 2 (Summer 2012): 359–84.

Newton, Adam Zachary. *Narrative Ethics*. Cambridge, MA: Harvard University Press, 1995.

Nikol'skii, S. A. "Smysly i tsennosti russkogo mirovozzreniia v tvorchestve L. N. Tolstogo." *Voprosy filosofii* 9 (September 2010): 117–35.

Nussbaum, Martha. *Love's Knowledge: Essays on Philosophy and Literature*. Oxford: Oxford University Press, 1999.

Nyiri, J. C. "Einleitung." In *Dostojewski: Notizen und Entwürfe*, edited by J. C. Nyiri, 7–34. Budapest: Akademiai Kiado, 1985.

Odesskaia, M. M. "Traktat Tolstogo 'Chto takoe iskusstvo?' v kontekste krusheniia idealisticheskoi estetiki." *Filologicheskie nauki* 2 (2009): 20–29.

Orvin, Donna. "Psikhologiia very v *Anne Kareninoi* i v *Bratiakh Karamazovykh*." In *Mir filologii: Posviashchaetsia Lidii Dmitrievne Gromovoi-Opul'skoi*, 235–45. Moscow: Nasledie, 2000.

Orwin, Donna Tussing. *Tolstoy's Art and Thought, 1847–1880*. Princeton, NJ: Princeton University Press, 1993.

Paige, Nicholas. *Before Fiction: The Ancien Régime of the Novel*. Philadelphia: University of Pennsylvania Press, 2011.

Paperno, Irina. *Chernyshevsky and the Age of Realism: A Study in the Semiotics of Behavior*. Stanford, CA: Stanford University Press, 1988.

———. *"Who, What Am I?": Tolstoy Struggles to Narrate the Self*. Ithaca, NY: Cornell University Press, 2014.

Perlina, Nina. "Rethinking Adolescence." In *Celebrating Creativity: Essays in Honour of Jostein Børtnes*, edited by Knut Andreas Grimstad and Ingunn Lunde, 216–26. Bergen: University of Bergen, 1997.

———. *Varieties of Poetic Utterance: Quotation in "The Brothers Karamazov."* Lanham, MD: University Press of America, 1985.

Phelan, James. *Reading People, Reading Plots: Character, Progression, and the Interpretation of Narrative*. Chicago: University of Chicago Press, 1989.

———. *Living to Tell about It: A Rhetoric and Ethics of Character Narration*. Ithaca, NY: Cornell University Press, 2005.

Piper, Andrew. "The Constraints of Character: Introducing a Character Feature-Space Tool." https://txtlab.org/2016/01/the-constraints-of-character-introducing-a-character-feature-space-tool/.

Plato. *Complete Works*. Edited by John M. Cooper. Indianapolis: Hackett, 1997.

Pliukhanova, M. B. "Tvorchestvo Tolstogo." In *L. N. Tolstoi: pro et contra*, edited by D. K. Burlaka, 822–57. Saint Petersburg: Izdatel'stvo Russkogo Khristianskogo gumanitarnogo instituta, 2000.

Pomerants, Grigorii. *Otkrytost' bezdne: Etiudy o Dostoevskom*. New York: Liberty Publishing House, 1989.

Prendergast, Christopher. *The Order of Mimesis: Balzac, Stendhal, Nerval, Flaubert*. Cambridge: Cambridge University Press, 1986.

"President Obama and Marilynne Robinson: A Conversation (II)." *New York Review of Books*, November 19, 2015. https://www.nybooks.com/articles/2015/11/19/president-obama-marilynne-robinson-conversation-2/.

Price, Martin. *Forms of Life: Character and Moral Imagination in the Novel*. New Haven, CT: Yale University Press, 1983.

Propp, V. *Morfologiia skazki*. Leningrad: Akademiia, 1928.

———. *Morphology of the Folktale*. Translated by Laurence Scott and edited by Louis A. Wagner. Austin: University of Texas Press, 1968.

Pumpianskii, L. V. *Dostoevskii i antichnost'*. Saint Petersburg, 1922. Reprint, *Studien und texte* no. 1. Bremen: K-Presse, 1973.

Pustygina, N. G. "O familii Dolgorukov v romane F. M. Dostoevskogo *Podrostok*." In *Problemy tipologii russkoi literatury: Trudy po russkoi i slavianskoi filologii*, 37–53. Tartu: Uchenye zapiski Tartuskogo gosudarstvennogo universiteta, 1985.

Ramey, James. "Parasitism and *Pale Fire*'s Camouflage: The King-Bot, the Crown Jewels, and the Man in the Brown Mackintosh." *Comparative Literature Studies* 41, no. 2 (2004): 185–213.

Rice, James L. "Dostoevsky's Endgame: The Projected Sequel to *The Brothers Karamazov*." *Russian History/Histoire Russe* 33, no. 1 (Spring 2006): 45–62.

Ricoeur, Paul. *Time and Narrative*. Translated by Kathleen McLaughlin and David Pellauer. 3 vols. Chicago: University of Chicago Press, 1984.

Rimmon-Kenan, Shlomith. *A Glance beyond Doubt: Narration, Representation, Subjectivity*. Columbus: Ohio State University Press, 1996.

———. *Narrative Fiction: Contemporary Poetics*. London and New York: Routledge, 2002.

Rogova, N. B. "Ideia dukhovnogo 'otechestva' i 'bratstva' v romane *Brat'ia Karamazovy*: K osmysleniiu obraza Pavla Fedorovicha Smerdiakova." *Dostoevskii i mirovaia kul'tura* 19 (2003): 189–99.

Ronen, Ruth. *Possible Worlds in Literary Theory*. Cambridge: Cambridge University Press, 1994.

Rosen, Nathan. "The Madness of Lise Khokhlakov." *Dostoevsky Studies* n.s., 6 (2002): 154–62.

Rosenshield, Gary. *"Crime and Punishment": The Techniques of the Omniscient Author*. Lisse: Peter de Ridder Press, 1978.

Rozenblium, L. M. "Tvorcheskaia laboratoriia Dostoevskogo romanista." In *Literaturnoe nasledstvo* 77, edited by I. I. Anisimov et al., 7–56. Moscow: Nauka, 1965.

Rubenstein, Rebecca. *Virginia Woolf and the Russian Point of View*. New York: Palgrave, 2009.

Ruttenberg, Nancy. *Dostoevsky's Democracy*. Princeton, NJ: Princeton University Press, 2008.

Ryan, Marie-Laure. *Narrative as Virtual Reality: Immersion and Interactivity in Literature and Electronic Media*. Baltimore: Johns Hopkins University Press, 2001 and 2015.

Rylkova, Galina. "The History of Natasha Rostova's Affair with Anatole Kuragin." *Canadian-American Slavic Studies* 31, no. 1 (Spring 1997): 51–63.

Rzhevsky, Nicholas. *Russian Literature and Ideology*. Urbana: University of Illinois Press, 1983.

Sankovitch, Natasha. *Creating and Recovering Experience: Repetition in Tolstoy*. Stanford, CA: Stanford University Press, 1998.

Scarry, Elaine. *Dreaming by the Book*. New York: Farrar, Straus, and Giroux, 1999.

Schiller, Friedrich. *On the Aesthetic Education of Man in a Series of Letters*. Edited and translated by Elizabeth M. Wilkinson and L. A. Willoughby. Oxford: Clarendon Press, 1967.

Schopenhauer, Arthur. *The World as Will and Representation*. Translated by E. F. J. Payne. 2 vols. New York: Dover, 1969.

Schultze, Sydney. *The Structure of "Anna Karenina."* Ann Arbor, MI: Ardis, 1982.

Semenov, E. I. *Roman Dostoevskogo "Podrostok": Problematika i zhanr*. Leningrad: Nauka, 1979.

Serpell, Namwali. "The Banality of Empathy." *NYR Daily*, March 2, 2019. https://www.nybooks.com/daily/2019/03/02/the-banality-of-empathy/.

Shevchenko, V. G. "Traktat o Smerdiakove." *Dostoevskii i mirovaia kul'tura* 10 (1998): 196–228.

Shklovskii, V. *Lev Tolstoi*. Moscow: Molodaia gvardiia, 1967.

———. *Mater'ial i stil' v romane L'va Tolstogo "Voina i mir."* Moscow: Federatsiia, 1928.

Shklovskii, Viktor. *O teorii prozy*. Moscow, 1929. Reprint, Ann Arbor, MI: Ardis, 1985.

———. *Povesti o proze: Razmyshleniia i razbory*. 2 vols. Moscow: Khudozhestvennaia literatura, 1966.

———. *Za i protiv: Zametki o Dostoevskom*. Moscow: Sovetskii pisatel', 1957.

Shklovsky, Victor. *Theory of Prose*. Translated by Benjamin Sher. Elmwood Park, IL: Dalkey Archive Press, 1990.

Shmid, Vol'f. *Proza kak poeziia: Pushkin, Dostoevskii, Chekhov, avangard*. Saint Petersburg: Inapress, 1998.

Silbajoris, Rimvydas. *Tolstoy's Aesthetics and His Art*. Columbus, OH: Slavica, 1991.

Slivitskaia, Ol'ga. *Istina v dvizhenii: O cheloveke v mire L'va Tolstogo*. Saint Petersburg: Amfora, 2009.

Solov'ev, V. S. *Sochineniia*. 2 vols. Edited by A. V. Gulyga and A. F. Losev. Moscow: Mysl', 1988.

Soloviev, V. S. *The Heart of Reality: Essays on Beauty, Love, and Ethics*. Edited and translated by Vladimir Wozniuk. Notre Dame, IN: University of Notre Dame Press, 2003.

Somoff, Victoria. *The Imperative of Reliability: Russian Prose on the Eve of the Novel, 1820s–1850s*. Evanston, IL: Northwestern University Press, 2015.

States, Bert O. *Dreaming and Storytelling*. Ithaca, NY: Cornell University Press, 1993.

Steinby, Liisa. "Concepts of Novelistic Polyphony." In *Bakhtin and His Others: (Inter)subjectivity, Chronotope, Dialogism*, edited by Liisa Steinby and Tintti Klapuri, 27–54. New York: Anthem Press, 2013.

Steiner, Lina. "The Ends of 'Personality': Tolstoy and the Problem of Modern Identity." In *From Petersburg to Bloomington: Studies Presented in Honor of Nina Perlina*, edited by J. Bartle et al., 355–72. Indiana Slavic Studies, no. 18. Bloomington, IN: Slavica, 2012.

———. *For Humanity's Sake: The Bildungsroman in Russian Culture*. Toronto: University of Toronto Press, 2011.

———. "Tolstoy, Liberal and Pluralist: On 'Personality' and the Protagonist in *War and Peace*." *Russian Literature* 36 (2009): 424–42.

Steinlight, Emily. *Populating the Novel: Literary Form and the Politics of Surplus Life*. Ithaca, NY: Cornell University Press, 2018.

Stenbock-Fermor, Elisabeth. *The Architecture of "Anna Karenina."* Lisse: Peter de Ridder Press, 1975.

Stepanian, Karen. *Iavlenie i dialog v romanakh F. M. Dostoevskogo*. Saint Petersburg: Kriga, 2010.

Stewart, Garrett. *Dear Reader: The Conscripted Audience in Nineteenth-Century British Fiction*. Baltimore: Johns Hopkins University Press, 1996.

Struve, Gleb. "Monologue Intérieure: The Origins of the Formula and the First Statement of Its Possibilities." *PMLA* 69, no. 5 (December 1954): 1101–11.

Suleiman, Susan Rubin. "Redundancy and the Readable Text." *Poetics Today* 1, no. 3 (1980): 119–42.

Sukhikh, I. N., ed. *Roman L. N. Tolstogo "Voina i mir" v russkoi kritike*. Leningrad: Izdatel'stvo Leningradskogo universiteta, 1989.

Terras, Victor. *A Karamazov Companion*. Madison: University of Wisconsin Press, 1981.

———. *Belinskij and Russian Literary Criticism: The Heritage of Organic Aesthetics*. Madison: University of Wisconsin Press, 1974.

Thompson, Diane Oenning. *"The Brothers Karamazov" and the Poetics of Memory*. Cambridge: Cambridge University Press, 1991.

Tihanov, Galin. "Ethics and Revolution: Lukács's Responses to Dostoevsky." *Modern Language Review* 94, no. 3 (July 1999): 609–25.

———. *The Master and the Slave: Lukács, Bakhtin, and the Ideas of Their Time*. Oxford: Clarendon, 2000.

Tikhomirov, B. N. "O 'khristologii' Dostoevskogo." *Dostoevskii: Materialy i issledovaniia* 11 (1994): 102–21.

———. "Khristos i istina v poeme 'Velikii Inkvizitor.'" *Dostoevskii i mirovaia kul'tura* 13 (1999): 147–77.

Todd, William Mills III. "The Ruse of the Russian Novel." In *The Novel*, edited by Franco Moretti, 1: 401–23. Princeton, NJ: Princeton University Press, 2006.

———. "Storied Selves: Constructing Characters in *The Brothers Karamazov*." In *Self and Story in Russian History*, edited by Laura Engelstein and Stephanie Sandler, 266–79. Ithaca, NY: Cornell University Press, 2000.

Todorov, Tzvetan. "Narrative-Men." In *The Poetics of Prose*, translated by Richard Howard, 66–79. Ithaca, NY: Cornell University Press, 1977.

Tolstoi, L. N. *Polnoe sobranie sochinenii*. Edited by V. G. Chertkov et al. 90 vols. Moscow and Leningrad: Gosudarstvennoe izdatel'stvo khudozhestvennoi literatury, 1928–58. http://tolstoy.ru/creativity/90-volume-collection-of-the-works/.

Tolstoy, Leo. *Anna Karenina*. Translated by R. Pevear and L. Volokhonsky. New York: Viking, 2000.

———. "Hadji-Murat." In *The Death of Ivan Ilyich and Other Stories*, translated by Richard Pevear and Larissa Volokhonsky. New York: Vintage Classics, 2009.

———. "Sevastopol in May." In *Collected Shorter Fiction*, translated by Louise and Aylmer Maude and Nigel J. Cooper, 1:97–137. New York and Toronto: Knopf, 2001.

———. *Tolstoy's Letters*. Translated by R. F. Christian. 2 vols. New York: Scribner, 1978.

———. *War and Peace*. Translated by Louise and Aylmer Maude and edited by Amy Mandelker. Oxford: Oxford University Press, 2010.

———. *What Is Art? and Essays on Art*. Translated by Aylmer Maude. London: Oxford University Press, 1930.

Tomashevskii, B. V. *Teoriia literatury. Poetika*. 4th ed. Moscow and Leningrad: Gosudarstvennnoe izdatel'stvo, 1928.

Tsimbaeva, E. "Istoricheskii kontekst v khudozhestvennom obraze: dvorianskoe obshchestvo v romane *Voina i mir*." *Voprosy literatury* 5 (October 2004): 175–215.

Tsiv'ian, T. V. "O strukture vremeni i prostranstva v romane Dostoevskogo *Podrostok*." *Russian Literature* 3 (1976): 203–56.

Ungurianu, Dan. *Plotting History: The Russian Historical Novel in the Imperial Age*. Madison: University of Wisconsin Press, 2007.

Vdovin, A. V. *Kontsept 'glava literatury' v russkoi kritike 1830–1860-kh godov*. Tartu: Dissertationes Philologiae Slavicae Universitatis Tartuensis 26, 2011. https://publications.hse.ru/mirror/pubs/share/folder/ut207e8849/direct/62727088.

Vermeule, Blakey. *Why Do We Care about Literary Characters?* Baltimore: Johns Hopkins University Press, 2010.

Vetlovskaia, V. E. *Poetika romana "Bratia Karamazovy."* Leningrad: Nauka, 1977.

———. "Poetika '*Anny Kareninoi*': Sistema neodnoznachnykh motivov." *Russkaia literatura* 4 (1979): 17–37.

Vinitsky, Ilya. "Behind the Door." *Tolstoy Studies Journal* 29 (2007): 80–86.

Vinogradov, V. V. "Dostoevskii i Leskov v 70-e gody XIX veka." In *Problema avtorstva i teoriia stilia*, 487–553. Moscow: Gosizdat. khudozhestvennoi literatury, 1961.

———. "K morfologii natural'nogo stilia: Opyt lingvisticheskogo analiza peterburgskoi poemy 'Dvoinik.'" In *Poetika russkoi literatury: Izbrannye trudy*, edited by M. P. Alekseev and A. P. Chudakov, 101–40. Moscow: Nauka, 1976.

———. "O iazyke Tolstogo (50–60-e gody)." In *Iazyk i stil' russkikh pisatelei ot Gogolia do Akhmatovoi: izbrannye trudy*, edited by A. P. Chudakov, 164–263. Moscow: Nauka, 2003.

Volgin, I. L. "Nravstvennye osnovy publitsistiki Dostoevskogo (Vostochnyi vopros v *Dnevnike pisatelia*)." In *Izvestiia AN SSSR*, Serial literatury i iazyka, 1971, vol. 30, vyp. 4, 317–18. http://feb-web.ru/feb/izvest/1971/04/714-312.htm.

Volgin, Igor'. *Poslednii god Dostoevskogo: Istoricheskie zapiski*, 4th ed. Moscow: AST/Zebra E, 2010.

Wachtel, Andrew Baruch. *The Battle for Childhood: Creation of a Russian Myth*. Stanford, CA: Stanford University Press, 1990.

———. *An Obsession with History: Russian Writers Confront the Past*. Stanford, CA: Stanford University Press, 1994.

Walsh, Richard. *The Rhetoric of Fictionality: Narrative Theory and the Idea of Fiction*. Columbus: Ohio State University Press, 2007.

Ware, Timothy. *The Orthodox Church: An Introduction to Eastern Christianity*. New York: Penguin Books, 2015.

Watt, Ian. *The Rise of the Novel*. Berkeley and Los Angeles: University of California Press, 1964.

Wellek, René. "The Concept of Realism in Literary Scholarship." In *Concepts of Criticism*, by René Wellek, 222–55. New Haven, CT: Yale University Press, 1963.

———. "The Essential Characteristics of Russian Literary Criticism." *Comparative Literature Studies* 29, no. 2 (1992): 115–40.

Wiggins, Kathleen Cameron. "The Drama in Disguise: Dramatic Modes of Narration and Textual Structure in the Mid-Nineteenth-Century Russian Novel." PhD diss., University of California, Berkeley, 2011.

Woloch, Alex. *The One vs. the Many: Minor Characters and the Space of the Protagonist in the Novel*. Princeton, NJ: Princeton University Press, 2003.

Woolf, Virginia. "The Russian Point of View." In *The Common Reader (First Series)*, edited by Andrew McNiellie, 173–82. New York and London: Harcourt Brace Jovanovich, 1984.

Young, Sarah. *Dostoevsky's "The Idiot" and the Ethical Foundations of Narrative: Reading, Narrating, Scripting*. London: Anthem Press, 2004.

Zaidenshnur, E. Ie. *"Voina i mir" L. N. Tolstogo: Sozdanie velikoi knigi*. Moscow: Kniga, 1966.

Zakharov, V. N. "Khristianskii realizm v russkoi literature: Postanovka problemy." In *Evangel'skii tekst v russkoi literature XVIII-XX vekov*, vyp. 3, edited by V. N. Zakharov, 5–20. Petrozavodsk: PetrGU, 2001.

Zhdanov, V. A., and E. Ie. Zaidenshnur. "Tekstologicheskie poiasneniia." In *Anna Karenina: Roman v vos'mi chastiakh*, by L. N. Tolstoi, edited by V. A. Zhdanov and E. Ie. Zaidenshnur, 834–55. Moscow: Nauka, 1970. http://feb-web.ru/feb/tolstoy/texts/selectpr/a70/a70-834-.htm.

Index

Page numbers in italics indicate figures.